W9-AEV-039

DISCARDED

ANNUAL REVIEW
OF NURSING RESEARCH

Volume 26, 2008

Annual Review
of Nursing Research

Volume 26, 2008

Focus on Rural Health

JOYCE J. FITZPATRICK, PhD, RN, FAAN
Series Editor

ELIZABETH MERWIN, PhD, RN, FAAN
Volume Editor

SPRINGER PUBLISHING COMPANY
New York

To purchase copies of other volumes of the *Annual Review of Nursing Research* at 10% off of the list price, go to www.springerpub.com/ARNR.

Springer Publishing Company, LLC
11 West 42nd Street
New York, NY 10036
www.springerpub.com

Acquisitions Editor: Allan Graubard
Production Editor: Julia Rosen
Cover design: Joanne E. Honigman
Composition: Apex CoVantage

08 09 10 11/ 5 4 3 2 1

ISBN-13: 978-0-8261-0126-6
ISSN: 0739-6686

ANNUAL REVIEW OF NURSING RESEARCH is indexed in *Cumulative Index to Nursing and Allied Health Literature* and *Index Medicus*.

Printed in the United States of America by Maple-Vail Book Manufacturing Group.

Contents

Contributors

Sandra L. Annan, PhD, RN
Research Assistant Professor
Acute & Specialty Care
School of Nursing
University of Virginia
Charlottesville, Virginia

Jennifer F. Brown, APRN-PMH
  BC, PhD
Assistant Professor
School of Nursing
Virginia Commonwealth University
Richmond, Virginia

Angeline Bushy, PhD, RN, FAAN
Professor and Bert Fish Chair
Community Health Nursing
College of Nursing
University of Central Florida
Orlando, Florida

Kathleen Cox, PhD, RN
Assistant Professor of Nursing
School of Nursing
University of Virginia
Charlottesville, Virginia

Pamela Stewart Fahs, DSN, RN
Associate Professor
Decker Chair in Rural Nursing
Decker School of Nursing
Binghamton University
Binghamton, New York

Doris F. Glick, PhD, RN
Associate Professor
School of Nursing
University of Virginia
Charlottesville, Virginia

Doris S. Greiner, PhD, RN
Associate Professor
School of Nursing
University of Virginia
Charlottesville, Virginia

Emily J. Hauenstein, PhD, LCP,
  MSN, RN
Thomas A. Saunders III Family
  Professor and Director
Southeastern Rural Mental Health
  Research Center
University of Virginia
Charlottesville, Virginia

Melanie Kalman, PhD, CNS, RN
Associate Professor
Director of Research
College of Nursing
State University of New York
Upstate Medical University
Syracuse, New York

Pamela A. Kulbok, DNSc, RN,
  APRN, BC
Associate Professor of Nursing
School of Nursing
University of Virginia
Charlottesville, Virginia

Irma H. Mahone, PhD, MSN, RN
Research Assistant Professor
School of Nursing
University of Virginia
Charlottesville, Virginia

Emma McKim Mitchell, MSN, RN
Doctoral Student
School of Nursing
University of Virginia
Charlottesville, Virginia

Deborah Shelton, PhD, RN, CNA, BC
Associate Professor, Director for Research and Evaluation
School of Nursing and School of Medicine
University of Connecticut Health Center
Storrs, Connecticut

Deirdre K. Thornlow, PhD, RN, CPHQ
Assistant Professor
School of Nursing
Duke University
Durham, North Carolina

Sharon Williams Utz, PhD, RN
Associate Professor
School of Nursing
University of Virginia
Charlottesville, Virginia

Foreword

The *Annual Review of Nursing Research (ARNR)* series was launched in 1983, more than a quarter of a century ago. Since the initial volume, throughout the years, I have participated as an editor with a number of distinguished nurse colleagues. I am indebted to them for their commitment to and vision for the *ARNR* series. Through the collective volumes, although we have charted the history of nursing science (including aspects of theory development), we have primarily focused on nursing research. Students of the developing discipline will be forever indebted to the nurse scientists and editors who contributed to the series.

In the *ARNR* series, two particular chapters are noteworthy because they include summaries of the first 20 years of content published in the series. In Volume 10, Joanne Stevenson analyzed the first decade of *ARNR* for content themes, identifying the changes in how the disciplinary content was organized and presented, and the areas in which there were significant scientific developments. In Volume 21, Fitzpatrick and Stevenson used the same framework for analysis of the second decade of nursing research content published in the *ARNR* series. In the analysis of the second decade of *ARNR* publication, attention also was paid to the societal forces, for example, the rapid expansion of research-oriented doctoral programs in nursing and the establishment of the National Institute of Nursing Research at the National Institutes of Health, and their effect on the development of the discipline.

Starting with Volume 20, emphasis was placed on theme issues of the series. Volume 20 included geriatric nursing research; Volume 21 included research on child health and development; Volume 22 included research on health disparities among minority populations; Volume 23 included research on substance use, misuse, and abuse; Volume 24 included research on patient safety; Volume 25 included research on vulnerable populations; and this Volume, 26, is focused on research on rural health. Each of these theme-related volumes was edited by distinguished colleagues in the content area.

Volume 26 is the final one in which I will participate. I am immensely proud of the contributions that have been made through the years. I am especially indebted to the founding editor of the *ARNR* series, Harriet Werley, for all that she contributed to the series through her vision and dedication to the rigor of scientific publishing. She taught me much of what I have subsequently applied throughout my career, including not to compromise quality and rigor in our science, to encourage others to maintain the vision, and to confront the challenges inherent in a developing discipline and redefine them as opportunities. I know that the *ARNR* series will be in able hands with the new series editor, Christine Kasper, and I welcome her enthusiastically.

It is important for me to reiterate the outstanding contributions that have been made by my colleagues throughout the years, including those serving as chapter authors, reviewers, advisory board members, and coeditors. I am indebted to all of you for making this historical *ARNR* series a reality, and for your significant contributions to the discipline of nursing.

Joyce J. Fitzpatrick, PhD, RN, FAAN
Series Editor

Preface

All nursing research and all rural health research contribute to the knowledge base of rural nursing research. Knowledge developed from nursing research in urban areas often informs the development of rural nursing studies. Understandings of clinical problems, systems problems, and rural culture and communities developed from general rural health care research inform the development of specific nursing studies. Of equal note is the role that nurse scientists serve, often as research leaders within the field of rural health. The integration of rural nursing research into the general nursing research and rural health literature makes identifying this research difficult. This constraint is magnified by the lack of consistent definitions of *rural* and the complete lack of consistency among authors in communicating how they decided to describe a particular setting or study as rural. Additionally, the paucity of rural nursing research makes it difficult to synthesize research findings on specific topics. Such are the challenges facing the nurse scientists who have contributed to this volume, challenges they have attempted to overcome by identifying and synthesizing the literature on important rural health problems and issues within the context of a comprehensive identification of relevant research, including contributions by nurse researchers from nonrural areas relevant to the problems and issues at hand.

As such, contributing authors of each chapter in this volume have developed a creative and effective strategy to identify relevant research, synthesize the literature, and present it within the context of the rural delivery system and what we know about the problem from the relevant research or policy literature. This enables the reader to situate available nursing knowledge within the broader context of knowledge about the problem or issue as a whole. In most chapters, the authors also have discussed the problems and issues they deal with within the context of recent rural and general health policy reports. We expect that readers will benefit from using such content as a basis for new research agendas within rural nursing research.

Certainly, rural nursing researchers have made important contributions toward meeting the health care needs of rural populations as well as toward improving the health care system within which care is delivered. Nonetheless, in chapters related to needs of particular population groups, we consistently note either limited intervention studies or the small sample sizes of such studies. The chapter "Diabetes Care Among Rural Americans," for example, presents mainly descriptive studies with only three intervention studies for this too prevalent health condition. In the chapter "Matters of the Heart: Cardiovascular Disease and Rural Nursing," contributing authors also report many descriptive studies while pointing out the small sample sizes of intervention studies. The chapter "Intimate Partner Violence in Rural Environments" identifies the major contributions of nursing researchers to the general field but also the lack of contributions to the specific area of rural nursing. In response, the authors provide an example of an approach that rural nursing researchers can use in developing a research program that builds on the general nursing and broader literature.

In Part II, contributors seek to improve the rural health care delivery system itself. Two particular components of the rural delivery system discussed are emergency and mental health care. In the chapter "Hospital-Based Emergency Nursing in Rural Settings," the author identifies some studies that fail to build on each other toward an evolving knowledge base. In contradistinction, the author uses the existing literature to propose an impressive research agenda to move the field forward and to contribute to solving some of the problems identified by a recent Institute of Medicine report that calls for improvements in emergency care. In one of the more developed areas of rural nursing research, mental health, the author of the chapter "Building the Rural Mental Health System: From De Facto System to Quality Care" presents results obtained by the successful implementation of research programs by a small group of researchers sustained for more than a decade. The chapter "Improving the Quality of Rural Nursing Care" describes studies that have been conducted in most areas of the health care setting with the aim of improving at least some aspect of quality of care. These studies provide discussions of workforce development and improving student experiences through innovative learning. The different dependent variables and outcomes that can come together under the broad concept of *quality* challenge the field to better conceptualize quality and to determine how it is operationalized in different settings. The recent Institute of Medicine focus on improving patient safety has stimulated rural nursing research in this regard, as reflected in the chapter "Nursing Patient Safety Research in Rural Health Care Settings." The author of this chapter calls for increasing interdisciplinary collaboration, as well as for collaborative research across the nation and the world. An important recommendation concerns the necessity for nurse researchers to sample rural hospitals in larger studies of patient safety. If this one recommendation were to be adopted as a funding criterion for large studies in general, then rural nursing research studies would expand dramatically, with a further result: the enlarging of the pool of nurse researchers conducting rural research also would prompt experienced researchers who work mainly in urban settings to assist in developing solutions to the more difficult methodological issues of recruitment, small samples, lack of resources and capacity of rural organizations to support research, and the role played by travel time and geographic distance to services in rural nursing research. These issues are discussed in some of the chapters in this volume and also throughout the rural health literature.

Part III focuses on the importance of cultural relevance in rural research and methodological issues facing the design and implementation of rural research. The issue of how *rural* is defined is one that limits the field of rural health research as a whole. The interaction between rural as a cultural concept and rural as a geographic measure thus prompts some reflection in the chapter "Conducting Culturally Competent Rural Nursing Research." A unique aspect of rural research is that researchers must understand the cultural values at work in a rural community in order to design a study that can be implemented successfully and contribute knowledge relevant to the unique needs of specific types of rural communities. Although *rural* is also considered a geographic concept, the availability of a variety of definitions of rural based on different aspects of geography, distance to urban areas, and so on, also serves as a methodological challenge for rural studies. This chapter thus provides an overview of cultural aspects of rural nursing research as well as methodological challenges common to rural research. Readers will witness how authors (both chapter authors and published studies being reviewed) consider the lack of consistency in the definition of *rural*, the common methodological challenges faced in recruitment, and the availability of small samples, as seen throughout this volume. The challenge to researchers, and to the capacity of researchers to generalize rural nursing research, is clear. As such, increasing the involvement of community leaders and members as collaborators in rural research is a subject that is clarified in "Establishing the Public's Trust Through Community-Based Participatory Research," which offers a case example of collaboration with an ethnic community. The potential of this approach to develop culturally meaningful rural studies is evident, as is the limited use of this approach within the rural nursing literature.

Clearly, the cultural aspects of rural nursing research are reflected in many of the chapters in this volume. The concluding special chapter, "Rural Health Nursing Research Review: Global Perspectives," provides an expanded view of the importance of cultures and characteristics of different countries with published rural nursing research. Here, the authors creatively presented the United Nations Human Development Programme's rating of development to contrast the countries represented by the nursing research studies reviewed in this chapter. This chapter differs from other chapters in the volume. The topic evolved from the identification of a large number of international studies identified in a review of the literature on quality of care, which provided the motivation to create a separate chapter with an international focus. Also at work here was a growing realization of the importance of contributions from international studies in several of the other chapters in this volume. The topics selected for focus in this volume were chosen and considered largely from the perspective of the United States. The major differences in types of rural communities within the United States pose challenges to the development of a relevant rural nursing knowledge base. The chapter on global perspectives, along with other chapters in the volume that incorporate international studies, points to analogous problems and issues that rural nursing research raises across countries, with the availability of resources being an important issue.

Many challenges face the nursing research community in its efforts to expand the empirical knowledge base to inform rural nursing practice. The approaches used in this volume of identifying an important problem or issue and identifying and critiquing the existing literature to determine what is known from research about the problem, what nursing research studies have been conducted, and what types of methods were used while identifying the strengths and limitations of the state of the science for a specific problem or issue offer direction for prioritizing the need for research and for formulating a research agenda or program of research that will contribute to solving the problem or addressing the issue. The general field of nursing research is asked to consider the recommendation of the author of the chapter on patient safety to include rural samples in general research studies. Nursing research journals should also solicit articles specifically on rural populations and include reviewers with backgrounds in conducting rural research on their review panels. In effect, to make informed decisions about contributions to the rural nursing research knowledge base, review panel members must understand the reason for small sample sizes and the methodological challenges of rural research. Similarly, funding agencies should do the same. With an increased focus on rural nursing research and with increased collaboration with the general nursing research community, the research questions and agendas proposed by authors of the chapters in this volume can improve the state of the science of rural nursing. This would allow nursing research to play a greater role in improving the health of rural populations as well as the effectiveness of the rural health care delivery system.

Elizabeth Merwin, PhD, RN, FAAN
Volume Editor

Acknowledgment

Thank you to the individuals who served as peer reviewers, for your thoughtful suggestions and contributions to the quality of this volume.

PART I

Nursing Research to Meet Health Care Needs of Rural Populations

Chapter 1

Diabetes Care Among Rural Americans

Sharon Williams Utz

ABSTRACT

The prevalence of diabetes in the United States is higher among those living in rural/ nonmetropolitan statistical areas than in urban centers. Managing this complex chronic illness is complicated by factors such as limited access to care, low socioeconomic status, aging, and membership in a racial or ethnic minority group. A review of the literature was conducted focusing on research about rural Americans with diabetes by searching databases of CINAHL, PubMed, and MEDLINE, and selecting articles in English that were published between 2000 and 2007. Search terms included: nursing, research, rural, rural nursing, rural health services/programs, and diabetes care. Additional search strategies included journal hand searching and networking. Twenty-six research reports were found and included qualitative and quantitative methods and program evaluations. All regions of the United States were represented except the Northwest. The vast majority of research reports were of descriptive studies (n = 16), with program evaluation reports (n = 7) and studies testing an intervention (n = 3) also represented. The quality of each study is examined and summarized.

Keywords: diabetes care; rural; nursing; research

INTRODUCTION

Diabetes mellitus (diabetes) is the sixth leading cause of death in the United States and is significantly underreported (Centers for Disease Control [CDC], 2005). Diabetes has become one of the major health concerns in the United States, often considered a public health crisis with a current incidence of 1.5 million new cases per year among people age 20 and older. The prevalence of diabetes is 20.8 million people, or 7% of the overall U.S. population. Highest rates are among older adults, with a rate of 20.9% among those ages 60 or older. Members of racial and ethnic minorities typically have rates that are two times those of non-Hispanic Whites. According to the CDC (2005), rates of diabetes are at epidemic levels, owing to factors such as longer life span, rising rates of obesity, inactivity, and possibly other factors. In addition to those already diagnosed with diabetes, estimates indicate that as many as 6.2 million people have a condition called *impaired glucose tolerance* or *prediabetes*, and are at significant risk for developing Type 2 diabetes mellitus (T2DM) (CDC, 2005). Among those living in rural areas, rates are higher than the national average. In their report, *Rural Healthy People 2010*, Gamm, Hutchinson, Dabney, and Dorsey (2003) note that the prevalence of diabetes is higher in nonmetropolitan statistical areas (non-MSAs) than in central cities. The authors indicate that the self-reported prevalence of diabetes in non-MSAs was 17% higher than in MSAs (Gamm et al., 2003). Of particular note is that diabetes is more common in the Southeast and the Southwest regions of the United States and, "Typically diabetes is a more serious problem in rural areas as they adopt a more 'developed' or urban lifestyle" (p. 110). The authors of *Rural Healthy People 2010* conclude that the higher prevalence of diabetes among rural residents is likely because of a complex set of factors such as low socioeconomic status among many rural residents, a high proportion of racial or ethnic minorities, and aging populations that are predominant in rural areas. The authors also note that the aspects that contribute to these health disparities are most pronounced among African Americans (Gamm et al., 2003, p. 110).

People living in rural areas also have many barriers to health care that complicate management of a complex illness such as diabetes. Barriers to care include cultural beliefs about seeking care, costs of care, distance and transportation, and few available specialists such as diabetologists and certified diabetes educators (typically nurses and dieticians). Therefore, with high rates of diabetes among rural populations and significant barriers to health care, it is important to review the nursing research literature to systematically examine studies that have been conducted among rural populations with diabetes and to identify results that inform nurses and other health care providers about offering high-quality health care to rural residents to manage the disease, prevent complications, and deal with the many implications of the illness.

Purpose

The purpose of this literature review was to systematically examine published research reports related to the nursing care of rural people with diabetes. It is recognized that there are numerous definitions of the term *rural* that may be chosen by researchers and policy makers (Stern, Merwin, Hauenstein, Hinton, Rovnyak, et al., in process). In the context of this review, published research reports were accepted if they used the term rural to describe the sample and/or population of the study as being derived from a rural area.

Methodology

Nursing and health care literature was examined by using the following search terms: research, nursing, diabetes, rural health, rural health centers/services, rural areas, rural health nursing, and diabetes mellitus (nursing). Databases that were searched were MEDLINE, PubMed, and CINAHL, via the National Library of Medicine. The search was limited to articles in English and to the years 2000 through 2007. In addition to searching national databases, additional strategies used to find relevant publications were networking and journal hand searching (particularly journals such as *Rural Health Care,* and journals focused on diabetes care such as *The Diabetes Educator* and *Diabetes Spectrum*). All published research reports were selected based on the previous parameters if they involved research relevant to nursing and people with diabetes living in rural areas in the United States. Although diabetes is increasingly being identified as a global epidemic by the World Health Organization (Ruder, 2007), the current review is limited to studies published about rural people residing in the United States.

LITERATURE REVIEW

Defining Rural Nursing

In the textbook about rural nursing, Long and Weinert (1998) define the term as, "the provision of health care by professional nurses to persons living in sparsely populated areas" (p. 4). In the first chapter of the text, Long and Weinert identify key concepts relevant to rural nursing such as, "work beliefs and health beliefs, isolation and distance, self-reliance, lack of anonymity, outsider/insider, and old timer/newcomer" (p. 9). These authors note the importance of the nurse recognizing the unique elements of rural life, and that perspectives of rural people often differ from people living in urban areas. Such perspectives must therefore be part of the understandings of nurses who offer health care to rural people. As previously noted, there are numerous ways to define *rural;* characteristics about rural communities are also numerous. Rural areas may be found within 50 miles of large urban centers, such as those near Atlanta, Georgia, or rural areas may be vast, frontier areas located hundreds of miles from urban areas such as in New Mexico. Rural Pennsylvania could be considered part of the Northeast, but some sections are part of Appalachian regions in terms of geography and culture. Rural Maine is very different from rural Virginia—and many more examples could be identified. Suffice it to say, a review about nursing research focusing on rural populations provides information that is varied in numerous ways. Of the 26 research reports examined in this review, the regions of the United States from which the samples were drawn are as follows: Appalachia ($n = 2$); Great Plains ($n = 6$); Northeast ($n = 1$); Midwest ($n = 2$); Southeast ($n = 12$); and Southwest ($n = 2$). There were no research reports of studies with rural samples of people with diabetes from the Northwest, nor from Alaska or Hawaii. Of the 12 research reports from the Southeast region, five studies were based in North Carolina, three in Virginia, and one from South Carolina. The predominance of studies from these regions most likely reflects the high rates of diabetes in the Southeast rural region of the United States (Gamm et al., 2003). There is a surprising paucity of studies from the other rural region with the highest reported rates of diabetes—the Southwest.

Use of Theory and Conceptual Frameworks

Review of nursing research about care of rural people with diabetes could be expected to reflect a variety of theories such as those of Orem and colleagues (2001) and Roy (1999), and midrange theories such as Health Behavior Model, Social Cognitive Theory, and Stages of Change Model. However, these theories or conceptual frameworks were rarely described in the articles selected for this review. Examples of studies that did report using a framework are: Morris (2007), who used Orem's Theory; Skelly and colleagues (2007), who used Kleinman's Explanatory Model of Illness; and Nagelkerk, Reick, and Meengs (2006), who used the Theory of Integration. The study by Tessaro, Smith, and Rye (2005) was reported by the authors to be based on a combination of theories—the Explanatory Model of Illness, Social Learning Theory, the Health Belief Model, and Social Support Theory (p. 3). Two of the three intervention studies were based on the Wagner Chronic Care Model, a framework for health care delivery to those with chronic illness (Bray, Roupe, Young, Harrell, Cummings, et al., 2005; Siminerio, Piatt, & Zgibor, 2005). Some research reports included elements that appeared to implicitly incorporate specific theories or frameworks such as the research of Utz and colleagues (2006), where elements of Orem's Theory of Self-Care Deficit Nursing and Bandura's Social Cognitive Theory implicitly underlie the exploration of barriers and facilitators to self-care, and examination of self-efficacy of rural African Americans with T2DM.

Research Designs

Of the 26 research reports analyzed in this review, the vast majority reported the use of quantitative research designs (*n* = 17) such as questionnaires, structured phone surveys, medical record reviews, cost-benefit analyses, and testing interventions using quasiexperimental designs. A total of eight studies reported predominately qualitative research designs. Seven research reports described the use of qualitative methods such as phenomenology (Struthers, Hodge, DeCora, & Geishirt-Cantrell, 2003), mapping and ethnographic survey combined with interviewing (Gesler, Hayes, Arcury, Skelly, Nash, et al., 2004), and focus group exploratory studies (Jones et al., 2006; Nagelkerk, Reick, & Meengs, 2006; Utz et al., 2006; Wenzel, Utz, Steeves, Hinton, & Jones, 2006). One researcher used a mix of both qualitative and quantitative methods, including a combination of open interviews with semistructured questionnaires (Heuer, Hess, & Batson, 2006).

Summary of Results of the Studies

Descriptive Studies

Studies examined for this review focused on the health problem of diabetes or aspects of caring for people with diabetes in rural areas. Search terms included *nursing*, and the research reports are highly relevant to nurses interested in the health problem of diabetes and the care of those living in rural areas. The majority of the research reports were authored by nurses (22 out of 26); however, most were published in journals intended for a variety of health professionals (e.g., *Family & Community Health, Journal of Rural Health, The Diabetes Educator*), while a smaller number were published in nursing journals (e.g., *Holistic Nursing Practice, Research in Nursing & Health, Western Journal of Nursing Research*). The majority of studies selected for this review—16 (*n* = 16) of the 26 studies (61.5%)—were descriptive in their design. Studies in this category are summarized and analyzed in detail in Table 1.1. In most cases, the purpose of these studies was to describe the experiences, perspectives, health care needs, health care practices, facilitators and barriers to care, impact of technology, and quality of care for individuals and groups with diabetes living in rural areas. Nearly all were cross-sectional, collecting data at only one point in time, with only a few reporting data collection over a long period of time or returning to collect additional data more than one time. Methods used for several studies were focus groups, but other approaches included surveys, interviews, medical record reviews, and mapping sites for potential diabetes care in a community using global positioning satellite (GPS) technology. The samples ranged in size from 23 to more than 1,420, with many having samples in the hundreds. Most were samples of convenience, reflecting the bias of self-selected samples. All except one study examined samples of people with diabetes or those at risk for developing diabetes. One study was of a sample of health care providers who used telehealth interventions for people with diabetes (Tudiver et al., 2007). Most of the studies reported diverse samples of African Americans, American Indians, Hispanics, and European Americans. None included samples of Asians or Pacific Islanders. A few studies did not describe racial and ethnic composition of the sample—presumably because the majority of people in the region are White. Only a few researchers described the population from which their sample was drawn—an important factor in determining how representative the sample was of those living in the area. In a few cases, researchers not only described the population in the region, but also gave geographic information to enhance the readers' understanding of the rural character of the area.

Program Evaluation Studies

The second most frequent research design characterizing studies in this review was program evaluation ($n = 8$, 30.8%). Program evaluation studies are analyzed in detail in Table 1.2. Each of these studies by definition included the testing of a programmatic approach to meeting the health care needs of adults with diabetes, or needs of providers. These studies are in some ways similar to an approach recently emphasized by the National Institutes of Heath as *translational research*. However, most of these program evaluation studies do not reflect rigorous designs and controls that typically characterize translational research, but are intended to test feasibility and acceptability of programs to address needs of patients living in rural areas with diabetes. The samples from the program evaluation studies reflect efforts to meet the needs of several different racial or ethnic groups for diabetes care. Only one study focused on a program to increase the number of certified diabetes educators in order to meet the needs of the rural population. Many of these studies collected data from medical records or electronic databases from the health care delivery sites. Evaluation data most often consisted of descriptive information about services provided to patients (e.g., number of patient encounters, percent seen by case manager, etc.), information from medical records to document outcomes (e.g., blood glucose levels, self-care goals met, etc.), and changes in processes of care (e.g., proportion of providers meeting the standards set by the American Diabetes Association, etc.). To their credit, many of the researchers reported the year(s) that data were collected. The most frequent limitation of this set of studies is the lack of a comparison group. Although it is recognized that these are program evaluation studies, rather than more highly controlled designs, researchers could enhance the strength of their findings by using comparisons to other groups in the community or the region, data that can often be drawn from state health department statistics or large data

TABLE 1.1 Analysis of Descriptive Studies (n = 16)

Source	Purpose	Design and Method	Rural Location	Sample Size, Demographics	Findings	Limitations
Neil (2002)	To report findings on self-care practices related to foot care of 61 rural people with diabetes mellitus.	Descriptive, using questionnaire (Siriraj Foot-Care Score Questionnaire) to compare self-care by those with and without foot ulcers. Administered verbally by researchers, 4 subscales: Inspection, cleaning, nail cutting, going barefoot.	Southeast Region of the United States. Southeastern North Carolina.	Convenience sample of 61 patients from treatment facility of Academic Medical Center serving 26 counties. Referred by MDs. n = 24 with foot ulcers, N = 37 without; 30 men, 31 women; 48 White, 14 African American, 2 Hispanic. Average age = 46 (range 18–81) Type 1 or T2DM.	Overall scores no difference between groups. No statistical differences on three subscales. Significant difference in "going barefoot" (p ≤ .004): those without ulcers more likely to go barefoot inside. Many could not see feet; most common reason for no foot care: can't reach feet.	Data collected in MD office: may have told researchers the "right answer": no information on representativeness of sample based on demographics of region. Instrument validated in Thailand and tests knowledge versus behavior.

(Continued)

TABLE 1.1 Analysis of Descriptive Studies (n = 16) (*Continued*)

Source	Purpose	Design and Method	Rural Location	Sample Size, Demographics	Findings	Limitations
Struthers et al. (2003)	To explore the experience of American Indian facilitators in a culturally appropriate intervention (Talking Circles) on two Northern Plains reservations.	Phenomenological. Examining Native American "Talking Circle"; Research Question: "What did Native talking circle facilitators experience?" Used constant comparative analysis and phenomenological data analysis techniques. Audiotapes transcribed for analysis.	Great Plains Region of the United States. South Dakota, Nebraska, Iowa	2 tribes 4 facilitators 147 participants	Describes "Powerful experiences" of peer facilitators and major concept of "a calling to do the work" (p. 176). Four themes: self-growth process, blending of two worldviews as a diabetes intervention strategy, importance of translating materials, commitment to tribal people and communities. Evidence of cultural mediation support and established network.	No demographic information about facilitators or participants in talking circle.

Author (Year)	Purpose	Method/Design	Location	Sample	Findings	Comments
Gesler et al. (2004)	To show how maps of location of daily activities can be used by health care providers to plan a diabetes prevention program.	Description of all activity locations of patients without diabetes using global positioning system (GPS) and geographic information system (GIS); interviews about where participants went; locations identified by GPS. Also interviewed providers to identify potential sites for diabetes medication.	Southeast Region of the United States. Central North Carolina	Ethnographic sampling from a rural southern town population 7,000 in year 2000. n = 121 working adults (not diagnosed with diabetes) 20 Latino men, 20 Latino women, 20 African American men, 22 African American women, 20 White men, 19 White women	Important differences found in standard deviational ellipses (SDEs) by ethnicity and gender; resulting maps of spatial patterns of people's movements have a strong visual impact and enable planners to see at a glance how intervention strategy would look on the ground.	No information about how questions were asked. Need to elicit and compare reports of where participants would like to get health education to care providers' ideas.
Anderson-Loftin et al. (2005)	To summarize literature and describe lessons learned by researchers regarding recruitment and retention of	Descriptive study; summary of literature and report of researchers' experience.	Southeastern Region of the United States. Central South Carolina	MEDLINE search of research and clinical literature. Report of researchers' studies with African Americans:	Successful strategies reported: collaboration with community leaders, get donations from local businesses, involve local health care	No description of how reviewed literature was selected from MEDLINE search.

(Continued)

TABLE 1.1 Analysis of Descriptive Studies (n = 16) (*Continued*)

Source	Purpose	Design and Method	Rural Location	Sample Size, Demographics	Findings	Limitations
	rural African American research participants.			(1) feasibility study of food habits and physical measures; convenience sample of 23 with retention 70%. (2) Pilot intervention with 97 adults from primary care sites.	providers, obtain funds to cover nurse care manager. Primary importance of cultural competence, caring, trust, incentives, and follow-up over time.	Doesn't make clear distinctions between own results versus others from literature reviewed.
Skelly et al. (2005)	To describe self-monitoring blood glucose (SMBG) practice of older adults with T2 DM; identify characteristics differentiating testers from nontesters; to identify personal and support-related predictors of monitoring frequency.	Population-based cross-sectional survey with in-home interviews. Used claim records from CMS of randomly selected patients. Conducted 11 two-hour interviews about diabetes self-care practices. Multiple logistic regression.	Southeastern Region of the United States. Central North Carolina.	n = 698 elders from two rural counties. African American, Native American, European American. Medicare recipients with diabetes. Men and women Response rate 89%	77% practiced SMBG previous week; 40% tested daily; no ethnic differences in SMBG. Significant predictors of SMBG were medication regimen, provider recommendation, duration of diabetes, receiving help with testing.	Researchers noted reliance on self-report as limited. Sample from only two rural counties in one region.

| Zulkowski & Coon (2005) | Descriptive study to examine congruence between rural patient self-reported and provider-documented information on American Diabetes Association (ADA) recommended guidelines. | From larger study to improve provider adherence to ADA guidelines. Questionnaire sent to patients. Data collected from records to compare to ADA recommendations. | Great Plains Region of the United States. Rural Montana | Patients n = 149 adults ages 45 or above diagnosed with diabetes (provider documented); 86 women. 65% response rate to questionnaire. Four rural health care providers. | Multiple barriers to care: lack of certified diabetes educators; gaps in patients' knowledge; lack of communication between provider and patient. Adherence to ADA guidelines suboptimal. | Noted no ethnic, educational, or socioeconomic information in records. Participants younger and had lower A1c levels compared to nonresponders. |
| Tessaro et al. (2005) | To gain culturally informed understanding of diabetes in an Appalachian region by determining cultural knowledge, beliefs, and attitudes about | Design: Focus groups. Qualitative analysis methods. Transcription of tapes and use of NUD*IST software. | Appalachian Region of the United States. West Virginia | 13 focus groups over 5 months from 16 counties. 7 groups with diabetes, n = 61; 6 groups without diabetes, n = 40; 73 women, 28 men. | Broad themes: Cultural beliefs and perceived susceptibility; Barriers to early detection; Knowledge about diabetes; Social relationships. | No description of racial/ethnic characteristic of sample. Data analysis would be better described as content analysis of previously |

(Continued)

13

TABLE 1.1 Analysis of Descriptive Studies (n = 16) (*Continued*)

Source	Purpose	Design and Method	Rural Location	Sample Size, Demographics	Findings	Limitations
	diabetes among those in region; identify concerns, barriers, and facilitators to developing interventions for prevention and early detection.				Socioeconomic factors were major influence on health-related decision-making; health care system provided little.	determined topics, rather than exploratory qualitative method.
Alverson & Kessler (2005)	To examine health concerns by individuals for themselves, families, and community.	Self-report instrument developed by researchers and clinic staff at health care center.	Midwest Region of the United States. Rural Northwestern Indiana	90 adults invited on random days at clinic to complete questionnaire. Total n = 82 Ages 19–64 80% women; 88% White; 7% Hispanic; 1% African American; 4% other.	Numerous health concerns listed—(1) for self, only three listed diabetes; most listed chronic conditions; (2) for community, health concerns varied from "general" to HIV/AIDS, addiction, etc.	Subjects tend to underreport concerns (i.e., diabetes prevalence in community is high); Subjects unable to explain nature of concern; limited participation. Self-selected sample.

| Nagelkerk et al. (2006) | To describe the perceived barriers to self-management of adults with T2DM in a rural setting and to identify effective strategies in self-management to highlight infrastructure needs or changes in clinical practice. Framework Theory of Integration | Exploratory focus groups. Interviews using key informant technique. Analysis Content evaluation. Ranked barriers and strategies. By expert panel and researchers. Data collected in 2002. | Midwest Region of the United States. Michigan | Three focus groups, 24 adults (>21) with T2DM recruited from rural primary care practice. Purposive sampling of fourth person on a list of 160 eligible. Age 26–78. Half women, men. All White. Approximately equal numbers with high school education, less than or more than. | Most frequent barriers: lack of knowledge, actions to take; feeling helpless/frustrated; lack of resources; poor quality DSME; daily struggles. Effective strategies: collaboration with provider, positive attitude, support, routines, group DSME. Recommend more individual tailoring. | One practice setting, all White, small sample. Not clear if participants could be anonymous from providers. |
| Utz et al. (2006) | Aims were to describe experience of self-managing Type 2 diabetes among rural dwelling | Focus groups. Taped/transcribed with line by line analysis. | Southeast region of the United States. Central Virginia | 10 Focus groups, 3 rural communities, n = 73 African American adults, 42 women, 31 men | Many diagnosed late in disease process. Individuals varied greatly in knowledge and skills for | Volunteer participants. Small sample from one region of the United States. |

(Continued)

TABLE 1.1 Analysis of Descriptive Studies (n = 16) (*Continued*)

Source	Purpose	Design and Method	Rural Location	Sample Size, Demographics	Findings	Limitations
	African Americans, to identify facilitators and barriers to self-management, to describe the use of prescribed and alternative therapies and elicit recommendations for programs of diabetes care. Framework Orem's Theory of Self-Care Deficit Nursing; Bandura's Social Cognitive Theory.	Content analysis, group centered. Analysis Folio Views software. Data collected 2003–2004		Age 23–89 Mean = 60 years old, 80% high school education or less. Sessions held in community sites.	self-care. Overall feeling of needing more DSME. Barriers: access to specialists, CDEs; costs. Facilitators: creative ways to seek care and cope; resilience, support from providers, family, and friends, close-knit community. Use of teas, supplements, dietary treatments, religion/spirituality. Recommended programs of care.	
Wenzel et al. (2006)	To examine experience of being diagnosed with diabetes as described by rural Blacks.	Descriptive exploratory study of focus groups. Part of a larger study (see Utz et al., 2006).	Mid Atlantic Region: Central Virginia	n = 73 African Americans from three rural communities (see Utz et al., 2006).	One quarter diagnosed by routine screen; most acutely ill (64%); many hospitalized.	Problem in accurate report, that is, many years with diagnosis (11.6 yrs).

	Purpose	Method	Setting	Sample	Findings	Limitations
		Methods: 10 focus groups Separate men and women. Transcriptions of taped sessions and analysis using Folio Views software.		31 women, 42 men. Average years with diabetes = 11.6.	Vivid memories of diagnoses, classic symptoms of DM. Many "expected" diagnosis (family history; high rates in community); a few "shocked"; many report difficult acceptance; illness rarely discussed with family/friends; men emphasize treatments; most use figurative, symbolic language; common use of religious, spiritual language. Focus groups facilitate rich descriptions.	Focus groups may limit disclosure of more personal nature. Only those comfortable with focus groups participate (self-select sample).
Jones et al. (2006)	To explore use of complementary and alternative modalities	Exploratory focus group method.	Southeast Region of the United States.	Two rural communities Eight focus groups	Most common remedies: prayer, diet-based, that	Small sample one region

(Continued)

TABLE 1.1 Analysis of Descriptive Studies (n = 16) (*Continued*)

Source	Purpose	Design and Method	Rural Location	Sample Size, Demographics	Findings	Limitations
	(CAM) therapies, and the role of religion and spirituality in dealing with diabetes among adult African Americans with Type 2 diabetes.	Part of larger study (see Utz et al., 2006).	Central Virginia	n = 68 African American adults with T2DM, 39 men, 29 women. Demographics: 20% 8th grade or less, 38% high school education. Most had health insurance. One quarter paid for health care "out of pocket."	is, teas from root, leaves, lemon juice, vinegar, "Natural" products and herbal dietary supplements. Some findings differ from other literature and others consistent. Women spoke more openly about CAM use. Some skeptical. Many took remedies for arthritis, hypertension. Confidence in own providers.	Group participation may limit disclosure though opposite appears to be true.

| Tudiver et al. (2007) | Purpose: to determine acceptability and perceived impact on primary care practices of a randomized clinical trial using telemedicine to deliver diabetes services to elderly Medicare patients (endocrinologist, nurses, dieticians). | Longitudinal phone survey. Part of larger project using telemedicine for diabetes education. Survey: 36 items using 5-point Likert scale with 3 foci: impact, acceptability, and communication. Six open-ended items for qualitative evaluation, content analysis. Two interviews identified key words, phrases, concepts, and list of themes. Conducted 2002–2004. Analysis: descriptive statistics, paired t-tests between year 1 | Northeast Region of the United States. Upstate New York | Primary care providers serving patients with diabetes in rural areas and small towns "medically underserved." n = 116 of 137 eligible potential participants, 65 completed both year 1 and year 2 surveys. Mean age 48. 84 women, 32 men. Family practice and internal medicine MDs, nurse practitioners, physician assistants with at least 1 year experience. Providers saw an average of three telemedicine patients per year (SD = 2.9). | Multiple regression showed only one variable predictive of acceptability with impact, number of patients enrolled showed an inverse relationship. Means and standard deviations. For year 1 and 2 surveys showed slight improvement in acceptability over time. Qualitative: Three themes: what worked best for patients and providers; what did not work; suggestions for improving diabetes education and telemedicine. | Survey tool developed by investigators (tested for content and face validity three iterations). Factors analysis, reliability, Cronbach's ok 0.88, etc. No verbatim transcripts. Analysis limited to 65 who did year 1 and 2 surveys. Modifications year 1 and 2 may affect validity of measures. |

(Continued)

TABLE 1.1 Analysis of Descriptive Studies (n = 16) (*Continued*)

Source	Purpose	Design and Method	Rural Location	Sample Size, Demographics	Findings	Limitations
		and year 2 data; multiple regression of outcomes.		Providers spent about 33 minutes/month on project-related tasks.	Overall: PCPs show increased quality of care but reported too much time consuming, too much paperwork.	
				One of first to do longitudinal analysis of telemedicine.		
Moore et al. (2006)	To compare quality of diabetes care provided to American Indian, Alaskan Natives (AI/AN) by urban and rural Indian Health Service (IHS) Programs	<u>Design:</u> cross-sectional study. Medical records review, Audit in 2002 by Indian Health Service. <u>Source of data</u> 70 demographic and quality of care variables collected in 2002 from those with complete data for covariants.	Researcher from Great Plains Region of the United States. New Mexico. Data from Indian Health Programs, 225 rural and 17 urban clinics.	20,102 individuals from 242 facilities from all 12 IHS service areas. From urban areas n = 841 patient records selected, all urban and random sample of rural. Final sample = 710 urban, 1,420 rural.	Average age rural, 55; urban, 51. Few differences among groups. Urban more likely to receive formal diabetes education. Diastolic BP only intermediate outcome different, slightly increased in urban residents. Rural more	Not clear why year 2002 chosen for analysis. Decisions about selection of larger number of rural patients not explained. Not all IHS Programs participated thus may overestimate quality of care. Note: Last 6 years New

Author	Purpose	Methods	Setting	Sample	Findings	Limitations
		Data analysis Descriptives, Logistic regression to compare odds of dichotomous outcomes of rural versus urban patients. Linear regression.		Complete explanation regarding analysis, that is, complex selection of variables, creation of intermediate outcomes, and so on.	likely to receive eye and dental exams. Rates of adherence to national guidelines same or higher than national norms for care providers overall.	"Special Diabetes Program for Indians" from Congress, making future comparisons difficult.
Heuer et al. (2006)	To describe Hispanic migrant farmer workers' perceptions of services provided at 37 multidisciplinary "Cluster Clinics" designed to serve rural populations with diabetes.	Questionnaire and interviews of clinic clients. Methods Descriptive statistics and individual interview of clinic clients (contact evaluation), 15-item English-Spanish eliciting perceptions of clinic services. Bilingual health outreach workers administer questionnaire and interviews.	Midwest Region of the United States. Northeast North Dakota to Southern Minnesota	Convenience samples from 37 clinics over 447 linear miles: n = 566 survey n = 12 in-depth interviews 91% had T2DM Age 23–77 Mean age = 51 14% = 55 or > 53% men.	High percent rated service at clinics as "excellent" (75%–88%); 21%–25% rated "good." Over 85% preferred "no changes." Content analysis—clients perceive quality service, six characteristics contributing to successful delivery and four challenges to be tackled.	No outcomes measured. Quality to uninformed may mean "nice, friendly providers." Data skewed by social desirability, fear of criticizing providers. Researcher developed instrument—provides no information on validity or reliability. Interview from only two clinics.

(Continued)

TABLE 1.1 Analysis of Descriptive Studies (n = 16) (*Continued*)

Source	Purpose	Design and Method	Rural Location	Sample Size, Demographics	Findings	Limitations
		Interview about benefits, barriers, and suggestions for improvement of clinic services (Clinics established between 1998 and 2003).				
Skelly et al. (2007)	To elicit views of African Americans and identify differences by gender and age about diabetes and its prevention; to design/plan a community-based intervention for prevention; to derive	Descriptive guided by Kleinman's Ethnographic interviewing—5 domains to develop interview guide. 1. etiology 2. time with mode for symptom onset 3. pathophysiology	Southeastern Region of the United States. Rural North Carolina	n = 42 African American adults Stratified for equal number of men (n = 20), women (n = 22); equal distribution of younger (18–30) and older (31–50) adults.	Findings similar to Utz et al. (2006), "Diabetes is your own personal business" (p. 22) (often not discussed). Respondents did not share a well-developed explanatory model for disease.	Small nonrepresentative sample. Nonrandom sample from one community.

| an explanatory model of diabetes from this population. Framework Kleinman's (1973, 1980) explanatory models of illness. Analysis Transcribed analysis using Ethnograph software. | 4. course of illness 5. treatment. Added an item on prevention of diabetes. 24 open-ended questions and probes. 45 minutes to 2 hours in homes or place of choice. Thorough in-depth interview and analysis. | Site-based sampling in community (stores, churches, agencies) working poor at risk for diabetes (*not* diagnosed). | More ideas about etiology than other domains of explanatory model. Some consistent themes within domains. Recommendations: focus on family involvement, build on belief about "taking care of oneself," recognize age and gender differences to develop programs to prevent diabetes. |

sets from studies by the federal government. Of particular note is an unusual study that is an in-depth cost-benefit analysis of a proposed case management program intended for low-income, high-risk people living in a rural county of Alabama (Crow, Lakes, & Carter, 2006). The latter study involved a detailed examination of the financial elements of a proposed program prior to testing. Such an approach is unique in the literature selected for this review and results may be important in future decisions about the kinds of programs that are effective and sustainable in rural areas.

Intervention Studies

The smallest percentage of study designs identified for this review was experimental or interventional—a design found in only three studies (11.5%). All three studies were quasiexperimental designs, and are analyzed in detail in Table 1.3. Samples for these studies reflect special populations—that is, African Americans in the rural South and women in the Great Plains. All deal with testing interventions that include one or more group approaches. All include outcomes that measured effective diabetes self-management, such as glycosolated hemoglobin (HbA1c) level (a measure of long-term glycemic control), blood pressure, body weight, and use of health care resources. Some included more subjective data such as patients' preferences or satisfaction with the approach. One included use of computers to deliver the intervention. While it is disappointing that such a small number of studies were conducted to test an intervention, this finding reflects the difficulties of conducting research in rural areas. Barriers to conducting such studies are consistent with the factors described previously by Long and Weinert (1998), in their description of major concepts associated with rural nursing. Categories of research barriers include logistical factors for both researchers and participants—such as distance, transportation difficulties, cost, communication barriers, and limited facilities. Cultural factors can also complicate research because of differences between rural residents and researchers as described by Long and Weinert (1998): "outsider/insider, old timer/newcomer" factors (p. 9). Researchers who lack an understanding of cultural differences between rural groups are unlikely to be successful in studies about rural people. Another factor that may be a barrier to research in rural areas is the lack of available health professionals and researchers in the region. While most nursing research is conducted by nurses in academic medical centers, such centers are rarely located in rural areas. All of these barriers to nursing research affect studies of every type (descriptive program evaluations and experimental interventions); however, they impact researchers most profoundly when they attempt to test an intervention and follow results over time—a type of study that is most needed to inform health care providers about diabetes care.

TABLE 1.2 Analysis of Program Evaluation Studies (n = 7)

Source	Purpose	Design and Method	Rural Location	Sample	Findings	Limitations
Heuer et al. (2004)	To describe migrant Health Services, Inc. (MHSI) Diabetes Program conceptual model and four types of outcomes achieved over three years.	Descriptive analysis of program records and documents. Methods Description of types, amounts of medical services and patient education offered. Qualitative: Data from program records and documents "to analyze the nature of the program" between 2000 and 2002. Information from electronic registry.	Great Plains Region of the United States. Minnesota North Dakota	Systematic sample of 451 Hispanic farm workers with every third patient served at each of nine health centers from 447 linear miles. Nurse-managed health centers. Comparisons of two annual subsamples: Year 2000: 165; Year 2002: 140; and preliminary data from 2003. Those with T2DM are 91% of sample. 9%: T1DM. Age range 23–77, Average age 51, Women = 53%.	Multicomponent program addressing barriers offering continuum of health services and education to meet ADA recommendations. Outcomes 1. 78% seen two times/ year or more 2. screenings offered at cluster clinics 3. specific medical care given statistically significant increase, by 2002 all but 6% had A1c measure: screened for complications. Extensive patient/ participant education with positive evaluations. Conducting research and educating providers. Conclusion: major increase from 2000 to 2002 in services provided.	Program evaluation with no comparison of those served elsewhere in this community or similar one elsewhere or to national norms.

(Continued)

TABLE 1.2 Analysis of Program Evaluation Studies (n = 7) (*Continued*)

Source	Purpose	Design and Method	Rural Location	Sample	Findings	Limitations
Bray, Roupe, et al. (2005)	To assess feasibility and potential for cost effectiveness of restructuring care in rural fee-for service practices for predominately minority patients with diabetes for over one year.	Business plan developed to examine costs and revenue for tailored intervention for 12 months with advanced practice nurse case manager (CM)—weekly visits and four group sessions with MD and CM. Electronic registry with reminders, "Circuit rider case manager" nurse. Care based on established overall goals following ADA guidelines; CM set individual goals with patients.	Southeast Region of the United States. North Eastern North Carolina	n = 314 patients with T2DM from five clinics serving 3,700 people with DB. Average age = 61. 72% African American, 54% men Targeted high-risk patients with HbA1c >7 and BP > 135/85, evidence of complications.	Increase in percentage of patients achieving diabetes care goals. Increase productivity and billable encounters. Increase average daily encounter rate. Significant improvement with both patient care and processes of care. Program continues to expand in five clinics. Cost/benefits analysis: increase charges offset 75% of costs of CM nurse. May be associated with lowered ER visits, hospitalization. Appears to be sustainable.	Didn't measure total use of health care system (e.g., emergency room or hospital visits). Lack of comparisons with control clinics. Can't separate effects of three different aspects of intervention. May not generalize to other settings.

| Siminerio et al. (2005) | Pilot study to determine impact of implementing elements of the Chronic Care Model (CCM) on provider's diabetes care practices and patient outcomes in rural practice setting. | Chart reviews and interviews to describe practices and outcomes. Methods: reviewed charts previous years; interviewed providers; repeated chart review. Intervention by CDE based on ADA guidelines. DSME at office site: held group sessions, series of five per group. For 12 months dieticians CDE came two times/month; phone call follow-up. Analysis McNemar's test, paired t-tests | Appalachian Region of the United States. Pennsylvania, South Central bordering Appalachia | County has 172 people diagnosed with diabetes; Sample eligible $n = 104$ adult patients with T2DM; $n = 29$ received intervention, $n = 17$ completed entire program. 99% White, Low formal education. Average age 65.4. Primary care practice with four MDs and a PA and NP. | Provider adherence to ADA standards increased significantly across all process measures. Patients increase knowledge, empowerment. Changes in clinical values nonsignificant except Alc<7; HDL cholesterol improved. Conclusion Implementing systems to support decisions and DSME has influence on practices and patient outcomes in rural areas. Practice site received ADA certification after patient study. | Small number completed entire program. Hawthorne effect. Small power to detect differences. |

(Continued)

TABLE 1.2   Analysis of Program Evaluation Studies (n = 7) (*Continued*)

Source	Purpose	Design and Method	Rural Location	Sample	Findings	Limitations
Balamurugan et al. (2006)	To describe barriers to diabetes self-management education (DSME) programs in medically underserved rural areas of Arkansas and describe lessons learned.	Chronic Care Model A coalition of groups developed a plan, recruited 12 sites to set up DSME programs of care; hired three certified diabetes educators (CDEs) to train staff of clinics and prepare them as CDEs; each clinic got resources/materials. Each patient got 10 hours DSME and three hours nutrition assistance—tailored to individual.	Southeastern Region of the United States. Rural Arkansas 12 DSME programs established by state health department.	Enrolled 734 between February 2003 to March 2004. Total n = 734 93% T2DM 25% age 45 or less 69% White 30% African American 50% High school education or less Only 20% completed the 13 hours DSME (n = 65). Total data on 43.	Clinical changes not statistically significant except increased foot exam rates. HbAlc decreased 0.5. Barriers to implement program at patient level and program level. Only significant change at six months = increased foot exam rates (p = 0.03). <u>Conclusions</u> • Met goal of establishing 12 sites for DSME. Increased number of CDEs by three • Doubled number received DSME over one year • Key problem—attrition. Lack of effort for retention of patients • Problems with reimbursement • Didn't have systematic evaluation early. • Planning six more sites of evaluation.	Barriers well summarized in table form. Recognition of lack of evaluation plan. No use of Planning model such as PRECEDE-PROCEED

| Butcher et al. (2006) | To increase access to quality diabetes self-management education (DSME) in rural Montana via a mentoring program with three levels (basic, intermediate, advanced). | Mentoring and technical assistance offered through state-wide initiative. Assessed each profile, learning needs, outlined course of self-study and matched with mentor. Most mentoring conducted via phone and email with occasional site visits. Lending library of materials on DB care/education. Program with ADA recognition held meeting and offered information documents, etc. HIS involved. | Great Plains Region of the United States.

Rural Montana | 90 nurses (76%) and dieticians (21%) participated.

30 facilities received technical assistance to achieve ADA certification.

Average number participating each of six years = 37. | 27 completed structured education and 13 achieved CDE. Satisfaction with program $n = 23$ "high." 25 of 30 facilities received ADA recognition. Number CDEs in state increased from 52 to 76 over five years. Number ADA recognized programs increased from 2 to 22. Strong network of diabetes educators developed across state. Minimal costs. Materials, lending library, Montana Diabetes control program DCP developed. Successful partnership between Montana DCP and Association of Diabetes Educators. | Small number evaluated program (self-selected).

No comparison to other states or national norms.

"Technical Assistance" not well explained.

No cost figures provided. |

(Continued)

TABLE 1.2 Analysis of Program Evaluation Studies (n = 7) (*Continued*)

Source	Purpose	Design and Method	Rural Location	Sample	Findings	Limitations
Morris (2007)	To address the social support and education needs of rural residents with diabetes by implementing an adult support group.	Telephone needs assessment. Goal: to provide specified rural population with education and social support to enable better self-care. Framework: Orem's Theory of Self-Care Deficit Nursing.	Southwest Region of the United States. Northwest Texas	Needs assessment survey conducted in five counties. Participants selected via telephone interview (no number given). Sample population: 87% White, 4.16% Black, 8.3% Hispanic (not proportional, too few Black and Hispanic). First group meeting, n = 32. Phone survey completed by 12 participants two weeks after meeting. Good discussion of evidence about importance of social support.	Services wanted: monthly meetings, speakers, talk with others with similar needs, and telephone resource list. 75% found information beneficial at first meeting. 40% stated information with meeting others beneficial.	Cites *Healthy People 2000* (vs. 2010) for objective for diabetes care. State data based on 1990 census. Hospital admission data from 1996. Goal of 20 people is too big for group process. Evaluation of one group session is very limited.

COST-BENEFIT ANALYSIS

Source	Purpose	Design/Methods	Rural Location	Sample	Results	Limitations
Crow et al. (2006)	Describes cost-benefit analysis. Proposed nursing case management (CM) program that provides care for low-income, high-risk diabetic population in a rural county.	Cost-benefit analysis based on case manager's caseload of 20 low-income, high-risk clients with diabetes. Part of Rural Health Mobile Medical Unit (RHMMA). Analysis of one year. Cost savings are estimates based on national averages established by Healthcare Costs and Utilization Project (AHRQ).	Southern Region of the United States. Alabama	Calculations based on sample of 941 patients with diabetes from total patients of 5,354 seen over four years by RHMMA.	Baseline Analysis: RHMMA projected to save local and community hospital (ER and hospital) $3.5 million over four years: – Program able to "break even" with costs and revenues at $808,307 in 2004 Analysis by adding CM: – Net benefit of $149,544 savings per year – Benefit-cost ratio 2:9 (a ratio of >1 generates more benefits than costs) – Assume other intangible benefits such as client and staff satisfaction, overtime, decrease complications.	Strengths: thorough literature review of CM and needs of rural people. Provides detailed description of CM job and organizational arrangement. Projected cost-benefit analysis not actual savings. Outcome evaluation planned after one year.

TABLE 1.3 Analysis of Experimental/Intervention Studies (n = 3)

Source	Purpose	Design and Method	Rural Location	Sample	Findings	Critique
Anderson-Loftin et al. (2002)	Test a culturally competent dietary education intervention.	Longitudinal quasi-experimental study to evaluate effectiveness, feasibility of intervention in rural area. One group pre-postintervention of four sessions with six groups, follow-up designed to improve physiologic outcomes and diabetes self-management. Costs of care analyzed using case management method for rural settings. Data collection, 1999. Independent Variable: dietary self-management education (low fat; peer group and professional follow-up). Dependent Variable: physiologic outcomes, diabetes self-management; Cost of care five months postintervention.	Southeast Region of the United States. South Carolina (Columbia)	n = 23 adult African Americans with T2DM. Convenience sample from one family practice office in rural medically underserved county. High-risk individuals with indicators modifiable by diet. Comprehensive description of community from which the sample was drawn.	1. Significant decrease in A1c and FBS not in weight, cholesterol, blood pressure. 2. Significant improvement in fat-related dietary habits. 3. No change in access or health services utilization except significant decrease in acute care visits. 4. Significant decrease in costs of care measured by number of visits.	Convenience sample. Outcomes of FBS not very useful. Some questions developed by researchers, e.g., health services utilization and costs of care (well-established instruments are available). Pilot study with small sample from one setting.

| Bray, Thompson, et al. (2005) | To explore efficiency of combining care management and interdisciplinary group visits for rural African Americans with diabetes. | Quasiexperimental intervention study comparing usual care to multidisciplinary group sessions.

APN visited the practice weekly for 12 months and facilitated diabetes education, patient flow, and management.

Patients participated in a four-session group visit education/support program led by nurse, physician, pharmacist, and nutritionist.

Compared to control patients in separate practice (usual care). | Southeast Region of the United States.

North Carolina (Eastern North Carolina, Greenville) | Rural African Americans with diabetes. Convenience sample from two adjacent counties.

Targeted those with high risk or poor management intervention, $n = 112$; control $n = 48$; Total 160

90% African American

Comprehensive description of population of counties used. | A1c not significantly different at baseline but significantly changed at 12 months. Decreased A1c in intervention group, increase in control group (median). No change in body weight or blood pressure in either group. Cost Analysis: increased number of visits due to guidelines in 10 randomly selected subjects reviewed, thus increased costs of intervention and increased patient volume. ≥ 60% of those in intervention group had decreased A1c. However, those achieving 7% increased from 32% to 45%. | Limited information on use of health care services/cost analysis.

Use of modified case management approach can be successful with rural African American circuit rider concept.

Findings similar to those with managed care system in urban areas. |

(Continued)

TABLE 1.3 Analysis of Experimental/Intervention Studies (n = 3) (*Continued*)

Source	Purpose	Design and Method	Rural Location	Sample	Findings	Critique
Smith & Weinert (2000)	To test the use of telecommunication technology to deliver diabetes education and social support to rural women with diabetes.	Quasiexperimental study with usual care compared to support group offered via computer over five-month period. Provided computers and software. Data collected from telephone interviews, mail questionnaires, and computer-use information. Measures collected at 2.5 months, 5 months, 7.5 months, and 10 months: Personal Resource Questionnaire, Quality of Life Index, Social Readjustment Rating Scale, and Psychosocial Adaptation to Illness Scale. Researcher developed score for utilization of computer. Information from software: number of times used and length.	Great Plains Region of the United States. Montana (South Central)	30 women randomized to computer and noncomputer groups. Recruited through health care providers and Montana Diabetes Association. Average age = 46.7 80% married 60% employed	Improving health and higher education attainment positively influenced social support scores and quality of life scores. Married women or those who reported greater support had higher Personal Resource Questionnaire scores. Employment may have significant effect on illness. Those in both groups tended to feel better adjusted to disease over time. Only five subjects had information about their A1c levels. Subjects spent more time using computer first month (average 129 minutes) vs. month 5 (average 37 minutes). Most positive evaluations were of "health chat" and "conversation" segments.	Not conceptually clear—"health" vs. "Quality of Life" measures? Length of time with diabetes not reported. Why women only? Multicollinearity of measures, with varied/overlapping measures of social support and adaptation to illness.

CONCLUSIONS

A critique of the research literature about nursing care of rural people with diabetes was conducted focusing on research published between 2000 and 2007 among rural populations of the United States. A total of 26 research reports were found that met the established criteria. The vast majority of research reports (22 of 26) were authored by nurses and published in journals intended for an audience of various health professionals. Results of this review are therefore informative for developing knowledge for nurses and other health professionals who care for those with diabetes, particularly those living in rural areas. Of the 26 studies examined, 16 were descriptive studies, 7 were program evaluations, and only 3 were intervention studies.

Findings indicate that with a few exceptions, researchers typically did not define *rural*, and rarely mentioned a conceptual framework. The studies reflected nearly every region of the continental United States with the exception of the Northwest; the majority were conducted in the Southeast. No studies were found from Alaska or Hawaii. The most significant methodological limitations include a lack of detailed information about recruitment of samples and/or populations from which they were drawn, a predominance of nonprobability sampling, and low statistical power that was the result of small sample size and/or too many variables. Additional methodological limitations identified in this review are the lack of longitudinal studies and the lack of adequate comparison groups in most studies. Thus, studies that use better research designs and that offer both valid and reliable results are needed. Because only three intervention studies were found, it is evident that there is a need for more experiments to test approaches to diabetes care among rural people, particularly because of the high rates of diabetes and high burden of disease in this population. Surprisingly, only a few of the studies used computers, telehealth, or other technological approaches to reach out to rural residents with diabetes.

Research Agenda for Rural Diabetes Care

It has been established for some time that good glucose control can reduce morbidity and mortality from diabetes—what remains to be determined for rural people in the United States is what kinds of strategies work in various settings with particular population groups. The research agenda for rural diabetes care should also include testing interventions that have already shown positive outcomes in urban populations. For example, studies have shown the importance of social, emotional, and informational support over the long term while individuals learn diabetes self-management (Funnell, Tang, & Anderson, 2007). More studies are needed to test ways of providing similar support to rural people for whom attending regular support group meetings may be difficult. Of those studies reviewed here, only one tested a support group in a rural area (Morris, 2007), and no outcomes such as glycemic control were measured. Studies are therefore needed to determine what kind of support is feasible to sustain diabetes management and whether such support is associated with key outcomes such as optimal glycemic control and improved quality of life.

As noted in a report by the Health and Human Services Task Force on Community Preventive Services, approaches such as case management and community-based self-management education programs need to be tested in rural populations (Evans & Kantrowitz, 2001). Studies that use such care processes to deal with barriers for rural people are particularly needed. For example, to overcome the barrier of distances and transportation, approaches should be tested that make use of technology such as computers, cell phones, and telehealth. Another barrier is the lack of multidisciplinary teams to offer comprehensive diabetes self-management education. Intervention studies need to be conducted that test creative ways to overcome insufficient numbers and types of health professionals. Examples might be the use of trained community health workers or other nonprofessional health care extenders. Only one study was found for this review that tested an approach to increasing the number of certified diabetes educators in a rural state (Butcher et al., 2006). Studies that implement new ways to train existing health care providers and to increase their ability to offer diabetes education are needed to test new approaches to rural diabetes care.

Financial barriers in the current health care system are another significant barrier to rural diabetes care. Limited reimbursement for diabetes self-management education by nurses and dieticians contributes to small numbers of health professionals in rural areas and throughout the United States (Siminerio, 2007). Studies are needed to test approaches that are financially viable in rural areas, such as the study reviewed here by Bray, Thompson, and colleagues (2005), which found 75% of the costs of a rural-based nurse case manager were offset by improvement in billable encounters and improved processes of care. Similarly, the study by Crow, Lakes, and Carter (2006) projected that a program will be able to break even with costs and revenues by using a nurse case manager. Follow-up studies are needed to determine actual cost-benefit analyses and the outcomes of diabetes care. Similarly, the circuit rider diabetes educator nurse who travels to several primary care sites is another approach that has promise in rural areas but has had minimal testing (Bray, Thompson, et al., 2005) as regards outcomes and cost-effectiveness. Studies are therefore needed to measure long-term savings that may be realized from case management diabetes care, circuit rider diabetes educators, and other kinds of care processes to determine if such approaches result in better clinical outcomes and fewer emergency room and hospital visits among those living in rural areas.

In summary, there is a great need for research to test many areas of diabetes care among rural people. Given the high rates of diabetes and the importance of improving the health of rural people with diabetes, there is an urgent need for nurses and other health care professionals to tackle the health disparities that currently plague this population.

REFERENCES

Alverson, E., & Kessler, T. (2005). Concerns expressed by underserved individuals regarding family & community healthcare needs. *Holistic Nursing Practice, 19*(4), 181–186.

Anderson-Loftin, W., Barnett, S., Bunn, P., & Sullivan, P. (2005). Recruitment and retention of rural African Americans in diabetes research: Lessons learned. *The Diabetes Educator, 31*(2), 251–259.

Anderson-Loftin, W., Barnett, S., Sullivan, P., Bunn, P., & Tavakoli, A. (2002). Culturally competent dietary education for southern rural African Americans with diabetes. *The Diabetes Educator, 28*(2), 245–257.

Balamurugan, A., Rivera, M., Jack, L., Allen, K., & Morris, S. (2006). Barriers to diabetes self-management education programs in underserved rural Arkansas: Implications for program evaluation. *Preventing Chronic Disease: Public Health Research, Practice and Policy, 3*(1). Retrieved June 12, 2007, from www.cdc.gov/pcd/issues/2006/jan/of_0129.htm

Bray, P., Roupe, M., Young, S., Harrell, J., Cummings, D., & Whetstone, L. (2005). Feasibility and effectiveness of system redesign for diabetes care management in rural areas: The Eastern North Carolina experience. *The Diabetes Educator, 31*(5), 712–718.

Bray, P., Thompson, D., Wynn, J., Cummings, D., & Whetstone, L. (2005). Confronting disparities in diabetes care: The clinical effectiveness of redesigning care management for minority patients in rural primary care practice. *The Journal of Rural Health, 21*(4), 317–321.

Butcher, M., Gilman, J., Meszaros, J., Bjorsness, D., Madison, M., McDowall, J., et al. (2006). Improving quality diabetes education in rural states: The Montana Quality Diabetes Education Initiative. *The Diabetes Educator, 32*(6), 963–968.

Center for Disease Control and Prevention (CDC). (2005). *Diabetes fact sheet.* Retrieved November 18, 2007, from http://www.cdc.gov/diabetes/pubs/factsheet05.htm

Crow, C., Lakes, S., & Carter, M. (2006). A nursing case management program for low-income high-risk diabetic clients. *Lippincott's Case Management, 11*(2), 90–98.

Evans, G. W., & Kantrowitz, E. (2001). Strategies for reducing morbidity and mortality from diabetes through health-care system interventions and diabetes self-management education in community settings. A report on recommendations of the Task Force on Community Preventive Services. *Morbidity and Mortality Weekly Report Recommendations and Reports, 50*, 1–15.

Funnell, M., Tang, R., & Anderson, R. (2007). From DSME to DSMS: Developing empowerment-based diabetes self-management support. *Diabetes Spectrum, 20*(4), 221–226.

Gamm, L., Hutchinson, L., Dabney, B., & Dorsey, A. (Eds.). (2003). *Rural healthy people 2010: A companion document to Healthy People 2010* (Vol. 1). Rockville, MD: The

Office of Rural Health Policy, Health Resources and Services Administration, United States Department of Health and Human Services.

Gesler, W., Hayes, M., Arcury, T., Skelly, A., Nash, S., & Soward, A. (2004). Use of mapping technology in health intervention research. *Nursing Outlook, 52,* 142–146.

Heuer, L., Hess, C., & Batson, A. (2006). Cluster Clinics for migrant Hispanic farm worker with diabetes: Perceptions, successes, and challenges. *Rural and Remote Health, 6,* 469. Retrieved June 12, 2007, from http://rrh.deakin.edu.au/

Heuer, L., Hess, C., & Klug, M. (2004). Meeting health care needs of a rural Hispanic migrant population with diabetes. *The Journal of Rural Health, 20*(3), 265–270.

Jones, R., Utz, S., Wenzel, J., Steeves, R., Hinton, I., Andrews, D., et al. (2006). Use of complementary and alternative therapies by rural African Americans with type 2 diabetes. *Alternative Therapies, 12*(5), 34–38.

Long, K. A., & Weinert, C. (1998). Rural nursing: Developing the theory base. In H. J. Lee (Ed.), *Conceptual basis for rural nursing.* Philadelphia: Springer Publishing.

Moore, K., Roubideaux, Y., Noonan, C., Goldberg, J., Shields, R., & Acton, K. (2006). Quality of diabetes care for urban & rural Indian Health Programs. *Ethnicity and Disease, 16,* 772–777.

Morris, D. (2007). A rural diabetes support group. *The Diabetes Educator, 24,* 493–497.

Nagelkerk, J., Reick, K., & Meengs, L. (2006). Perceived barriers & effective strategies to diabetes self-management. *Journal of Advanced Nursing, 54*(2), 151–158.

Neil, J. (2002). Assessing foot care knowledge in rural population with diabetes. *Ostomy Wound Management, 48*(1), 50–56.

Orem, D., Taylor, S., & Renpenning, K. M. (2001). *Nursing: Concepts of practice.* St. Louis, MO: Mosby.

Roy, C. (1999). *The Roy adaptation model.* Philadelphia: Appleton and Lange.

Ruder, K. (2007). Fighting the epidemic: A United Nations resolution on diabetes. *Diabetes Forecast, February Issue, 47,* 50–51.

Siminerio, L. M. (2007). Is the diabetes educator our next endangered species? Lessons from the American Bald Eagle. *Diabetes Spectrum, 20*(4), 197–198.

Siminerio, L., Piatt, G., & Zgibor, J. (2005). Implementing the Chronic Care Model for improvements in diabetes care and education in a rural primary care practice. *The Diabetes Educator, 31*(2), 225–234.

Skelly, A., Arcury, T., Snively, B., Bell, R., Smith, S., Wetmore, L., et al. (2005). Self-monitoring of blood glucose in a multiethnic population of rural older adults with diabetes. *The Diabetes Educator, 31*(1), 84–90.

Skelly, A., Dougherty, M., Gesler, W., Soward, A., Burns, D., & Arcury, T. (2007). African American beliefs about diabetes. *Western Journal of Nursing Research, 28*(9), 9–29.

Smith, L., & Weinert, C. (2000). Telecommunication support for rural women with diabetes. *The Diabetes Educator, 26*(4), 645–655.

Stern, S., Merwin, E., Hauenstein, E., Hinton, I., Rovnyak, V., Wilson, M., et al. (in process). *The effect of rurality on mental and physical health.*

Struthers, R., Hodge, R., DeCora, L., & Geishirt-Cantrell, B. (2003). Experience of Native peer facilitators in the Campaign Against Type 2 Diabetes. *The Journal of Rural Health, 19*(2), 174–180.

Tessaro, I., Smith, S., & Rye, S. (2005). Knowledge & perceptions of diabetes in an Appalachian population. *Public Health Research, Practice, and Policy, 2*(2), 1–9.

Tudiver, F., Wolff, L., Morin, P., Teresi, J., Palmas, W., Starren, J., et al. (2007). Primary care providers' perceptions of home diabetes telemedicine care in the IDEATel Project. *The Journal of Rural Health, 23*(1), 55–61.

Utz, S., Steeves, R., Wenzel, J., Hinton, I., Jones, R., Andrews, D., et al. (2006). "Working hard with it": Self-management of type 2 diabetes by rural African Americans. *Family & Community Health, 29*(3), 195–205.

Wenzel, J., Utz, S., Steeves, R., Hinton, I., & Jones, R. (2006). Stories of diagnosis from rural Blacks with diabetes. *Family and Community Health, 29*(3), 206–213.

Zulkowski, K., & Coon, P. (2005). Patient perceptions & provider documentation of diabetes care in rural areas. *Ostomy Wound Management, 51*(3), 50–58.

Chapter 2

Matters of the Heart: Cardiovascular Disease and Rural Nursing

Pamela Stewart Fahs and Melanie Kalman

ABSTRACT

Cardiovascular disease (CVD) is the leading cause of death in the United States and around the world. Most of the work done on CVD among rural populations uses mortality versus prevalence rates because prevalence data for rural populations is difficult, if not impossible, to find in national data sets as currently published. Cardiovascular disease is a significant threat to rural dwellers and those in rural nursing need evidence on which to base their practice. This chapter provides an examination of the CVD literature as it relates to rural populations with an emphasis on studies that include or are limited to rural women as subjects. Topics reviewed included: awareness and symptoms of heart disease among women, heart failure (HF) in rural women, hypertension (HTN) in rural areas, stroke in rural populations, quality care in acute myocardial infarction (MI) in rural facilities, mortality and CVD, and CVD risk factors in rural populations. The authors reviewed 134 research articles published between 2000 and 2007. Overall, the CVD research literature in rural populations has small sample sizes, except for epidemiologic studies, and tends to be descriptive in nature. There is a dearth of literature on prevalence among rural populations from a national perspective and little is written on interventions to reduce CVD risks and physiological markers that include large samples from rural populations. Future nursing research on CVD in rural populations needs to move beyond the descriptive to intervention studies, which need to be robust in power to guard against Type II errors.

Keywords: rural; women; men; awareness; cardiovascular disease (CVD); coronary heart disease (CHD); hypertension (HTN); stroke; myocardial infarction (MI); acute myocardial infarction (AMI)

OVERVIEW

The purpose of this chapter is to review research conducted in rural populations or on factors of rurality in the area of cardiovascular disease (CVD) that has meaning to the nursing care of this group. In addition, the reviewers examined the state of the science in CVD and nursing as it relates to rural populations. Cardiovascular disease is the leading cause of death in the United States. According to the American Heart Association (AHA) 1 in 3 American adults are diagnosed with CVD (Rosamond, Flegal, Friday, et al., 2007; Rosamond, Flegal, Furie, et al., 2008). This translated into an estimated 80,700,000 adults in the United States (U.S.) with one or more types of CVD from 1999 to 2004 extrapolated to 2005 population estimates, which is the most recent data available (Rosamond, Flegal, Furie, et al., 2008). Despite the fact that geographic location has been identified as one possible factor in health disparities, prevalence data for CVD among rural Americans is difficult to find at the national level. The most recent national extrapolations of rural health disparities were published more than five years ago (Eberhardt et al., 2001; Ricketts, 1999). These sources were extremely helpful for researchers and need to be updated to maintain relevance. The prevalence of people with CVD in the United States is now more than 80 million, and of those, 38 million are age 60 or older (Rosamond, Flegal, Furie, et al., 2008). Seventy-three million are hypertensive, 16 million have coronary heart disease (CHD), more than 5 million have heart failure (HF), and more than 5.5 million have had a stroke (Kisely, Campbell, & Skerritt, 2005; Rosamond, Flegal, Furie, et al., 2008). Men are at greater risk for CVD until women reach menopause (Douglas & Poppas, 2007). Estimates of yearly myocardial infarction (MI) range from more than 700,000 to 1 million in the United States (United States Preventative Services Task Force [USPSTF], 2004). Interestingly, better treatment of CVD and longer life expectancy have led to an increase in the prevalence of HF (Vasan & Wilson, 2007). As Americans age, the number of people with CVD will increase.

Risk factors for CVD are age, gender, and smoking (USPSTF, 2004). Other risk factors include: HTN, dsylipidemia, abnormal glucose metabolism, and a sedentary lifestyle. The modifiable risk factors are often associated with each other and with obesity (Jackson & Ockene, 2007; USPSTF, 2004). Obesity, which is endemic in the United States, is associated with cardiac mortality. The authors of the Women's Health Study (Manson et al., 1995) found that among women with a body mass index (BMI) of 32 kg/m2 or higher who had never smoked, the relative risk (RR) of death from CVD was 4.1 compared with women in the lowest group, with a BMI below 19.0. Overweight is defined as a BMI between 25 and 29 kg/m2, from 30 to 39 is considered obese, and 40 and higher is defined as extreme or morbid obesity (Association of Women's Health Obstetric and Neonatal Nurses, 2003). Obesity rates are influenced by rurality more for women than men. The highest percentage of obese women was in rural areas (23%) compared to large fringe metropolitan areas (16%) (Eberhardt et al., 2001). In the northeast and south, obesity is highest in non-metropolitan counties (25%), yet in the Midwest about 25% of obese women live in large metropolitan areas. Visceral or abdominal obesity is associated with insulin resistance and is more likely to result in CVD (Jackson & Ockene, 2007).

There are racial disparities related to CVD. The prevalence for having two or more risk factors for heart disease or stroke was highest for African Americans (48.7%) and next highest for American Indians and Alaskan Natives (46.7%). Asians had the lowest prevalence (25.9%) (Rosamond, Flegal, Friday, et al., 2007). High mortality rates among African Americans may be explained in part by treatment-seeking behaviors (McSweeney, Lefler, Fischer, Naylor, & Evans, 2007). McSweeney and colleagues (2007) found that Black women (n = 509) with MI symptoms seek treatment in a less timely manner than White women (n = 500). Racial disparities may be more related to socioeconomic status (SES) factors, such as poverty, than race itself. Poverty is a common occurrence in rural populations, thus disparities in SES along the rural–urban continuum may explain some of the crude mortality rate differentiation as well as CVD risk factors seen in rural populations (Taylor, Hughes, & Garrison, 2002).

The crude mortality rates for rural dwellers in the category of CHD are higher than those of nonrural populations (Ricketts, 1999). However, in data that are age-adjusted, this difference often disappears, indicating that because rural areas tend to have a heavier proportion of elders, the differences in mortality data from heart disease may be more age than geographic location dependent. The literature is replete with data that indicates that those in rural locations have less access to specialty care including services provided by cardiologists (Eberhardt et al., 2001; Morgan & Fahs, 2007; Ricketts, 1999), and that transportation and isolation can be a factor in time to treatment as well as access to treatment for CVD. According to the Centers for Disease Control and Prevention (CDC), the mortality from heart disease is 652,486 annually (National Center for Health Statistics [NCHS], 2007). Cardiovascular disease is the underlying cause of death in 1 out of 2.8 deaths and CVD is listed 58% of the time as a contributing cause of death in the United States. This translates into 2,400 Americans dying every day or 1 death every 37 seconds from a CVD-associated illness (Rosamond, Flegal, Furie, et al., 2008).

Heart disease is the most costly component of health care spending in the United States. Chest pain is the most frequent reason for emergency department (ED) visits and admissions (Kisely et al., 2005). According to the AHA, the cost of CVD in 2007 alone would reach $431.8 billion (Rosamond, Flegal, Friday, et al., 2007) and the 2008 estimate for direct and indirect costs will be $448.5 billion (Rosamond, Flegal, Furie, et al., 2008). The overall costs of CHD and stroke in 2003 were estimated to be greater than $350 billion (USPSTF, 2004). The information on the economic burden of CVD is particularly relevant to rural dwellers, health care providers, and scientists interested in geographic health disparities because rural areas often have issues of poverty and limited resources that make health care delivery and compliance with health care management an important issue.

Women and Cardiovascular Disease

Disease of the heart, or CHD, is the number one cause of death and stroke is the number three cause of death in women overall (NCHS, 2007). Although heart disease is often thought of as a disease of men or older women, in addition to being the number one cause of death for women age 65 and older, it is ranked second for women age 45–65, and is the third leading cause of death in women age 25–44. Symptoms of CVD start to develop between the ages of 45 and 64 for one in nine women (CDC, 2004). After age 65, the ratio climbs to one in three women (Miller, 2007). In addition, the morbidity and mortality from MI is higher for women than men (McSweeney & Coon, 2004).

Until the late 1980s, CVD research sampled predominately men, so the picture of so-called normal cardiac symptoms is skewed toward a male diagnostic picture. Lack of significant chest pain and symptomology that is different from the typical male presentation may be a major reason why women have more unrecognized acute myocardial infarction (AMI) than men or are mistakenly diagnosed and discharged from the ED without appropriate treatment (McSweeney, Cody, O'Sullivan, Elberson, Moser, et al., 2003). Healy (1991) supports this view, claiming that "women are not considered different from men as far as health. . . . The problem is women have different symptoms and react to treatment differently. This is the 'Yentl Syndrome' " (p. 275).

METHODOLOGY

Literature searches for this chapter were conducted through two State University of New York campuses. The major search engines used were CINAHL, MEDLINE, and PubMed using the subject heading *Cardiovascular Diseases* combined with *rural, rural nursing, rural health services, rural health centers,* or *rural areas.* In addition the keywords *rural* and *hypertension* or *blood pressure* were searched. This produced more than 5,000 citations. Limiters were set including *English language, research,* and *peer reviewed* articles after the year 2000, producing 210 relevant articles on CINAHL. MEDLINE and PubMed produced similar results although the journal titles on these search engines were more often, but not limited to, medical journals. The Cochrane and UpToDate databases were also searched using the keywords *cardiovascular disease* and *rural.* In addition, nurse authors known to write in the area of CVD were searched specifically through CINAHL and Web of Science, bringing forth another small group of articles. Finally, to ensure an exhaustive search, journals known to publish in the area of rural health were searched for articles using the keywords CVD, HD, HTN, stroke, or diseases of the heart. These included: the *Journal of Rural Health,* which produced 10 articles; the *Online Journal of Rural Nursing and Health,* which produced three articles; and *Rural and Remote Health,* which produced three articles. Reviewing all search results, articles were maintained for analysis if: (a) the topic was cardiovascular; (b) a research method was used; (c) they explicitly mentioned sampling from rural populations, were geographically located in a rural area, or if personal communication indicated rural populations were included; or (d) if they were from a national database where statistical notes indicated inclusion of rural samples. Exclusion criteria used were: (a) topic was specific to specific risk factor(s) such as obesity; (b) an intervention looked at one outcome, such as a change in physical activity (PA) without examining commensurate changes in cardiovascular status; (c) literature review or meta-analysis; and (d) male only. The decision to limit this analysis to the general topic of CVD in rural populations with a focus on rural women was made when it became apparent that literature on specific risk factors and specific interventions alone would broaden the search and analysis beyond limitations of space and time for this analysis. Most intervention studies that focused on reducing one risk factor of CVD tended to use only the measurement of that variable, such as amount of PA, as the outcome rather than looking at the improved cardiovascular (CV) status including biological markers of CVD risks. Excluding studies of CVD and rural men alone was done because only eight articles were found on CVD and rural men. This was considered too small a pool of studies from which to draw accurate conclusions, other than the obvious, which is that more work is needed in this area. This chapter highlights the work of nurse scientists in the literature on CVD and rural populations but is not limited to nurse researchers alone. The inclusion and exclusion criteria produced 134 articles, which were reviewed.

LITERATURE REVIEW

Cardiovascular Disease and Rural Populations

Awareness and Symptoms of Heart Disease in Women

Awareness of the fact that CVD is a killer of women, how to recognize and treat heart disease in women, and disparities in awareness and treatment of CVD has been an issue permeating the literature throughout the past decade (Christian, Rosamond, White, & Mosca, 2007; Mosca, Jones, King, Ouyang, Redberg, et al., 2000). A national representative sample ($n = 1,005$) that presumably includes rural women found that there had been a statistically significant increase in the knowledge of CVD as a leading cause of death (LCOD) among women since 1997 (Christian et al., 2007). These authors conclude "a significant increase in awareness of heart disease as the LCOD among women has been documented since 1997, suggesting that efforts by several organizations to educate women about CVD have been effective in raising awareness . . . important racial/ethnic disparities persists, and future initiatives should target these high-risk populations" (p. 80). This work does not identify whether there is a gap in awareness of CVD as the LCOD among rural women.

McSweeney and colleagues have a body of work (McSweeney, 1998; McSweeney & Crane, 2000; McSweeney, Cody, & Crane, 2001; McSweeney et al., 2003; McSweeney & Crane, 2004; McSweeney, O'Sullivan, Cody, & Crane, 2004; McSweeney, Lefler, & Crowder, 2005; McSweeney et al., 2007) that has included rural women within their samples (personal communication, J. McSweeney's office manager, November 2007). It is unclear if the rural women were seen in tertiary care centers or in their rural localities and there is no breakdown of any rural versus urban differences in either their perception of risk of CHD or their ability to identify prodromal or acute symptoms of MI. McSweeney and colleagues (2001) noted: "We need to change women's perceptions about their risk for developing CHD by revising educational materials and increasing publicity about the impact of CHD on women's health" (p. 35). In addition, they cautioned that practitioners must also be aware of the dangers and develop a more comprehensive treatment plan for women with CHD and that more work needed to be done on both the prodromal and AMI symptoms of women. In a secondary analysis of a qualitative study ($n = 40$) describing prodromal and AMI symptoms in women, McSweeney and colleagues (2005) uncovered five themes: (1) awareness, (2) seeking treatment, (3) frustration,

(4) treatment decisions, and (5) anger. These themes spanned the prodromal stages and acute stages of MI. The themes for the prodromal stage were: awareness, seeking treatment, and frustration. The theme for the acute stage was treatment decisions. The final theme, anger, was expressed in both the prodromal and acute stages. Of interest is that the women sought help initially and then when the problem was not resolved. Because they did not have crushing chest pain they felt that they were not taken seriously. Health care professionals do not always recognize women's symptoms of MI, but most are aware that women have CVD risks. However, women themselves do not always recognize their risk for CHD (McSweeney et al., 2004). McSweeney and Coon (2004) reported that only 7% of women identify CHD as a health threat.

Being diagnosed with an MI often requires lifestyle changes. McSweeney and Coon (2004), using a semistructured interview, explored the inhibitors and facilitators to making behavioral changes in women after an MI. The behavioral changes were diet, exercise, smoking cessation, and medication adherence. In their sample of mostly White women (n = 40), they found the perceived inhibitors were: (a) financial, environmental, and physical problems; (b) social support; and (c) reduced quality of life. Perceived facilitators were: (a) social support, (b) finances, (c) motivation, and (d) environment. The authors concluded that while interventions are necessary to decrease risk factors and prevent reoccurrence of MI, "women are often of lower SES, have more risk factors and co-morbidities, and are typically older by ten years than men at the time of their first MI" (p. 49). These differences require different interventions for women than for men to help change behavior. It would be interesting to see if the facilitators and inhibitors would be different for a sample composed entirely of rural women because there are discussions in the rural literature about rurality, quality of life, and barriers to access to care.

Another contribution of McSweeney and colleagues (2004) to the literature of women and CVD has been the development of the instrument, the McSweeney Acute and Prodromal Myocardial Infarction Symptom survey, for assessing acute and prodromal MI symptoms. Because many women are unaware of their risk for CVD or do not relate their symptoms to cardiac problems, they often ignore prodromal symptoms. The tool was developed from four studies (McSweeney et al., 2004). In-depth interviews and a naturalistic design were used to explore women's perception of their symptoms after they were diagnosed with an MI (McSweeney, 1998; McSweeney & Crane, 2000). The most consistent symptom was unusual fatigue. Only 30% of women in this study described severe chest pain and 25% reported no chest pain at all (McSweeney, 1998). In the second study, the most frequent prodromal symptoms were unusual fatigue and discomfort in the shoulder blade and chest areas and the most frequent acute symptoms were chest sensations, shortness of breath, feeling hot and flushed, and unusual fatigue (McSweeney & Crane, 2000).

Instrument development was discussed in the third and fourth studies and the instrument now includes 38 acute and 35 prodromal symptoms (McSweeney et al., 2003, 2004). Although the tool is designed to be given to women who have had an MI, it may also be useful in identifying education needs for both the lay public and health care providers about prodromal and acute MI symptoms in women, as well as being used to understand that the prodromal symptom score is an important predictor of acute symptoms. Future research is needed to determine if this tool can be used to predict MI based on the prodromal symptoms, whether these symptoms are predictive of future cardiac events, and how other risk factors and comorbidities affect the prodromal symptoms in this instrument (McSweeney et al., 2004). Because most of the women in these studies were White, future research should explore instrument psychometrics for use with other ethnicities and geographic locations. The work of McSweeney and colleagues (McSweeney, 1998; McSweeney & Crane, 2000; McSweeney et al., 2001; McSweeney et al., 2003; McSweeney & Crane, 2004; McSweeney et al., 2004; McSweeney et al., 2005; McSweeney et al., 2007) is a strong body of literature that began with qualitative studies and has moved to tool development in the area of identification of prodromal and acute MI symptoms in women. Although this is an issue pertinent to all women at risk for CVD, an area of investigation into rural influences on women's awareness of MI symptoms and patterns in seeking medical attention in the case of prodromal or acute symptoms would greatly benefit the care of rural women with CVD.

One author wrote specifically about the ability of a rural sample to recognize symptoms of AMI and their patterns in seeking treatment (Morgan, 2005). Morgan examined whether the symptoms of AMI were incongruent with their expectations of MI symptoms. This study reports a sample of 98 rural dwellers, which provided a power level of 0.80. There were 62 men and 36 women in this study. Symptoms that limited activity and resulted in anxiety led to shorter treatment times compared to those who were able to go about their normal activities of daily living (ADL) and had less anxiety. Both men and women had incongruence between expected and actual symptoms, with many reporting they had expected to have shortness of breath or fatigue, which did not occur. It is the reviewers' opinion that this study demonstrates a possible problem with campaigns to raise awareness. Individuals may get part, but not all, of the message with unintended consequences, such as women not seeking help because they had chest pain, but had been educated to expect shortness of breath and fatigue or vice versa. Education efforts need to clearly reflect that different people may have different symptoms and if in doubt immediate help should be sought for MI, which is a medical emergency.

One study (Struthers, Savik, & Hodge, 2004) looked at how Native American women on three rural and geographically isolated reservations in Minnesota and Wisconsin responded to chest pain. The sample included 866 rural Native

American women age 22 and older. This quantitative, descriptive study included face-to-face interviews and secondary data analysis of the Inter-Tribal Heart Project. Two sources, the Indian Health Service (IHS) outpatient clinic and an IHS hospital, provided care to 87% of the subjects in this study. Other sources included: traditional healers (0.6%), private doctors (5.3%), non-IHS or non-tribal health care facility (6.1%), and ED (0.01%). Distance to health care varied, but 93.2% lived within 30 miles of a health care facility. Health care was reported as not available in the past two years for 12.9% of the respondents and reasons for nonavailability for this group with publicly funded health care were explored. The majority of women had been told they had not had an MI (93%) at the health clinic or hospital; however, 13% were told they had other cardiac problems and 3.6% had a history of stroke. When asked "What would you do if you experienced crushing pain in your chest that lasted longer than 15 minutes?" (p. 161), more than two-thirds (68%) reported they would go for medical care or call an ambulance while about one-third (32%) had a more passive response, such as sitting down to rest until it passed (23%), seeking medical care when it was convenient (3%), or hoping it would go away (2%). Only 0.1% reported they would seek the help of a traditional healer. Analysis showed that the more passive group was younger and had less education at a statistically significant level than the group that responded with more active options. This study did not include MI symptoms beyond crushing chest pain. This is a limitation because research shows that although women have the more typical crushing chest pain about one-third of the time, female symptoms can be more insidious and less clear, such as unusual fatigue (McSweeney et al., 2004; Morgan, 2005).

This review indicates that education efforts in helping rural dwellers identify possible acute MI symptoms and the importance of seeking immediate emergency care are needed, particularly among rural women. This is an area that could benefit from nurse-developed programs to improve knowledge and appropriate response to MI symptoms among rural populations. Research on various approaches to define effective and appropriate programs for increasing awareness of MI symptoms and facilitating appropriate responses in rural populations is needed.

Heart Failure and Rural Populations

Heart failure is another issue that was explored during this review of CVD and rural populations. Six studies were reviewed on the topic of HF (Clark & Lan, 2004; Clark, McLennan, Eckert, Dawson, Wilkinson, et al., 2005; Granmyr, Ball, Curran, & Wang, 2007; Pierce, 2005, 2007; Wagnild, Rowland, Dimmler, & Peters, 2004). Wagnild and colleagues (2004) compared frontier and urban elders (n = 284) with HF residing in Montana. Of those, 52% were urban and 48% frontier. This retrospective medical record review included data on depression, quality of life (QoL), the New York Heart Association (NYHA) classification of HF, comorbid conditions, and sociodemographic data (p. 14); although data were incomplete for depression and QoL because some subjects did not return these forms. Frontier dwellers had significantly lower scores on the Minnesota Living with Heart Failure Questionnaire (LlhFE), which the authors say indicates that "frontier patients were having more symptoms that interfered with their lives than did urban patients" (p. 15). The second component of the study was a review by the researchers with three cardiac specialty nurses at the tertiary care center after subject discharge. These nurses speculated that (a) frontier primary care providers may not be up-to-date on HF treatment guidelines; (b) there is lack of communication between the hospital specialist, the community generalist, and the patient; (c) frontier patients tend to develop high thresholds of pain and only see themselves as sick when they cannot function, possibly preventing recognition of when symptoms indicate a critical problem; and (d) self-reliance may influence care in subtle ways, such as patients are thought to be more likely to change their medication regimen without consultation. In this study, the 28 frontier counties had population densities that ranged from 2.2 to 6 persons per square mile. Frontier in the United States is generally defined as counties of seven or fewer persons per square mile (United States Department of Agriculture, 2008). There were 17 hospitals serving these frontier counties of MT, while six counties did not have hospital services. Specialty care for HF patients ranged from 37 to 440 miles away, one way, with the average distance to care being 200 miles. These authors suggested that providing more accessible and frequent specialty care could be accomplished through technological and communication advances. They also suggested better communication links between specialty CV nurses and clinic and home health nurses in the community as well as with primary care providers. Home monitoring devices are another avenue that could use further exploration based on the findings of this study (Wagnild et al., 2004).

Clark and Lan (2004) conducted a study in the United States of small community hospitals serving surrounding rural areas on learning needs of HF patients after discharge. An aside revealed during the study enrollment was that 13 rural elderly who were diagnosed with HF on admission to the hospital did not know they had HF at discharge (Clark et al., 2005). These subjects indicated that learning about adherence to medications was most important in their perspective, and behavioral changes in areas of diet, PA, as well as psychological factors were the least important to them. Two studies (Pierce, 2005, 2007) related specifically to rural women with HF and were reports on different aspects of the same study (personal communication, C. Pierce, December 16, 2007). The author studied a sample of 45 rural women in upstate New York. This was a descriptive study that focused on predicting health promotion behaviors (HPB; Pierce, 2005) and explicating the effect of distance and weather on accessing health care (Pierce, 2007). Diabetes mellitus (DM) ($r = .431$, $p < 0.05$) and the NYHA classification level ($r = -.275$, $p < 0.01$) were most predictive of who participated in HPB. The author speculates that with DM there is an increase in health education and more contact with health care providers and that these factors should be further studied to see if they influence the improved HPB seen among subjects with DM in this sample. Those with less impact of HF, thus a better score on the NYHA scale, had better HPB. On the topic of distance and isolation (Pierce, 2007), the mean distance to obtain primary care was six miles while the average distance for cardiology care was 33 miles. The rural county in upstate New York used in this study does have an adjacent metropolitan area that influences the distance to specialty care over the distances reported in some rural studies, particularly in rural states where metropolitan areas are further apart and fewer in number. Of note in this study is that only 50% of the subjects actually had follow-up care provided by a cardiologist. Weather and distance did not have a significant effect on seeking care, although with the advancing age of the women, weather was more likely to have an influence ($p = 0.59$). The limited sample size in this study may contribute to a Type II error or false negative.

In the area of HF, further studies with larger sample sizes and more rigorous designs are needed. Heart failure is an area where the work of nurse researchers interested in rural health is evident in the literature. This body of work to date is primarily descriptive. Future studies need to focus on interventions to reduce both mortality and morbidity from HF in rural populations. Ideally these interventions should consider the influence of rural life to improve the care of clients with HF. In terms of the large variation across studies seen in the distances traveled to specialty care, a system to help readers identify the level of rurality of study locations, such as the Rural-Urban Commuting Area Codes (RUCA), would be helpful in standardizing rural research.

Hypertension

Hypertension is a category of CVD but it is also considered a risk factor for stroke and diseases of the heart. Several articles were reviewed in this section (Agyemang, 2006; Ahmad & Jafar, 2005; Bassett, Fitzhugh, Crespo, King, & McLaughlin, 2002; Bjerregaard et al., 2003; Borges-Yanez, Irigoyen-Camacho, & Maupom, 2006; Boutain, 2001; Brown, Etrata, Aki, Cardines, & James, 2001; Brown, James, Aki, Mills, & Etrata, 2003; Brown, Sievert, et al., 2001; Charlton et al., 2005; Huang, Niu, et al., 2004; Huang, Wildman, Gu, Muntner, Su, et al., 2004; Hunter, Sparks, Mufunda, Musabayane, Sparks, et al., 2000; James & Bovbjerg, 2001; Lancaster, Smiciklas-Wright, Weitzel, Mitchell, Friedmann, et al., 2004; Nyholm, Merlo, Rastam, & Lindblad, 2005; Ohira et al., 2002; Peltzer,

2004; Pizent, Jurasovic, & Telisman, 2001; Silva, James, & Crews, 2006; Skliros et al., 2007; Tazi et al., 2003; Tsutsumi, Kayaba, Tsutsumi, & Igarashi, 2001; Wijewardene et al., 2005; Yamagishi, Iso, Tanigawa, Cui, Kudo, et al., 2004; Yamagishi et al., 2007; Yan, Gu, Yang, Wu, Kang, et al., 2005; Yang, Sun, Zhang, Wu, Zhang, et al., 2007; Zhang et al., 2005, 2007). The literature in this area covered many aspects of HTN and blood pressure (BP), from prevalence to bio-chemical markers involved in the hypertensive process. Several foreign stud-ies found that rural populations had lower incidence of HTN in places where subsistence living was still a mainstay of the culture; however, rural dwellers of higher SES or with more industrialization had increasing levels of HTN as well as other cardiovascular risk factors (Agyemang, 2006; Huang, Niu, et al., 2004; Hunter et al., 2000). A few studies looked at dietary intake and HTN (Charlton et al., 2005; Lancaster et al., 2004; Yamagishi et al., 2007). These studies exam-ined dietary elements such as sodium (Na), calcium (Ca), and potassium (K). In general Na intake was high while Ca and K intakes were lower than desired. One study (Yamagishi et al., 2007) found that dietary Na intake can strengthen the association between an angiotensin-converting gene and higher BP. These authors speculate that differing dietary habits may explain why previous works on the association of this gene and HTN have produced varied outcomes. Much of the literature reviewed in this section used *rural* as a keyword but in most cases this referred only to where the sample was recruited. There was only one article where the researcher was easily identified as a nurse (Boutain, 2001). In this qualitative study, rural Louisiana residents discussed their perceptions of worry, stress, and high BP. These participants felt that worry and stress were factors that influenced their BP and mismanagement of their HTN increased these elements. This author notes that in this sample the average control rate for HTN was only 27%. Of note to this discussion is an article that compared CVD risk factors among rural, suburban, and urban women (Fahs, Grabo, James, Neff-Smith, & Spencer, 2001), the details of which can be found in Table 2.1. On the issue of HTN control, eight (24% of rural sample) rural women, nine suburban (19%), and six (22%) urban subjects reported having a history of HTN on screening. Six of the eight (75%) rural known hypertensive subjects were using antihyperten-sives compared to 15 (100%) of their more urban counterparts. Reasons for not using antihypertensives among the rural women were explored in this study. One could ask, is the disparity between diagnosis and treatment that occurred in rural but not urban women in this study a sample variant or does this issue deserve further study? On the whole, articles that reflect nursing research in the area of HTN were conspicuously absent in the search results. Many of the nursing stud-ies reviewed in the CVD risk section included prevalence and identification of HTN or high BP as just one aspect of their studies. Control and management of HTN among rural populations is an area where more nursing work is needed.

TABLE 2.1 References and Details of Articles Reviewed on the Topic of CVD Risk Factors

References	Sample Size/Location/ Gender/Ethnicity/ Rurality	Method/Significant Findings
Appel et al., 2002	n = 1,110; North Carolina; African American and White; women; rural	Quantitative: Descriptive, Survey. Significant predictive risk factors for CVD were BMI and lower education levels, there was no ss difference for race in the association of CVD.
Borges-Yanez et al., 2006	n = 315; Mexico; men and women; rural and urban	Quantitative: Descriptive/Correlational.* Urban, lower SES, and elders had the worse periodontitis disease. Only 29% of the rural sample had periodontal problems.
Carter et al., 2005	n = 27; Alabama; African American and White; men and women; rural	Qualitative: Focus groups. Employees identified screening and health education as helpful. Self-report of changes in dietary intake and ways of preparing food.
Chikani et al., 2004	n = 1,500; Marshfield, Wisconsin; White women; rural	Quantitative: Epidemiological: Cohort. Among overweight women, only anger-discussion score had an effect on lipids with elevated triglycerides, elevated risks ratio, and low levels of high density lipids (HDL).
Chikani et al., 2005	n = 1,500; Wisconsin (MESA); White women; rural	Quantitative: Epidemiological: Cohort. Job demands were associated with higher DBP, insulin, TG, TC, and ratios but were inversely associated with insulin sensitivity. Decision latitude was inversely associated with BMI and insulin level but positively associated with insulin sensitivity. Job demand predicted more CVD risk factors among farm residents, who had more CVD risks than nonfarm residents.
Eyler et al., 2002	n = 305; African American, Latina, and White; women; rural and urban	Qualitative: Focus Groups. This report sets the stage for the other reports on the same study (Eyler & Vest, 2002; Sanderson et al., 2002) found in the literature. Discusses purpose, method, and sampling for the 42 focus groups conducted in this study.

(Continued)

TABLE 2.1 References and Details of Articles Reviewed on the Topic of CVD Risk Factors (*Continued*)

References	Sample Size/Location/ Gender/Ethnicity/ Rurality	Method/Significant Findings
Eyler & Vest, 2002	n = 33; Missouri and Illinois women; rural	Qualitative: Focus Groups. Social environment, guilt, and family responsibilities, social support, and environmental and policy barriers to being PA were identified with fewer opportunities to exercise in rural areas. Few and inconvenient facilities; lack of sidewalks and safe walking areas, and cost were barriers. Worksite exercise facilities were seen as an appealing potential intervention.
Deskins et al., 2006	n = 142; West Virginia; 14 community leaders; 36 parents; and 92 students; women, men, and children; rural	Qualitative: Focus Groups. Adult-generated barrier themes: concerns about testing outcomes and lack of knowledge about cholesterol/heart disease in children; traditional Appalachian cultural beliefs; costs, availability; and lack of time. Child-identified themes: (1) concerns about testing outcomes; (2) privacy; (3) fear of needles; (4) lack of concern about health and cholesterol; (5) parental beliefs; and (6) lack of social pressure to engage in preventive health.
Fahs et al., 2001	n = 108; New York; White women; rural, suburban, and urban	Quantitative: Descriptive/Correlational. SBP was higher for rural women (ss) but not after controlling for age. Fewer rural women with HTN went untreated or were not taking their antihypertensive medications. Women in all three groups had higher than desired levels of CVD risk factors.
Fiandt et al., 1999	n = 102; Nebraska; women; rural	Quantitative: Descriptive: Survey* Women underestimated their risk for chronic illnesses including CVD. Actual risk factors, such as high BP, were most likely to be associated with higher perceived risk of chronic illnesses.
Fu, 2001	n = 1,432; Hong Kong, China; men and women; rural and urban	Quantitative: Epidemiological: Cohort. Prevalence of risk factors increased with age and was higher for men than women. The overall level of risk factors in this study was lower than those reported for Australia and the Peoples Republic of China.
Gaetano et al., 2007	n = 1,458; n = 315 screened for CHD; New York; women and men; rural	Quantitative: Descriptive/Correlational. Of the 315 screened for CHD, 52% had increased CHD risk on the FCHDRS. Thirty-nine later saw a primary care provider or cardiologist with 26 (67%) getting pharmacological, surgical, or other interventions.

Grubbs & Frank, 2004	n = 76; Florida; African American, Hispanic, White, and other; women and men; rural and migrant	Quantitative, cross-sectional survey. Self-report data indicated 25% smoked and used alcohol, 44% were overweight, and 36% obese; although 67% reported exercising. Most (78%) reported eating vegetables, 62% ate fruits, and 50% ate fried foods. More than one-quarter reported having two or more symptoms indicative of CVD in the past 12 months.
Gu et al., 2005	n = 19,012; China; women and men; rural and urban	Quantitative: Epidemiological: Cohort. Older women more likely to be overweight. HTN and DM increased for both genders as they aged. Men had higher rates than women of HTN and smoking. Rural residents more likely to smoke, but faired better on other CVD risk factors.
Jackson et al., 2004	n = 1,660 cohort. Jamaica; women and men; rural and urban	Quantitative: Epidemiological cross-sectional cohort. Older, unemployed, and less educated were less likely to have BP screened. Males with hx of DM, HD, and stroke were underscreened. Logistic Regression: DM and increasing age best explained recent BP screening behaviors.
Jafar, 2006	n = 9,942; Pakistan; women and men; rural and urban	Quantitative: Secondary analysis of National Data Set. 1,496 patients had two or more of the following: HTN, DM, proteinuria, hyperlipidemia, or central obesity. Women's CVD risks increased with age; had a higher burden of CVD risk factors; with obesity and saturated fat intake increasing the risk.
Jelinek et al., 2006	n = 71; New South Wales; women and men; rural	Quantitative Descriptive. ECG abnormalities found in 45 (64%) of subjects, even though only 7 had previous abnormal ECG. Thirteen percent had newly discovered ECG changes that required further evaluation. The conclusion, that routine 3-lead ECG testing in rural and remote areas may improve health by providing early recognition of CVD prior to symptoms.
Kettle et al., 2005	n = 540; Canada; women and men; rural and urban	Quantitative: Epidemiological: Cohort. No difference between rural and urban subjects in smoking status or BMI. More female rural residents had a WC above the accepted cutoff than female urbanities.
Kieu et al., 2002	n = 286; Vietnam; women and men; rural, suburban, and urban	Quantitative: Epidemiological: Mean BMI was lowest in rural areas for both genders. No site had BMI averages above normal. The authors conclude that rural populations living by the sea consume more fish than vegetable oils. SFA especially 16:0 is seen in lard, and men in urban areas have less lard consumption than those in suburban or rural areas.

(Continued)

TABLE 2.1 References and Details of Articles Reviewed on the Topic of CVD Risk Factors (*Continued*)

References	Sample Size/Location/ Gender/Ethnicity/ Rurality	Method/Significant Findings
Lewis et al., 2000	n = 44,500; women and men; rural	Quantitative: Epidemiological: Cohort.* SES gradient for health care practices such as BP screenings. Uninsured without Medicaid had lower use of health screening tests, higher tobacco use, and more obesity. This short abstract does not provide much detail on findings. A more full report of the study would be helpful.
Martinez et al., 2004	n = 72; +n = 130 school-children; women, men, and children; rural	Qualitative: Ethnographic: Participant observation. "Causes" of 8 identified CVD were: coming from weather, elevation, "frozen winds," humidity, and low temperature. Severe cases of Chagas often sent to regional centers by Traditional Healers. Natural remedies for Chagas are taken not to cure but to control symptoms. Of traditional medicines, 70% identified as "new world," which are typically gathered in the wild.
Messner et al., 2003	n = 6,167; Sweden; women and men; rural and urban	Quantitative: Epidemiological: Cohort. Educational status decreased gradually with size of town. The smaller communities had ss higher TC, SBP, prevalence of DM and BMI.
Ng et al., 2006	n = 2,963; Indonesia; women and men; rural (n = 2,600) and urban (n = 363)	Quantitative: Epidemiological: Cohort. More men smoke, regardless of age and more likely to smoke if rural. Women rarely smoked. More women had NTN when cut point 160/95 and above was used. Urbanites, or rural classified in the highest SES, more likely to have high BP and be overweight. CVD seen in urban and rural areas (especially higher SES within rural communities).
Niemann et al., 2000	n = 896,954; Denmark: women and men; rural (1/3) and urban (2/3)	Quantitative: Epidemiological: Cohort. Distance to angiography capability 44 to 80 miles from the rural county and 37.2 furthest distance urban. Angiogram rates differed (ss) between the counties. More rural males had 3-vessel disease and left main stenosis and were referred for CABG than urban men. Rural residents had about half of the angiogram activity as urbanites; yet, rural men had more severe findings indicating angiograms in this rural Denmark setting may be underperformed.

Ohira et al., 2001	$n = 901$ with 879 at 10-year follow-up. Kyowa, Ibaraki prefecture, Japan; women and men; rural	Quantitative: Epidemiological: Cohort. Stroke pts had higher depression scores and SBP, regardless of gender. Age- and sex-adjusted data: mild depression was two times higher among those with stroke. Weak inverse relationship between depression and BP or BMI at baseline. Controlling for BMI, SBP, TC, alcohol intake, smoking, use of antihypertensives, and hx of DM reduced the relative risk (RR) to 1.9; however, depression scores remained ss related to ischemic stroke. How depression can increase ischemic stroke is not well understood at this time.
Ohira et al., 2002	$n = 4,734$; Kyowa and Yao; women and men; rural and suburban/urban	Quantitative: Epidemiological: Cross-sectional cohort. Mean anger out values were higher for men and women regardless of rurality. For both genders, anger out scores higher in the urban cohort. For men only, the higher the anger out score, the lower the SBP, with this association stronger in rural males and strongest in the low-coping group. There was no association with anger and DBP or between stress coping and BP levels by gender.
Ohmori-Matsuda et al., 2007	$n = 12,340$; National Health Insurance Beneficiaries Japan; women and men; rural	Quantitative: Epidemiological: Prospective Cohort. Medical cost increased as the number of CVD risk factors rose, ss. No-risk group had mean medical costs of 193.4 per month. HTN increased costs by 33% (ss) and hyperglycemia increased costs by 48.3% (ss). Combinations of CVD risk factors exponentially increased cost with subjects with all three risks having a 91% higher monthly medical cost. During the study $192.6 million was spent on medical cost.
Ortiz et al., 2004	$n = 271$; Texas; Latinos of Mexican descent residing in 2 border rural TX towns; women and men; rural	Quantitative: Descriptive: Oral Survey. Over half reported getting their health care in Mexico. Transportation time to care averaged 30 minutes. Those whose usual care was in Mexico were less likely to have regular physicals ($p < 0.05$). Neither age nor birth country was associated with getting usual care in Mexico. Those getting care in Mexico were less likely to get checks of BP, glucose, or cholesterol ($p < 0.05$). About one-third reported using herbal substances for preventive care and prayer for healing.

(Continued)

57

TABLE 2.1 References and Details of Articles Reviewed on the Topic of CVD Risk Factors (*Continued*)

References	Sample Size/Location/Gender/Ethnicity/Rurality	Method/Significant Findings
Pappas et al., 2001	n = 49,626; Pakistan; women and men; rural, sub-urban, and urban	Quantitative: Epidemiological: Comparative Study. Forty-two percent rural low income, 35% middle class equally divided between rural and urban areas. Nutritional status is poor in Pakistan with underweight common in the rural dwellers. Overweight (RR < .33), HTN, and high TC were more common in upper SES rural and urban dwellers. Male smokers more likely to be urban and of low or middle SES. HTN was only slightly more likely in U.S. men and rates for women were equal. More Pakistanis with HTN are unaware of their dx than Americans. There was little difference in HTN rates but Americans are better screened and treated.
Pizent et al., 2001	n = 26 Croatia; Istra and Podravina; women; rural	Quantitative: Descriptive, Cross Section. Stepwise regression: Lower age, higher alcohol consumption, Pb, and DBP were found in the women with Low Ca intake (ss). An increase in DBP was best explained by BMI, age, and Ca intake. Croatian Pb levels may be higher because of the leaded gas used in that country; however, Cd levels are similar to those seen in other countries. Female alcohol consumption and low Ca intake can increase Pb, which contributes to an increase in DBP in nonsmokers even at relatively low-level Pb exposure.
Pladevall et al., 2003	n = 410; Spain; women and men; rural	Quantitative: Epidemiological: Cohort. Increased LVM related to higher glucose, TC, and uric acid in males (ss). Strongest correlations for increased LVM were SBP, BMI, and WC and weakest were HDL, TC, and leptin. Leptin had a weak inverse relationship with SWT and was inversely associated with LVM after adjustments for age, BMI, SBP, gender, and insulin resistance (p < 0.01). Findings contradict previous study that linked leptin, SWT, and CHD.
Pullen et al., 2005	n = 225; Nebraska; women; rural	Quantitative: Descriptive Correlational. Obese women consumed more calories, fewer fruit servings, and more meat (ss). Normal weight (NW) had higher HDL levels. NW and overweight (OW) had lower resting HR and SBP than obese women. NW also had lower DBP than obese. NW had higher VO2max scores than either OW or obese. NW had fewer CVD risk factors.

Sanderson et al., 2002	$n = 61$; Alabama, 6 focus groups; African American; women; rural	Qualitative: Focus Groups. Major pattern in personal theme: being too tired to exercise (work and family schedules). Both enablers and barriers identified. Rural specific barriers were living too far from facilities for exercise and transportation issues. Rural roads were seen by some as an enabler, yet lack of sidewalks, lighting, traffic, and other factors were seen as barriers. Subject suggestions for possible PA interventions can be seen in a chart (p. 84).
Skliros et al., 2007	$n = 221$; subjects with DM in 4 rural Greece locations; women and men; rural	Quantitative: Epidemiological: Cohort. BP was higher in men, no gender difference in HTN rates. More than 80% of DM subjects had HTN. 34.1% with HTN were unaware of the HTN dx. Of those aware, 100% treated. Of treated only 5.6% had BP < 130/85 while 38.7% had BP readings < 140/90. This indicates inadequate control for HTN. Multivariate analysis indicated that age, hx of CHD, and family hx of HTN were associated with a dx of HTN.
Tazi et al., 2003	$n = 1,802$; Morocco women and men; rural and urban	Quantitative: Epidemiological: Cohort. HTN (33.6%). BP means higher in women ($p < 0.02$) and did not vary by rural/urban residence. HTN prevalence was higher in rural areas ($p < 0.04$). Mean TC was higher among women ($p < 0.02$) and in urban areas ($p < 0.0001$). Dyslipidemia was higher in women ($p < 0.05$) and urban areas ($p < 0.0001$), and increased with age. BMI and the prevalence of obesity were higher in women ($p < 0.0001$) and higher in urban areas ($p < 0.0001$). No difference in smoking in rural and urban areas ($p < 0.23$). Smoking rates increased until 35–44 years (42.9%) and then decreased.
Thommasen & Zhang, 2006	$n = 675$; Bella Coola, Canada; women and men; rural	Quantitative: Descriptive/Correlational with Retrospective Chart Review + Survey. Prevalence was HTN 17%; depression/anxiety 13%; and hyperlipidemia 11%. Fifty percent of those with DM also had HTN and 31% with HTN had DM. Chronic illness decreased HRQOL and was associated with more unhealthy days. Tools published in appendix (pp. 15–17).
Tsutsumi et al., 2001	$n = 6,994$; 12 rural communities in Japan; women and men; rural	Quantitative: Epidemiological: Cohort. Age-adjusted higher HTN rates were associated with family hx of HTN, inactivity, and higher BMI. This study indicates job strain is implicated in HTN among rural Japanese men but not women.

(Continued)

TABLE 2.1 References and Details of Articles Reviewed on the Topic of CVD Risk Factors (*Continued*)

References	Sample Size/Location/Gender/Ethnicity/Rurality	Method/Significant Findings
van der Sande et al., 2001	n = 5,373; Gambia, Africa; women and men; rural and urban	Quantitative: Epidemiological: Cohort. Obesity was a problem with urban women; however, rural women were more likely to suffer from severe undernutrition. Within the obese population there was the emergence of data indicative of metabolic syndrome.
Vrentzos et al., 2006	n = 203; Crete, Greece; women and men; rural	Quantitative: Descriptive/Correlational. Sixty-seven (33%) had normal tHcy levels, 85 (42%) mildly, and 51 (25%) moderate to very high levels. Only serum folate and vitamin B(12) and age associated with tHcy independently (ss). Dietary changes and increased levels of tHcy implicated in rising Crete CVD rates.
Wang et al., 2004	n = 158; China; men and women with CHD; rural	Qualitative: Prospective with Open-Ended Questions. CHD patients were ss more likely to be overweight and smoke in this sample.
Wijewardene et al., 2005	n = 6,047; Western, North Central, Southern, and Uva, Sri Lanka; women and men; rural and urban	Quantitative: Epidemiological: Cohort. HTN prevalence was 18.8% (men) and 19.3% (women). Mean (SD) BMI scores were 21.5 kg/m2 (3.7) in men and 23.2 (4.5) in women. Women were much more likely to be obese (36.5%) than men (20.3%). The authors conclude CVD risk factors are common in Sri Lankans with regional differences.
Wong et al., 2007	n = 590; China; women and men; rural	Quantitative: Epidemiological: Cohort. Prevalence of intracranial atherosclerosis was 6.9% with 41 subjects being positive for this abnormality. HTN, glycosuria, heart disease, and family hx of stroke were risk factors for intracranial atherosclerosis. Conclusion, intracranial atherosclerosis is not uncommon among the rural asymptomatic population.
Yamagishi et al., 2004	n = 2,823; Kyowa, Ibaraki prefecture, Japan; women and men; rural	Quantitative: Epidemiological: Cohort. "The frequencies of adducin genotypes were 21.2% (GG), 48.4% (GW), and 30.4% (WW)" (p. 386). Mean SBP in WW groups vs. GG groups were 133.3 vs. 130.3 mm Hg for men, 137.4 vs. 130.8 mm Hg for men with higher Na excretion (ss). This study strengthens the concept of gene, environment links in HTN.

Yamagishi et al., 2007	n = 2,823; Kyowa, Ibaraki prefecture, Japan; women and men; rural	Quantitative: Epidemiological: Cohort. "The frequency of ACE genotypes was 12.3% for DD genotypes, 45.4% for ID genotype, and 42.3% for II genotype equilibrium" (p. 753). "High sodium intake strengthens the association of ACE I/D polymorphism with BP levels in community-based samples" (p. 751) as the authors had hypothesized.
Yan et al., 2005	n = 671; rural Uygur and Kazak, China; women and men with HTN; rural	Quantitative: Epidemiological: Case Control. Mean age of case vs. control group was 4 years higher (ss). Several other variables such as tea consumption, lipids, glucose, Na intake, SBP, and DBP were also higher in the case vs. control group. The authors note the findings are inconsistent with previous research. An obvious limitation is the variance between case and control groups that could have skewed the findings.
Yang et al., 2007	n = 5,549; XinYang County, China; women and men; rural	Quantitative: Epidemiological: Cross-sectional. PAD = ABI < 0.9 in either leg. Multiple logistical regression, adjusting for gender, age, and other CVD factors: PAD was still associated with current smoking, 1.65 odds ratio (OR), hx of stroke (OR 1.50), serum uric acid (OR 1.21), and TC (OR 1.12).
Yokoyama et al., 2000	n = 1,121; Kadani-Ijimino, Japan; women and men; rural	Quantitative: Epidemiological: Cohort. Mean vitamin C concentrations were higher in women and lower in the elderly (ss). Sex- and age-adjusted risk of stroke was decreased at higher vitamin C levels. Before one can assume that controlling low vitamin C levels prevents CVD such as stroke, intervention studies must be performed.
Zhang et al., 2007	n = 6,412; Liaoning, China; women and men; rural	Quantitative: Epidemiological: Cohort. More than one-third had borderline elevated TC, 16.9% high cholesterol, and 8.8% low HDL. LDL prevalence for borderline high, high, and very high LDL was 15.7, 3.5, and 0.9%, respectively. TG results in the same categories were 15.9%, 17.8%, and 2.0%. Dyslipidemia prevalence was relatively high in rural China and HTN, impaired glucose metabolism, and BMI were all risk factors for dsylipidemia in this sample of rural hypertensives.

*Indicates no electronic version available, abstract only used. Chart abbreviations not used elsewhere in text: diagnosis (dx), history (hx), symptom/s (sx), statistically significant (ss), not statistically significant (ns), and treatment (tx).

Stroke and Rural Populations

One study (Cuellar, 2002) compared African American (n = 36) and White (n = 38) caregivers in a descriptive correlational study conducted in rural Mississippi with a convenience sample (n = 74), female caregivers. These 74 women cared for 44 male and 30 female, bed-bound stroke survivors. The ADL scale; Social Support Questionnaire, short form revised (SSQSR); Revised Ways of Coping Checklist (RWCCL); Centers for Epidemiologic Studies Depression Scale (CES-D); and the Life Satisfaction Index Z (LSI-Z) scales were used in this study. The ADL dependency of the survivors on the caregiver did not vary between groups. All caregivers lived in a rural area. In 69% of the cases, others also lived in the household. Only 13.5% of the caregivers worked full time out of the home while 40% reported that becoming a caregiver had necessitated their retirement from paid employment. The mean number of hours reported giving care was 132.42 and did not differ between groups. More than half (55.4%) reported no help from immediate family, other family members (54.1%), neighbors (93.2%), or church (94.6%). Home health agencies were used more frequently by African American caregivers with the number of visits reported by group as 19.56 (African American) and 18.34 (White). Statistically significant differences between the African American and White caregivers were found on the self-efficacy, stress, and life satisfaction scales, with African American caregivers scoring lower on self-efficacy and stress but higher on life satisfaction. There was no difference in social support between the two groups. The higher the satisfaction with their social support, the higher the self-efficacy, network size, and life satisfaction and the lower the depression symptomology scores for African American caregivers. There was no difference in coping between the two groups. Cuellar (2002) suggests that although social support may differ by race among caregivers, nurses should identify the social support system and use that system in nursing interventions in caring for the caregiver.

Three reports of research (Eaves, 2000, 2002, 2006) address rural African American stroke survivors and/or their primary and secondary caregivers. Eaves notes that two of the reports are different aspects of findings from one study (Eaves, 2000, 2002); it is difficult to tell whether the third report is data originating from the same or a different study (Eaves, 2006). Eaves (2000) noted five themes in this initial report that focused mostly on the stories of the stroke survivors themselves. These themes were: (1) discovering stroke, (2) delaying care, (3) living with uncertainty, (4) discovering the impact of stroke, and (5) reconstructing life. The author suggests that nurses can use the information gained from the study to improve their education efforts for rural African Americans on stroke signs and symptoms as well as prevention strategies. The first three themes do point out the lack of knowledge many rural elders have about the signs and symptoms of stroke and the necessity to call 911 immediately if stroke symptoms occur. The next report (Eaves, 2002) focuses on the findings pertinent to the satisfaction of rural African American caregivers and stroke survivors with health care. The themes here included: professional (formal) care, familial (informal) care, and insufficient care. The patterns associated with professional care were those of uncertainty and mistrust. They did not always trust the diagnosis and plan of care in place. There was also uncertainty about home care, timing of appointments, and whether appropriate care was being given. These subjects also felt they did not have enough information about referrals and follow-up plans. Some subjects did have positive experiences with caring providers who were compassionate in their care. Many of the caregivers recognized the need for more services. There was dissatisfaction with the level and type of help from community agencies. This dissatisfaction was apparent when financial assistance was sought. Often the survivors and caregivers felt that in order to get services they were being asked to give up precious resources. The second theme dealt with the informal or familial care. In the pattern of complaining, both primary caregivers and those family members who were not caregivers complained about each other. On a more positive note, a call for help from the primary caregiver often brought an appropriate response from other family members. Another pattern in this theme was the need for caregiver respite, which was greatly needed and appreciated. The third theme, insufficient care, had three patterns: (1) rising costs, (2) being vulnerable, and (3) limited access. Limited resources contributed to decisions such as using a less appropriate medication such as aspirin (ASA) instead of Coumadin because of costs and lack of coverage. Cost of health care visits was also an issue for some subjects in this study. The subjects recognized rurality as a factor in limited access issues, for example, the issue of distance and transportation to specialty care can be a barrier for rural dwellers.

The third study in this series (Eaves, 2006) found that transitions for both stroke survivors and caregivers emerged as a major theme. Eaves expounds on theory that was developed from the data that includes a four-stage process that helped these subjects work toward striking a balance. This process included: (1) deciding to care, (2) dividing the care, (3) protective care, and (4) coming to terms. A figure of this theory is provided by Eaves (2006, p. 273). Some limitations identified by Eaves include the theoretical sampling; homogeneity of the sample, which included only southern rural African American stroke survivors and caregivers; and the lack of testing for the theory at this stage. Regardless of the limitations, the work of Eaves adds a great deal to the knowledge base of nurses as they work with rural African American stroke survivors and their caregivers. This work is qualitative in nature and uncovers themes that deal with many aspects of the stroke experience. This has led to the identification of a theory for rural African American family caregiving for elderly stroke survivors. Some of the issues uncovered in both the Eaves (2000, 2002, 2006) and Cuellar (2002) studies are worsened by rural poverty. Rural poverty may influence the type and quality of care available as well as influence caregiver support. This type of burden will only worsen in the current climate of continued rise in transportation and energy costs. Transportation for rural dwellers has always been a barrier to health care but may well be an overwhelming issue for rural elders who often have to rely on family or community informal support for transportation to distant tertiary care sites. Rural poverty is often thought of as an issue in the rural south but it is a persistent characterization of rural living throughout many rural regions of the country (Eberhardt et al., 2001). As nurses develop and test theories to improve care for stroke survivors and lighten the load for family caregivers, they need to take into consideration ways to improve cost efficiency and build on the positive rural values and characteristics. For example in upstate New York, there is the Neighbors Helping Neighbors project, funded through an Appalachian Regional Commission (Rural Health Network of South Central New York, 2007) where volunteers work with rural elders to help transport them to health care appointments, make calls to check in, and provide other volunteer services that help make life more pleasant for those with limited resources or disabilities. Even those that receive services often volunteer to return services that they can provide. For example, someone that relies on the project to pick up groceries or provide transportation to health care providers may volunteer to make daily calls to elders who live alone.

One study of stroke symptom knowledge (Alkadry, Wilson, & Nicholson, 2005) used a survey mailed to 1,114 citizens in West Virginia. These authors found that although 83% of the participants said they would call 911 for stroke symptoms, only 20% could correctly identify major stroke symptoms. A national survey (Christian et al., 2007) of women's awareness of heart disease and stroke uncovered that 23% of the women considered themselves to have less knowledge of stroke than heart disease, while 11% felt they had less knowledge of heart disease than stroke. Hispanic women were more likely than White women to consider themselves as lacking knowledge about stroke. There is no indication of knowledge level of rural women regarding stroke or heart disease in this study. In general, women's knowledge of some stroke symptoms has increased during the past decade but not as much as awareness of women's symptoms of a heart attack. The most recognized of stroke symptoms was numbness or weakness in a limb or face (42%) while the least recognized symptoms were sudden dimness or loss of vision, often in one eye (16%), and unexplained dizziness (17%).

Two studies reported on intervening to reduce the cardiovascular burden of stroke on rural populations (Fahs, 2006; Riggs, Libell, Brooks, & Hobbs, 2005). Both studies included data on males and females. The Fahs (2006) report is an overview of the effectiveness of a nurse-run stroke intervention program known as Facts for Action to Stroke Treatment (FAST). The program used the acronym FAST to highlight changes that may occur in the face, arm, or with speech and that any symptoms in these areas indicate it is time to call 911. The program had more than 500 participants during a year and a half and there was an increase in the knowledge of rural dwellers on the symptoms of stroke, immediately post-test, that was sustained at the two-month follow-up testing. Those age 75 and older did not maintain their knowledge at a statistically significant level at the two-month mark. One limitation in this study was that only knowledge of stroke symptoms and the appropriate response were measured. The study did not include a measure to see if actual behavior had changed in the area. Riggs and colleagues (2005) looked at referral bias in the transfer of intracerebral hemorrhage (ICH), which has the highest risk of in-hospital mortality in the acute phase. A clinical acute stroke program instituted at a rural tertiary care referral center, which receives patients from rural facilities in three states, resulted in a statistically significant decrease in referral bias from rural facilities to the medical center. Both of these studies highlight issues of stroke in rural communities. Both (Fahs, 2006; Riggs et al., 2005) descriptive studies indicate further work is needed in the areas of raising awareness of stroke symptoms and the usefulness of rapid treatment and or transfer to stroke-designated facilities. Issues of telemedicine may also have implications for rapid treatment of rural patients suffering from stroke but articles on this subject did not surface in this literature review. Future reviews in the area of stroke should specifically induce the terms *telemedicine* and *telehealth*.

The availability of diagnostic and treatment services for acute stroke in frontier counties of Montana and northern Wyoming was the subject of the final stroke study reviewed (Okon et al., 2006). These researchers used a survey mailed to hospital administrators in the two states and had an 87% return rate. Of the respondents, 79% were from frontier hospitals with an average of 18 beds. Less than half (44%) of the frontier hospitals had prehospital stroke identification programs. Thirty-nine percent had computed tomography capability (CAT scan) 24 hours a day and 44% had an ED stroke protocol. More than two-thirds (61%) reported a recombinant tissue plasminogen activator protocol.

The work in this section is again primarily descriptive. These 11 studies indicate that more work is needed in increasing the knowledge of stroke symptoms as well as increasing the number of people who seek immediate emergency medical care with a stroke. Ideally, treatment for stroke should occur within three hours of the first symptoms for the best outcomes, especially if the stroke is the result of a blood clot. Rural living often includes barriers such as lag in EMS response time, geographic isolation and distance to stroke centers, bad driving conditions, and lack of ability to intervene at small rural hospitals, factors that make stroke care an area of importance to rural individuals and an area that needs more study. Nursing is in a unique role in rural settings, and rural nurses are often trusted health care professionals that are never off duty. Further studies are needed on nurse-run stroke education programs in rural areas, such as the one reported by Fahs (2006), to explore avenues for improving both knowledge and appropriate care-seeking behaviors of rural individuals when stroke occurs. It is time for nursing research to move past describing and into testing interventions that will improve knowledge, care-seeking behaviors, and actual outcomes of stroke treatment for those living in rural areas.

Quality of Care in Acute Myocardial Infarction in Rural Facilities

Five studies examined quality of care for MI patients in rural facilities (Baldwin, MacLehose, Hart, Beaver, Every, et al., 2004; Domes, Szafran, Bilous, Olson, & Spooner, 2006; Ellerbeck, Bhimaraj, & Perpich, 2004; Hedges, Adams, & Gunnels, 2002; James, Li, & Ward, 2007). Three used existing data bases: (1) Medicare (Baldwin et al., 2004); (2) Oregon State (Hedges et al., 2002); and (3) Iowa State (James et al., 2007). One used a retrospective chart review of 12 Canadian facilities in the Alberta region (Domes et al., 2006) and one (Ellerbeck et al., 2004) surveyed 45 urban and 12 rural facilities in Kansas. All concluded that protocols can improve quality of care for AMI patients whether in rural or urban settings. Baldwin and colleagues (2004) had the largest cohort with a sample of 4,085 acute care hospitals, with 893 facilities coded as small rural and 619 coded as large rural hospitals. They found that "substantial proportions of ideally eligible admissions in both urban and rural hospitals did receive the recommended treatments for AMI" (p. 102). However, patients admitted to rural hospitals were significantly less likely to get aspirin (ASA), heparin, intravenous nitroglycerin, or to be reperfused. The more remote the facility, the less likely those admitted would receive the recommended treatments. It should also be noted that there was a statistically significant difference in age with the oldest mean age being seen by remote small rural hospitals. There was no discussion as to whether variables such as decisions regarding lifesaving measures or advanced directives with older patients may have influenced the differences in adherence to protocols of care seen in remote smaller rural hospitals with elders. Rates of death within a month of admission increased with the rurality of the hospital; here it is noted that this difference persisted even after controlling for patient characteristics. The researchers in this study (Baldwin et al., 2004) did not address issues of nurse staffing patterns among the hospitals evaluated. They did conclude that efforts are needed in both rural and urban facilities to improve adherence to the guidelines for care for AMI patients. The Iowa state inpatient database (James et al., 2007) was used to explore the effect of controlling for unmeasured cofounders in calculating MI mortality rates. Independent variables used included payer (Medicare, Medicaid, private insurance, self-pay, no charge, other); race (Black or not); admission type (emergency, urgent, other); two comorbidity indices (the Charlson Comorbidity Index and the All Patient Refined DRG risk index); and distance between patient's home and all urban hospitals in Iowa. The outcome variable was in-hospital mortality. These researchers concluded that there were no statistically significant differences in mortality rates in Iowa between rural and urban hospitals once these confounding variables, such as age, were controlled. The Canadian study (Domes et al., 2006) assessed quality of care of AMI patients using standards from the American College of Cardiology and AHA as well as guidelines from the Canadian Cardiovascular Outcomes Research Team and the Canadian Cardiovascular Society in 12 East Central Health Region (ECHR) facilities in a rural health region in Alberta, Canada. These authors concluded that ED care was high in quality for most audit elements. Exceptions were found in the areas of rapid ECG, urinalysis, and provision of nitroglycerin and morphine. The average time from "door to needle" for thrombolytic therapy was 102.5 minutes. In-hospital care, again, was judged to be high on most elements with the exception of nitroglycerin, angiotensin-converting enzyme (ACE) inhibitors, daily ECG, and counseling regarding smoking cessation and diet. Male and younger patients were found to be treated more aggressively for AMI than older and female patients. Stress testing was not readily available in the more rural facilities. Facilities that used care protocols had better initial AMI outcomes than those who did not implement protocols. Again, there was no discussion of the role of nurses in caring for AMI patients in either rural or urban facilities.

Care of patients with AMI in a sampling of rural and urban Kansas hospitals (Ellerbeck et al., 2004) found that 911 systems were available in both rural and urban locations. However, EMS personnel were more likely to be volunteers in rural areas and less trained resulting in fewer paramedics and less advanced cardiac life support (ACLS) available prehospital in rural locations. Few rural hospitals in this study were able to provide cardiac catheterization, angioplasty, or coronary artery bypass surgery. Cardiologists were often available by phone but not on site in the more rural locations. Ambulances were not usually permitted to bypass local facilities and most rural AMI patients were later transferred to more urban centers with an average transfer distance of 78 miles. The numbers of rural and urban hospitals using protocols for care of the AMI patient were not significantly different. This study also included nursing measure of quality for care of the AMI patient and found that nursing capabilities in rural hospitals were equivalent to those in more urban hospitals with almost all ED nurses trained in ACLS and capable of obtaining ECG readings without physician orders. The nursing staff in rural facilities did operate under protocols that allowed them to immediately administer ASA for AMI patients. Ellerbeck and colleagues concluded that "this expertise and empowerment of nurses may be particularly important in rural emergency departments that do not always have physicians in-house" (p. 366). Limitations of this study include the lack of data on time from door to needle or event to treatment and in-hospital mortality rates were not given as an outcome. Further exploration of the nurse's role in quality of care for CVD patients in rural hospitals as well as regional tertiary care centers is needed in this country. Magnet status is giving many nursing departments a new voice with hospital administrators in urban centers as nurses use research to build evidence-based practice and to explore quality outcomes. Rural hospitals, nursing homes, and health departments can also look at the role nursing care, qualifications, and personnel mix have on quality outcomes for clients. Standards of nursing as well as medical care should be examined by rural administrators as they work to improve quality care in rural settings.

Mortality and Cardiovascular Disease

Nine studies (Aiello & Fahs, 2001; Barnett & Halverson, 2000, 2001; Cort & Fahs, 2001; James et al., 2007; Minh, Byass, & Wall, 2003; Mussolino & Armenian, 2007; Strand & Tverdal, 2004; Weinehall, Hellsten, Boman, Hallmans, Asplund, et al., 2001) were identified that described the mortality of CVD either as associated heart disease and/or stroke alone or in combination with other mortality data that included rural populations. Two studies were secondary analyses of the CDC interactive atlas of women and heart disease, a national data set that addressed mortality data from diseases of the heart from 1991 to 1995 for women age 35 and older. These authors (Aiello & Fahs, 2001; Cort & Fahs, 2001) extrapolated the mortality data specific to rural Native American and African American women. They noted that it is often difficult to get mortality data for rural areas. This data set used age and spatial smoothing that helped minimize these problems and allowed mortality for rural women to emerge from the data. Spatial smoothing is a statistical method that takes an average of mortality in a given year for a county and the counties that border it. This protects privacy of individuals as well as statistically avoids large spikes and drops that can occur in small places where there can be a great deal of variation in mortality rates from year to year. Aiello and Fahs (2001) report that the CVD mortality rates were 57% higher among Native American women residing in rural locations as compared to those residing in urban settings. One rural reservation in South Dakota may have skewed the rural mortality rate for Native American women since it had the highest mortality rate in the country: 1,000 deaths per 100,000 persons. Cort and Fahs (2001) found that the mortality rate for rural African American women in selected states in the eastern United States was higher than that of White rural women in the same areas but not significantly different than the overall mortality rate of the general population of African American women.

Another secondary analysis (Kim, Eby, & Piette, 2005) used the National Longitudinal Mortality study, which links the U.S. Census Bureau population surveys with the National Death Index for the years 1979–1989 to examine mortality rates from CVD and breast cancer for women, comparing Black and

White women. They examined how education, as an indicator of SES, related to both sources of mortality. Unadjusted incidence of CVD mortality was 4.2% for Black women and 2.3% among White women. This study concludes there is an association between lower levels of education, income, and CVD mortality even when controlling for age, marital status, and urban or rural residence among both Black and White women. The third National Health and Nutrition Examination survey (NHANES III) was used to determine the long-term association between bone mineral density (BMD) and CVD mortality, including CHD and stroke mortality in one study that included both men and women (Mussolino & Armenian, 2007). These authors divided BMD into quartiles and found that those in the first quartile were more likely to report less PA, be older, have lower BMI, higher total cholesterol (TC), HTN, DM, less calcium and alcohol intake, and be current smokers than those in the fourth quartile. Analysis of BMD and CHD deaths was nonsignificant for those age 50 and older when both genders were included in the analysis. The strength of this study is the large sample size and the fact that BMD was calculated using dexascans (DXI), which are technologically superior to other methods of measuring bone density, such as heel scans. This study is more generalizable to the U.S. population than studies with smaller samples and studies that use less sophisticated measurements of BMD. There were three studies that examined mortality rates from CVD in foreign countries (Minh et al., 2007; Nyholm et al., 2005; Strand & Tverdal, 2004).

The studies in this section examine factors that contribute to CVD mortality, primarily on a national level. One feature in these national databases is that often minority populations can either be oversampled or the data weighted to give a picture of disparities in CVD mortality that might not be available from more local or regional data. Foreign countries, particularly those with publicly funded health care systems, can more easily complete large epidemiologic studies on the health of their rural populations. In this country, secondary analysis of national data sets or breakdown of geographic data for rural dwellers would be very helpful in moving the science of rural nursing forward. It is very difficult to extrapolate pertinent information from national data sets specific to rural dwellers because of the statistical blinding of data in rural places. Those data can be very useful to investigators and practitioners alike. Those creating national data sets should take a cue from the CDC and use statistical strategies such as spatial smoothing to make rural data on morbidity and mortality more accessible. Two sources often used by those working in the field of rural health care are becoming dated (Eberhardt et al., 2001; Ricketts, 1999); at the very least these resources need to be updated to help provide a picture of geographic health disparities and the health status of rural dwellers. In addition, national databases should begin to explore geographic variations in health as well as racial and economic disparities.

Cardiovascular Risk Factors in Rural Populations

The largest number of articles reviewed deal with CVD risk factors (Appel, Harrell, & Deng, 2002; Borges-Yanez et al., 2006; Chikani, Reding, Gunderson, & McCarty, 2004, 2005; Deskins et al., 2006; Eyler et al., 2002; Eyler & Vest, 2002; Fahs, 2001; Fahs et al., 2001; Fiandt, Pullen, & Walker, 1999; Fu, 2001; Gaetano et al., 2007; Grubbs & Frank, 2004; Gu et al., 2005; Jackson, Coombs, Wright, Carney, Lewis-Fuller, et al., 2004; Jafar, 2006; Jelinek, Warner, King, & De Jong, 2006; Kettle, Roebothan, & West, 2005; Kieu et al., 2002; Lewis et al., 2000; Martinez, Pochettino, & Cortella, 2004; Messner, Lundberg, & Stegmayr, 2003; Ng, Stenlund, Bonita, Hakimi, Wall, et al., 2006; Niemann, Lous, Thorsgaard, & Nielsen, 2000; Ohira et al., 2001; Ohira et al., 2002; Ohmori-Matsuda, Kuriyama, Hozawa, Nakaya, Shimazu, et al., 2007; Ortiz, Arizmendi, & Cornelius, 2004; Panagiotakos et al., 2006; Pappas, Akhtar, Gergen, Hadden, & Khan, 2001; Pizent et al., 2001; Pladevall et al., 2003; Pullen, Walker, Hageman, Boeckner, & Oberdorfer, 2005; Sanderson, Littleton, & Pulley, 2002; Skliros et al., 2007; Tazi et al., 2003; Thommasen & Zhang, 2006; Tsutsumi et al., 2001; van der Sande et al., 2001; Vrentzos et al., 2006; Wang, Yao, & Wu, 2004; Wijewardene et al., 2005; Wong et al., 2007; Yamagishi et al., 2004; Yamagishi et al., 2007; Yan et al., 2005; Yang et al., 2007; Yokoyama, Date, Kokubo, Yoshiike, Matsumura, et al., 2000; Zhang et al., 2007). Table 2.1 gives a brief overview of these studies. One of the most interesting articles in this section was an ethnographic study of rural villagers where Chagas disease is endemic (Martinez, Pochettino, & Cortella, 2004). Study details can be found in Table 2.1; however, background information gleaned from the report is provided here. American trypanosomiasis (Chagas) is a parasitic disease that affects the heart causing chronic cardiomyopathy as well as enlargement of the esophagus and colon. Vinchuca or barbeiro are common names of the species *Triatoma infestans*, an endemic vector for *Trypanosoma cruzi*, the cause of Chagas. The houses in rural Central and South America are often made of mud with thatched roofs, which are breeding grounds for the parasite. Treatment must be given in the acute stage to eradicate the disease. Many children die of Chagas and if they do live beyond the acute stage, chronic CVD results. After the acute stage the parasite is not evident for 15–20 years and then reemerges in the bloodstream to cause symptoms. It is estimated that 30% of adults in this region suffer from chronic Chagas. Principal public health actions include education about eradicating the vector for prevention of the disease and the need to treat in the acute phase of the illness.

The majority of studies in this section measured traditional CVD risks, which included BP, cholesterol, smoking, obesity, and so on. Most of the studies were descriptive correlational with the majority (54%) using an epidemiologic design. Many were conducted outside the United States.

TABLE 2.2 Summary of Nursing and Public Health Intervention Studies

References	Sample/Purpose or Question	Design/Project Name/Findings
Carter et al., 2005	n = 27 women and men in a rural small industry in Alabama. An employee wellness program focused on improving CVD risk factors.	Qualitative: Focus Group. Four themes were uncovered in the analysis. These included: benefits, changes in behaviors, follow-up care and tx, and future needs.
Meng et al., 2007	n = 281 community-living Medicare patients with heart conditions, in a randomized controlled trial (RCT). The purpose was to examine the impact of a nurse intervention program on physical function and health expenditures among elderly with heart conditions and the effect of rural residence on the intervention effect (p. 322). Standardized protocols were used.	Quantitative: RCT. The nurse intervention resulted in fewer impairments in ADL ($p = .055$) at the end of 2 years. Average total health care expenditures were 6.5% ($1,981, 95% CI: −$8,048, $4,087) lower in the nurse group (p. 322). These authors conclude that the nurse intervention led to better physical functioning and has potential to reduce total health care expenditures among high-risk Medicare beneficiaries with heart conditions.
Nafziger et al., 2001	n = 158,000 rural inhabitants in upstate New York in the intervention cohort compared to a similar but separate population for reference. Purpose was to evaluate the effectiveness of a rural, 5-year, hospital-based public health intervention program on CVD risk factors.	Quantitative: Epidemiologic: Random Sample 3-stage Cluster Intervention design. Smoking declined by 10%. SBP was reduced while DBP remained stable. BMI increased significantly in both groups. Conclusion, the rural community intervention program decreased smoking in the rural sample. RCT studies are needed to support these findings.

(Continued)

TABLE 2.2 Summary of Nursing and Public Health Intervention Studies (*Continued*)

References	Sample/Purpose or Question	Design/Project Name/Findings
Perry et al., 2007	n = 46 rural women with random assignment. Purpose was to test a 12-week walking program for rural women.	Heart-to-Heart (HTH) program. Women in HTH group had a greater improvement in cardiorespiratory fitness ($p = 0.057$) and social support ($p = 0.004$) compared to the comparison group. These authors conclude: HTH was effective in improving cardiorespiratory fitness in a sample of rural women.
Tessaro et al., 2006	n = 48 women in two rural West Virginia counties (nonrandom sample) participated in four focus groups to guide the development of a culturally sensitive and individually tailored program. Cookin' Up Health is the intervention that resulted from this study. It uses a computer-based interactive format (touch screen presentation).	Qualitative: Focus Groups; Cookin' Up Health project. Focus group feelings regarding heart disease and rural women presented (p. 2006). This report whets the appetite for more information on the Cookin' Up Health intervention. Unfortunately no articles evaluating the intervention were found in this search.
Williams et al., 2004	n = 294 African American rural and urban women in Georgia. Purposes: (1) to compare CVD risk factors among low-income African American women (LAAW) in a rural and urban site, comparing that data with national risk data for African American women; and (2) test a worksite intervention designed to reduce CVD risks.	Quantitative: Quasiexperimental. Pender's Health Promotion model used. The two LAAW groups had higher or similar CVD RR as compared with a national sample of AAW. Pretest TC and fat intake for the rural women were higher than for the urban women ($p < 0.05$). Posttest changes in TC and fat intake risks were more significant in rural LAAW than in urban LAAW ($<.05$). Study limitations: lack of control group, although comparison to national data is helpful, and the sampling methods used.

Intervention Studies

Only 17 intervention studies were found in this review (Aoun & Rosenberg, 2004; Carter, Gaskins, & Shaw, 2005; Gaetke, Stuart, & Truszczynska, 2006; Kuhajda et al., 2006; Lupton, Fonnebo, & Sogarrd, 2003; Meng, Wamsley, Eggert, & Van Nostrand, 2007; Nafziger, Erb, Jenkins, Lewis, & Pearson, 2001; Panagiotakos et al., 2006; Perry, Rosenfeld, Bennett, & Potempa, 2007; Rudholm, 2006; Sanchez & Khalil, 2005; Santos, Gillies, Vartiainen, Dunbar, & Nettleton, 2004; Tessaro et al., 2006; Verrill, Barton, Beasley, Lippard, & King, 2003; Weinehall et al., 2001; Williams, Wold, Dunkin, Idleman, & Jackson, 2004; Zhang et al., 2005). These studies range from using the screening process as an intervention (Sanchez & Khalil, 2005) to large epidemiologic community-level interventions (Lupton et al., 2003). The studies identified as nursing or public health interventions are summarized in Table 2.2.

CONCLUSIONS

Nursing's Contribution to Literature on Cardiovascular Disease and Rural Populations

The contribution of nurses to the state of the science of cardiovascular health in rural populations can be seen in Table 2.3, which shows the number and percentage of studies authored by nurses and those published in what is thought of as nursing journals. The discipline was represented in the literature with 39 of the first authors identifiable as nurses and nursing journals published a little more than one-quarter of the studies reviewed. Although nurses are making a contribution to the research, it was disappointing to find that the study (Meng et al., 2007) on nursing interventions to reduce health care costs did not have an author identifiable as a nurse. Another disappointment was the low number of nurse authors found published in a journal dedicated to rural health issues (see Table 2.4).

The majority of studies reviewed were quantitative at the descriptive level and sample sizes varied appropriately by method. The few intervention programs

TABLE 2.3   Discipline Representation in the CVD Research Literature in Rural Populations

Number of Articles Reviewed	Number (%) of First Authors Identifiable as Nurse	Number (%) Subsequent Author Identifiable as Nurse or Associated with a School of Nursing	Number (%) of Journals Known as Nursing Journals
134	39 (29.1%)	17 (12.7%)	35 (26.1%)

TABLE 2.4   Nurse Authorship in Journals Specific to Rural Health Issues

Journal Title	Number of Articles in Review	Nurse as First Author	Nurse in Any Authorship Position	Percentage of Nurse Authorships in Review
Online Journal of Rural Nursing and Health Care	3	3	3	100%
Rural and Remote Health	3	1	1	33%
Journal of Rural Health	10	0	2	20%

reviewed had what appeared to be adequate sample sizes for the analysis and method used, but none discussed whether a power analysis was calculated to guide sample size and protect against error. Awareness of CVD risk for women as well as their unique symptom patterns is increasing; however, women are still being underdiagnosed and undertreated for CVD. Heart failure studies need to include awareness of diagnosis and interventions using health promotion habits to improve outcomes. Prehospital stroke issues in rural populations were addressed; however, more work is needed to both raise awareness of stroke symptoms and to find the most effective method for getting rural stroke victims to treatment in a timely manner. Caregiver burden for stroke survivors is an important topic where some initial qualitative work has been done and theory testing from that work is warranted. Research in quality of care in AMI cases in rural hospitals indicates that the use of protocols can significantly increase the quality of care. Nursing expertise should be included in assessments of quality of care for AMI patients. Protocols that allow nurses to act autonomously may be one means of improving AMI quality of care. Mortality studies from CVD are evident in the literature but most do not allow identification of mortality in rural areas. Large national data sets should address and illuminate the issues of geographic disparities in disease and mortality patterns to allow researchers working with rural dwellers to have good sources of data on the issue of CVD in rural populations. Finally, there is a good deal of literature on CVD risk factors in rural populations. Rural people have higher than acceptable levels of CVD risk factors including obesity. In most cases, living in rural places does not put one at more risk of CVD, but neither does rural dwelling protect individuals from the epidemic of CVD risks seen in this and other countries today. One conceptual article (Appel, Giger, & Davidhizar, 2005) offers a model for a way to move forward with theory-based interventions to reduce CV health disparities. The model was developed for use with low-income rural African American women; however, expansion and testing with rural populations in general should be explored because rural poverty and CVD risks are not limited to the rural south or minority groups.

This review indicates that there are many opportunities for nurses to become involved in research and develop research trajectories in cardiovascular health of rural populations. As a discipline, we need to move beyond describing the risks to intervening in reducing risks and improving the health of those with CVD. Studies need to be conducted with rigor, whatever the methodology used. Cardiovascular research is one area where the question of substance for the discipline is easily answered; study of this topic can generate and test knowledge that has the potential to reduce mortality and improve health for millions of people worldwide.

ACKNOWLEDGMENTS

The authors wish to acknowledge the assistance of Virginia Young, Librarian at SUNY Upstate Medical University, and Deandra Hinds, Student Nurse at the Decker School of Nursing, Binghamton University, for their assistance in conducting searches for the literature reviewed.

REFERENCES

Agyemang, C. (2006). Rural and urban differences in blood pressure and hypertension in Ghana, West Africa. *Public Health, 120*(6), 525–533.

Ahmad, K., & Jafar, T. H. (2005). Prevalence and determinants of blood pressure screening in Pakistan. *Journal of Hypertension, 23*(11), 1979–1984.

Aiello, M. O., & Fahs, P. S. (2001). A secondary analysis of cardiovascular mortality among rural Native American women. *Journal of Multicultural Nursing & Health, 7*(2), 42–47.

Alkadry, M. G., Wilson, C., & Nicholson, D. (2005). Stroke awareness among rural residents: The case of West Virginia. *Social Work in Health Care, 42*(2), 73–92.

Aoun, S., & Rosenberg, M. (2004). Are rural people getting HeartSmart? *Australian Journal of Rural Health, 12*(2), 81–88.

Appel, S. J., Giger, J. N., & Davidhizar, R. E. (2005). Opportunity cost: The impact of contextual risk factors on the cardiovascular health of low-income rural southern African American women. *Journal of Cardiovascular Nursing, 20*(5), 315–324.

Appel, S. J., Harrell, J. S., & Deng, S. (2002). Racial and socioeconomic differences in risk factors for cardiovascular disease among southern rural women. *Nursing Research, 51*(3), 140–147.

Association of Women's Health Obstetric and Neonatal Nurses [AWHONN]. (2003). *Evidence-based clinical practice guideline. Cardiovascular health for women: Primary prevention* (2nd ed.). Washington, DC: Author.

Baldwin, L. M., MacLehose, R. F., Hart, L. G., Beaver, S. K., Every, N., & Chan, L. (2004). Quality of care for acute myocardial infarction in rural and urban U.S. hospitals. *Journal of Rural Health, 20*(2), 99–108.

Barnett, E., & Halverson, J. (2000). Disparaties in premature coronary heart disease mortality by region and urbanicity among black and white adults ages 35–64, 1985–1995. *Public Health Reports, 115*(1), 52–64.

Barnett, E., & Halverson, J. (2001). Local increases in coronary heart disease mortality among blacks and whites in the United States, 1985–1995. *American Journal of Public Health, 91*(9), 1499–1506.

Bassett, D. R., Fitzhugh, E. C., Crespo, C. J., King, G. A., & McLaughlin, J. E. (2002). Physical activity and ethnic differences in Hypertension prevalence in the United States. *Preventive Medicine, 34*(2), 179–186.

Bjerregaard, P., Dewailly, E., Young, T. K., Blanchet, C., Hegele, R. A., Ebbesson, S. E. O., et al. (2003). Blood pressure among the Inuit (Eskimo) populations in the Arctic. *Scandinavian Journal of Public Health, 31*(2), 92–99.

Borges-Yanez, S. A., Irigoyen-Camacho, M. E., & Maupom, G. (2006). Risk factors and prevalence of periodontitis in community-dwelling elders in Mexico. *Journal of Clinical Periodontology, 33*(3), 184–194.

Boutain, D. M. (2001). Discourses of worry, stress, and high blood pressure in rural south Louisiana. *Journal of Nursing Scholarship, 33*(3), 225–230.

Brown, D. E., Etrata, M. B., Aki, S. L., Cardines, K. L., & James, G. D. (2001). Anxiety state vs trait as predictors of ambulatory blood pressure at work: A test case among school teachers in Hawaii. *American Journal of Human Biology, 13*(1), 113–114.

Brown, D. E., James, G. D., Aki, S. L., Mills, P. S., & Etrata, M. B. (2003). A comparison of awake-sleep blood pressure variation between normotensive Japanese-American and Caucasian Women in Hawaii. *Journal of Hypertension, 21*(11), 2045–2051.

Brown, D. E., Sievert, L. L., Aki, S. L., Mills, P. S., Etrata, M. B., Paopao, R. N. K., et al. (2001). Effects of age, ethnicity and menopause on ambulatory blood pressure: Japanese-American and Caucasian school teachers in Hawaii. *American Journal of Human Biology, 13*(4), 486–493.

Carter, M., Gaskins, S., & Shaw, L. (2005). Employee Wellness Program in a small rural industry: Employee evaluation. *AAOHN Journal, 53*(6), 244–248.

Centers for Disease Control and Prevention (CDC). (2004). *Women and heart disease fact sheet*. Retrieved March 2005 from http://www.cdc.gov

Charlton, K. E., Steyn, K., Levitt, N. S., Zulu, J. V., Jonathan, D., Veldman, F. J., et al. (2005). Diet and blood pressure in South Africa: Intake of foods containing sodium, potassium, calcium, and magnesium in three ethnic groups. *Nutrition, 21*(1), 39–50.

Chikani, V., Reding, D., Gunderson, P., & McCarty, C. A. (2004). Wisconsin Rural Women's Health Study psychological factors and blood cholesterol level: Difference between normal and overweight rural women. *Clinical Medicine & Research, 2*(1), 47–53.

Chikani, V., Reding, D., Gunderson, P., & McCarty, C. A. (2005). Psychosocial work characteristics predict cardiovascular disease risk factors and health functioning in rural women: The Wisconsin Rural Women's Health Study. *Journal of Rural Health, 21*(4), 295–302.

Christian, A. H., Rosamond, W., White, A. R., & Mosca, L. (2007). Nine-year trends and racial and ethnic disparities in women's awareness of heart disease and stroke: An American Heart Association national study. *Journal of Women's Health, 16*(1), 68–81.

Clark, J. C., & Lan, V. M. (2004). Heart failure patient learning needs after hospital discharge. *Applied Nursing Research, 17*(3), 150–157.

Clark, R. A., McLennan, S., Eckert, K., Dawson, A., Wilkinson, D., & Stewart, S. (2005). Chronic heart failure beyond city limits. *Rural Remote Health, 5*(4), 443.

Cort, N. A., & Fahs, P. S. (2001). Heart disease: The hidden killer of rural black women. *Journal of Multicultural Nursing & Health, 7*(2), 37–41.

Cuellar, N. G. (2002). A comparison of African American & Caucasian American female caregivers of rural, post-stroke, bedbound older adults. *Journal of Gerontological Nursing, 28*(1), 36–45.

Deskins, S., Harris, C. V., Bradlyn, A. S., Cottrell, L., Coffman, J. W., Olexa, J., et al. (2006). Preventive care in Appalachia: Use of the theory of planned behavior to identify barriers to participation in cholesterol screenings among West Virginians. *Journal of Rural Health, 22*(4), 367–374.

Domes, T., Szafran, O., Bilous, C., Olson, O., & Spooner, G. R. (2006). Acute myocardial infarction: Quality of care in rural Alberta. *Canadian Family Physician, 52,* 69–76.

Douglas, P. S., & Poppas, A. (2007). Determinants and management of cardiovascular risk in women. In B. D. Rose (Ed.), *UpToDate.* Waltham, MA: UpToDate.

Eaves, Y. D. (2000). "What happened to me": Rural African American elders' experiences of stroke. *Journal of Neuroscience Nursing, 32*(1), 37–48.

Eaves, Y. D. (2002). Rural African American caregivers' and stroke survivors' satisfaction with health care. *Topics in Geriatric Rehabilitation, 17*(3), 72–84.

Eaves, Y. D. (2006). Caregiving in rural African American families for older adult stroke survivors. *Journal of Neuroscience Nursing, 38*(4 Suppl.), 270–281, 330.

Eberhardt, M. S., Ingram, D. D., Makuc, D. M., Pamuk, E. R., Freid, V. M., Harper, S. B., et al. (2001). *Health, United States, 2001 urban and rural health chartbook.* Hyattsville, MD: Center for Health Statistics.

Ellerbeck, E. F., Bhimaraj, A., & Perpich, D. (2004). Organization of care for acute myocardial infarction in rural and urban hospitals in Kansas. *Journal of Rural Health, 20*(4), 363–367.

Eyler, A. A., Matson-Koffman, D., Vest, J. R., Evenson, K. R., Sanderson, B., Thompson, J. L., et al. (2002). Environmental, policy, and cultural factors related to physical activity in a diverse sample of women: The Women's Cardiovascular Health Network Project—introduction and methodology. *Women & Health, 36*(2), 1–15.

Eyler, A. A., & Vest, J. R. (2002). Environmental and policy factors related to physical activity in rural white women. *Women & Health, 36*(2), 111–121.

Fahs, P. S. (2001). Health risks and practices of rural women residing in Delaware County, New York. *Journal of Multicultural Nursing & Health, 7*(1), 41–49.

Fahs, P. S. (2006). Raising stroke awareness in rural communities. *American Journal of Nursing, 106*(11), 42.

Fahs, P. S., Grabo, T. N., James, G. D., Neff-Smith, M., & Spencer, G. (2001). A comparison of the cardiovascular risks of rural, suburban, and urban women. *Online Journal of Rural Nursing and Health Care, 2.* Retrieved November 2007 from http://www.rno.org/journal

Fiandt, K., Pullen, C. H., & Walker, S. N. (1999). Actual and perceived risk for chronic illness in rural older women. *Clinical Excellence for Nurse Practitioners, 3*(2), 105–115.

Fu, F. H. (2001). The prevalence of cardiovascular disease risk factors of Hong Kong Chinese. *Journal of Sports Medicine & Physical Fitness, 41*(4), 491–499.

Gaetano, D. E., Ackerman, S., Clark, A., Hodge, B., Hohensee, T., May, J., et al. (2007). Health surveillance for rural volunteer firefighters and emergency medical services personnel. *AAOHN Journal, 55*(2), 57–63.

Gaetke, L. M., Stuart, M. A., & Truszczynska, H. (2006). A single nutrition counseling session with a registered dietitian improves short-term clinical outcomes for rural Kentucky patients with chronic diseases. *Journal of the American Dietetic Association, 106*(1), 109–112.

Granmyr, J., Ball, P., Curran, S., & Wang, L. (2007). Evidence-based use of medications in patients with coronary artery disease in a rural Australian community. *Australian Journal of Rural Health, 15*(4), 241–246.

Grubbs, L., & Frank, D. (2004). Self-care practices related to symptom responses in African-American and Hispanic adults. *Self-Care, Dependent-Care & Nursing, 12*(1), 4–9.

Gu, D., Gupta, A., Muntner, P., Hu, S., Duan, X., Chen, J., et al. (2005). Prevalence of cardiovascular disease risk factor clustering among the adult population of China: Results from the International Collaborative Study of Cardiovascular Disease in Asia (InterAsia). *Circulation, 112*(5), 658–665.

Healy, B. (1991). The Yentl syndrome. *New England Journal of Medicine, 325*(4), 274–276.

Hedges, J. R., Adams, A. L., & Gunnels, M. D. (2002). ATLS practices and survival at rural level III trauma hospitals, 1995–1999. *Prehospital Emergency Care, 6*(3), 299–305.

Huang, G., Niu, T., Peng, S., Ling, D., Liu, J., Zhang, X., et al. (2004). Association between the interleukin-1[beta] C(-511)T polymorphism and blood pressure in a Chinese hypertensive population. *Immunology Letters, 91*(2–3), 159–162.

Huang, J., Wildman, R. P., Gu, D., Muntner, P., Su, S., & He, J. (2004). Prevalence of isolated systolic and isolated diastolic hypertension subtypes in China. *American Journal of Hypertension, 17*(10), 955–962.

Hunter, J. M., Sparks, B. T., Mufunda, J., Musabayane, C. T., Sparks, H. V., & Mahomed, K. (2000). Economic development and women's blood pressure: Field evidence from rural Mashonaland, Zimbabwe. *Social Science & Medicine, 50*(6), 773–795.

Jackson, E., & Ockene, I. S. (2007). Obesity, weight reduction, and cardiovascular disease. In B. D. Rose (Ed.), *UpToDate.* Waltham, MA: UpToDate.

Jackson, M. D., Coombs, M. P., Wright, B. E., Carney, A. A., Lewis-Fuller, E., & Reizo, M. (2004). Self-reported non-communicable chronic diseases and health-seeking behaviour in rural Jamaica, following a health promotion intervention: A preliminary report. *International Congress Series, 1267,* 59–68.

Jafar, T. H. (2006). Women in Pakistan have a greater burden of clinical cardiovascular risk factors than men. *International Journal of Cardiology, 106*(3), 348–354.

James, G. D., & Bovbjerg, D. H. (2001). Age and perceived stress independently influence daily blood pressure levels and variation among women employed in wage jobs. *American Journal of Human Biology, 13*(2), 268–274.

James, P. A., Li, P., & Ward, M. M. (2007). Myocardial infarction mortality in rural and urban hospitals: Rethinking measures of quality of care. *Annals of Family Medicine, 5*(2), 105–111.

Jelinek, H., Warner, P., King, S., & De Jong, B. (2006). Opportunistic screening for cardiovascular problems in rural and remote health settings. *Journal of Cardiovascular Nursing, 21*(3), 217–222.

Kettle, S. M., Roebothan, B. V., & West, R. (2005). Prevalence of specific cardiovascular disease risk factors in young Newfoundland and Labrador adults living in urban and rural communities. *Canadian Journal of Rural Medicine, 10*(2), 81–85.

Kieu, N. T., Yasugi, E., Hung, N. T., Kido, T., Kondo, K., Yamamoto, S., et al. (2002). Serum fatty acids, lipoprotein (a) and apolipoprotein profiles of middle-aged men and women in South Vietnam. *Asia Pacific Journal of Clinical Nutrition, 11*(2), 112–116.

Kim, C., Eby, E., & Piette, J. D. (2005). Is education associated with mortality for breast cancer and cardiovascular disease among black and white women? *Gender Medicine, 2*(1), 13–18.

Kisely, S., Campbell, L. A., & Skerritt, P. (2005). *Psychological interventions for symptomatic management of non-specific chest pain in patients with normal coronary anatomy*. Retrieved December 2007 from http://www.mrw.interscience.wiley.com/cochrane

Kuhajda, M. C., Cornell, C. E., Brownstein, J. N., Littleton, M. A., Stalker, V. G., Bittner, V. A., et al. (2006). Training community health workers to reduce health disparities in Alabama's black belt. *Family & Community Health, 29*(2), 89–102.

Lancaster, K. J., Smiciklas-Wright, H., Weitzel, L. B., Mitchell, D. C., Friedmann, J. M., & Jensen, G. L. (2004). Hypertension-related dietary patterns of rural older adults. *Preventive Medicine, 38*(6), 812–818.

Lewis, C., Gadomski, A., Nafziger, A., Reed, R., Jenkins, P., Dennison, B., et al. (2000). Insights from a large rural population laboratory: Health census '89 and '99. *Annals of Epidemiology, 10*(7), 454–455.

Lupton, B. S., Fonnebo, V., & Sogarrd, A. J. (2003). The Finnmark Intervention Study: Is it possible to change CVD risk factors by community-based intervention in an Arctic village in crisis? *Scandinavian Journal of Public Health, 31*(3), 178–186.

Manson, J. E., Willett, W. C., Stampfer, M. J., Colditz, G. A., Hunter, D. J., Hankinson, S. E., et al. (1995). Body weight and mortality among women. *New England Journal of Medicine, 333*(11), 677–685.

Martinez, M. R., Pochettino, M. L., & Cortella, A. R. (2004). Environment and illness in the Calchaqui Valley (Salta, Argentina): Phytotherapy for osteo-articular and cardio-circulatory diseases. *Journal of Ethnopharmacology, 95*(2–3), 317–327.

McSweeney, J. C. (1998). Women's narratives: Evolving symptoms of myocardial infarction. *Journal of Women Aging, 10*(2), 67–83.

McSweeney, J. C., Cody, M., & Crane, P. B. (2001). Do you know them when you see them? Women's prodromal and acute symptoms of myocardial infarction. *Journal of Cardiovascular Nursing, 15*(3), 26–38.

McSweeney, J. C., Cody, M., O'Sullivan, P., Elberson, K., Moser, D. K., & Garvin, B. J. (2003). Women's early warning symptoms of acute myocardial infarction. *Circulation, 108*(21), 2619–2623.

McSweeney, J. C., & Coon, S. (2004). Women's inhibitors and facilitators associated with making behavioral changes after myocardial infarction. *Medical-Surgical Nursing, 13*(1), 49–56.

McSweeney, J. C., & Crane, P. B. (2000). Challenging the rules: Women's prodromal and acute symptoms of myocardial infarction. *Research in Nursing & Health, 23*(2), 135–146.

McSweeney, J. C., Lefler, L. L., & Crowder, B. F. (2005). What's wrong with me? Women's coronary heart disease diagnostic experiences. *Progress in Cardiovascular Nursing, 20*(2), 48–57.

McSweeney, J. C., Lefler, L. L., Fischer, E. P., Naylor, A. J., Jr., & Evans, L. K. (2007). Women's prehospital delay associated with myocardial infarction: Does race really matter? *Journal of Cardiovascular Nursing, 22*(4), 279–285.

McSweeney, J. C., O'Sullivan, P., Cody, M., & Crane, P. B. (2004). Development of the McSweeney Acute and Prodromal Myocardial Infarction Symptom Survey. *Journal of Cardiovascular Nursing, 19*(1), 58–67.

Meng, H., Wamsley, B. R., Eggert, G. M., & Van Nostrand, J. F. (2007). Impact of a health promotion nurse intervention on disability and health care costs among elderly adults with heart conditions. *Journal of Rural Health, 23*(4), 322–331.

Messner, T., Lundberg, V., & Stegmayr, B. (2003). Cardiovascular risk factor levels differ between communities of different sizes in the Northern Sweden MONICA Project. *Scandinavian Journal of Public Health, 31*(5), 359–366.

Miller, D. D. (2007). Stress testing for the diagnosis of coronary heart disease in women. In B. D. Rose (Ed.), *UpToDate.* Waltham, MA: UpToDate.

Minh, H. V., Byass, P., & Wall, S. (2003). Mortality from cardiovascular diseases in Bavi District, Vietnam. *Scandinavian Journal of Public Health, 31*(Suppl. 60), 26–31.

Morgan, D. M. (2005). Effect of incongruence of acute myocardial infarction symptoms on the decision to seek treatment in a rural population. *Journal of Cardiovascular Nursing, 20*(5), 365–371.

Morgan, L. L., & Fahs, P. S. (2007). *Conversations in the disciplines: Sustaining rural populations.* Binghamton, NY: Global Academic Publishing.

Mosca, L., Jones, W. K., King, K. B., Ouyang, P., Redberg, R. F., & Hill, M. N. (2000). Awareness, perception, and knowledge of heart disease risk and prevention among women in the United States. American Heart Association Women's Heart Disease and Stroke Campaign Task Force. *Archives of Family Medicine, 9*(6), 506–515.

Mussolino, M. E., & Armenian, H. K. (2007). Low bone mineral density, coronary heart disease, and stroke mortality in men and women: The Third National Health and Nutrition Examination Survey. *Annals of Epidemiology, 17*(11), 841–846.

Nafziger, A. N., Erb, T. A., Jenkins, P. L., Lewis, C., & Pearson, T. A. (2001). The Otsego-Schoharie healthy heart program: Prevention of cardiovascular disease in the rural U.S. *Scandinavian Journal of Public Health* (Suppl. 56), 21–32.

National Center for Health Statistics (NCHS). (2007). *Fast stats A to Z.* Hyattsville, MD: Centers for Disease Control and Prevention (CDC).

Ng, N., Stenlund, H., Bonita, R., Hakimi, M., Wall, S., & Weinehall, L. (2006). Preventable risk factors for noncommunicable diseases in rural Indonesia: Prevalence study using WHO STEPS approach. *Bulletin of the World Health Organization, 84*(4), 305–313.

Niemann, T., Lous, J., Thorsgaard, N., & Nielsen, T. T. (2000). Regional variations in the use of diagnostic coronary angiography. *Scandinavian Cardiovascular Journal, 34*(3), 286–292.

Nyholm, M., Merlo, J., Rastam, L., & Lindblad, U. (2005). Overweight and all-cause mortality in a Swedish rural population: Skaraborg Hypertension and Diabetes Project. *Scandinavian Journal of Public Health, 33*(6), 478–486.

Ohira, T., Iso, H., Satoh, S., Sankai, T., Tanigawa, T., Ogawa, Y., et al. (2001). Prospective study of depressive symptoms and risk of stroke among Japanese. *Stroke, 32*(4), 903–908.

Ohira, T., Iso, H., Tanigawa, T., Sankai, T., Imano, H., Kiyama, M., et al. (2002). The relation of anger expression with blood pressure levels and hypertension in rural and urban Japanese communities. *Journal of Hypertension*, 20(1), 21–27.

Ohmori-Matsuda, K., Kuriyama, S., Hozawa, A., Nakaya, N., Shimazu, T., & Tsuji, I. (2007). The joint impact of cardiovascular risk factors upon medical costs. *Preventive Medicine*, 44(4), 349–355.

Okon, N. J., Rodriguez, D. V., Dietrich, D. W., Oser, C. S., Blades, L. L., Burnett, A. M., et al. (2006). Availability of diagnostic and treatment services for acute stroke in frontier counties in Montana and northern Wyoming. *Journal of Rural Health*, 22(3), 237–241.

Ortiz, L., Arizmendi, L., & Cornelius, L. J. (2004). Access to health care among Latinos of Mexican descent in colonias in two Texas counties. *Journal of Rural Health*, 20(3), 246–252.

Panagiotakos, D. B., Arapi, S., Pitsavos, C., Antonoulas, A., Mantas, Y., Zombolos, S., et al. (2006). The relationship between adherence to the Mediterranean diet and the severity and short-term prognosis of acute coronary syndromes (ACS): The Greek Study of ACS (The GREECS). *Nutrition*, 22(7–8), 722–730.

Pappas, G., Akhtar, T., Gergen, P. J., Hadden, W. C., & Khan, A. Q. (2001). Health status of the Pakistani population: A health profile and comparison with the United States. *American Journal of Public Health*, 91(1), 93–98.

Peltzer, K. ((2004). Health beliefs and prescription medication compliance among diagnosed hypertension clinic attenders in a rural South African hospital. *Curationis*, 27(3), 15–23.

Perry, C. K., Rosenfeld, A. G., Bennett, J. A., & Potempa, K. (2007). Heart-to-heart: Promoting walking in rural women through motivational interviewing and group support. *Journal of Cardiovascular Nursing*, 22(4), 304–312.

Pierce, C. (2005). Health promotion behaviors of rural women with heart failure. *Online Journal of Rural Nursing and Health Care*, 5, 28–37. Retrieved November 24, 2007, from http://www.rno.org/journal/index.php/online-journal/issue/view/16

Pierce, C. (2007). Distance and access to health care for rural women with heart failure. *Online Journal of Rural Nursing and Health Care*, 7, 27–34. Retrieved November 24, 2007, from http://www.rno.org/journal/index.php/online-journal

Pizent, A., Jurasovic, J., & Telisman, S. (2001). Blood pressure in relation to dietary calcium intake, alcohol consumption, blood lead, and blood cadmium in female nonsmokers. *Journal of Trace Elements in Medicine and Biology*, 15(2–3), 123–130.

Pladevall, M., Williams, K., Guyer, H., Sadumi, J., Falces, C., Ribes, A., et al. (2003). The association between leptin and left ventricular hypertrophy: A population-based cross-sectional study. *Journal of Hypertension*, 21(8), 1467–1473.

Pullen, C. H., Walker, S. N., Hageman, P. A., Boeckner, L. S., & Oberdorfer, M. K. (2005). Differences in eating and activity markers among normal weight, overweight, and obese rural women. *Women's Health Issues*, 15(5), 209–215.

Ricketts, T. C. (Ed.). (1999). *Rural health in the United States*. New York: Oxford University Press.

Riggs, J. E., Libell, D. P., Brooks, C. E., & Hobbs, G. R. (2005). Impact of institution of a stroke program upon referral bias at a rural academic medical center. *Journal of Rural Health*, 21(3), 269–271.

Rosamond, W., Flegal, K., Friday, G., Furie, K., Go, A., Greenlund, K., et al. (2007). Heart disease and stroke statistics—2007 update: A report from the American Heart Association Statistics Committee and Stroke Statistics Subcommittee. *Circulation, 115*(5), e69–e171.

Rosamond, W., Flegal, K., Furie, K., Go, A., Greenlund, K., Haase, N., et al. (2008). Heart disease and stroke statistics—2008 update: A report from the American Heart Association Statistics Committee and Stroke Statistics Subcommittee. *Circulation, 117*, e25–e146. Retrieved April 1, 2008, from http://www.americanheart.org

Rudholm, N. (2006). Comparison of population versus individual based cardiovascular disease prevention programs in Vasterbotten, Sweden. *Health Policy, 78*(1), 70–76.

Rural Health Network of South Central New York. (2007). *Annual report 2006–2007.* Retrieved January 20, 2008, from http://www.ruralhealthnetwork.org

Sanchez, R. J., & Khalil, L. (2005). Badger Heart Program: Health screenings targeted to increase cardiovascular awareness in women at four northern sites in Wisconsin. *Wisconsin Medical Journal, 104*(6), 24–29.

Sanderson, B., Littleton, M., & Pulley, L. (2002). Environmental, policy, and cultural factors related to physical activity among rural, African American women. *Women & Health, 36*(2), 75–90.

Santos, D., Gillies, J., Vartiainen, E., Dunbar, J., & Nettleton, B. (2004). Implementing the evidence: A disease management system for secondary prevention of coronary heart disease in the Scottish Borders. *Quality in Primary Care, 12*(1), 65–72.

Silva, H. P., James, G. D., & Crews, D. E. (2006). Blood pressure, seasonal body fat, heart rate, and ecological differences in Caboclo populations of the Brazilian amazon. *American Journal of Human Biology, 18*(1), 10–22.

Skliros, E., Sotiropoulos, A., Vasibossis, A., Xipnitos, C., Chronopoulos, I., Razis, N., et al. (2007). Poor hypertension control in Greek patients with diabetes in rural areas. The VANK study in primary care. *Rural Remote Health, 7*(3), 5.

Strand, B. H., & Tverdal, A. (2004). Can cardiovascular risk factors and lifestyle explain the educational inequalities in mortality from ischaemic heart disease and from other heart diseases? 26 year follow up of 50 000 Norwegian men and women. *Journal of Epidemiology & Community Health, 58*(8), 705–709.

Struthers, R., Savik, K., & Hodge, F. S. (2004). American Indian women and cardiovascular disease: Response behaviors to chest pain. *Journal of Cardiovascular Nursing, 19*(3), 158–163.

Taylor, H. A., Hughes, G. D., & Garrison, R. J. (2002). Rural health and women of color. Cardiovascular disease among women residing in rural America: Epidemiology, explanations, and challenges. *American Journal of Public Health, 92*(4), 548–551.

Tazi, M. A., Abir-Khalil, S., Chaouki, N., Cherqaoui, S., Lahmouz, F., Srairi, J. E., et al. (2003). Prevalence of the main cardiovascular risk factors in Morocco: Results of a national survey, 2000. *Journal of Hypertension, 21*(5), 897–903.

Tessaro, I., Rye, S., Parker, L., Trangsrud, K., Mangone, C., McCrone, S., et al. (2006). Cookin' up health: Developing a nutrition intervention for a rural Appalachian population. *Health Promotion Practice, 7*(2), 252–257.

Thommasen, H. V., & Zhang, W. (2006). Impact of chronic disease on quality of life in the Bella Coola Valley. *Rural and Remote Health, 6*, 18. Retrieved January 2008 from http://www.rrh.org.au

Tsutsumi, A., Kayaba, K., Tsutsumi, K., & Igarashi, M. (2001). Association between job strain and prevalence of hypertension: A cross sectional analysis in a Japanese working population with a wide range of occupations: The Jichi Medical School cohort study. *Occupational & Environmental Medicine, 58*(6), 367–373.

United States Department of Agriculture. (2008). *Rural information center.* Retrieved January 20, 2008, from http://www.nal.usda.gov/ric/ricpubs/what_is_rural.htm#DF

United States Preventative Services Task Force (USPSTF). (2004). Screening for coronary heart disease: Recommendation statement. *Annals of Internal Medicine, 140*(7), 569–572.

van der Sande, M. A. B., Ceesay, S. M., Milligan, P. J. M., Nyan, O. A., Banya, W. A. S., Prentice, A., et al. (2001). Obesity and undernutrition and cardiovascular risk factors in rural and urban Gambian communities. *American Journal of Public Health, 91*(10), 1641–1644.

Vasan, R. S., & Wilson, W. F. (2007). Epidemiology and causes of heart failure. In B. D. Rose (Ed.), *UpToDate.* Waltham, MA: UpToDate.

Verrill, D. E., Barton, C., Beasley, W., Lippard, M., & King, C. N. (2003). Six-minute walk performance and quality of life comparisons in North Carolina cardiac rehabilitation programs. *Heart & Lung, 32*(1), 41–51.

Vrentzos, G. E., Papadakis, J. A., Malliaraki, N., Bampalis, D. E., Repa, A., Lemonomichelaki, V., et al. (2006). Serum homocysteine concentration as a marker of nutritional status of healthy subjects in Crete, Greece. *Journal of Human Nutrition & Dietetics, 19*(2), 117–123.

Wagnild, G., Rowland, J., Dimmler, L., & Peters, D. (2004). Differences between frontier and urban elders with chronic heart failure. *Progress in Cardiovascular Nursing, 19*(1), 12–18.

Wang, L., Yao, D., & Wu, T. (2004). Prevalence of overweight and smoking patients with coronary heart disease in rural China. *Australian Journal of Rural Health, 12*(1), 17–21.

Weinehall, L., Hellsten, G., Boman, K., Hallmans, G., Asplund, K., & Wall, S. (2001). Can a sustainable community intervention reduce the health gap?—10-year evaluation of a Swedish community intervention program for the prevention of cardiovascular disease. *Scandinavian Journal of Public Health, 29*(Suppl. 56), 59–68.

Wijewardene, K., Mohideen, M. R., Mendis, S., Fernando, D. S., Kulathilaka, T., Weerasekara, D., et al. (2005). Prevalence of hypertension, diabetes and obesity: Baseline findings of a population based survey in four provinces in Sri Lanka. *Ceylon Medical Journal, 50*(2), 62–70.

Williams, A., Wold, J., Dunkin, J., Idleman, L., & Jackson, C. (2004). CVD prevention strategies with urban and rural African American women. *Applied Nursing Research, 17*(3), 187–194.

Wong, K. S., Huang, Y. N., Yang, H. B., Gao, S., Li, H., Liu, J. Y., et al. (2007). A door-to-door survey of intracranial atherosclerosis in Liangbei County, China. *Neurology, 68*(23), 2031–2034.

Yamagishi, K., Iso, H., Tanigawa, T., Cui, R., Kudo, M., & Shimamoto, T. (2004). Alpha-adducin G460W polymorphism, urinary sodium excretion, and blood pressure in community-based samples. *American Journal of Hypertension, 17*(5), 385–390.

Yamagishi, K., Tanigawa, T., Cui, R., Tabata, M., Ikeda, A., Yao, M., et al. (2007). High sodium intake strengthens the association of ACE I/D polymorphism with blood pressure in a community. *American Journal of Hypertension, 20*(7), 751–757.

Yan, W., Gu, D., Yang, X., Wu, J., Kang, L., & Zhang, L. (2005). High-density lipoprotein cholesterol levels increase with age, body mass index, blood pressure and fasting blood glucose in a rural Uygur population in China. *Journal of Hypertension*, *23*(11), 1985–1989.

Yang, X. M., Sun, K., Zhang, W. L., Wu, H. Y., Zhang, H. M., & Hui, R. T. (2007). Prevalence of and risk factors for peripheral arterial disease in the patients with hypertension among Han Chinese. *Journal of Vascular Surgery*, *46*(2), 296–302.

Yokoyama, T., Date, C., Kokubo, Y., Yoshiike, N., Matsumura, Y., & Tanaka, H. (2000). Serum vitamin C concentration was inversely associated with subsequent 20-year incidence of stroke in a Japanese rural community: The Shibata study. *Stroke*, *31*(10), 2287–2294.

Zhang, S., Mao, G., Zhang, Y., Tang, G., Wen, Y., Hong, X., et al. (2005). Association between human atrial natriuretic peptide Val7Met polymorphism and baseline blood pressure, plasma trough irbesartan concentrations, and the antihypertensive efficacy of irbesartan in rural Chinese patients with essential hypertension. *Clinical Therapeutics*, *27*(11), 1774–1784.

Zhang, X., Sun, Z., Zheng, L., Li, J., Liu, S., Xu, C., et al. (2007). Prevalence of dyslipidemia and associated factors among the hypertensive rural Chinese population. *Archives of Medical Research*, *38*(4), 432–439.

Chapter 3

Intimate Partner Violence in Rural Environments

ABSTRACT

The purpose of this chapter is to review nursing and other research related to rural intimate partner violence. The author presents a review of research in the area of intimate partner violence in the rural setting. The findings indicate that there is limited nursing research related to intimate partner violence in rural communities. The review describes the prevalence and types of abuse, the rural service issues, and the consequences of battering. The chapter also discusses the health implications of violence in the rural setting. The author concludes with a presentation of a research agenda for nursing research in rural environments.

Keywords: rural; domestic violence; health effects; barriers

OVERVIEW

People living in rural areas constitute about one-fourth of the U.S. population (U.S. General Accounting Office, 2003). Yet, the majority of studies of intimate partner violence (IPV) focus on nonrural settings. The amount of scientific data collected on IPV in rural areas is minimal. A recent literature review of rural violence revealed only 11 published articles (Annan, 2006). Many of the articles in that review were limited to adolescent populations; moreover, the review focused only on sexual violence, not speaking to other types of rural intimate partner violence. Few nursing researchers have examined violence in the rural setting. To fully examine the state of the science related to rural IPV, it is therefore important to include articles in this review that were conducted by other disciplines as well as by nurses. Researchers must study the potentially unique problems associated with rural living, especially for vulnerable populations such as women experiencing IPV, to facilitate caring for victims and their families.

The National Institute of Justice and the Centers for Disease Control and Prevention call violence against women a major public health and criminal justice concern (Tjaden & Thoennes, 2000). Definitions of intimate partner violence vary, but often include physical, psychological, sexual, and economic abuse (Murray & Graybeal, 2007). Physical violence against women often occurs in conjunction with other types of abuse. For the population of women experiencing physical violence, however, the prevalence of sexual violence is high; studies have reported varying rates from 42% to 72% (Abraham, 1999; Campbell, 1989; Campbell & Soeken, 1999; Resnick et al., 2000; Ullman & Brecklin, 2000). Overall, American women experience one million acts of violence per year (Rennison & Welchans, 2000). Yet, only one-third of domestic violence victims obtained a restraining order and received police assistance (CDC, 2000).

Violence against women is a significant health issue affecting physical, sexual, and psychological aspects of health. An increased susceptibility to illness appears to occur in women who have experienced IPV, and this vulnerability often continues even after they leave the abusive relationship. An association exists between exposure to IPV and poor physical health, increased physical disability, chronic pain, sexually transmitted diseases, and gastrointestinal symptoms (Campbell, 2002; Carbone-Lopez, Kruttschnitt, & Macmillan, 2006; El-Mouselhy, 2004). Almost half (45.5%) of female victims of IPV receive mental health services (Coker, Derrick, Lumpkin, Aldrich, & Oldendick, 2000; Gerlock, 1999). Common mental health problems associated with IPV include depression, posttraumatic stress disorder, substance abuse, and suicide (Acierno, Lawyer, Rheingold, Kilpatrick, Resnick, et al., 2007; Campbell & Soeken, 1999; Dienemann, Boyle, Baker, Resnick, Wiederhorn, et al., 2000; Koss, Bailey, Yuan, Herrera, & Lichter, 2003; Reviere et al., 2007; Romito, Turan, & De Marchi, 2005; Woods & Isenberg, 2001).

There is also an important economic impact for victims of IPV and some victims pay the ultimate price. Studies suggest that women who have experienced IPV are more likely to be currently unemployed, to experience more job turnover, and to have used welfare-type programs (Byrne, Resnick, Kilpatrick,

Best, & Saunders, 1999; Lloyd & Taluc, 1999). Unfortunately, homicide is also an outcome of domestic violence (Garcia, Soria, & Hurwitz, 2007). In 2005, one in three homicides in Virginia was attributed to domestic violence (Virginia Department of Health, 2007).

Studies consistently show that women who experience violent relationships have more physical, mental, and sexual health problems than a nonabused cohort. This likely translates into poorer overall health and more health care visits, which results in a significant economic impact for the health care system. Nursing research examining these health issues in the rural setting will provide information about effective screening methods and assist in identifying victims. Prevalence statistics suggest that nurses will care for many victims of abuse during their career, and studies examining screening for IPV suggest that most victims proceed unidentified through the health care system (D'Avolio et al., 2001; Glass, Dearwater, & Campbell, 2001).

Limited research suggests that there are many social, economic, and access to care differences for victims of IPV in the rural setting, compared to an urban setting. Rural communities tend to be close knit with a shared sense of community and with important social ties among nearby friends and family (Ames, Brosi, & Damiano-Teixeira, 2006). This characteristic closeness of rural areas may make it difficult for health care professionals and others to maintain confidentiality about sexual assault. In rural areas, there is a likelihood that someone the woman encounters in the process would likely know the victim, the perpetrator, or family members, and potentially could compromise confidentiality (Websdale, 1995b). Generally, many people, including the police officer, physician, dispatcher, ambulance crew, court personnel, and hospital registration clerks, have some knowledge of a reported assault. This is not to suggest that people in rural areas are predisposed to breaches of confidentiality, but that living in a smaller community means having closer ties to a greater percentage of people in that community than in a nonrural setting. These potential differences in community relationships may make it more difficult for victims to report or to share their experiences with others. Continuing in a violent relationship would likely increase their health risks, as previously described.

Economic difficulties are common in rural settings. Many rural women have limited access to jobs and are therefore not employed (Van Hightower & Gorton, 2002). Job opportunities are often restricted to seasonal, service, and laborer work with low wages often necessitating both a long-distance commute and a need to work multiple jobs (Ames, Brosi, & Damiano-Teixeira, 2006; Fishwick, 1993; Zunz, Wichroski, & Hebert, 2005). Rural household incomes are often low. From 40% to 45% of rural people live in poverty (DeLeon, Wakefield, Schultz, Williams, & VandenBos, 1989; Foshee, 1996; Stommes & Brown, 2002). These economic conditions may also make women less likely to report an assault because economic stress (e.g., paying a hospital bill or missing time from work for court appearances) may result, although no studies were found examining this relationship.

Isolation is a common characteristic of rural areas (Navin, Stockum, & Campbell-Ruggaard, 1993; Websdale, 1995b, 1998). Long commutes to services make transportation difficult for many rural people and complicate escape for IPV victims (Fishwick, 1998). Public transit was only available in approximately half of rural counties nationwide, according to one source (Stommes & Brown, 2002). Rural inhabitants who did not have access to public transportation had to drive long distances to work, to purchase groceries, and to access social or medical services (National Rural Health Association, 2002; Van Hightower & Gorton, 2002). Many rural households had no phone and only 6.1% of rural families had a computer in the home compared to 66% of urban families (O'Hare & Johnson, 2004). Cell phones often did not receive a signal in rural areas (Stommes & Brown, 2002). Victims isolated by a lack of transportation or no phone or Internet service would seem to be at higher risk of further abuse.

Moreover, in the rural setting there are generally fewer public services (Navin et al., 1993). Some rural towns may have no local police coverage, relying on the sheriff to patrol an entire county (Royse, 1999). Approximately 50% of police departments in the United States retained 10 or fewer officers, and often these officers worked only part time (Weisheit, Falcone, & Wells, 1994). Rural officers often protected a wider geographic area than urban officers resulting in slower response times (Weisheit et al., 1994). Economic hardships and isolation make victims of IPV in the rural setting more vulnerable than nonrural victims. Social, economic, transportation, and service problems suggest an increased need for services in rural areas. Rural women, therefore, who are living with violence in this isolated setting, may have greater difficulty seeking help and are at a higher risk for health problems. Research studies conducted in rural settings related to IPV by nursing and non-nursing researchers were critiqued. The results of this review are considered together with an understanding of the needs of rural people and communities to guide the development of a nursing research agenda. This agenda will aim to expand and improve the knowledge base to guide the development of nursing actions and interventions aimed at reducing IPV in rural settings and to assist nurses in effective interventions with clients treated throughout the rural health system.

METHODOLOGY

For this review, studies were located through a search of eight academic databases in disciplines associated with IPV including nursing, counseling, public health, social work, education, women's studies, and psychology. The databases searched were CINAHL, ERIC, MEDLINE, PsycINFO, Science Direct, InfoTrac, Academic OneFile, JSTOR, and EBSCOhost and covered the past 20 years (1987–2007). Searches were limited to articles in English and to those where the research took place in the United States. A variety of search terms were used to capture studies: *abuse, intimate partner violence, domestic violence, abused women, interpersonal violence, battering, rape, forced sex,* and *sexual assault* were all combined with the keyword *rural*. In addition, government Web sites including the U.S. Department of Justice (Bureau of Justice Statistics, National Institute of Justice, Office of Justice Programs), the Centers for Disease Control and Prevention (National Sexual Violence Resource Center, National Center for Injury Prevention and Control), and the Federal Bureau of Investigation (Uniform Crime Reporting) were searched. Articles were also sought through the invisible college (the use of e-mail lists and word of mouth) and the ancestry approach (the examination of an article's reference list).

This review is limited to research examining physical, sexual, and emotional abuse of adult females in the rural setting. Studies with a primary focus on child abuse, male victims, adolescents, perpetrators, or acquaintance assault were excluded. Studies that included children or adolescents were retained only if the study primarily focused on adults. The term *rural* must have occurred in either the title, abstract, or keyword of every article included in this review. All of the 50 articles found that met these parameters were included in this review.

LITERATURE REVIEW

Intimate partner violence, overall, has been well investigated by nursing researchers (Campbell & Parker, 1999). On this rural-specific issue, however, it was not worthwhile to perform a review of research performed only by nurses as most of the articles in this review were interdisciplinary in nature. In fact, only seven of the articles included in this review were authored solely by nurses (Averill, Padila, & Clements, 2007; Boyd, Mackey, Phillips, & Tavakoli, 2006; Boyd, Phillips, & Dorsey, 2003; Coyer, Plonczynski, Baldwin, & Fox, 2006; Denham, 2003; Evanson, 2006; Zust, 2000). Another six articles had at least one nurse author (Champion, Artnak, Shain, & Piper, 2002; Gray, Lesser, Rebach, Hooks, & Bounds, 1988; Kershner, Long, & Anderson, 1998; Krishnan, Hilbert, & Pase, 2001; Persily & Abdulla, 2000; Thomas, Miller, Hartshorn, Speck, & Walker, 2005). The majority of the articles were not specific to nurse authors; therefore, inclusion criteria were expanded to incorporate non-nurse authors.

Definition of Terms

Rural

The studies in this review often defined important concepts differently, especially the most two relevant concepts: *rural* and *abuse*. The concept of rurality may be defined in many ways. Generally, the articles reviewed defined rural by certain characteristics such as a particular geographic location, population density, distance to urban areas, existence of communication barriers, or the amount of farming, mining, or forestry work occurring in a particular area.

The U.S. Census Bureau defined rural areas as, essentially, all areas not urban. Specifically, it was defined as "all territory, population, and housing units located outside of urbanized areas and urbanized clusters" (U.S. Bureau of Census, 2002, p. 1). The U.S. Census Bureau labeled as urban those areas that have more than 2,500 people living in a region, and rural those areas with less than 2,500 people (U.S. Bureau of Census, 2002).

The Economic Research Service (ERS) of the U.S. Department of Agriculture classifies counties on an urban-rural continuum. This classification system has nine codes: Code One being metropolitan with a population of more than one million to Code Nine, which is completely rural, an area with no adjacent city and a population of less than 2,500 (ERS, 2003). In 2004, the ERS added typology codes to further designate counties based on economic indicators (e.g., farming dependent, mining dependent, etc.) and policy types (e.g., housing stress, low education, population loss, etc.; ERS, 2004).

Many of the rural IPV studies reviewed defined rural using the U.S. Census Data (Boyd et al., 2006, 2003; Grossman, Hinkley, Kawalski, & Margrave, 2005; Ruback & Menard, 2001). However, most studies took other factors into account, such as area size, proximity to urban settings, cultural factors, economic factors, or predominant type of work (e.g., agricultural) found in the setting (Eastman & Bunch, 2007; Grossman, Hinkley, Kawalski, & Margrave, 2005; Johnson & Elliott, 1997; Logan, Walker, Cole, Ratliff, & Leukefeld, 2003; Ulbrich & Stockdale, 2002; Websdale & Johnson, 1997). One study, for example, defined rural as an area "where people know each other's business, come into regular contact with each other and share a larger core of values than is true of people in urban areas" (DeKeseredy & Joseph, 2006). Some studies did not specifically define rural at all, although they provided the location of the study and implied that the reader would know that the location was rural.

Abuse

Many of the articles included in this review did not formally define abuse, except through the tools utilized to screen participants. Well-known standardized scales, such as the Conflict Tactics Scale, the Abuse Assessment Screen, or the

Severity of Violence Against Women Scale were often used (e.g., see Bailey & Daugherty, 2007; Boyd et al., 2003; Denham et al., 2007). Other investigators created their own mechanism for inquiring about abuse in their research, usually either developing questions for participants or devising a new and untested scale (DeKeseredy & Joseph, 2006; Johnson & Elliott, 1997; Krishnan, Hilbert, & Pase, 2001). Some studies selected participants from women in a domestic violence shelter (Few, 2005; Feyen, 1989; Krishnan, Hilbert, & VanLeeuwen, 2001; Websdale & Johnson, 1997; Willis, 1998), women who had obtained protective orders (Logan, Shannon, & Walker, 2005; Logan et al., 2003), or through word-of-mouth inquires (Bosch & Bergen, 2006).

Critique of the Research and Theory

There were many methodological strengths in this body of research. First, researchers used all types of study design: qualitative, quantitative, and mixed-methods. Of the 50 studies, approximately half used qualitative methods of some type and approximately half used quantitative methods. A handful of studies used mixed methods. A variety of quantitative methods were used such as retrospective chart reviews, mailed surveys, and intervention studies. A few studies performed secondary data analyses based on national studies and one article used a case study design. Most of the quantitative studies used convenience samples. Second, researchers used a variety of survey instruments to conduct their studies. Many of these instruments were well-known, such as the Abuse Assessment Screen, although others were created for a given study. Most studies utilized self-administered instruments, although a few used surveys that were read to participants and the answers recorded by the interviewers. Third, although rural settings often have limited minority populations, such groups were a primary focus in a number of the studies.

On the other hand, the body of rural IPV research also had several design flaws. First, only four of the studies in this review were experimental in design (Coyer et al., 2006; Thomas et al., 2005; Ulbrich & Stockdale, 2002; Zust, 2000). These intervention studies were all pretest–posttest in design; none had experimental and control group sections. However, true experimental design is difficult to obtain in vulnerable populations. Quasiexperimental designs are more practical and are often still generalizable.

Second, there were not any longitudinal studies; most quantitative studies were cross sections, descriptive studies, or comparisons of some type, and none were prospective. In addition, although the number of participants in the nonqualitative studies ranged from 14 to more than 2,000, there were several studies with participant numbers ranging between 15 and 35. Depending on the statistical analyses being performed, studies with less than 30 subjects generally do not hold sufficient power to detect differences in or make comparisons among the population examined (Burns & Grove, 1997). Also, most of the research documented in this review occurred in the eastern half of the United States. Studies examining the western United States would be useful to fully comprehend rural IPV and to inform nursing research aimed at building a knowledge base to guide interventions.

Safety issues are an important concern in research design with such a vulnerable population. Study methods must pose minimal risk for participants. Women in violent relationships could be at risk if their assailants discovered they had been talking to others about their experiences. A few studies posed potential safety issues. In one study, the researcher went into the town and asked people if they knew of any women who had experienced IPV (Bosch & Bergen, 2006). Another researcher called participants at home if the survey form was not completed (Denham et al., 2007). Parker and Ulbrich's (1990) safety guidelines do provide recommended procedures for calling subjects at home; however, these guidelines are not addressed in the Denham et al. (2007) article.

Among many of the qualitative studies there were also methodological problems. Many studies did not fully discuss their frameworks or theoretical basis. A number of studies simply used questionnaires read to participants with the investigator recording answers. This is not rigorous qualitative research. Several of the qualitative studies did not state the method of data analysis and appeared to be content analysis only (Lewis, 2003; Logan, Shannon, et al., 2005), as contrasted with the ethnographic (Websdale, 1995a, 1998) and focus group methods (Logan, Evans, Stevenson, & Jordon, 2005) used by other studies in the review. More often than not, however, many articles portray semistructured interviews as qualitative research with no further properties of qualitative framework or data analysis described (Johnson & Elliott, 1997; Logan, Shannon, et al., 2005; Moracco, Hilton, Hodges, & Frasier, 2005; Sudderth, 2006). For example, Strauss and Corbin's (1998) Grounded Theory approach to data analysis involves moving from specific patterns noted in the data to produce a generalizable explanation of events, grounded within the data. The end product of a Grounded Theory analysis is the development of a new theory. Yet, one so-called Grounded Theory study in this review had only general findings and quotations in the results section without substantive discussion of themes and no theory was proposed. Methodological issues similar to these were not uncommon in the review of research.

Many unique challenges exist in conducting IPV research; however, future nursing research should attempt to avoid methodological deficiencies. The adequacy of methodology should be carefully evaluated in future nursing research before study initiation. Improvements in methodology, such as the use of psychometrically sound instruments and more rigorous experimental and qualitative study designs, will increase the strength of the findings.

Findings That Have Implications for Clinical Application and for Nursing Research

Demographics

In the studies reviewed, victims tended to be young and married or cohabitating with limited education and few financial resources. The typical rural IPV victim was younger than age 35 (Denham et al., 2007; DeKeseredy & Joseph, 2006; Feyen, 1989; Kershner et al., 1998; Krishnan, Hilbert, & VanLeeuwen, 2001; Logan et al., 2003; Persily & Abdulla, 2000; The Center for Rural Pennsylvania, 2004; Zweig, Crockett, Sayer, & Vicary, 1999). As with urban victims, older rural women experienced less risk of violence than younger rural women (Kershner et al., 1998). However, IPV was reported across all age groups (18–72) (Bosch & Bergen, 2006; Boyd et al., 2006; Krishnan, Hilbert, & VanLeeuwen, 2001; Van Hightower & Gorton, 1998; Websdale & Johnson, 1998).

The majority of rural women experiencing violence were married to or cohabitating with their abuser (Feyen, 1989; The Center for Rural Pennsylvania, 2004) and had at least one child (Denham et al., 2007; Few, 2005; Feyen, 1989; Johnson & Elliott, 1997; Krishnan, Hilbert, & Pase, 2001; Krishnan, Hilbert, & VanLeeuwen, 2001). In particular, among rural pregnant women, those who were abused were more likely to be married (Bailey & Daugherty, 2007; Dye, Tolliver, Lee, & Kenney, 1995; Persily & Abdulla, 2000). Conversely, one study concluded that married women were less likely to be experiencing IPV than unmarried women (Kershner et al., 1998). However, this study reported that single women who agreed to marriage were more likely to experience IPV than married women in the process of separation. Because Kersher, Long, and Anderson (1998) examined these specific subgroups of the unmarried and married populations, their conclusions cannot necessarily be applied broadly to the entire married and unmarried population.

Victims of IPV in rural areas had limited education and limited financial resources. Approximately half of rural victims had a high school education or less (Krishnan, Hilbert, & VanLeeuwen, 2001; Logan et al., 2003). The typical rural IPV victim was unemployed or, if employed, was employed in a low-wage position (Feyen, 1989; Krishnan, Hilbert, & VanLeeuwen, 2001; Van Hightower & Gorton, 2002), and lived at or below poverty level (Few, 2005; Logan et al., 2003; The Center for Rural Pennsylvania, 2004). Logan et al. (2003) noted that 88% of their participants, women with protective orders, considered themselves to be homeless. By comparison, urban victims of IPV were less likely to be married or cohabitating, to have children, to consider themselves homeless, or to have low income (Logan et al., 2003; The Center for Rural Pennsylvania, 2004). These findings support the need for further nursing research into IPV in the rural setting as a separate distinct focus of research from nonrural settings.

A better understanding of the demographics of this population, such as age, marital status, and income levels, may allow an increased rate of identification of victims by nurses and others and may be used to focus interventions and guide future nursing research.

Prevalence and Types of Abuse

A comparison of the percentages of women reporting IPV in rural versus nonrural settings revealed inconsistent findings. Some studies reported higher percentages of rural IPV (Johnson & Elliott, 1997; Logan et al., 2003). However, one study reported higher percentages of urban IPV (Lewis, 2003), and another reported similar percentages of IPV in both rural and urban settings (Websdale & Johnson, 1998). However, the majority of articles did not have prevalence as a primary focus.

Prevalence varied among subgroups of rural women experiencing IPV. The highest percentage of recent IPV reported was noted among rural African American women struggling with substance abuse (77%) (Boyd et al., 2006). Of those who recently experienced IPV, 15%–19% were pregnant women (Denham, 2003; Dye et al., 1995; Persily & Abdulla, 2000), 29% were rural female emergency department patients (Krishnan, Hilbert, & Pase, 2001), 21% were women attending local rural clinics (Kershner et al., 1998), 19% were Hispanic migrant farm workers (Van Hightower & Gorton, 1998), and 6% were women from a rural healthy-worksite program (Denham et al., 2007). In another study, approximately 3% of women living in a rural county reported severe physical abuse such as being hit with a fist and being injured with a knife or gun (Murty, Peek-Asa, Zwerling, Stromquist, Burmeister, et al., 2003).

Lifetime adult IPV prevalence was also reported for rural women. Twenty-nine percent of pregnant women (Bailey & Daugherty, 2007), and 28% of working women (Denham et al., 2007) reported IPV during adulthood. Seven percent of health care workers (Denham, 2003) reported abuse while pregnant. Similar to urban studies, previous abuse (both prior to age 18 or in a previous relationship) was a strong predictor of later abuse (Kershner et al., 1998). Teaster, Roberto, and Dugar (2006) found that for older rural victims of IPV, the violence started while the participants were dating and continued to occur throughout the relationship.

Not all abuse reported in these studies was physical. Although sexual violence is often also physically violent, it is typically separated out in research studies into categories such as physical, sexual, psychological, and sexual violence. Women reported psychological and emotional abuse (Bailey & Daugherty, 2007; Bosch & Bergen, 2006; Krishnan, Hilbert, & VanLeeuwen, 2001; Persily & Abdulla, 2000), stalking (Krishnan, Hilbert, & VanLeeuwen, 2001), and intimate partner sexual assault (Bailey & Daugherty, 2007; Bosch & Bergen, 2006;

Krishnan, Hilbert, & VanLeeuwen, 2001; Van Hightower & Gorton, 1998). Further, economic abuse, dependence, sabotage, and forced isolation were also reported (Bosch & Bergen, 2006). Rural IPV women were more likely than nonrural IPV women to report threatened or actual harm to their pets (Faver & Strand, 2003). One ethnographic study found that every participant interviewed in rural Kentucky experienced emotional abuse (Websdale, 1998).

Compared to urban participants, rural participants were more likely to report physical abuse and reported the highest incidence of abuse, although the actual prevalence statistics were not published (Mattson & Rodriguez, 1999). Logan et al. (2003) found more severe physical abuse, that the abuse started much earlier in the relationship, more threats to kill, more property destruction, and more reports of abuse among the rural women than among urban victims of IPV. Among the 23 women in the Logan et al. study (2003) the urban women (73%) were much more likely to seek a protective order after the first incidence of abuse than the rural women (0%); however, only 8 rural women and 15 urban women were interviewed in this study (Logan et al., 2003). Another study compared prevalence of intimate partner murders (Gallup-Black, 2005). For every year from 1980 to 1999, femicide was significantly greater in the rural counties compared to urban counties (Gallup-Black, 2005).

A significant number of abused women in rural communities have been documented in a variety of settings such as emergency departments, clinics, and worksites (Coyer et al., 2006; Denham et al., 2007; Krishnan, Hilbert, & Pase, 2001). This review suggests that rural women experience varied types of abusive experiences and that there are important differences between abused women in the rural as opposed to nonrural settings. Further, the rural IPV population makes up a significant proportion of women in any health care setting as rural women often present at urban hospitals and clinics. Further nursing research to corroborate these findings is called for to develop effective and specific nursing interventions.

Results of Battering

Although urban studies of IPV have documented the health effects of domestic violence, only 11 of 48 articles examined this issue in the rural context. Similar health concerns appear to exist in the rural population, but these effects may be more prevalent and consequential in the rural setting.

Almost two-thirds (64%) of sheltered rural battered women have two or more psychiatric diagnoses (Thomas et al., 2005). Rural women who had experienced IPV reported symptoms of depression, anxiety, and posttraumatic stress disorder (Krishnan, Hilbert, & Pase, 2001; Logan et al., 2003). In the Logan et al. (2003) study, an urban comparison group reported fewer symptoms of mental illness than the rural women. Similarly, among rural women presenting to the emergency department, women with a history of IPV were more likely to report suicide attempts than a nonabused rural comparison group (Krishnan, Hilbert, & Pase, 2001). Low self-esteem was common among rural battered women (Feyen, 1989; Zust, 2000). Self-blame was greatest among those participants who knew the perpetrator (Gray et al., 1988). Many rural women have experienced abuse in a previous relationship and the abuse began early their current relationship (Krishnan, Hilbert, & Pase, 2001). Many rural women reported that they had known nothing other than abusive relationships in their lifetime (Willis, 1998).

For many rural women, alcohol or illegal drugs were a factor in the violent relationship. Violence was more likely to occur when the partner drank alcohol or used illegal drugs (Denham, 2003; Feyen, 1989; Van Hightower & Gorton, 2002; Willis, 1998). In many instances illegal drugs or alcohol was used by both the women and the abusers (Teaster, Roberto, & Dugar, 2006; Wingood, DiClemente, & Raj, 2000). Among rural women, some studies found that abused women were more likely to use tobacco, alcohol, and other drugs than nonabused women (Bailey & Daugherty, 2007; Dye et al., 1995; Persily & Abdulla, 2000). Another study reported that rural women with protective orders were less likely to abuse substances than urban women with protective orders (Logan et al., 2003). Yet, one study found no differences in drug and alcohol use between abused and nonabused rural women presenting to the emergency department (Krishnan, Hilbert, & Pase, 2001).

Several studies examined aspects of physical health and IPV. Rural women with protective orders reported more stress and poorer overall health than their urban counterparts (Logan et al., 2003). Abused rural pregnant women were also more likely to experience fetal distress and fetal death and were more likely to have low birth weight babies than nonabused rural women even after controlling for smoking and maternal age (Dye et al., 1995). Abused pregnant rural women were more likely to have a history of sexually transmitted diseases (Persily & Abdulla, 2000), less likely to start prenatal care in the first trimester (Bailey & Daugherty, 2007), and more likely to be homeless (Dye et al., 1995) than nonabused rural pregnant women. These are all conditions that contribute to other physical health problems. Rural victims of IPV were more likely to complain of gastrointestinal symptoms compared to nonrural victims of IPV (Logan et al., 2003).

Although Logan et al. (2003) did not find any significant differences for lifetime emergency department or hospital visits between urban and rural victims, it is likely that rural victims are less likely to obtain needed health care because of access difficulties and financial stress in the rural setting. Importantly, most rural victims of IPV did not seek medical care for their injuries (Denham, 2003; Krishnan, Hilbert, & VanLeeuwen, 2001; Van Hightower & Gorton, 2002). The physical health effects reported among victims of rural

IPV suggest a real need for nursing researchers to develop secondary interventions, which attempt to prevent illness, to develop tertiary prevention interventions, and to reduce disability or relieve symptoms. The need for rural-specific interventions is demonstrated well in one article, which applies an ethical framework to a case study, demonstrating the unique complexities of caring for this population (Champion, Artnak, Shain, & Piper, 2002). The victim in the case study was experiencing poverty, limited health care access, and was afraid to tell her husband about acquiring a sexually transmitted disease. This article focuses on the clinical dilemmas occurring for rural providers in providing safe interventions for victims of IPV in the rural setting.

Rural IPV Services

Services available in the rural setting included counseling, shelter, protective orders, and medical attention (Bogal-Allbritten & Daughaday, 1990; Krishnan, Hilbert, & VanLeeuwen, 2001; Teaster, Roberto, & Dugar, 2006; Willis, 1998). Many (38%) sheltered battered rural women sought counseling services (Krishnan, Hilbert, & VanLeeuwen, 2001), and this was one of the most common services offered in the rural setting (The Center for Rural Pennsylvania, 2004). However, urban shelters were more likely to offer in-house counseling than rural shelters (Bogal-Allbritten & Daughaday, 1990). Participants reported that counseling was safe, helpful, and supportive (Willis, 1998).

Rural shelters offered many services for victims. A national study found that rural shelters were more likely to offer crisis phone counseling, transportation assistance, food, legal information, child care, and financial assistance, while urban shelters were more likely to offer clothing and employment help (Bogal-Allbritten & Daughaday, 1990). Other services offered were legal accompaniment and medical accompaniment (The Center for Rural Pennsylvania, 2004). Rural programs were more likely to offer services to those outside of their regional area, but were also more likely to be required by their funding source to serve a particular area or region (Bogal-Allbritten & Daughaday, 1990). Further, sheltered rural victims were more likely than urban sheltered victims to need education, training, transportation, medical, and employment assistance (Grossman, Hinkley, Kawalski, & Margrave, 2005). Awareness of available services and the efficacy of services, through nursing research, will guide nurses and others in developing effective supports for victims in the rural setting.

Barriers to Accessing Assistance

Despite the various resources available in rural communities, studies revealed that barriers to help seeking existed. Rural women were often not aware that a shelter was available within their community before deciding to leave their abuser and were often given misleading information about the shelter by their abuser (Few, 2005). Interestingly, access to resources inversely predicted severity of abuse (Bosch & Bergen, 2006). Services not generally offered by rural agencies within a community included alcohol and drug assistance, mental health services, and family planning services (The Center for Rural Pennsylvania, 2004). Although rural agencies would refer women to other locations that offered these services, many rural women needed assistance with transportation (Websdale, 1995b).

Family and social support for IPV victims had an effect on accessing care. One study found that families gave financial, emotional, and housing support (Van Hightower & Gorton, 2002). Two other studies, however, reported that for some victims their family was unhelpful (Bosch & Bergen, 2006; Teaster, Roberto, & Dugar, 2006). In the rural setting women often lived among or near the abuser's family rather than their own (Few, 2005). Community support was uneven and religious supports were minimal (Few, 2005; Feyen, 1989; Teaster, Roberto, & Dugar, 2006). Religious and community expectations led the victim to stay with the abuser (Few, 2005). Bosch and Bergen (2006) reported that friends and neighbors were often the most supportive, and the absence of supportive persons was a significant barrier to victim's access of services. Rural victims of IPV needed more emotional support (Grossman, Hinkley, Kawalski, & Margrave, 2005) and reported more loneliness and less social support than urban victims (Logan et al., 2003). With lack of information about resources and inadequate support, a rural woman experiencing a violent relationship will often not report it to anyone.

About half (56%) of sheltered battered rural women had reported their abuse to police (Krishnan, Hilbert, & VanLeeuwen, 2001). Rural women were more likely to have told a health or mental professional about their abuse than nonrural women and were also more likely to have been screened for abuse than urban women (Logan et al., 2003). Rural women related that they did not report their abuse if they felt that doing so would place them in more danger or if they felt that the service providers would not believe them (Teaster, Roberto, & Dugar, 2006).

Only six studies examined women's experiences with rural service providers. Victims reported inadequate police protection and response, discourteous treatment from law enforcement officials, and a lack of information on legal options (Few, 2005; Teaster, Roberto, & Dugar, 2006; Van Hightower & Gorton, 2002). Rural women experiencing IPV also reported that prosecuting attorneys often did not file charges, reduced the severity of the charges against the victim's wishes, and failed to inform the victim when the accused was being released (Van Hightower & Gorton, 2002). While interviewing rural service providers, Van Hightower and Gorton (2002) found that providers often questioned victim credibility, were reluctant to make arrests, imposed lenient sanctions on abusers, and expressed victim-blaming statements. Those in advocacy roles, such as directors of rural shelters, had more concerns about the way cases were handled than urban shelter directors (The Center for Rural Pennsylvania, 2004).

Shelters were not always reasonably accessible for rural victims, although rural victims reported that they were a safe option (Few, 2005; Van Hightower & Gorton, 2002). Victims reported that they did not use the local shelter because of transportation issues and a desire to stay near their support system and home (Van Hightower & Gorton, 2002). Rural shelter clients were less likely to be referred by police or by social service agencies to a shelter but were more likely to be self-referred or referred by a legal provider, friend, or relatives (Grossman, Hinkley, Kawalski, & Margrave, 2005).

The research included in this review examined many factors influencing victim help seeking, including available services, family and social support, reporting, frustrations with some providers, and location of shelters and other services. Nurses in rural settings must inquire about abuse, encourage victims to seek help, and acknowledge victims' experiences. Nursing research must broaden understanding of barriers to help seeking in rural victims of IPV in order to develop appropriate nursing care. Victims that are unidentified by legal and service providers may not receive needed care.

Culture-Related Research

Many rural areas are not ethnically diverse, which is oftentimes reflected in the populations included in rural research. For example, Logan et al. (2003) reported only a 2% African American population in the county studied, and none of these women participated in this study (Logan et al., 2003). However, ethnic homogeneity is not always the case and it is important to study cultural differences to create effective interventions appropriately. Of the 50 studies included in this review, only seven examined specific ethnicities (Boyd et al., 2003; Denham et al., 2007; Few, 2005; Krishnan, Hilbert, & VanLeeuwen, 2001; Mattson & Rodriguez, 1999; Moracco et al., 2005; Van Hightower & Gorton, 1998). Three of these studies examined African Americans and five examined rural Hispanics.

Among ethnic groups in the studies comparing IPV, prevalence was similar across Latina or Hispanic, African American, and White rural women (Boyd et al., 2003; Denham et al., 2007; Van Hightower & Gorton, 1998), although other differences among the groups were noted. Boyd et al. (2003) found 65%–70% of rural African American and White women with substance abuse disorders had experienced violence within their current relationships. Adult lifetime prevalence of Latinas was 19% and of African Americans and Whites was 28%, although this difference was not statistically significant (Denham et al., 2007).

Nineteen percent of low-income rural Hispanics had experienced IPV within the past year (Van Hightower & Gorton, 1998).

African American and Latina or Hispanic women may have less support than White rural women when both experienced IPV. When comparing rural Latinas experiencing abuse to those not abused, the abused women were more likely to report a lack of nearby friends, family, or other social supports (Denham et al., 2007). Rural African American women were more likely to state that IPV and shelter life could not be talked about with their family; however, they were also were more likely than White women to report relying on family for help (Few, 2005).

When comparing rural non-Latinas experiencing IPV to rural Latinas experiencing IPV, the Latinas had less education, were less likely to have health insurance (Denham et al., 2007), were more likely to report suicidal thoughts or attempts, were more likely to stay in their abusive relationships longer, and were less likely to report alcohol or drug use (Krishnan, Hilbert, & VanLeeuwen, 2001). One study found that most rural Latinas had not heard of a protective order, although most knew it was against the law for a man to hit his spouse or partner (Moracco et al., 2005). However, another study found that Latinas were more likely to seek a protective order than non-Latinas, but this study was among a group of sheltered women (Krishnan, Hilbert, & VanLeeuwen, 2001). Only one study compared rural and urban Latina women experiencing IPV. Here, the participants in rural areas were more likely to report physical abuse and reported the highest incidence of abuse, although the urban women reported more severe abuse (Mattson & Rodriguez, 1999). The rural women in this study, however, were more likely to have been born in the United States, and the urban women were more likely to be new immigrants. This lack of assimilation could explain why the urban women experienced more severe abuse (Mattson & Rodriguez, 1999). Likely, there are fewer social supports and less-developed social service infrastructures to help Latinas and African Americans in the rural setting. Language and social barriers may present additional impediments to help seeking in this population.

Intervention Studies

Four rural domestic violence intervention studies were found; two studies were screening based and two were treatment based (Coyer et al., 2006; Thomas et al., 2005; Ulbrich & Stockdale, 2002; Zust, 2000). The screening studies were pretest–posttest in design and examined the effectiveness of an intervention to increase screening of domestic violence (Coyer et al., 2006; Ulbrich & Stockdale, 2002). Clinical and nonclinical staff at rural family planning clinics were selected for a 5-hour workshop on the cycle of violence, power, and control, why women stay, how to screen, shelter services, and a specific model (RADAR) to screen women (Ulbrich & Stockdale, 2002). Six months after the training, participants self-reported increased comfort in asking patients about IPV and self-reported that 100% of patients were screened (Ulbrich & Stockdale, 2002). This research was a pilot study with 40 participants throughout four different sites; a small sample size. Moreover, although the posttest survey protected the identity of the participants, the responses were self-reported. A chart review to compare rates of screening could be more accurate.

Similarly, Coyer et al. (2006) examined screening via a retrospective chart review both before and after an educational intervention that consisted of lectures performed by local advocates and aimed at nurse practitioners. Screening at the study clinic consisted of one question, "Is anyone hurting you" (p. 51), and abuse was added to the list of identified health risks on the clinics history form and into the electronic medical record. Coyer reported 100% screening in the postintervention period, although only six women were identified out of 859 (far below normal prevalence percentages) and the 100% screening was at least in part the result of a computer prompt that required an answer in order to continue with charting. The low prevalence noted in this study may have been influenced by the lack of specificity of the screening process.

Thomas et al. (2005) completed a treatment intervention aimed at a convenience sample of rural battered women staying at a shelter. The women who scored a certain number on the SCR-90-R were offered psychiatric treatment through an electronic telepsychiatry program. Those women meeting eligibility criteria for the study were also offered a physical examination, lab work, and psychological intake. The study authors reported on successes and difficulties associated with the program as well as types of disorders identified. At the end of a year, just over half of the subjects were still in treatment. However, no testing to examine the success of the program was performed and the authors label the study observational in nature. The cost of setting up a telehealth program and the planning, preparation, and coordination of services involved could be prohibitive to some areas.

Zust (2000) examined the effectiveness of a 20-week program of cognitive-behavioral group therapy in both battered and nonbattered rural women. Both pretesting and posttesting were performed on several variables including anxiety, loneliness, and self-esteem. Half of the battered women dropped out before study completion, but posttest results suggest a decrease in loneliness and depression and an increase in self-esteem for the battered rural women. Zust, a nurse, did include a conceptual framework, critical feminist theory paired with the INSIGHT Holistic Ecological model, in her research study. The screening questionnaire used was not validated, however, and a convenience sample was used. This was a pilot study, and the small sample size ($n = 27$) likely influenced the power of data analysis.

Sexual Violence

Intimate partner sexual assault is relatively unexamined in the rural setting. Most studies of rural sexual assault did not differentiate between intimate partner assault and stranger assault. In the one study that addressed this question, almost half of battered rural women reported sexual assault from partners (Wingood et al., 2000). However, given that most rural sexual assaults are not stranger assaults (Annan, 2006; Gray et al., 1988; Ruback & Menard, 2001), rural studies of all types of sexual assault were examined in this review.

Approximately 30%–40% of rural women reported an unwanted sexual experience in their lifetime (DeKeseredy & Joseph, 2006; Gray et al., 1988; Zweig et al., 1999). One study found that rates of sexual assaults were similar in urban, rural, and suburban areas (Duhart, 2000). Data from the Federal Uniform Crime Reports and Pennsylvania Rape Crisis Centers, however, found that rural counties had higher percentages of sexual victimization than urban counties (Ruback & Menard, 2001). Specific numbers, however, were not reported. Ruback and Menard (2001) speculated that rural isolation and a higher likelihood of knowing people in the community increased opportunities for offenders.

Many articles focused on other aspects of rural sexual assault. Gray et al. (1988) found that 78% of victims had not reported the assault to police, 56% reported the use of alcohol at the time of assault, and only 11% sought counseling after the assault. Logan, Evans, et al. (2005) conducted focus groups with 18 rural and 12 urban women from rape crisis centers to examine barriers to services. Rural women complained about the limited hours of services, problems with distance to services, lack of advocate availability, health professionals being unfamiliar with the rape exam, and having to wait a long time for police assistance or to see mental health professionals. Further, participants reported experiencing significant adverse stigma associated with sexual assault, self-blame, and avoiding sharing their experience. Other difficulties included perceived political influences over legal outcomes, lack of control over the process, and gossip by criminal justice personnel (Logan, Evans, et al., 2005). Lewis (2003) interviewed rural service providers in four states. Participants reported the need for additional personnel, travel assistance to care facilities, and training and outreach. This qualitative study, however, did not report coding or other data analysis procedures.

Although some of these issues, such as law enforcement complaints, the use of alcohol during an assault, and the effect of legal outcomes, may not seem to be nursing-related issues, good patient care comes from a holistic understanding of the issues surrounding a given population. Further, nursing specialties, such as forensic nurses, have a close tie to these seemingly non-health-related issues surrounding IPV. However, the experiences of victims, especially negative experiences aside from the abuse itself, likely compound the victim experience, adversely affecting physical and mental health. In fact, for some women, social, legal, and medical systems that projected negative or judgmental attitudes, including blaming the woman, led to psychological distress above and beyond the assault (Campbell, Sefl, Barnes, Ahrens, Wasco, et al., 1999; Campbell, Wasco, Ahrens, Sefl, & Barnes, 2001).

Rural-Specific Issues Related to IPV

The literature suggests that there are social conditions in the rural setting that differ from urban areas. The small size of rural populations often produces a tight network of long-term acquaintances among rural residents. Rural nurses frequently see their clients in nonprofessional settings (Evanson, 2006). The impact of the rural acquaintance factor on reporting has not been thoroughly examined, although one study found that lack of anonymity was a concern among rural abused women (Kershner & Anderson, 2002). Many victims lived in their county for more than 20 years on average, making it likely that they would know most of the people within their small community (Logan et al., 2003).

A sense of traditional values and conservative social beliefs could contribute to some level of normalization of violence between intimate partners. One study found victim reports of familial patriarchy, male peer support for abuse, and traditional feminine roles in the rural setting (DeKeseredy & Joseph, 2006). Many rural women have experienced abuse in a prior relationship and the abuse began early in the relationship (Krishnan, Hilbert, & Pase, 2001). Rural women reported that they knew nothing other than abusive relationships in their lifetime (Willis, 1998). These findings may suggest community acceptance of some level of abuse. Future nursing research should examine this issue directly.

Geography produces isolation for abuse victims in the rural community. Rural houses are often far back from the road and located farther apart than urban houses (Websdale, 1995a). Many victims live too far from town to walk for help or for services if needed (Bosch & Bergen, 2006; Feyen, 1989; Van Hightower & Gorton, 2002). One study noted that participants lived, on average, 78 miles from shelter services (Bosch & Bergen, 2006).

Transportation via car was also more difficult in rural areas. Many (20%–43%) rural victims did not have access to a car or were prevented by the abuser from using their car by tactics such as fuel siphoned from vehicles, car keys hidden, and parts removed from car engines (Bosch & Bergen, 2006; Logan et al., 2003; Websdale, 1995a; Willis, 1998). Comparatively, only 10% of urban victims had no access to a car (Logan et al., 2003). Half of rural victims reported having no transportation available at the time of the abuse (Feyen, 1989).

Access disparities related to telephone services exist in the rural setting. Compared to 6% of urban victims without a phone, many (20%–33%) rural victims of IPV do not own a phone (Feyen, 1989; Logan et al., 2003; Websdale,

1995a). Unfortunately, even for victims with a dependable car or phone service, other barriers to help seeking remain. Studies documented phones pulled off of the wall, phone cords removed from the home each day, and the abuser standing next to the victim when talking on the phone (Bosch & Bergen, 2006; Websdale, 1995a; Websdale & Johnson, 1998). These simple problems present insurmountable barriers to escape or to seek assistance in the rural setting.

Weapons were often used in rural assaults (Teaster, Roberto, & Dugar, 2006). Rural women were more likely to report the use of weapons during an assault than urban women (Logan et al., 2003; Websdale & Johnson, 1998). This may be in part because of the fact that rural communities are more likely to have a hunting lifestyle than urban communities, which entails having guns in the home. A weapon in the home is a predictor of femicide (Campell, 2001). And, as noted previously, nationally, femicide is greater in rural counties compared to urban counties (Gallup-Black, 2005). These are worrisome findings.

About Providers

Unique service provider problems also exist in rural areas. Rural police are often stretched thin with only one officer on patrol to cover a large area (Feyen, 1989). This makes it more difficult for quick police response during an assault. Victim advocates reported that police did not always conduct thorough investigations (Teaster, Roberto, & Dugar, 2006) and victims reported that police sometimes refuse to come when called or take a long time to arrive (Feyen, 1989; Websdale, 1995a; Websdale & Johnson, 1997). Rural women were less likely to report that police responded when called and were less likely to call police than nonrural women (Websdale & Johnson, 1997).

Interviews with rural police suggest that they view equally the protection of the victim and the alleged batterer and that they have limited flexibility in their protocols because they are dictated by law (Sudderth, 2006; Van Hightower & Gorton, 2002). Study participants reported, however, that the law was applied haphazardly (Willis, 1998) and that they felt that law enforcement and the court process was affected by who the assailant knew (Logan, Evans, et al., 2005; Willis, 1998). In the rural setting, victim credibility and the severity of assault influenced police decision making (Van Hightower & Gorton, 2002; Websdale & Johnson, 1998). State police were viewed more favorably by victims compared to local police; this may be because of greater community detachment and more training in domestic violence issues (Websdale, 1995b; Websdale & Johnson, 1997).

Advocacy agencies in the rural setting were busier in many ways than urban centers. Rural agencies were open less hours per week and had half as many staff employed, but attended to twice as many clients than urban agencies (The Center for Rural Pennsylvania, 2004).

Typically, rural providers had less training and less equipment than urban providers (Lewis, 2003; Van Hightower & Gorton, 2002). Yet these service providers were often responsible for a wider range of activities than in urban areas. For example, law enforcement officers were often responsible for firefighting rescue operations (Lewis, 2003), and public health nurses were often responsible for at-home visits; immunization clinics; and Women, Infants and Children (WIC) programs (Evanson, 2006). Frequent personnel turnover contributed to a lack of knowledge of domestic violence issues (Sudderth, 2006). Rural providers were more likely to report difficulty in finding training opportunities in IPV, difficulty accessing the latest IPV developments, and to report that there were not enough resources locally compared to urban providers (Eastman & Bunch, 2007). Rural health care providers reported that they needed more education to prepare them for working with the IPV population (Denham, 2003).

Two of the three rural studies that interviewed health care providers examined IPV screening issues (Centers for Disease Control, 1998; Denham, 2003; Evanson, 2006). Most physicians, physician's assistants, nurse practitioners, and nurses in the rural setting reported that their facility adequately screened, counseled, and referred IPV victims, yet less than a third of these providers actually indicated that they routinely screened for IPV themselves (Centers for Disease Control, 1998). In addition, most health care providers were not comfortable discussing suspicions of abuse with the victim and did not document these suspicions in the chart (Denham, 2003).

Already spread thin by multiple roles and fewer resources, providers likely prioritize their work based on the facts of each case and the intensity of other demands on them. Given the issues that often cloud cases related to intimate partner violence, service providers, especially police, in rural areas with fewer resources may tend to not pursue certain cases that might be pursued in areas with more resources. This lack of support for rural IPV victims likely contributes to the health problems experienced.

CONCLUSIONS

Suggested Nursing Research Agenda and Needed Follow-Up Studies

The research of IPV is not in its infancy but is in its toddlerhood. A strong comprehensive foundation of rural IPV is needed. There are two main problems with the existing research. First, large-scale mixed-method studies do not appear to exist. Second, existing research lacks methodological strength to allow confidence to be placed in conclusions. A discussion of these two issues is warranted.

This research review suggests that there are a number of studies that could be undertaken in the examination of IPV in rural areas. First, further qualitative studies are needed. Qualitative studies are ideal for examining the subtle differences and concerns that may exist for this population. One such study would employ hermeneutical phenomenology to establish a baseline understanding of the unique problems and lived experiences of the rural IPV victim. Such experiences should include the victim's experiences from childhood through the present day.

Second, an ethnographic study would be useful. The foundation of ethnography is cultural anthropology. Here, the researcher participates in daily life, learns the local language, and becomes familiar with societal customs and traditions. This, too, would provide information about the life and needs of victims of IPV in rural settings and should focus on the unique cultural life in rural communities in America.

Third, a four-group study examining rural versus urban and abused versus nonabused women in multiple communities is needed. This study would demand a large sample size in order to obtain the power necessary to give a definitive look at rural versus urban characteristics. This study should include an examination of physical, sexual, and emotional health effects of IPV, prevalence, types of violence experienced, the influence of social supports, and barriers to help seeking, among other issues. Further examination is also warranted into the influence of weapons in rural IPV. A study of this magnitude would require cooperation between the research team and the communities involved, as well as a coordinating interdisciplinary research team to oversee the project. Such a study almost certainly would need to involve more than one institution and because no such interinstitutional research organization appears to exist, one seems to be called for.

Improvements in the science of IPV research must come through careful methodological procedures. This examination of the literature found that often the research that does exist on rural IPV lacks methodological rigor. The qualitative research violated standard methodological procedures more often than quantitative research. For a scientifically valid qualitative study, a discussion of the guiding framework, how data was manipulated, and the data analysis procedures is required. All too often, some or all of these essential elements were missing from the qualitative articles reviewed. The researcher's analysis from data to conclusion was often simply not discussed.

Many of the quantitative studies reviewed were descriptive in design and used convenience samples. Descriptive designs certainly have a valid place in quantitative research, and admittedly it is difficult to design some types of quantitative studies with vulnerable human subjects; however, there is a need for other kinds of quantitative studies, especially experimental designs, such as pretest–posttest control group designs. Descriptive designs alone do not provide sufficient knowledge to guide nursing practice. Nursing knowledge is developed as part of a long process to examine phenomena, test hypotheses, reassess phenomena, and examine its properties.

It is important to understand the culture of a given community and to tailor services and interventions to the needs of that particular community (Edelson & Frank, 1991). There appear to be many social, economic, educational, and environmental differences for victims in rural communities. Victims of IPV in rural communities face obstacles to reporting and care that differ from urban communities. An exploration by nurse researchers of factors unique to the rural setting may shed light on elements influencing the experience of rural IPV and improve effectiveness of interventions.

REFERENCES

Abraham, M. (1999). Sexual abuse in south Asian immigrant marriages. *Violence Against Women, 5*, 591–618.

Acierno, R., Lawyer, S. R., Rheingold, A., Kilpatrick, D. G., Resnick, H. S., & Saunders, B. E. (2007). Current psychopathology in previously assaulted older adults. *Journal of Interpersonal Violence, 22*(2), 250–258.

Ames, B. D., Brosi, W. A., & Damiano-Teixeira, K. M. (2006). "I'm just glad my three jobs could be during the day": Women and work in a rural community. *Family Relations, 55*, 119–131.

Annan, S. (2006). Sexual violence in rural areas: A review of the literature. *Family & Community Health, 29*(3), 164–168.

Averill, J. B., Padilla, A. O., & Clements, P. T. (2007). Frightened in isolation: Unique considerations for research of sexual assault and interpersonal violence in rural areas. *Journal of Forensic Nursing, 3*(1), 42–46.

Bailey, B. A., & Daugherty, R. A. (2007). Intimate partner violence during pregnancy: Incidence and associated health behaviors in a rural population. *Maternal Child Health, 11*, 495–503.

Bogal-Allbritten, R., & Daughaday, L. R. (1990). Spouse abuse program services: A rural-urban comparison. *Human Services in the Rural Environment, 14*(2), 6–10.

Bosch, K., & Bergen, M. B. (2006). The influence of supportive and nonsupportive persons in helping rural women in abusive partner relationships become free from abuse. *Journal of Family Violence, 21*, 311–320.

Boyd, M. B., Mackey, M. C., Phillips, K. D., & Tavakoli, A. (2006). Alcohol and other drug disorders, comorbidity and violence in rural African-American women. *Issues in Mental Health Nursing, 27*, 1017–1036.

Boyd, M. R., Phillips, K., & Dorsey, C. J. (2003). Alcohol and other drug disorders, comorbidity, and violence: Comparison of rural African American and Caucasian women. *Archives of Psychiatric Nursing, 17*(6), 249–258.

Burns, N., & Grove, S. K. (1997). *The practice of nursing research: Conduct, critique, and utilization* (3rd ed.). Philadelphia: W. B. Saunders.

Byrne, C. A., Resnick, H. S., Kilpatrick, D. G., Best, C. L., & Saunders, B. E. (1999). The socioeconomic impact of interpersonal violence on women. *Journal of Consulting and Clinical Psychology, 67*(3), 362–366.

Campbell, J., & Parker, B. (1999). Clinical nursing research on battered women and their children: A review. In A. Hinshaw, S. Freetham, & J. Shaver (Eds.), *Handbook of clinical nursing research* (pp. 535–559). Newbury Park, CA: Sage.

Campbell, J. C. (1989). Women's responses to sexual abuse in intimate relationships. *Health Care for Women International, 10,* 335–346.

Campbell, J. C. (2001). *The Danger Assessment: Research validation from the 12 city femicide study.* Oral Presentation given at Southern Nursing Research Society Annual Conference, February 2001.

Campbell, J. C. (2002). Health consequences of intimate partner violence. *The Lancet, 359,* 1331–1336.

Campbell, J. C., & Soeken, K. (1999). Forced sex and intimate partner violence: Effects on women's risk and women's health. *Violence Against Women, 5*(9), 1017–1035.

Campbell, R., Sefl, T., Barnes, H. E., Ahrens, C. E., Wasco, S. M., & Zaragoza-Diesfeld, Y. (1999). Community services for rape survivors: Enhancing psychological well-being or increasing trauma? *Journal of Consulting & Clinical Psychology, 67*(6), 847–858.

Campbell, R., Wasco, S. M., Ahrens, C., Sefl, T., & Barnes, H. E. (2001). Preventing the "second rape": Rape survivor's experiences with community service providers. *Journal of Interpersonal Violence, 16*(12), 1239–1259.

Carbone-Lopez, K., Kruttschnitt, C., & Macmillan, R. (2006). Patterns of intimate partner violence and their associations with physical health, psychological distress and substance use. *Public Health Reports, 121,* 382–392.

The Center for Rural Pennsylvania. (2004, November). *Survey of domestic violence, sexual assault victim service agencies.* Retrieved September 24, 2007, from www.ruralpa.org

Centers for Disease Control. (1998, August 21). Rural health-care provider's attitudes, practices and training experience regarding intimate partner violence, West Virginia, March 1997. *Morbidity and Mortality Weekly Report, 47*(32), 670–671.

Centers for Disease Control. (2000, June 9). Use of medical care, police assistance, and restraining orders by women reporting intimate partner violence—Massachusetts, 1996–1997. *Morbidity and Mortality Weekly Report, 49,* 485–488.

Champion, J. D., Artnak, K., Shain, R. N., & Piper, J. (2002). Rural women abuse and sexually transmitted disease: An ethical analysis of clinical dilemmas. *Issues in Mental Health Nursing, 23,* 305–326.

Coker, A. L., Derrick, C., Lumpkin, J. L., Aldrich, T. E., & Oldendick, R. (2000). Help-seeking for intimate partner violence and forced sex in South Carolina. *American Journal of Preventative Medicine, 19*(4), 316–320.

Coyer, S. M., Plonczynski, D. J., Baldwin, K. B., & Fox, P. G. (2006). Screening for violence against women in a rural health clinic. *Online Journal of Rural Nursing and Health Care, 6*(1), 47–54.

D'Avolio, D., Hawkins, J., Haggerty, L., Kelly, U., Barrett, R., Toscano, S., et al. (2001). Screening for abuse: Barriers and opportunities. *Health Care for Women International, 22*(4), 349–362.

DeKeseredy, W. S., & Joseph, C. (2006). Separation and/or divorce sexual assault in rural Ohio: Preliminary results of an exploratory study. *Violence Against Women, 12*(3), 301–311.

DeLeon, P. H., Wakefield, M., Schultz, A. J., Williams, J., & VandenBos, G. R. (1989). Rural America: Unique opportunities for health care delivery and health services research. *American Psychologist, 10,* 1298–1306.

Denham, A. C., Frazier, P. Y., Hooten, E. G., Belton, L., Newton, W., Gonzalez, P., et al. (2007). Intimate partner violence among Latinas in Eastern North Carolina. *Violence against Women, 13,* 123–140.

Denham, S. A. (2003). Describing abuse of pregnant women and their healthcare workers in rural Appalachia. *The American Journal of Maternal Child Nursing, 28*(4), 264–269.

Dienemann, J., Boyle, E., Baker, D., Resnick, W., Wiederhorn, N., & Campbell, J. (2000). Intimate partner abuse among women diagnosed with depression. *Issues in Mental Health Nursing, 21,* 499–513.

Duhart, D. T. (2000). Urban, suburban, and rural victimization, 1993–1998. *Bureau of Justice Statistics: Special Report* (NCJ 182031). Washington, DC: U.S. Department of Justice, Office of Justice Programs, National Crime Victimization Survey.

Dye, T., Tolliver, N., Lee, R., & Kenney, C. (1995). Violence, pregnancy and birth outcome in Appalachia. *Paediatric and Perinatal Epidemiology, 9,* 35–47.

Eastman, B. J., & Bunch, S. G. (2007). Providing services to survivors of domestic violence: A comparison of rural and urban service provider perceptions. *Journal of Interpersonal Violence, 22,* 465–473.

Economic Research Service (ERS), U.S. Department of Agriculture. (2003). *Measuring rurality: New definitions in 2003.* Retrieved March 6, 2005, from www.ers.usda.gov/briefing/rurality/NewDefinitions

Economic Research Service (ERS), U.S. Department of Agriculture. (2004, December 15). *State fact sheets: Virginia.* Retrieved March 6, 2005, from www.ers.usda.gov/statefacts/VA.htm

Edelson, J. L., & Frank, M. D. (1991). Rural interventions in woman battering: One state's strategies. *Families in Society: The Journal of Contemporary Human Services, 72,* 543–551.

El-Mouselhy, M. (2004). Violence against women: A public health problem. *The Journal of Primary Prevention, 25*(2), 289–303.

Evanson, T. (2006). Intimate partner violence and rural public health nursing practice: Challenges and opportunities. *Online Journal of Rural Nursing and Health Care, 6*(1), 7–20.

Faver, C. A., & Strand, E. B. (2003). To leave or to stay? Battered women's concern for vulnerable pets. *Journal of Interpersonal Violence, 18*(12), 1367–1377.

Few, A. L. (2005). The voices of black and white rural battered women in domestic violence shelters. *Family Relations, 54,* 488–500.

Feyen, C. (1989). Battered rural women: An exploratory study of domestic violence in a Wisconsin county. *Wisconsin Sociologist, 26*(1), 17–32.

Fishwick, N. (1993). Nursing care of battered women. *AWHONN's Clinical Issues in Perinatal and Women's Health Nursing, 4*(3), 441–448.

Fishwick, N. (1998). Issues in providing care for rural battered women. In J. C. Campbell (Ed.), *Empowering survivors of abuse: Health care for battered women and their children* (pp. 280–290). Thousand Oaks, CA: Sage.

Foshee, V. A. (1996). Gender differences in adolescent dating abuse prevalence, types and injuries. *Health Education Research, 11*(3), 275–286.

Gallup-Black, A. (2005). Twenty years of rural and urban trends in family and intimate partner homicide: Does place matter? *Homicide Studies, 9*(2), 149–173.

Garcia, L., Soria, C., & Hurwitz, E. L. (2007). Homicides and intimate partner violence: A literature review. *Trauma, Violence and Abuse*, 8(4), 370–383.

Gerlock, A. A. (1999). Health impact of domestic violence. *Issues in Mental Health Nursing*, 20, 373–385.

Glass, N., Dearwater, S., & Campbell, J. (2001). Intimate partner violence screening and intervention data from eleven Pennsylvania and California community hospital emergency departments. *Journal of Emergency Nursing*, 27(2), 141–149.

Gray, M. D., Lesser, D., Rebach, H., Hooks, B., & Bounds, C. (1988). Sexual aggression and victimization: A local perspective. *Response to the Victimization of Women & Children*, 11(3), 9–13.

Grossman, S. F., Hinkley, S., Kawalski, A., & Margrave, C. (2005). Rural versus urban victims of violence: The interplay of race and religion. *Journal of Family Violence*, 20(2), 71–81.

Johnson, M., & Elliott, B. A. (1997). Domestic violence among family practice patients in midsized and rural communities. *Journal of Family Practice*, 44(4), 391–401.

Kershner, M., & Anderson, J. (2002). Barriers to disclosure of abuse among rural women. *Minnesota Medical Association*, 85, 1–10.

Kershner, M., Long, D., & Anderson, J. (1998). Abuse against women in rural Minnesota. *Public Health Nursing*, 15(6), 422–431.

Koss, M. P., Bailey, J. A., Yuan, N. P., Herrera, V. M., & Lichter, E. L. (2003). Depression and PTSD in survivors of male violence: Research and training initiatives to facilitate recovery. *Psychology of Women Quarterly*, 27, 130–142.

Krishnan, S. P., Hilbert, J. C., & Pase, M. (2001). An examination of intimate partner violence in rural communities: Results from a hospital emergency department study from southwest United States. *Family & Community Health*, 24(1), 1–14.

Krishnan, S. P., Hilbert, J. C., & VanLeeuwen, D. (2001). Domestic violence and help-seeking behaviors among rural women: Results from a shelter-based study. *Family & Community Health*, 24(1), 28–38.

Lewis, S. (2003, April). Sexual assault in rural communities. *Unspoken crimes: Sexual assault in rural America*. Retrieved January 6, 2005, from www.nsvrc.org

Lloyd, S., & Taluc, N. (1999). The effects of male violence on female employment. *Violence against Women*, 5(4), 370–392.

Logan, T. K., Evans, L., Stevenson, E., & Jordan, C. E. (2005). Barriers to services for rural and urban survivors of rape. *Journal of Interpersonal Violence*, 20(5), 591–616.

Logan, T. K., Shannon, L., & Walker, R. (2005). Protective orders in rural and urban areas: A multiple perspective study. *Violence against Women*, 11(7), 876–911.

Logan, T. K., Walker, R., Cole, J., Ratliff, S., & Leukefeld, C. (2003). Qualitative differences among rural and urban intimate violence experiences and consequences: A pilot study. *Journal of Family Violence*, 18(2), 83–92.

Mattson, S., & Rodriguez, E. (1999). Battering in pregnant Latinas. *Issues in Mental Health Nursing*, 20(4), 405–422.

Moracco, K. E., Hilton, A., Hodges, K. G., & Frasier, P. Y. (2005). Knowledge and attitudes about intimate partner violence among immigrant Latinos in rural North Carolina: Baseline information and implications for outreach. *Violence Against Women*, 11, 337–352.

Murray, C., & Graybeal, J. (2007). Methodological review of intimate partner violence prevention research. *Journal of Interpersonal Violence, 22,* 1250–1269.

Murty, S., Peek-Asa, C., Zwerling, C., Stromquist, A., Burmeister, L., & Merchant, J. (2003). Physical and emotional partner abuse reported by men and women in a rural community. *American Journal of Public Health, 93,* 1073–1075.

National Rural Health Association. (2002). *What's different about rural health care?* Retrieved June 19, 2004, from http://www.nrharural.org

Navin, S., Stockum, R., & Campbell-Ruggaard, J. (1993). Battered women in rural America. *Journal of Humanistic Education and Development, 32,* 9–16.

O'Hare, W. P., & Johnson, K. M. (2004). Child poverty in rural America. *Population Reference Bureau Reports on America, 4*(1), 1–21.

Parker, B., & Ulbrich, Y. (1990). A protocol of safety: Research on abuse of women. *Nursing Research, 39*(4), 248–250.

Persily, C. A., & Abdulla, S. (2000). Domestic violence and pregnancy in rural West Virginia. *Online Journal of Rural Nursing and Health Care, 1*(3), 11–20.

Rennison, C. M., & Welchans, S. (2000). *Bureau of Justice Statistics special report: Intimate partner violence* (NCJ 178247). Washington, DC: U.S. Department of Justice, Office of Justice Programs.

Resnick, H. S., Holmes, M. M., Kilpatrick, D. G., Clum, G., Acierno, R., Best, C. L., et al. (2000). Predictors of post-rape medical care in a national sample of women. *American Journal of Preventative Medicine, 19*(4), 214–219.

Reviere, S. L., Farber, E. W., Twomey, H., Okun, A., Jackson, E., Zanville, H., et al. (2007). Intimate partner violence and suicidality in low-income African-American women: A multi-method assessment of coping factors. *Violence Against Women, 13,* 1113–1129.

Romito, P., Turan, J. M., & De Marchi, M. (2005). The impact of current and past interpersonal violence on women's mental health. *Social Science & Medicine, 60,* 1717–1727.

Royse, B. (1999, September). *Non-stranger sexual assault: Rural realities.* Paper presented at the Denver Sexual Assault Interagency Council: National Non-stranger Sexual Assault Symposium (50–52, 249). Retrieved January 6, 2005, from denversaic.org

Ruback, R. B., & Menard, K. S. (2001). Rural-urban differences in sexual victimization and reporting: Analyses using UCR and crisis center data. *Criminal Justice & Behavior, 28*(2), 131–155.

Stommes, E. S., & Brown, D. M. (2002). Transportation in rural America: Issues for the 21st century. *Rural America, 16*(1), 2–10.

Strauss, A., & Corbin, J. (1998). *Basics of qualitative research: Techniques and procedures for developing grounded theory* (2nd ed.). Thousand Oaks, CA: Sage.

Sudderth, L. K. (2006). An uneasy alliance: Law enforcement and domestic violence victim advocates in a rural area. *Feminist Criminology, 1*(4), 329–353.

Teaster, P. B., Roberto, K., & Dugar, T. A. (2006). Intimate partner violence of rural aging women. *Family Relations, 55,* 636–648.

Thomas, C. R., Miller, G., Hartshorn, J. C., Speck, N. C., & Walker, G. (2005). Telepsychiatry program for rural victims of domestic violence. *Telemedicine and e-Health, 11*(5), 567–573.

Tjaden, P., & Thoennes, N. (2000). *Full report of the prevalence, incidence, and consequences of violence against women* (NCJ 183781). Washington, DC: U.S. Department of Justice and Centers for Disease Control and Prevention.

Ulbrich, P. M., & Stockdale, J. (2002). Making family planning clinics an empowerment zone for rural battered women. *Women & Health, 35*, 83–100.

Ullman, S. E., & Brecklin, L. R. (2000). Alcohol and adult sexual assault in a national sample of women. *Journal of Substance Abuse, 11*(4), 405–420.

U.S. Bureau of Census. (2002, March). *Urban and rural classification.* Retrieved March 6, 2005, from http://www.census.gov/geo/www/ua/ua_2k.html

U.S. General Accounting Office. (2003). Rural development: Profile of rural areas. *U.S. GAO: Fact sheet for Congressional requesters.* GAO/RCED-93-40FS, 1–32. Washington, DC: Author.

Van Hightower, N. R., & Gorton, J. (1998). Domestic violence among patients at two rural health care clinics: Prevalence and social correlates. *Public Health Nursing, 15*(5), 355–362.

Van Hightower, N. R., & Gorton, J. (2002). A case study of community-based responses to rural woman battering. *Violence against Women, 8*, 845–872.

Virginia Department of Health. (2007). *Family and intimate partner homicide: Virginia 2005.* Office of the Chief Medical Examiner, Commonwealth of Virginia. Retrieved September 2007 from www.VDOH.gov

Websdale, N. (1995a). An ethnographic assessment of the policing of domestic violence in rural eastern Kentucky. *Social Justice, 22*(1), 102–123.

Websdale, N. (1995b). Rural woman abuse: The voices of Kentucky women. *Violence Against Women, 1*(4), 309–338.

Websdale, N. (1998). *Rural woman battering and the justice system: An ethnography.* Thousand Oaks, CA: Sage.

Websdale, N., & Johnson, B. (1997). The policing of domestic violence in rural and urban areas: The voices of battered women in Kentucky. *Policing and Society, 6*, 297–317.

Websdale, N., & Johnson, B. (1998). An ethnostatistical comparison of the forms and levels of woman battering in urban and rural areas of Kentucky. *Criminal Justice Review, 23*(2), 161–196.

Weisheit, R. A., Falcone, D. N., & Wells, L. E. (1994). Rural crime and rural policing. *National Institute of Justice: Research in Action* (NCJ 150223). Washington, DC: National Institute of Justice.

Willis, S. M. (1998). Recovering from my own little war: Women and domestic violence in rural Appalachia. *Journal of Appalachian Studies, 4*, 255–270.

Wingood, G. M., DiClemente, R. J., & Raj, A. (2000). Adverse consequences of intimate partner abuse among women in non-urban domestic violence shelters. *American Journal of Preventive Medicine, 19*(4), 270–275.

Woods, S., & Isenberg, M. A. (2001). Adaptation as a mediator of intimate abuse and traumatic stress in battered women. *Nursing Science Quarterly: Theory, Research, and Practice, 14*(3), 215–221.

Zunz, S. J., Wichroski, M. A., & Hebert, S. M. (2005). Challenges faced by rural TANF recipients: Regional differences in the outcomes of a lifeskills program. *Journal of Human Behavior in the Social Environment, 12*(1), 39–57.

Zust, B. L. (2000). Effect of cognitive therapy on depression in rural battered women. *Archives of Psychiatric Nursing, 14,* 51–63.

Zweig, J. M., Crockett, L. J., Sayer, A., & Vicary, J. R. (1999). A longitudinal examination of the consequences of sexual victimization for rural young adult women. *The Journal of Sex Research, 36*(4), 396–409.

PART II

Improving Systems, Quality of Care, and Patient Safety

Chapter 4

Hospital-Based Emergency Nursing in Rural Settings

Jennifer F. Brown

ABSTRACT

In 2006, the Institute of Medicine (IOM) released a series of reports that highlighted the urgent need for improvements in the nation's emergency health services. This news has provided new energy to a growing body of research about the development and implementation of best practices in emergency care. Despite evidence of geographical disparities in health services, relatively little attention has been focused on rural emergency services to identify environmental differences. The purpose of this chapter is to summarize the contributions of nursing research to the rural emergency services literature. The research resembles a so-called shotgun effect as the exploratory and interventional studies cover a wide range of topics without consistency or justification. Emergency nursing research has been conducted primarily in urban settings, with small samples and insufficient methodological rigor. This chapter will discuss the limitations of the research and set forth an agenda of critical topics that need to be explored related to emergency nursing in rural settings.

Keywords: rural emergency nursing; disaster nursing; nursing research

INTRODUCTION

In 2006, the Institute of Medicine's (IOM) release of a series of reports titled "Future of Emergency Care" stimulated the widespread engagement of U.S. health care professionals, legislators, and the general public in conversations about the problems and the dire need for improvements in the nation's emergency health services. One of the reports, "Hospital-Based Emergency Care: At the Breaking Point," identifies overcrowding, fragmentation, and a general scarcity of resources as negative influences on quality of care and suggests the existence of geographical disparities. Already, these documents have yielded a significant impact by raising awareness and interest in this area of health care, and the potential for promoting sustainable progress is promising. Because nurses are the largest group of health professionals and the primary providers of hospital-based emergency care, it stands to reason that substantial nursing research and practice efforts should be devoted to the improvement of emergency health services. The purpose of this chapter is to summarize the contributions of nursing research to the rural emergency services research literature and to propose an agenda of critical topics that need to be explored related to hospital-based emergency nursing in rural settings. The chapter begins by reviewing the broad scope of emergency services research undertaken during the past decade and then focuses more specifically on the research related to emergency nursing in rural settings.

Emergency Health Care Services

Emergency health care services deliver care to all types of patients and conditions ranging from serious injury to common ailments and trauma to primary care. The unique premise under which emergency services are delivered, that care is provided to the person who needs it most rather than who came first, sets it apart from other areas of health care. In recent years, increased attention has been paid to the role of emergency health services in disaster preparedness and response. Thus an additional paradigm, to provide care that offers the greatest good for the greatest number, drives the delivery of these services (NeSmith, 2006). Moreover, the specialty does not discriminate by income, insurance status, age, or race in terms of who is eligible to receive services.

The recognition of emergency health care services as a specialty area has been relatively recent. Prior to the 1950s, emergency care was delivered by health care providers from a wide range of clinical backgrounds on the basis of availability rather than expertise. Recognizing the distinct challenges clinicians face in the emergency setting, physicians were the first to formalize specialty education and training. Emergency nursing emerged as a distinct specialty in 1970 (IOM, 2006a). Emergency health care services are delivered through several venues including hospital (emergency department) services, mobile response and transport (ambulance, flight) units, and community-based crisis response teams, all of which utilize nurses.

Emergency health care has been recognized as a cornerstone of primary and secondary illness prevention worldwide (Anderson, Petrino, Halpern, & Tintinalli, 2006). Arnold and colleagues (2001) conducted a survey of emergency medical services across 36 countries and found this area of health care to be widely available but in varying levels of sophistication. The majority of the countries in the sample had hospital-based emergency departments (97%); emergency medical transport systems (75%); a system of triage (67%); and specialized care for pediatrics (81%), obstetrics (63%), and psychiatry (71%). In the United States, emergency medical services have become the fastest-growing area of health care with the number of annual emergency department (ED) visits equal to roughly one-third of the national census (IOM, 2006b). The rapid, widespread development of hospital-based emergency health care has generated tremendous variation in services. Research has shown that variability exists in the following areas: access to treatment; provider availability and expertise; triage and care processes; and patient volumes, characteristics, and outcomes. Identified influences include geographic, economic, political, and social forces.

The IOM (2006b) reports that the U.S. emergency health care system is overburdened, underfunded, and fragmented. The shortage of health care professionals, hospital consolidations, and legislation mandating open access to care (Emergency Medical Treatment and Labor Act, 1986) have stimulated an increase in the number of annual ED visits while the number of care providers and hospitals offering emergency services has decreased (McCaig & Burt, 2005). Prior to a study conducted by Sullivan and colleagues (2006), the number, distribution, and general characteristics of U.S. EDs was not well documented. The National Emergency Department Inventory, which Sullivan and his team created by integrating several secondary databases, highlighted geographic disparities in visit volume and service access. Emergency department staffing is another concern: approximately 75% of EDs report difficulty finding medical specialists to take emergency and trauma calls, most EDs do not have pediatric specialists or even the appropriate equipment to manage pediatric emergencies, and there is a pronounced shortage of nurses to care for the increased volume of patients. While emergency health care providers are recognized as integral responders to disasters, the Homeland Security funding that was allocated to emergency services (4% of the total Homeland Security budget) is not sufficient to develop appropriate response infrastructures, leaving most EDs inadequately prepared to handle the expected increased volume and special needs of patients in disaster situations (IOM, 2006a). Overly cautious interpretations of the Healthcare Insurance Portability and Accountability Act (HIPAA) have contributed to system fragmentation as providers, who restrict critical patient information in attempts to avoid liability, leave emergency workers without access to any prior medical records for the clients they treat.

The IOM report (2006b) claims that emergency care research is a broad field involving many disciplines and overlapping themes, which makes it difficult to define. Too few adequately trained investigators, poorly defined professional research tracks, limited interdisciplinary collaboration, and lack of specific funding streams are named as challenges to the field of emergency services research. The IOM task force recommends that the Department of Health and Human Services conduct a study of the research needs and gaps in emergency care, and determine the best strategy for closing the gaps, which may include a center or institute for emergency care research (IOM, 2006b). Well-designed research that compares emergency services, including disaster preparedness and response activities, across multiple agencies and geographic regions is necessary to fully understand how the aforementioned factors influence the quality of emergency health care.

Nursing is identified in the IOM report (2006a) as a critical component of emergency health care that must be addressed in future research. Recommendations highlight the need for greater understanding of nursing supply issues. Clinical staff shortages on hospital units lead to overcrowding within the ED and, ultimately, to diversions and backups for transport and response units as well. Nursing position vacancies are third highest in ED settings. Implementation of standardized staffing ratios in the ED has been controversial because of ever-changing patient census and complexity. The IOM report suggests that the impact of these conditions has not been effectively evaluated. In addition, the report illuminates demographical disparities in the composition of ED nurses (88.5% non-Hispanic White, 86% female) and says that little is known about the characteristics of advanced-practice nurses who work in emergency settings. The adequacy of nurses' training for responding to disasters, and how such preparation should differ across clinical and geographical settings, is largely unknown. The Emergency Nurses Association (ENA) supported an extensive investigation for the purpose of establishing national emergency nursing research priorities and identified nursing workforce issues, pain management, and patient education as the research areas of greatest interest to emergency nurse leaders (Bayley, MacLean, Desy, & McMahon, 2004). The responsibility for conducting further emergency research to address these aspects of nursing in rural settings rests with three major entities: emergency nursing, disaster nursing, and other disciplines whose research makes contributions that impact emergency nursing care (the overlapping interests of these entities are depicted in Figure 4.1).

METHODOLOGY

Alpi (2006) conducted a library indexing search to find the core emergency nursing literature and found PubMed and CINAHL to be the most comprehensive

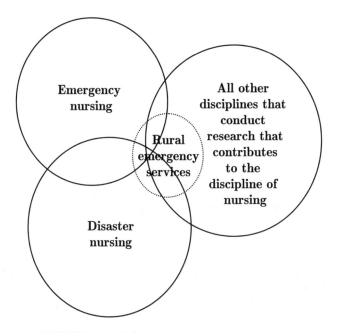

FIGURE 4.1   Defining emergency nursing research.

databases for this topic. To identify the body of literature relevant to this review, the author performed several searches of PubMed and CINAHL electronic databases using different combinations of the keywords *emergency nursing, disaster nursing, rural,* and *research,* limiting articles to those published since 1997 in English. Initial PubMed and CINAHL searches using the search phrase *emergency nursing* or *disaster nursing* yielded 3,248 and 4,440 articles, respectively. Adding *research* to each term reduced the number of articles to 608 in PubMed and 440 in CINAHL. Adding *rural* before each term, *emergency nursing research* or *disaster nursing research,* yielded 15 articles in PubMed and 20 in CINAHL. There was an overlap of articles (3 duplicates) across the two databases. Only research-based articles related to rural emergency nursing were selected for full review (3 articles found in PubMed and 7 articles in CINAHL were eliminated). A review of the cited reference lists for these 22 articles revealed 10 additional articles that met inclusion criteria. A large portion of the research comes from countries other than the United States, including Australia, England, and Canada; thus this is a review of international rural emergency nursing research. The articles are summarized in Table 4.1. In addition, the author searched the CRISP database of federally funded biomedical research projects conducted at universities, hospitals, and other research institutions within the United States and identified six rural emergency nursing research studies that are in progress or recently completed.

Recognizing that nursing is one component of the broad field of emergency research, the author conducted an electronic exploration (using PubMed) of the *rural emergency research* literature published in English throughout the past two years and identified 13 additional studies that addressed nursing. These articles are summarized in Table 4.2.

LITERATURE REVIEW

Research on Emergency Services in Rural Settings

Despite the acknowledgment of significant geographical disparities (Lutfiyya, Bhat, Gandhi, Nguyen, Weidenbacher-Hoper, et al., 2007), a disproportionately insignificant effort has been taken to systematically compare rural and urban emergency services. The body of literature related to rural emergency health care spans the globe including studies in Africa, Australia, Europe, North America, and the Middle East (Ali, Ayaz, Rizwan, Hashim, & Kuroiwa, 2006; Bennett, Moore, & Probst, 2007; Marcin et al., 2007; Otchere & Kayo, 2007; Sweetman & Brazil, 2007; Vinson, 2007; Wamwana, Ndavi, Gichangi, Karanja, Muia, et al., 2006; Wright, McGrail, & Disler, 2007). The focus of research has included access and cost of care, use of technology, provider training, treatment of common ED clinical presentations, and disaster preparedness. In the United States, the Office of Rural Health Policy/Health Resources and Services Administration has funded several national studies that have addressed similar topics (Casey, Wholey, & Moscovice, 2007; Hartley, Ziller, Loux, Gale, Lambert, et al., 2005; Schur, 2004). The studies have been descriptive in nature, which has limited the extent to which the results are generalizable or transferable to practice.

The IOM "Future of Emergency Care" report identifies the predominant focus on a single intervention or health problem rather than broader system-level issues as a significant limitation to the published emergency services research. To create the recommended coordinated regionalized accountable system, the report calls for system-level emergency research to address the following needs: development of evidence-based indicators of emergency care system performance; improvement of the hospital-based service classification system; evaluation of the rural hospital-academic medical center linkages; and assessment of rural and urban differences in relation to ED staffing, triage, technology, and disaster preparedness. Moreover, previous studies have focused on a single type of health professional or patient in isolation. Given the complexity of the patient population and the interdisciplinary collaboration within emergency services, researchers must design studies that identify the implications for *all* stakeholders—patients and their families, physicians, nurses, and other care providers.

TABLE 4.1 Summary of Rural Emergency Nursing Research

Authors	Year	Topic	Study Design/ Location/Sample	Rural (R) and Urban (B)
Andersson, Omberg, & Svedlund	2006	Factors influencing triage decision-making by ED nurses	Qualitative, observations & interviews/ Sweden/1 site, $n = 19$	R
Bates & Brown	1998	Surveyed staff knowledge & attitudes towards victims of domestic violence	Survey/ Australia/ 4 sites, $n = 111$	B
Chang et al.	1999	Compared pt satisfaction with NP & MD in a major rural ED	RCT, qualitative & quantitative data, telephone interview/ U.S./1 site	R
Considine, Ung, & Thomas	2001	Tested reliability of nurse decision-making with triage tool	Standardized patient scenarios/Australia/ $n = 31$	B
Danielson & Kuntz	2006	Disaster: all-hazard rural readiness and response nurses	Descriptive analysis, novel survey/ Montana/convenience sample	R
Davis & Bush	2003	Patient satisfaction with ED nursing care	Consumer Emergency Care Satisfaction Scale (CECSS) survey/U.S., Slovenia, Australia/6 sites, $n > 600$	B
Davis & Duffy	1999	Patient satisfaction w/ nursing care in rural & urban EDs	CECSS survey, descriptive comparison/ Australia/2 sites, $n = 103$	B
Dello Stritto	2005	Exploration of the experiences of ED triage nurses	Phenomenological study/Texas/$n = 10$	B
Elder et al. .	2004	Patient satisfaction with triage nursing in a rural ED	CECSS survey of nurses & patients/ U.S./1 site, $n = 76$	R

(*Continued*)

TABLE 4.1   Summary of Rural Emergency Nursing Research (*Continued*)

Authors	Year	Topic	Study Design/ Location/Sample	Rural (R) and Urban (B)
Ferrier et al.	2006	Skill development in the rural ED	Survey/Australia/ 1 site	R
Fry	2001	Development of triage tool in rural ED	Delphi technique/ Australia/1 region	B
Göransson et al.	2005	Nursing triage in EDs	Survey/Sweden/ multisite, national	B
Graham & Dellinger	2001	Descriptive study to identify ED patients who could be managed by an FNP	Retrospective chart review/Ohio/1 site	R
Griswold*	2006	Nursing challenges during health emergencies in rural areas	Multiple data sources, descriptive/ Australia	R
Hawkins	2000	Triage in rural hospitals	Australia	R
Hawley	2000	ED patient perceptions of nursing care	Qualitative/Canada/ 1 site, $n = 14$	R
Hayes	1998	Comparison of two ED patient medication teaching interventions	Random group assign- ment, use of existing assessment tool/ Kansas/3 sites, $n = 60$	R
Hayes	2000	Nurse practitioner education of adult patients and caregivers in a rural ED	Standardized assessment tool/ U.S./3 sites, $n = 195$	R
Henderson	2006	Telemedicine and use of nurse practitioners in rural EDs	Patient & adminstrator questionnaires/ Mississippi/10 sites	R
Hogenbirk & Pong	2004	Audit of rural nursing teletriage	Canada – 1 site	R

(*Continued*)

TABLE 4.1   Summary of Rural Emergency Nursing Research (*Continued*)

Authors	Year	Topic	Study Design/ Location/Sample	Rural (R) and Urban (B)
Kinsman et al.	2007	Evaluation of dissemination strategy for use of evidence-based thrombolytic therapy guideline in EDs	Retrospective chart audit before-after design/Australia/1 site, $n = 170$	R
Luck et al.*	2006	Exploration of violence in rural ED	Ethnographic case study/Australia/ 1 site	R
Lyneham & Nancarrow	1997	Examination of the nature and content of telephone calls received in EDs — rural/urban comparison	Call Audit/ Australia/2 sites	B
Middleton	2006	Examined APRN suturing skills, compared EDs in different geographical settings	Prospective questionnaire, convenience sample/Australia/ 3 sites, $n = 31$	B
Mills & McSweeney	2005	Characteristics of patients seen by ED nurse practitioners	Secondary analysis of 4 years of National Hospital Ambulatory Medical Care Survey/U.S./ nationally representative sample	B
Nielson	2004	Nurse communication intervention to improve patient satisfaction	Intervention, before-after design/ Michigan/1 site	R
Pardey	2006	ED triage: application of the Australasian Triage Scale	Intervention/ Australia/ 1 site	R
Smith et al.	2001	Examination of the outcomes of emergency nurse phone consults for nonurgent 911 calls	2 phases, retrospective record review/ U.S./1 region, $n = 171$	B

(*Continued*)

TABLE 4.1   Summary of Rural Emergency Nursing Research (*Continued*)

Authors	Year	Topic	Study Design/ Location/Sample	Rural (R) and Urban (B)
Timmings	2006	Rural ED nurse skills	Survey/Australia	R
Van Kon- kelenberg & O'Connor*	1997	Workforce planning study for emergency department and men- tal health nurses	Delphi survey/ Australia	R
Way et al.	2006	Nursing care of chest pain in a rural ED	Retrospective chart review, intervention with comparison groups/Australia/1 site, $n = 115$	R

* Indicates a published conference abstract; study details not available.

TABLE 4.2   Other Research That Addresses Rural Emergency Nursing

Authors	Year	Topic	Study Design/ Location/Sample	Rural (R) and Urban (B)
Ali et al.	2006	Rural emergency obstetric care avail- ability, accessibility, and utilization	Survey/Pakistan/ 8 sites	R
Australian Nurses & Midwives Association	2007	Rural nurses' responses to mental health emergencies	Descriptive survey and intervention/ Australia/$n = 3,683$	R
Brown	2005	Examination of emergency department psychiatric services (surveyed nurse managers)	Descriptive survey and secondary data/ United States/two states, $n = 102$	B
Casey et al.	2007	Rural ED staffing	Survey/United States/ nationally representa- tive sample	R

(*Continued*)

TABLE 4.2   Other Research That Addresses Rural Emergency Nursing (*Continued*)

Authors	Year	Topic	Study Design/ Location/Sample	Rural (R) and Urban (B)
Chandy et al.	2007	Tested effectiveness of intervention training rural providers of complicated deliveries	Self-assessment rating/Cambodia/ $n = 196$	R
Galli et al.	2008	Implementation of telemedicine program in rural EDs using NPs	Intervention, survey and outcomes data/ United States— Louisiana/10 sites	R
Kildea et al.	2006	Management of maternity emergencies for rural health staff with no midwifery qualifications	Descriptive survey/ Australia/1 site	R
Manley et al.	2006	Disaster preparedness in rural hospitals	Descriptive survey/United States/ nationally representative sample	R
Marcin et al.	2007	Medication errors among children treated in rural EDs	Chart audits/ United States/ multiple sites	R
Otchere & Kayo	2007	Challenges of improving rural emergency obstetric care	Descriptive survey/ Africa/2 sites	R
Sullivan et al.	2006	Profile of U.S. EDs in 2001	Secondary dataset/ United States/ nationally representative sample	B
Sweetman & Brazil	2007	Videoconference education links between the rural and tertiary EDs	Intervention and outcomes data/Australia/ multiple sites	R
Vinson	2007	Managing bioterrorism mass casualties in a rural ED	Intervention and evaluation/United States/1 site	R
Wamwana et al.	2006	Characteristics of patients with gynecological emergencies in rural area	Chart audits/Africa/ 1 site	R

Nursing Research on Emergency Services

In most cases, nurses offer the first and most frequent contact to patients who present to the hospital-based emergency care setting; yet, the contributions of nursing research related to emergency services is limited. The literature will be presented by first discussing selected examples of nursing research related to emergency care and then describing nursing research related specifically to emergency services in rural settings.

The emergency nursing literature focuses on several key topics: workforce issues, triage and standards of care for specific illnesses, patient satisfaction, the role of the advanced practice nurse, and hospital emergency and disaster preparedness. Studies of the ED nursing workforce address staffing, resources, and workplace conditions. Almeida (2004) identified the influence of organizational and contextual factors on the ED environment and proposed the appropriate skill set of an ED nurse manager. Tanabe and colleagues (2004) used a triage system to predict ED resource consumption. Erickson and Williams-Evans (2000) surveyed ED nurses' incidence of and attitudes toward assault and found that 82% had been assaulted; the majority believed it "went with the job" and very few felt that reporting was beneficial. In a survey of ED nurses ("Tension in the waiting room," 2007), researchers addressed workplace violence and safety. Alarmingly, 87% of respondents (n = 1,000) reported violence in the past three years and more than 40% said their ED is only somewhat safe or not safe at all. The most comprehensive study of the U.S. ED nursing workforce was undertaken by the ENA in 2001. The researchers conducted a survey of 1,380 EDs to benchmark ED staffing indicators, patterns of service delivery and patient utilization, and vital service characteristics (Ray, Jagim, Agnew, McKay, & Sheehy, 2003). They created staffing guidelines based on study findings; however, it is estimated that less than 25% of EDs actually follow these guidelines, and their applicability to rural settings remains in question (Robinson, Jagim, & Ray, 2005). The ENA survey data allowed researchers to describe ED nursing workforce issues and to recommend strategies for improving patient care as well as for staff recruitment and retention (Robinson et al., 2005). These strategies still need to be tested. The CRISP database reveals two studies in progress that are exploring the relationship between ED staffing and patient outcomes (Bickell & New York University, 2005–2007) and ED patient flow processes (Burdick & Banner Health, 2005–2007).

Recognizing triage as predominantly a nursing responsibility, numerous international researchers have examined ED nurse triage processes to determine best practices (Arslanian-Engoren, 2005; Broadbent, Jarman, & Berk, 2002; Chan & Chau, 2005; Chung, 2005; Considine, LeVasseur, & Charles, 2002; Daniels, 2007; Dello Stritto, 2005; Fry, 2001; Fry & Burr, 2001; Gurney, 2003; Wollaston, Fahey, McKay, Hegney, Miller, et al., 2004). The results have been informative; for example, Crellin and Johnston (2003) found that a widely accepted triage tool used in Australian EDs was not valid or reliable when tested on a pediatric population, and Travers and colleagues (2002) confirmed that a five-level triage system was more effective than a three-level system in a tertiary ED.

Researchers have examined the accuracy of ED nurses' knowledge, assessment, and decision-making skills with various patient illnesses and age groups. Tippins (2005) used standardized patients to evaluate ED nurses' assessment and intervention activities and revealed a need for skill enhancement in the management of patient deterioration. Furthermore, to assess the adequacy of the triage and treatment process, nurses have conducted surveys to identify characteristics of patients who refused to wait to be seen in the ED (Lee, Endacott, Flett, & Bushnell, 2006). Findings suggest that the majority of patients who leave without treatment present during the night, wait for more than two hours, and do not consider their problem emergent. Nairn and colleagues (2004) performed a review of the literature and identified five significant themes affecting surveyed patients' perceptions of their ED experience: waiting times, communication, cultural aspects of care, pain, and the environment. Other studies have explored ED nurses' management of acute conditions including myocardial infarction and stroke in the elderly, domestic violence and other psychosocial issues in families, complicated labor in women, and asthma in children (Andersson, Omberg, & Svedlund, 2006; Bates & Brown, 1998; Campbell, Dennie, Dougherty, Iwaskiw, & Rollo, 2004; "EDs aren't following," 2005; Fry, 2001; Gerdtz & Bucknall, 2001; Hughes, Fritsch, & Calder, 2007; Middleton, 2006). In addition, the CRISP database reveals projects under way related to pain in ED patients (Puntillo & University of California, San Francisco, 1998–2001), the effectiveness of a tele-EKG intervention in prehospital care for cardiac patients (Drew & University of California, San Francisco, 2003–2008), ED use by African American patients who have diabetes (Jenkins & Medical University of South Carolina, 2006–2008), and ethical issues for ED nurses in treating the critically ill (Zeitzer & University of Pennsylvania, 2007–2009).

Patient satisfaction has been another focus of emergency nursing research. The literature supports the quality of nursing interactions as a significant indicator of patient satisfaction. This has been confirmed further by empirical studies ("Tiered structure helps," 2006). Researchers have explored the influence of specific nursing roles on ED patient satisfaction including the use of ED-based mental health liaison nurses (Eales, Callaghan, & Johnson, 2006) and nurse discharge coordinators (Guttman et al., 2004). Researchers have also examined patient satisfaction with advanced-practice nurses in the ED setting and found it to be comparable with physicians (Carter & Chochinov, 2007; Fry, Borg, Jackson, & McAlpine, 1999). Considine and colleagues (2001) determined a postgraduate education is not necessary for triage effectiveness.

Another key area within emergency nursing literature is research related to disaster and crisis preparedness. This fairly new focus of inquiry is diverse.

Studies have evaluated nurses' ability to handle the expected surges in ED volume during disasters (Danielson & Kuntz, 2006), have assessed the availability of resources for managing emergencies in the school setting (Olympia, Wan, & Avner, 2005), and have considered appropriate crisis interventions for the pediatric population (Rassin et al., 2007).

Nursing Research on Emergency Services in Rural Settings

For the most part, emergency nursing research has been conducted in large nonrural hospitals; however, the body of rural emergency nursing research covers the same general topics as the nonrural emergency nursing research: workforce issues, triage, standards of care for specific illnesses, patient satisfaction, the role of the advanced practice nurse, and disaster preparedness and response. Following, organized by topic, is a discussion of the emergency nursing research that has been conducted in rural settings.

Workforce Issues. Most of the research related to rural emergency nursing workforce issues has been conducted in Australia. Ferrier and colleagues (2006) examined skill development among ED nurses in rural areas of Australia but the selection of a rural ED was by convenience rather than an intentional effort to address a gap in research. Other Australian researchers have examined ED nurses' skills (Timmings, 2006) and used the Delphi technique to identify staffing and training needs (Van Konklenberg & O'Connor, 1997) in the rural setting. Two workforce studies conducted in the United States included an analysis of nursing staff. Sullivan and colleagues (2006) used secondary data to profile the U.S. ED workforce and identified disparities in nursing supply-and-demand present across the nation, particularly in rural areas. In a study funded by the Upper Midwest Rural Research Center, Casey, Wholey, and Moscovice (2007) examined rural ED staffing across the United States and found that rural EDs commonly staff nurse practitioners. In addition, they identified a need for continuing education related to pediatric and trauma patients and effective teamwork.

Triage. Numerous studies have explored the triage process employed by ED nurses in rural settings and demonstrate that significant variability exists (Elder, Neal, Davis, Almes, Whittledge, & Littlepage, 2004; Fry, 2001; Hogenbirk & Pong, 2004; Pardey, 2006). Research suggests that triage decision-making is influenced by the nurse's level of training and use of different tools. Crellin and Johnston (2003) found the Australasian Triage Scale (ATS) was not reliable with pediatric patients whereas Considine, Ung, and Thomas (2001) tested the ATS with adult scenarios and attributed rater inconsistency to their study method rather than the tool. Moreover, the findings related to rural triage processes are not conclusive because the majority of studies were conducted in other countries (Sweden and Australia) and the choice of rural setting appears to be one of convenience rather than intention (Andersson et al., 2006; Hawkins, 2000). Several studies include both rural and urban settings (Dello Stritto, 2005; Göransson, Ehrenberg, & Ehnfors, 2005; Smith et al., 2001) but these are largely descriptive, utilize a qualitative design, and do not offer any conclusive comparisons between rural and urban practices.

Standards of Care for Specific Illnesses. Oftentimes researchers include rural and nursing components in their investigations of specific illnesses that are treated in the ED. Brown (2005) assessed variation in the psychiatric services available to ED patients and found that rural hospitals were less likely to have ED psychiatric specialists. Way and colleagues (2006) explored the effectiveness of an implementation strategy for a nurse-initiated chest-pain management guideline in a rural ED and reported that the intervention provided a means for safe and effective care in the absence of a doctor. Kinsman, Tori, Endacott, and Sharp (2007) tested the effectiveness of a standardized strategy for disseminating a thrombolytic therapy evidence-based care guideline across rural and urban EDs and attributed the failure of the intervention to site-specific influences, suggesting the need for strategies that are tailored to the particular setting. Surveys of ED nurse and physician attitudes toward and knowledge about domestic violence illuminated the need for additional staff training across rural and urban settings (Bates & Brown, 1998; Luck, Jackson, & Usher, 2006). No articles could be found that address nursing management of common clinical issues including pain and traumatic injury, or specific patient populations (e.g., age or racial group) within the rural ED setting.

Patient Satisfaction. Several nursing studies explore ED patient satisfaction with the inclusion of a rural setting, sometimes by intention and other times by convenience. The emergency nursing literature that compares patient satisfaction in rural and urban settings offers contradictory results. Elder and colleagues (2004) intentionally selected a rural ED to replicate an urban study of patient satisfaction with triage. The results were similar across the two settings—there was a significant amount of nurse-patient agreement in patient acuity ratings and that when patients perceived themselves as more seriously ill, they were less satisfied. Davis and Duffy (1999) compared a rural and an urban ED with respect to patient satisfaction and found that urban patients were more satisfied with nurse *caring* and *teaching* behaviors, but admitted that further research was necessary to substantiate these conclusions. A few years later, Davis and Bush (2003) completed a meta-analysis of six studies to explore patient satisfaction with emergency nursing care at rural and urban hospitals located in three countries (United States, Australia, and Slovenia) with the intent to capture cultural differences; however, culture was defined primarily by nationality rather than geographic descriptors. The results showed that patients reported no differences in satisfaction with caring, but the U.S. and Slovenian groups reported greater satisfaction with teaching than the Australian group. In a qualitative study of a Canadian rural ED service, Hawley (2000) explored patient perceptions of nurse comforting strategies and found nurses' technical competency the most highly regarded characteristic. In another study, Nielsen (2004) implemented a communication intervention that significantly improved patient satisfaction with triage nurses in rural ED. But again, in both the aforementioned studies, the selection of rural setting was by convenience and not addressed.

The Role of the Advanced Practice Nurse. Given the widespread use of nurse practitioners in rural EDs, the bulk of rural emergency nursing research has focused on the advanced practice role. In a study that took place in England, Chang and colleagues (1999) explored the potential utilization of nurse practitioners as primary providers in a rural ED. They evaluated the quality of care provided by nurse practitioners and found no significant differences when compared to physicians. However, the study results must be interpreted with caution because, in consideration of time constraints on sample selection, the researchers selected patients with medical conditions typical of rural settings in place of actually conducting the study in a rural ED. Graham and Dellinger (2001) conducted a retrospective chart review at one rural ED in Ohio to assess the extent to which ED patients could be appropriately managed by a family nurse practitioner (FNP) and found the majority of presentations to be well within the scope of FNP practice. Again, this conclusion was projected rather than based on actual care provided by FNPs. Other researchers have examined the quality of services provided by rural ED nurse practitioners as well (Hayes, 2000; Hogenbirk & Pong, 2004). In a study of 10 rural Mississippi EDs, Henderson (2006) evaluated the outcomes (patient and hospital administrator satisfaction as well as financial impact) of a telemedicine program in which onsite nurse practitioners, with access to guidance from a remote physician, treated patients. The patients, administrators, and financial data supported continuation of the program. At a national level, Mills and McSweeney (2005) utilized four years of National Hospital Ambulatory Medical Care Survey data to examine the practice patterns of ED nurse practitioners. Although comprehensive, the proportionally representative sample of rural and urban hospitals was more than 75% urban and did not compare hospital geographic characteristics, thereby limiting the extent to which the findings were applicable to rural settings.

Disaster Preparedness and Response. Recently, nurse researchers have begun to explore rural disaster preparedness and response, with the bulk of the literature coming from Australia. Based on the findings from a survey of rural nurses' emergency mental health skills training needs, the rural nurses and midwives from the Australian Nurses and Midwives Association (2007) created an educational program that has provided 22 workshops for 350 participants across rural areas in Australia. In a report of research in progress, Griswold (2006) compared a variety of data including case studies, organizational policies, and best-practice guidelines to identify challenges Australian rural ED nurses face when patients require transfer to a tertiary care facility. Several general studies of health disasters that were conducted in the United States have considered the role of nurses. Researchers conducted a nationwide survey to describe rural ED experience with specific incidents, as well as the frequency of occurrence of these events (Manley et al., 2006). Danielson and Kuntz (2006) surveyed a small group of disaster nurse volunteers in Montana to characterize their experiences. Vinson (2007) developed and pilot-tested an evidence-based plan for ED and hospital management of contaminated patients in a rural ED and evaluated the plan as effective.

Limitations of Emergency Nursing Research in Rural Settings

The literature related to rural emergency nursing encompasses notable weaknesses that limit its value. First, the majority of relevant research has taken place in Australia and other countries with the comparability to services in the United States largely unknown. The literature is replete with exploratory accounts of single services in isolation and no comparison group. Samples lack in heterogeneity or volume. Of the studies conducted in a combination of rural and urban settings, often site selection was by convenience and geographic differences were not analyzed. Finally, the body of existing research fails to address key components of emergency nursing service structure, delivery, and outcomes. Researchers have begun to address aspects of care for some health problems common in the rural ED setting including mental illness and psychosocial issues and cardiovascular illnesses; however, no research could be found related to other high-frequency presentations such as asthma, trauma, and chronic pain.

CONCLUSIONS

Future Agenda for Emergency Nursing Research in Rural Settings

In recent years, deficiencies in our nation's emergency health care services have become a matter of public concern. Federal and private entities have responded by making funds available to encourage research about the development and implementation of best practices in emergency care; however, the contributions of the nursing profession to this effort have been nominal. This review high-lights the need for more nursing research related to emergency services including increased consistency and rigor in capturing all aspects of ED nursing. While continuing to expand research related to aspects of emergency nursing that are shared by nurses in rural and urban settings, intentional exploration and recognition of geographical differences are critical. The "Future of Rural Health" report calls for rural-specific comparative data to guide quality improvement (IOM, 2004). As the subspecialty of disaster nursing gains momentum, there is a need for emergency services researchers to explore the unique resource and training needs for disaster nurses practicing in rural localities. To advance the nursing research related to rural emergency care, we must follow the IOM "Future of Emergency Care" (2006b) recommendations to design system-level and outcomes research. Nurse researchers should utilize the recommendations strategically to identify areas of research that are of specific interest to the state and federal entities that are responsible for providing the much-needed resources and support to improve this area of health care. For example, questions have been raised about the influence of nurse staffing or training on the quality of care provided in EDs; consequently, EDs in urban and academic medical settings have responded by implementing standards and examining outcomes. Nurse researchers could use similar approaches in rural EDs to identify appropriate staffing ratios and core competencies for the rural setting. This review has aided in the development of an agenda for future rural emergency nursing research that proposes the follow-ing activities.

1. Explore and compare the variety of emergency service arrangements in rural settings: freestanding EDs, critical access hospitals (CAHs), as well as hospitals that have no emergency department. Examine the relationship of service arrangement with factors that affect the nursing environment such as patient acuity on arrival, overcrowding and vol-ume fluctuations, and boarding.

2. Evaluate the value and appropriate use of technological innovations in rural settings including the use of electronic medical records and tele-triage. How widespread is the use of such technological innovations in rural settings and do these strategies improve nursing care?

3. Examine the effectiveness of the advanced practice nurse role as primary provider in the rural emergency setting. A common criticism related to physicians practicing in rural EDs is their lack of emer-gency specialization. If this is a valid concern, is there a need to create a specialty certification for advanced practice nurses in this setting? Further, the IOM report, "Future of Rural Health," implies that the dependence on nurse practitioners to provide rural emergency care is a

"compromise to quality" (2004, p. 227), providing a research question that needs to be empirically tested.

4. Compare triage processes and tools to identify best practice. Examine the typical levels of patient acuity in rural EDs to determine how emergency services are being utilized—emergent, urgent, or routine care?

5. Continue to evaluate patient satisfaction with nursing care. To really identify rural patient needs, studies must include larger heterogeneous samples.

6. Examine workforce issues including: staffing, use of resources and cost containment, continuing education opportunities, availability of physicians, nurse satisfaction, and workplace violence. Moreover, there is a need for research that explores methods to address ED nursing shortage in rural areas—the scope of prior research related to rural shortages has been focused primarily on physician supply.

7. Continue research on clinical issues relevant to the rural emergency patient population—identify patient demographical and diagnostic characteristics to prioritize the development of best practice standards. Given the evident lack of cultural diversity or pediatric expertise among rural ED staff, identify training needs related to pediatric populations and cultural competence.

8. Assess the extent to which rural ED nurses are prepared for disasters or crises—identify special training needs and resources relevant to the geographical setting.

In conclusion, as the predominant care providers in rural EDs, nurses must take the initiative to advance the knowledge and science of emergency health care. As noted in the "Future of Rural Health" (IOM, 2004), the types of issues that rural areas confront are distinctly different from those of urban areas; thus, solutions that work for one may be counterproductive to another. The emergency nursing literature has begun to address critical topics in rural settings; however, we must improve the extent to which the research identifies and analyzes geographical disparities in emergency staff, patients, and services so that valid conclusions can be drawn about rural emergency care. As Bernardo (2007) states, "the ultimate goal is the application of best evidence to guide clinical practice in the care of patients seeking emergency care" (p. 376).

REFERENCES

Ali, M., Ayaz, M., Rizwan, H., Hashim, S., & Kuroiwa, C. (2006). Emergency obstetric care availability, accessibility and utilization in eight districts in Pakistan's North West Frontier Province. *Journal of Ayub Medical College Abbottabad, 18*(4), 10–15.

Almeida, S. L. (2004). Nursing perspectives on the emergency department. *Emergency Medical Clinics of North America, 22*, 117–129, vii.

Alpi, K. M. (2006). Mapping the literature of emergency nursing. *Journal of Medical Library Associates, 94*(2 Suppl.), E107–E113.

Anderson, P., Petrino, R., Halpern, P., & Tintinalli, J. (2006). The globalization of emergency medicine and its importance for public health. *Bulletin of World Health Organizations, 84*, 835–839.

Andersson, A., Omberg, M., & Svedlund, M. (2006). Triage in the emergency department— A qualitative study of the factors which nurses consider when making decisions. *Nursing in Critical Care, 11*(3), 136–145.

Arnold, J. L., Dickenson, G., Tsai, M. C., & Han, D. (2001). A survey of emergency medicine in 36 countries. *Canadian Journal of Emergency Medicine, 3*, 109–118.

Arslanian-Engoren, C. (2005). Patient cues that predict nurses' triage decisions for acute coronary syndromes. *Applied Nursing Research, 18*, 82–89.

Australian Nurses and Midwives Association, The ARNM Mental Health Emergencies Project. (2007). *Australian Journal of Rural Health, 15*, 142.

Bates, L., & Brown, W. (1998). Domestic violence: Examining nurses' and doctors' management, attitudes and knowledge in an accident and emergency setting. *Australasian Journal of Advanced Nursing, 15*(3), 15–22.

Bayley, E. W., MacLean, S. L., Desy, P., & McMahon, M. (2004). ENA's Delphi study on national research priorities conducted for emergency nurses in the United States. *Journal of Emergency Nursing, 30*, 12–21, 96–102.

Bennett, K. J., Moore, C. G., & Probst, J. C. (2007). Estimating uncompensated care charges at rural hospital emergency departments. *Journal of Rural Health, 23*, 258–263.

Bernardo, L. M. (2007). Evidence-based emergency nursing practice: The journey begins. *Journal of Emergency Nursing, 33*, 375–376.

Bickell, N., & New York University. (2005–2007). *ED staffing and patient outcomes.* Funded by Agency for Healthcare Quality and Research #1R03HS013464–01.

Broadbent, M., Jarman, H., & Berk, M. (2002). Improving competence in emergency mental health triage. *Accident & Emergency Nursing, 10*, 155–162.

Brown, J. F. (2005). An examination of emergency department psychiatric consultation arrangements. *Health Care Management Review, 30*, 251–261.

Burdick, T. L., & Banner Health, Phoenix, AZ. (2005–2007). *Banner Health/ASU partnership for ED patient safety.* Funded by Agency for Healthcare Quality and Research #1U18HS015921–01.

Campbell, P., Dennie, M., Dougherty, K., Iwaskiw, O., & Rollo, K. (2004). Implementation of an ED protocol for pain management at triage at a busy level I trauma center. *Journal of Emergency Nursing, 30*, 431.

Carter, A. J., & Chochinov, A. H. (2007). A systematic review of the impact of nurse practitioners on cost, quality of care, satisfaction and wait times in the emergency department. *Canadian Journal of Emergency Medicine, 9*, 286–295.

Casey, M., Wholey, D., & Moscovice, I. (2007). *Rural emergency department staffing: Potential implications for the quality of emergency care provided in rural areas* (Final report #7). Minneapolis: Upper Midwest Rural Health Research Center.

Chan, J. N., & Chau, J. (2005). Patient satisfaction with triage nursing care in Hong Kong. *Journal of Advanced Nursing, 50*, 498–507.

Chandy, H., Steinholt, M., & Husum, H. (2007). Delivery life support: A preliminary report on the chain of survival for complicated deliveries in rural Cambodia. *Nursing Health Sciences, 9*, 263–269.

Chang, E., Daly, J., Hawkins, A., McGirr, J., Fielding, K., Hemmings, L., et al. (1999). An evaluation of the nurse practitioner role in a major rural emergency department. *Journal of Advanced Nursing, 30*, 260–268.

Chung, J. Y. (2005). An exploration of accident and emergency nurse experiences of triage decision making in Hong Kong. *Accident & Emergency Nursing, 13*, 206–213.

Considine, J., LeVasseur, S. A., & Charles, A. (2002). Development of physiological discriminators for the Australasian Triage Scale. *Accident & Emergency Nursing, 10*, 221–234.

Considine, J., Ung, L., & Thomas, S. (2001). Clinical decisions using the National Triage Scale: How important is postgraduate education? *Accident & Emergency Nursing, 9*, 101–108.

Crellin, D. J., & Johnston, L. (2003). Poor agreement in application of the Australasian Triage Scale to pediatric emergency department presentations. *Contemporary Nurse: A Journal for the Australian Nursing Profession, 15*, 48–60.

Daniels, J. H. (2007). Outcomes of emergency severity index five-level triage implementation: Clinical and operational metrics. *Advanced Emergency Nursing Journal, 29*, 58–67.

Danielson, L., & Kuntz, S. W. (2006). Disaster: All-hazard rural readiness and response: Descriptive analysis of Montana disaster nurse volunteers. *Communicating Nursing Research, 39*, 120.

Davis, B. A., & Bush, H. A. (2003). Patient satisfaction of emergency care in the United States, Slovenia, and Australia. *Journal of Nursing Care Quality, 18*, 267–274.

Davis, B. A., & Duffy, E. (1999). Patient satisfaction with nursing care in a rural and urban emergency department. *Australian Journal of Rural Health, 7*, 97–103.

Dello Stritto, R. A. (2005). *The experiences of the emergency triage nurse: A phenomenological study.* Unpublished PhD thesis, Texas Woman's University, Denton, TX.

Drew, B. J., & University of California, San Francisco. (2003–2008). *Tele-electrocardiography in emergency cardiac care.* Funded by National Institute for Nursing Research # 5R01NR007881–05.

Eales, S., Callaghan, P., & Johnson, B. (2006). Service users and other stakeholders' evaluation of a liaison mental health service in an accident and emergency department and a general hospital setting. *Journal of Psychiatric & Mental Health Nursing, 13*, 70–77.

EDs aren't following heart attack guidelines: Revamp protocols now: Even smallest ED can meet recommendations for time frames. (2005). *ED Nursing, 8*(11), 121–123.

Elder, R., Neal, C., Davis, B. A., Almes, E., Whitledge, L., & Littlepage, N. (2004). Patient satisfaction with triage nursing in a rural hospital emergency department. *Journal of Nursing Care Quality, 19*, 263–268.

Emergency medical treatment and labor act. (1986). Title 42. Chapter 7. Subchapter XVIII. Part E. § 1395dd. Legal Information Institute. Retrieved April 1, 2008, from http://www4.law.cornell.edu/uscode/42/1395dd.html

Erickson, L., & Williams-Evans, S. A. (2000). Attitudes of emergency nurses regarding patient assaults. *Journal of Emergency Nursing, 26*, 210–215.

Ferrier, M., Coombs, S., & Chapman, R. (2006). Heading bush: Skill development in the rural setting. CENA 2006 National Conference abstracts. *Australasian Emergency Nursing Journal*, 9, 129.

Fry, M. (2001). Using a survey tool to explore the processes underpinning the triage role: A pilot study. *Australian Emergency Nursing Journal*, 4, 27–31.

Fry, M., Borg, A., Jackson, S., & McAlpine, A. (1999). The advanced clinical nurse a new model of practice: Meeting the challenge of peak activity periods. *Australasian Journal of Emergency Nursing*, 2(3), 26–28.

Fry, M., & Burr, G. (2001). Current triage practice and influences affecting clinical decision-making in emergency departments in NSW, Australia. *Accident & Emergency Nursing*, 9(4), 227–234.

Galli, R., Keith, J. C., McKenzie, K., Hall, G. S., & Henderson, K. (2008). TelEmergency: A novel system for delivering emergency care to rural hospitals. *Annals of Emergency Medicine*, 51, 275–284.

Gerdtz, M. F., & Bucknall, T. K. (2001). Triage nurses' clinical decision making: An observational study of urgency assessment. *Journal of Advanced Nursing*, 35(4), 550–561.

Göransson, K. E., Ehrenberg, A., & Ehnfors, M. (2005). Triage in emergency departments: National survey. *Journal of Clinical Nursing*, 14, 1067–1074.

Graham, M. C., & Dellinger, R. W. (2001). Emergency department patients within the scope of nurse practitioner practice. *American Journal for Nurse Practitioners*, 5, 29.

Griswold, P. A. (2006). From presentation to evacuation: Nursing challenges during health emergencies in isolated and remote Australian aboriginal communities—A research in progress paper. CENA 2006 National Conference abstracts. *Australasian Emergency Nursing Journal*, 9, 128.

Gurney, D. (2003). Comparing triage decisions for the same patients with a five-level and a three-level triage scale: A quick exercise for nurses orienting to triage. *Journal of Emergency Nursing*, 29(2), 29.

Guttman, A., Afilalo, M., Guttman, R., Colacone, A., Robitaille, C., Lang, E., et al. (2004). An emergency department-based nurse discharge coordinator for elder patients: Does it make a difference? *Academic Emergency Medicine*, 11, 1318–1327.

Hartley, D., Ziller, E., Loux, S., Gale, J., Lambert, D., & Yousefian, A. (2005). *Mental health encounters in critical access hospital emergency rooms: A national survey* (Working Paper #32). Portland, ME: University of Southern Maine, Edmund S. Muskie School of Public Service, Institute for Health Policy, Maine Rural Health Research Center. Retrieved October 15, 2007, from http://muskie.usm.maine.edu/Publications/rural/wp32.pdf

Hawkins, A. (2000). Triage in rural hospitals. *Australasian Emergency Nursing Journal*, 3, 19–20.

Hawley, M. P. (2000). Nurse comforting strategies: Perceptions of emergency department patients. *Clinical Nursing Research*, 9, 441–459.

Hayes, K. S. (1998). Randomized trial of geragogy-based medication instruction in the emergency department. *Nursing Research*, 47, 211–218.

Hayes, K. S. (2000). Literacy for health information of adult patients and caregivers in a rural emergency department. *Clinical Excellence in Nurse Practice*, 4, 35–40.

Henderson, K. (2006). TelEmergency: Distance emergency care in rural emergency departments using nurse practitioners. *Journal of Emergency Nursing*, 32, 388–393.

Hogenbirk, J. C., & Pong, R. W. (2004). An audit of the appropriateness of teletriage nursing advice. *Telemedicine Journal and E-Health*, 10, 53–60.

Hughes F. G., Fritsch, K., & Calder, S. (2007). Psychosocial response in emergency situations—The nurse's role. *International Nursing Review, 54*, 19–27.

Institute of Medicine (IOM), Committee on the Future of Emergency Care in the U.S. (2006a). *Hospital-based emergency care: At the breaking point*. Washington, DC: National Academies Press.

Institute of Medicine (IOM), Committee on the Future of Emergency Care in the U.S. (2006b). *The future of emergency care*. Washington, DC: National Academies Press.

Institute of Medicine (IOM), Committee on the Future of Rural Health Care. (2004). *Quality through collaboration: The future of rural health*. Washington, DC: National Academies Press.

Jenkins, C. M., & Medical University of South Carolina. (2006–2008). *ED use—African Americans with diabetes*. Funded by the National Institute for Nursing Research #1R15NR009486–01A1.

Kildea, S., Kruske, S., & Bowell, L. (2006). Maternity emergency care: Short course in maternity emergencies for remote area health staff with no midwifery qualifications. *Australasian Journal of Rural Health, 14*, 111–115.

Kinsman, L., Tori, K., Endacott, R., & Sharp, M. (2007). Guideline implementation fails to improve thrombolytic administration. *Accident & Emergency Nursing, 15*, 27–33.

Lee, G., Endacott, R., Flett, K., & Bushnell, R. (2006). Characteristics of patients who did not wait for treatment in the emergency department: A follow up survey. *Accident & Emergency Nursing, 14*, 56–62.

Luck, L., Jackson, D., & Usher, K. (2006). The exploration of violence in a remote and rural ED. CENA 2006 National Conference abstracts. *Australasian Emergency Nursing Journal, 9*, 136–137.

Lutfiyya, M. W., Bhat, D. K., Gandhi, S. R., Nguyen, C., Weidenbacher-Hoper, V. L., & Lipsky, M. S. (2007). A comparison of quality of care indicators in urban acute care hospitals and rural critical access hospitals in the United States. *International Journal for Quality in Health Care, 19*, 141–149.

Lyneham, J., & Nancarrow, M. (1997). The nature and content of telephone calls received in rural and metropolitan emergency departments. *Australian Emergency Nursing Journal, 1*(2), 64–68.

Manley, W. G., Furbee, P. M., Coben, J. H., Smyth, S. K., Summers, D. E., Althouse, R. C., et al. (2006). Realities of disaster preparedness in rural hospitals. *Disaster Management Response, 4*(3), 80–87.

Marcin, J. P., Dharmar, M., Cho, M., Seifert, L. L., Cook, J. L., Cole, S. L., et al. (2007). Medication errors among acutely ill and injured children treated in rural emergency departments. *Annals of Emergency Medicine, 50*, 361–367.

McCaig, L. F., & Burt, C. W. (2005). *National hospital ambulatory medical care survey: 2003 emergency department summary*. Hyattsville, MD: National Center for Health Statistics.

Middleton, R. (2006). Suturing as an advanced skill for registered nurses in the emergency department. *Australasian Journal of Rural Health, 14*, 258–262.

Mills, A. C., & McSweeney, M. (2005). Primary reasons for ED visits and procedures performed for patients who saw nurse practitioners. *Journal of Emergency Nursing, 31*, 145–149.

Nairn, S., Whotton, E., Marshal, C., Roberts, M., & Swann, G. (2004). The patient experience in emergency departments: A review of the literature. *Accident & Emergency Nursing, 12*, 159–165.

NeSmith, E. G. (2006). Defining "disasters" with implications for nursing scholarship and practice. *Disaster Management & Response, 4,* 59–63.

Nielson, D. (2004). Improving ED patient satisfaction when triage nurses routinely communicate with patients as to reasons for waits: One rural hospital's experience. *Journal of Emergency Nursing, 30,* 336–338.

Olympia, R. P., Wan, E., & Avner, J. R. (2005). The preparedness of schools to respond to emergencies in children: A national survey of school nurses. *Pediatrics, 116,* e738–e745.

Otchere, S. A., & Kayo, A. (2007). The challenges of improving emergency obstetric care in two rural districts in Mali. *International Journal of Gynaecology & Obstetrics, 99,* 173–182.

Pardey, T. G. (2006). The clinical practice of emergency department triage: Application of the Australasian Triage Scale—An extended literature review part 1: Evolution of the ATS. *Australasian Emergency Nursing Journal, 9,* 155–162.

Puntillo, K. A., & University of California, San Francisco. (1998–2001). *Analgesic therapy outcomes in the emergency department.* Funded by the National Institute for Nursing Research #1R55NR004451–01A2.

Rassin, M. A., Nasi-Bashari, A., Idelman, S., Peretz, Y., Morag, S., Silner, D., et al. (2007). Emergency department staff preparedness for mass casualty events involving children. *Disaster Management Response, 5,* 36–44.

Ray, C., Jagim, M., Agnew, J., McKay, J., & Sheehy, S. (2003). ENA's new guidelines for determining emergency department nurse staffing. *Journal of Emergency Nursing, 29,* 245–253.

Robinson, K. S., Jagim, M. M., & Ray, C. E. (2005). Nursing workforce issues and trends affecting emergency departments. *Nurse Manager, 36*(9), 46–53.

Schur, C. L. (2004, April). *Understanding the role of the rural hospital emergency department in responding to bioterrorist attacks and other emergencies: A review of the literature and guide to the issues.* Bethesda, MD: NORC Walsh Center for Public Analysis.

Smith, W. R., Culley, L., Plorde, M., Murray, J. A., Hearne, T., Goldberg, P., et al. (2001). Emergency medical services telephone referral program: An alternative approach to nonurgent 911 calls. *Prehospital Emergency Care, 5,* 174–180.

Sullivan, A. F., Richman, I. B., Ahn, C. J., Auerbach, B. S., Pallin, D. J., Schafermeyer, R. W., et al. (2006). A profile of U.S. emergency departments in 2001. *Annals of Emergency Medicine, 48,* 694–701.

Sweetman, G., & Brazil, V. (2007). Education links between the Australian rural and tertiary emergency departments: Videoconference can support a virtual learning community. *Emergency Medicine Australasian, 19,* 176–177.

Tanabe, P., Gimbel, R., Yarnold, P. R., Kyriacou, D. N., & Adams, J. G. (2004). The Emergency Severity Index (version 3) 5-level triage system scores predict ED resource consumption. *Journal of Emergency Nursing, 30,* 22–29.

Tension in the waiting room—86% of ED nurses report recent violence: Crowded waiting rooms "bring out the worst" in patients. (2007). *ED Nursing, 10*(5), 49–52.

Tiered structure helps ED improve flow, satisfaction: Department cuts LOS 40 minutes. (2006). *ED Management, 18,* 6–8.

Timmings, R. W. (2006). Rural and isolated practice registered nurse (RIPRN)—Emergency nurses of the Queensland "bush." *Australasian Emergency Nursing Journal, 9,* 29–34.

Tippins, E. (2005). How emergency department nurses identify and respond to critical illness. *Emergency Nurse, 13*(3), 24–33.

Travers, D. A., Waller, A. E., Bowling, J. M., Flowers, D., & Tintinalli, J. (2002). Five-level triage system more effective than three-level in tertiary emergency department. *Journal of Emergency Nursing, 28,* 395–400.

Van Konkelenberg, R., & O'Connor, K. (1997). The political scene: Workforce planning study for emergency department and mental health nurses. *Australian Emergency Nursing Journal, 1*(2), 6–13.

Vinson, E. (2007). Managing bioterrorism mass casualties in an emergency department: Lessons learned from a rural community hospital disaster drill. *Disaster Management Response, 5,* 18–21.

Wamwana, E. B., Ndavi, P. M., Gichangi, P. B., Karanja, J. G., Muia, E. G., & Jaldesa, G. W. (2006). Socio-demographic characteristics of patients admitted with gynecological emergency conditions at the provincial general hospital, Kakamega, Kenya. *East African Medical Journal, 83,* 659–665.

Way, P., Aylward, R., Thompson, C., & Corke, G. (2006). Nurse initiated care of chest pain, the rural experience. *Australasian Emergency Nursing Journal, 9,* 19–22.

Wollaston, A., Fahey, P., McKay, M., Hegney, D., Miller, P., & Wollaston, J. (2004). Reliability and validity of the Toowoomba adult trauma triage tool: A Queensland, Australia study. *Accident & Emergency Nursing, 12,* 230–237.

Wright, A., McGrail, M., & Disler, P. (2007). Rural organization of Australian stroke teams: Emergency department project. *Internal Medicine Journal,* doi:10.1111/j.1445-5994.2007.01475.x.

Zeitzer, M., & University of Pennsylvania. (2007–2009). *Ethical issues for emergency nurses during resuscitation of injured patients.* Funded by National Institute for Nursing Research #1F3NR010432–01.

Chapter 5

Building the Rural Mental Health System: From De Facto System to Quality Care

Emily J. Hauenstein

ABSTRACT

About 20% of Americans live in rural America, yet the rural mental health infrastructure has yet to be firmly established. This is due in part to a pervasive belief about the tranquility of rural places and the relatively stress-free environment that they produce. In this chapter an adaptation of the Rural De Facto Mental Health Systems Model produced by Fox and her associates at the Southeastern Rural Mental Health Research Center is presented and used to organize the scientific state of the field of rural mental health services research. As many nurses have stood at the forefront of that research, the research of several prominent rural mental health nurse researchers and the innovative research they have produced are reviewed. The chapter concludes with a discussion of research that is needed to move the science of rural mental health services research forward, as well as a discussion of policy initiatives that may be necessary to foster the development and implementation of that research agenda.

Keywords: rural; mental health; health services research; nursing

INTRODUCTION

Prevailing beliefs about idyllic rural life and violence and other urban stressors have contributed to significant urban-rural mental health treatment disparities and poor mental health outcomes for rural dwellers. The field of rural mental health is significant for the challenges it poses—from few facilities, providers, and researchers to inequity in the financing of the treatment of mental health conditions. As a consequence, there is much to be done in both basic and translational research to improve the mental health and well-being of the 20% of Americans who are rural residents. Still, rural people and health care systems have shown remarkable resilience in the face of these significant challenges. This strength of purpose among rural residents and rural communities, coupled with the leadership of nurses, can lead to better integrated rural health systems delivering quality and culturally sensitive mental health care.

In this chapter a model of the rural mental health service delivery system is proposed, the supporting research for the model is reviewed and critiqued with an emphasis on the important contributions and leadership of nurse scientists in developing the field, and a research agenda that will build on the strengths of rural communities and health care systems to foster the delivery of quality mental health care is outlined. Particular attention is paid to integrating the scarce resources of rural places and the leadership nurses can provide in designing, testing, and evaluating innovative service delivery to this underserved population. Because of differences in the financing of health care internationally, studies referenced relative to health services use in this review are only based on rural health care systems in the United States. International contributions with regard to rural mental health theory are included in the overall review.

The De Facto Rural Mental Health System

Mental health services in rural areas are fragmented and underresourced. In response to the dearth of mental health professionals and facilities, a loosely woven network of formal and informal providers has emerged in rural settings (Merwin, Hinton, Dembling, & Stern, 2003; Merwin, Snyder, & Katz, 2006). Dubbed the de facto mental health system of care, it provides mental health care of varying quality across such diverse settings as community mental health services boards, primary care, social services, and rural churches (Fox, Merwin, & Blank, 1995; Norquist & Regier, 1996). Fox and her collaborators at the Southeastern Rural Mental Health Research Center (SRMHRC) at the University of Virginia School of Nursing first depicted the de facto mental health system in rural places in a model of the processes and outcomes of care in rural communities. This model was recently reconfigured based on research conducted by SRMHRC investigators, rural policy and quality initiatives (Institute of Medicine, 2001, 2005, 2006), and empiricism from other utilization models (Figure 5.1). The main concepts in the revised rural mental health systems (RMHS) are access to care; integration of consumer, community, and community organizations; implementation of evidence-based treatments and quality process; and population and consumer outcomes. The RMHS is used to organize a review of extant research in the field and underpins a proposed agenda for research that will support an integrated rural mental health service delivery system and build policy that informs that system.

Access Need

Mental Health Problems in Rural Areas

The National Institute of Mental Health Epidemiologic Catchment Area studies were the first attempt to quantify the extent of poor mental health in rural areas and found lower rates of mental illness among rural Americans than among their urban counterparts (Fichter, Narrow, Roper, Rehm, Elton, & Rae, 1996). Epidemiologic Catchment Area data was obtained in five sites; data for this report was for a mix of urban and rural residents. The first National Comorbidity Study (NCS) provided urban-rural comparisons and showed no differences in morbidity from mental illness (Kessler et al., 1994). The comparison was based on the Office of Management and Budget's metropolitan statistical area classification, which dichotomizes counties as urban or rural (Anonymous, 2007). The NCS was replicated in 2005 (NCS-R) using better diagnostic techniques and more sensitive measures of rurality. The data showed that externalizing disorders characterized by alcohol and drug use and intermittent explosive disorder were more common among rural residents than urban residents (Kessler, Chiu, Demler, Merikangas, & Walters, 2005). A recent reanalysis of the original NCS data comparing urban and remote rural residents showed that rural residents who were found to have either alcohol or drug use problems were also more likely to have comorbid major depression, lifetime antisocial disorder, or generalized anxiety disorder (Simmons & Havens, 2007).

There is some evidence that rural residents are more at risk for poor mental health than the national epidemiologic surveys suggest. High prevalence rates of depression have been detected in primary care settings serving rural and impoverished populations (Boyd, 2000; Hauenstein & Peddada, 2007; McCrone, Cotton, Jones, Hawkins, Costante, et al., 2007; Sears, Danda, & Evans, 1999). Rates of major depression ranging from 28% to 44% were shown in these studies. Another study showed a lifetime prevalence of 60% for any psychiatric

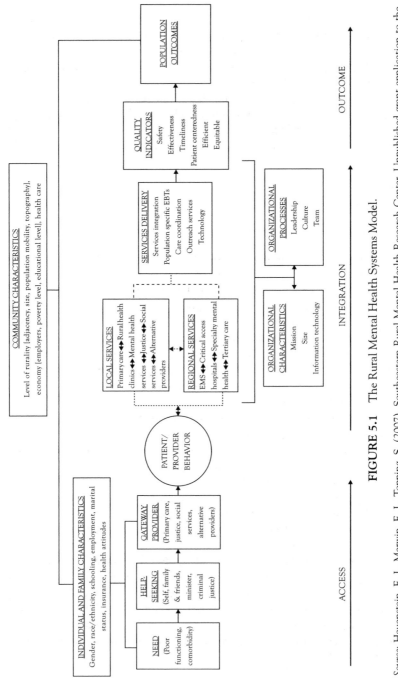

FIGURE 5.1 The Rural Mental Health Systems Model.

Source: Hauenstein, E. J., Merwin, E. I., Topping, S. (2007), Southeastern Rural Mental Health Research Center. Unpublished grant application to the National Institutes of Health, June 2007.

disorder among a sample of young adults in rural Iowa (Rueter, Holm, Burzette, Kim, & Conger, 2007). Psychiatric disorder was present among 19.4% of African American and 20.8% of White young people ages 9–17 participating in the Great Smokey Mountains mental health study conducted in rural North Carolina (Angold, Erkanli, Farmer, Fairbank, Burns, et al., 2002; Costello, Keeler, & Angold, 2001). Two studies show that on self-report measures rural residents perceive their mental health problems to be much worse than those living in urban settings (Hauenstein, Petterson, Merwin, Rovnyak, Heise, et al., 2007; Wallace, Weeks, Wang, Lee, & Kazis, 2006).

While sampling and diagnostic techniques have improved over the years, there are significant methodological issues in conducting both national and more local studies of prevalence of mental disorder and the evaluation of groups at risk. While the national studies have more precision in their sampling and estimation, sample sizes in the most remote rural areas remain small, and representation across rural typologies is inconsistent (Hauenstein et al., 2007). The regional and local studies described here suggest that among known risk groups like the impoverished, sizeable rates of poor mental health exist, but these studies lack comparison groups in urban areas. Further, the definitions of rurality used across these studies vary considerably. What is needed are national studies that obtain sufficiently large samples across varying levels of rurality and include ample ethnic minority representation.

Help Seeking

There is some evidence that rural residents are reluctant to seek treatment for their mental health problems. Evidence from the NCS has shown that rural residents are less likely than urban residents to report that they have sought treatment for emotions or "nerves" or a substance abuse condition (Simmons & Havens, 2007). In a large study conducted in the rural South, Fox and her associates found that only 13% of those who had been diagnosed with a mental health condition and received an educational intervention about the condition and how to obtain help actually sought help for that condition (Fox, Blank, Berman, & Rovnyak, 1999). When queried, respondents with mental health conditions who did not seek care indicated that they saw no need for that care. Attitudes toward the health care system and stigma have been cited as reasons for diminished health care seeking by rural residents. For example, research in another Southern state showed that rural residents are more likely to label mental health help seekers negatively and perceive cultural dissimilarities between providers and consumers (Rost, Smith, & Taylor, 1993b).

Other studies have noted the contribution of limited social networks found in rural communities in reinforcing negative attitudes toward the mentally ill and the systems that serve them (Bushy, 1998; Ekeland & Bergem, 2006; Esters,

Cooker, & Ittenbach, 1998; Gamm, 2004; Hemard, Monroe, Atkinson, & Blalock, 1998; Hill & Fraser, 1995; Kirkwood & Stamm, 2006; Logan, Stevenson, Evans, & Leukefeld, 2004; Pulice, McCormick, & Dewees, 1995; Rost et al., 1993b; Rost, Burnam, & Smith, 1993a). Because it can be difficult to obtain mental health care in rural areas without drawing attention to oneself, the effects of negative attitudes and stigma may have especially marked effects on the use of mental health services by rural residents (Bachrach, 1983; Philo, Parr, & Burns, 2003; Rost, Fortney, Fischer, & Smith, 2002a).

Even when rural residents perceive a need for mental health treatment, it may not be evident how they are to obtain those services. There is some evidence that in rural areas, entry into the mental health treatment sector is mediated by "gateway providers." Gateway providers are influential professionals and nonprofessionals who affect perceived need and who recommend appropriate service sectors (Leslie, Hurlburt, James, Landsverk, Slymen, et al., 2005; Stiffman et al., 2001; Stiffman, Pescosolido, & Cabassa, 2004). Gateway providers include family, friends, primary care providers, social service workers, and religious organizations, and these gateway agents can both facilitate and inhibit uptake of services (den Ouden, van der Velden, Grievink, Morren, Dirkzwager, et al., 2007; Givens, Katz, Bellamy, & Holmes, 2007; Kang, Wallace, Hyun, Morris, Coffman, et al., 2007; Nicholson & Biebel, 2002; Richardson, Lewis, Casey-Goldstein, McCauley, & Katon, 2007). Fox's study, cited earlier, showed that rural individuals can inhibit the use of mental health services by family members (Fox et al., 1999). African American churches in the rural South have been shown to provide mental health services but don't always act as a bridge to formal mental health care services (Blank, Mahmood, Fox, & Guterbock, 2002; Sexton, Carlson, Siegal, Leukefeld, & Booth, 2006; Wang, Lane, Olfon, Pincus, Wells, et al., 2005). National surveys have shown that rural residents are more likely to identify a "usual source of care," typically a primary care provider, than a mental health care provider, but little is known about the effect of this relationship on obtaining specialty mental health care (Hauenstein, Petterson, Merwin, Rovnyak, Heise, et al., 2006a; Larson & Fleishman, 2003). Further research is needed to determine how rural gateway providers affect mental health access and to evaluate the effect of targeted interventions on their recommendations with regard to obtaining mental health services.

Integration

Health care organizations are considered integral to rural communities, yet few descriptions of them, their relationship with the larger community, or intra- and inter-organizational relationships are available. One exception is a study conducted in the Mississippi River Delta that showed rural treatment networks to be smaller and flatter and to have fewer interagency linkages than urban systems

(Topping & Calloway, 2000). Because rural community characteristics vary, so do the rural mental health treatment networks embedded in those communities (Calloway, Fried, Johnsen, & Morrisey, 1999; Moscovice & Wholey, 2001; Topping & Calloway, 2000). For example, the Mississippi study also showed more centrality of organizations in a resource-poor rural community than in a better-resourced rural community (Topping & Calloway, 2000). A survey of Virginia community health centers showed little reciprocity between primary care and mental health care providers (Merwin, Hinton, Harvey, Kimble, & Mackey, 2001), a problem reported as widespread (New Freedom Commission on Mental Health Subcommittee on Rural Issues, 2004). Another report showed that residents of nonmetropolitan counties were about half as likely as their metropolitan counterparts to obtain mental health treatment from both the primary care and mental health specialty care system, indicating a greater dependence of rural consumers on one system of care (Hauenstein, Petterson, Merwin, Rovnyak, & Wagner, 2006b). While collaborative and integrated care have been advocated to improve mental health care overall (Gask, 2005; Gilbody, Whitty, Grimshaw, & Thomas, 2003; New Freedom Commission on Mental Health Subcommittee on Rural Issues, 2004; Sederer, Silver, McVeigh, & Levy, 2006), integration of rural agencies in resource-poor rural environments may be ineffective because of the diversity of organizations' primary missions (Calloway et al., 1999; Merwin et al., 2001; Moscovice & Wholey, 2001; Provan & Milward, 1995; Provan, Veazie, Staten, & Teufel-Shone, 2005). Research that provides basic descriptive data on mental health care systems serving rural communities with varying characteristics is needed to inform rural mental health policy. Further, researchers must understand the structural and social characteristics of health care organizations that serve rural communities to design effective systems of rural mental health care.

The overall goal of integration is the provision of quality mental health care in rural places. To improve both access and quality treatment in the rural de facto system, interventions must be evidence based, population specific, provided proximate to where consumers live, acceptable to consumers and providers, integrated within settings, and sustainable in resource-poor rural communities and health care organizations. They must also permit easy collaboration among health care providers and use technology (Arcury, Preisser, Gesler, & Powers, 2005; Farmer, Clark, Sherman, Marien, & Selva, 2005; Fortney, Rost, Zhang, & Warren, 1999; National Institute of Mental Health, 2006). Much needs to be learned and changed so that these services delivery objectives can be realized. For example, services integration requires the availability of both primary care and mental health care providers, but both of these are in short supply in rural areas (Merwin et al., 2003, 2006; Rosenblatt, Andrilla, Curtin, & Hart, 2006). Even with adequate personnel, recent reviews have observed only modest success in the implementation of evidence-based treatments in primary care. For example, there have been several randomized controlled trials and effectiveness studies of evidence-based treatments for major depression using collaborative care models with modest positive outcomes (Asarnow, Jaycox, Duan, LaBorde, Rea, et al., 2005; Brown, Schulberg, Madonia, Shear, & Houck, 1996; Bush, Rutter, Simon, Von Korff, Katon, et al., 2004; Miranda et al., 2003; New Freedom Commission on Mental Health Subcommittee on Rural Issues, 2004; Rosenblatt et al., 2006; Rost, Nutting, Smith, & Werner, 2000b; Rost, Nutting, Smith, Werner, & Duan, 2001; Rost, Pyne, Dickinson, & LoSasso, 2005b; Rost, Smith, & Dickinson, 2004). Only one of these evaluated rural-urban differences. It showed a positive treatment effect for urban consumers only (Adams, Xu, Dong, Fortney, & Rost, 2006; Rost, Dickinson, Dickinson, & Smith, 2006; Rost et al., 2004). These multicomponent interventions requiring extensive and specialized staffing are unlikely to be implemented and sustained in rural health care agencies. Evidence-based treatments implemented by individuals other than doctoral-level mental health care providers, supported by lay community workers, and delivered electronically are more likely to be sustained in resource-poor rural health care agencies. While these kinds of intervention supports have received research attention, significant research still needs to be done to determine if they result in quality outcomes and are sustainable in rural health care systems.

OUTCOMES OF THE DE FACTO RURAL MENTAL HEALTH SYSTEM

Urban-Rural Treatment Disparities

There is mounting evidence that rural residents receive less treatment for their mental health problems than do urban residents and that they receive those treatments in general health care settings. A large national survey using data from the Medical Expenditure Panel Survey revealed that residents of the most rural areas were less likely than urban residents to obtain any treatment for a mental health condition or treatment from a specialty mental health care provider for that condition (Hauenstein et al., 2007). In this study, "any" treatment referred to any visit for a mental health problem regardless of the treatment provider. In a subsequent study, the team of investigators who conducted the Medical Expenditure Panel Survey also showed that rural women were also less likely to obtain any treatment for a reported mental health condition, but this was not true for men. Data from the NCS-R showed that residents residing in a rural area not adjacent to an urban setting were less likely to obtain "any" treatment for a diagnosed mental health problem or to receive specialty mental health care (Wang et al., 2005). Similarly, urban-rural mental health treatment disparities were evident in data from the Community Tracking Study Physician and Household Surveys (Kemper et al., 1996), which showed that rural residents of counties not adjacent to urban centers were less likely to obtain treatment for their mental health problems (Reschovsky & Staiti, 2005). Mental health treatment disparities also have been reported in several studies in which the Office of Management and Budget dichotomous indicator of rurality was used (Freiman & Zuvekas, 2000; Petterson, 2003).

There also is evidence that rural residents do not receive the same kinds of services for their mental health problems as do individuals living in more urban settings. The NCS-R showed that rural residents were much more likely to obtain treatment for psychiatric disorders in primary care and other generalist health care settings (Wang et al., 2005). In a more complex analysis using both NCS and NCS-R data, the same research team showed that rural residents used multiple nonspecialty service sectors and that their services-use profile decreased their likelihood of obtaining evidence-based treatments (Wang, Demler, Olfson, Pincus, Wells, et al., 2006). There is some evidence that rural residents are less likely to be prescribed a psychotropic medication for their mental health problems (Rigler et al., 2003; Sewitch, Blais, Rahme, Bexton, & Galarneau, 2005; Zuvekas, 2005) and that the use of selective serotonin receptor inhibitors, with their more benign side effect profile, has not been completely adopted by rural health care providers (Ganguli, Mulsant, Richards, Stoehr, & Mendelsohn, 1997; Ng, Bardwell, & Camacho, 2002).

Outcomes of Treatment Disparities

There is ample evidence that rural residents enter the care system later in the illness trajectory and when they are more urgently ill than do urban residents. Several investigators have shown that rural residents with mental disorders are more likely than urban residents to be hospitalized for their disorder (Rost, Adams, Xu, & Dong, 2007; Rost, Fortney, Zhang, Smith, & Smith, 1999; Rost, Zhang, Fortney, Smith, Coyne, et al., 1998a; Rost, Zhang, Fortney, Smith, & Smith, 1998b; Simmons & Havens, 2007; Yuen, Gerdes, & Gonzales, 1996). Even more disturbing is the finding that suicide attempts are higher among rural residents than among urban populations and that among rural men, rates of suicide have been climbing steadily over the past 20 years (Rost et al., 1998b; Singh & Siahpush, 2002). While research has shown mixed outcomes for untreated psychiatric disorders, it would appear that nontreatment has negative outcomes for those rural residents who may have heightened risk for chronic psychiatric illness (Bonari, Bennett, Einarson, & Koren, 2004; Posternak & Miller, 2001; Rost et al., 1998a, 1998b; Simon, Chisholm, Treglia, Bushnell, & LIDO Group, 2002; Wang, 2004). Simmons and Havens (2007) assert that their finding of greater comorbid alcohol and drug use among rural residents is due to residents' attempts to self-treat their primary mental disorder.

These findings show real consequences from a system of care that apparently is inadequate to meet the demand of rural residents.

Rural Mental Health Nursing Research

Many disciplines have contributed to rural mental health care practice, research, and policy. Nurses stand out among these as voices that have consistently advocated the improvement of mental health outcomes in rural areas. In this next section, selected contributions of nurses who have devoted their careers to mental health research and policy are reviewed. These nurses were identified through professional relationships, and through the use of MEDLINE and CINAHL databases. Because of the breadth of these contributions, some nurses who are committed to the improvement of rural mental health are not reviewed here but are acknowledged as critical to efforts to move the science in this area forward. Nurses' contributions to understanding rural mental health systems, rural primary care, the seriously mentally ill, depression, substance abuse, women, geriatric mental health, and policy are discussed.

Rural Mental Health Systems

Rural Health Care Workforce

Merwin is among the most visible of nurse researchers contributing to theory and new knowledge with regard to rural health and mental health systems. Along with Fox and colleagues (1995) and later with Hauenstein, Merwin, and Topping (2007) (Figure 5.1), Merwin has developed a systematic theoretical framework for the use of mental health services in rural places. Using the de facto model as a point of departure, Merwin developed a model of community and health systems organization characteristics and their effect on the supply of and demand for nurses in traditional shortages areas, including rural areas (Merwin et al., 2003). Following that, she used secondary data and the rural-urban continuum codes (Butler & Beale, 1993) to test a supply-and-demand model and document the nearly linear relationship between rurality and deficits of health care providers. Further, Merwin demonstrated that the percentage of counties designated as having primary care and mental health care provider shortages increased significantly in areas more remote from urban places. A subsequent study showed that the odds of a county having a Medicare-certified community health center or community mental health center declined significantly as rural areas became more remote (Merwin et al., 2006). The complexity of modeling the impact of provider shortages using secondary data has led Merwin and her research team to improve research methods in this area (Dembling, Li, Chang,

Mackey, & Merwin, 2001; Holt, Merwin, & Stern, 1996). The absence of data on mental health care providers prompted Merwin and other representatives of mental health care professional groups to collaborate over a 15-year period with the Center for Mental Health Services to produce a series of volumes on human resources regarding the nation's mental health workforce.

The Use of Mental Health Services by Rural Residents

Nurses also have provided leadership in documenting service-use patterns. Rost and her research team have offered a competing services-use model, the Determinants of Use, Quality, and Outcomes of Care model, that specifies variables related to entry into a service sector and treatment engagement (Rost et al., 2002a). Much work has focused on entry into care. Using survey research, Rost found that rural residents labeled people who sought professional help for their depressive symptoms more negatively than urban residents and that negative labeling was associated with obtaining less treatment (Rost et al., 1993b). Rost's team also showed that treatment rates for depression were adversely affected by distance to care among rural residents (Fortney et al., 1999). Hauenstein also has shown that despite perceptions that their mental health is poor, rural women obtain substantially less of any kind of treatment for their mental health conditions and less mental health specialty care than urban women (Hauenstein et al., 2006a). In a sample of both urban and rural caregivers of elders with dementia, Buckwalter and associates found that 64% of caregivers of individuals with dementia did not use professional services and 79% did not use respite services (Robinson, Buckwalter, & Reed, 2005). Fox documented that rural residents perceive multiple barriers to obtaining mental health services, including cost, lack of transportation, unavailability of services, and rural residents' perceptions of health care providers as uncaring (Fox, Blank, Rovnyak, & Barnett, 2001). Fox found that providing information on a rural client's actual mental health problem and on how to obtain services reduced these perceived barriers to care. In this same study, however, reductions in perceived access did not lead to actual use of services for the mental health condition (Fox et al., 1999).

The conceptual enhancement of distinguishing between services entry and treatment offered by the Outcomes model is important because it suggests that the factors that lead someone in a rural area to seek treatment may not be the same as those that enable him or her to stay engaged in treatment long enough to obtain a benefit. In her Quality Enhancement by Strategic Teaming (quEST) study, Rost designed a two-part intervention that included a component intended to increase rural participants' engagement in treatment (Rost, Nutting, Smith, Coyne, Cooper-Patrick, et al., 2000a; Rost, Nutting, Smith, Elliott, & Dickinson, 2002b; Rost et al., 2001). The intervention facilitated treatment by educating respondents about their depressive disorder, obtaining information about preferences for treatment, and systematically addressing barriers to treatment. Treatment engagement strategies resulted in 85.1% of those receiving the intervention in both urban and rural settings receiving either medication or psychotherapy (Rost et al., 2000a).

The role of family, friends, and health care professionals as gateway providers in fostering treatment entry and engagement is illustrated in other studies conducted by nurses who are rural mental health researchers and their research teams. Buckwalter's team found, for example, that the use of professional and respite services decreased among spouses of elders with dementia (Robinson et al., 2005). In another study of community-dwelling rural elders, being married was positively associated with the use of psychiatric inpatient services (Neese, Abraham, & Buckwalter, 1999). Fox showed that the presence of a family member during an educational intervention to promote services use actually reduced subsequent services use (Fox et al., 1999). Variations in results are likely due to different populations accessed and measures used; however, rural nurse researchers have demonstrated the critical role family can play in members of rural populations accessing care for their mental health problems.

The gatekeeping activities of health care professionals can also facilitate or inhibit the use of services. For example, Fox's research team examined the consequences of follow-up practices of case managers when one of their seriously mentally ill clients failed to appear for services (Blank, Chang, Fox, Lawson, & Modlinski, 1996). They showed that in-home follow-up of clients resulted in 100% attendance in the next scheduled clinic visit, compared with 68% for either telephone or letter follow-up and 46% with no follow-up. This study also showed that for 18% of those without any follow-up service, the next contact was with emergency services. Merwin surveyed community health centers located in rural Virginia and found that primary care providers consistently made referrals to specialty mental health services: 25% had referred to state psychiatric hospitals, 64% to private psychiatric hospitals, 97% to community mental health centers, and 75% to private specialty providers or clinics within the last two years (Merwin et al., 2001). Unfortunately, referral and follow-up contact from specialty mental health care settings to rural community health centers was far lower, demonstrating a gap in services with the potential to reduce clients' participation in ongoing treatment for their psychiatric conditions.

Research on Specific Populations

Depression

Rural mental health nurse researchers Hauenstein and Rost have examined the effects of major depression on rural populations. Hauenstein, for example, has described high prevalence rates of depression in rural women receiving rural primary care. In two studies drawn from similar rural and impoverished populations, Hauenstein found rates of major depression that exceeded 40% among rural women visiting a physician for routine primary care (Hauenstein & Boyd, 1994; Hauenstein & Peddada, 2007). In the second study, Hauenstein used probability estimation to determine rates; these high rates were attributed to poverty and to high rates of previous emotional, physical, and/or sexual abuse by participants. Boyd and Hauenstein (1997) also showed that significant psychiatric comorbidity existed in another sample of rural women with substance abuse problems, and similar to Hauenstein's prevalence studies, the study showed that a substantial proportion reported a history of some kind of emotional, physical, and/or sexual abuse.

Rost and her research team have completed numerous studies on the detection and treatment of depressive disorders in rural primary care settings. For example, she developed an outcomes module that had 100% sensitivity and 77.8% specificity in detecting depression in these settings (Rost, Smith, Burnam, & Burns, 1992b). In a later study, she validated the use of a two-item screener in detecting depression in community, medical, and mental health patients, thus establishing a sensitivity between 83% and 92% (Rost et al., 1993b). Rost's research team conducted several studies examining the diagnostic and treatment process for depression in rural primary care (Rost, Humphrey, & Kelleher, 1994a). In one study they showed that 32% of patients with current major depression were not identified as such by their primary care physician despite one or more visits over a 6-month time period; nearly half developed suicidal ideation during that time period (Rost et al., 1998a). This research team showed that when physicians did detect depression in their clients, more than half of the time they would substitute a diagnosis other than depression in the patient record (Rost, Smith, Matthews, & Guise, 1994c). Substitutions were most likely to occur when physicians were uncertain of the diagnosis and because of limited reimbursement for mental health problems. Examining the treatment of depression by primary care physicians practicing in small towns, Rost and her team found that while 63% of patients with major depression received a prescription for an antidepressant, only 28.9% actually received guideline-concordant pharmacologic treatment (Rost, Williams, Wherry, & Smith, 1995). In another study of depressed patients in primary care, Rost and her associates found that depression was less likely to be evaluated and treatment modified when patients presented with concomitant physical problems or with new health problems (Rost et al., 2000b). They also showed that rural physicians preferred prescribing medication for depression to recommending psychotherapy, although 26% reported providing some kind of counseling service. Rost's team also found that rural physicians could identify few mental health treatment referrals for their depressed patients. Completing the picture of nontreatment and undertreatment of depression in rural primary care, Rost and her associates showed that rural residents had fewer outpatient expenditures for depression treatment than their urban counterparts. While costs for rural residents were lower for outpatient care, Rost demonstrated that depressed rural residents were more likely to be hospitalized for both physical and mental health problems, resulting in greater costs overall (Rost et al., 1999). Rost's extensive contribution to our understanding of treatment access and barriers for people with depression is also discussed elsewhere in this review (Rost et al., 1993a, 1998b, 2002a, 2007). Rost also has conducted similar studies in patients with a variety of mental health problems (Rost et al., 1992a, 1993b, 1994b, 2002a, 2006; Rost, Ross, Humphrey, Frank, Smith, et al., 1996; Rost & Smith, 1997).

The Seriously Mentally Ill

Research with individuals with serious mental illness offers significant challenges; the limited knowledge in this area has been developed primarily by nurse investigators at the SRMHRC. In using different methods and examining different targets in evaluating the outcome of community tenure, SRMHRC investigators have been unable to determine a consistent pattern of client and community characteristics associated with hospitalization for mental health problems among rural residents with serious mental illness (Downs & Fox, 1993; Francis, Merwin, Fox, & Shelton, 1995; Stern, Merwin, & Holt, 2001). In another approach, Kane and other SRMHRC investigators developed and tested a theoretical model identifying several factors that predict community adjustment (Kane, Blank, & Hundley, 1999). The test of the model on 40 rural community-dwelling consumers with serious mental illness showed that life stressors and their direct and indirect effects on consumers and informal care providers were most predictive of consumers' satisfaction with their quality of life. In another study conducted by Kane, rural community-dwelling clients with serious mental illness were found to have poor health habits and co-occurring physical problems for which they were not receiving treatment (Holmberg & Kane, 1999). While the SRMHRC investigators provided a concentrated focus on the issues associated with the care of rural residents with serious mental illness in the community, more studies examining both individual and community variables associated with community tenure of this vulnerable group are needed.

Substance Abuse

Boyd has profiled the antecedents and outcomes of alcohol abuse among rural White and African American women. In several studies, Boyd documented substantial psychiatric comorbidity among White and African American rural women and high rates of reported violence by both (Boyd, 2000; Boyd, Bland,

Herman, Mestler, Murr, et al., 2002; Boyd, Mackey, Phillips, & Tavakoli, 2006). In these comparison studies, Boyd notes greater drug use of all types and more reports of violence by rural White women and differing patterns of comorbidity between the two racial groups. Boyd's research also has demonstrated that women of both racial/ethnic backgrounds experienced more stressors, used fewer coping strategies associated with controlling their emotions, and were more likely to have positive expectancies associated with the use of alcohol and lower self-esteem than women who did not abuse alcohol and drugs, although the patterns varied to some degree by race/ethnic group. Using grounded theory techniques, Boyd also showed that rural women diagnosed with alcohol and drug abuse problems experienced self-alienation and could not understand the purpose of their lives; these women used several strategies, including drinking, to escape this negative valuation of their lives (Boyd & Mackey, 2000a, 2000b).

Dementia

Buckwalter was one of the originators of the Progressively Lowered Stress Threshold Model of Dementia (PLST), which has spawned a series of descriptive and intervention research projects (Hall & Buckwalter, 1987; Schultz, Hoth, & Buckwalter, 2004; Smith, Gerdner, Hall, & Buckwalter, 2004; Smith, Hall, Gerdner, & Buckwalter, 2006). PLST describes a cluster of behaviors, including agitation, night wakening, late day confusion, and combative actions, that emerge when environmental demands, external or internal, exceed a person's ability to cope and adapt. Identification of these behaviors and their antecedents has stimulated research on the presence of psychiatric disorders among rural elders and their effects on functioning. Using three measures of depression, Buckwalter and her research team identified depression in 21.3%–39.1% of rural elders living in residential care; the lowest rates were based on a single item abstracted from residents' charts (Kerber, Dyck, Culp, & Buckwalter, 2005). In another study, Buckwalter showed that 34.6% of rural elders living in residential care had mild to moderate anxiety and that the presence of these symptoms had significant effects on their physical and cognitive functioning (Schultz et al., 2004). The PLST was used in another study to profile how stressors of different sources contributed to agitation in residents of rural residential care facilities. Stressors including urinary tract infections, environmental stimuli such as noise, and changes in routine and emotional demands all led to observable increases in agitation in these residents. Using an innovative 12-step psychophenomenological qualitative research design, Buckwalter's research team described the enduring stress and suffering of caregivers of patients with dementia, as well as the meaning they derived from the experience (Butcher, Holkup, & Buckwalter, 2001).

RESEARCH ON TREATMENT OF MENTAL HEALTH PROBLEMS

Intervention Studies for Depression

Rural mental health nurse researchers have consistently demonstrated the feasibility of delivering evidence-based treatment for individuals with mental health problems in rural places by adapting treatments to the realities of the rural service delivery system. Both Rost and Hauenstein have designed treatments for rural residents with depression seeking care in rural primary care. Rost recruited 12 primary care practices in both metropolitan and nonmetropolitan areas for the quEST study (Rost et al., 2000a, 2001, 2002b). The aim of the study was to provide patients presenting with major depression with two years of guideline-concordant treatment. Nurses in each of the practices enhanced depression care by providing psychoeducation designed to increase patients' readiness to participate in treatment and reduce perceived barriers to obtaining treatment. Continuing intervention involved telephone contacts by nurses, who monitored symptoms and resolved treatment adherence problems. Results showed that enhanced care led to significantly more depression-free days over a two-year period than usual care. In terms of employment outcomes, enhanced care led to 6.1% greater work productivity and 22.8% less absenteeism over the two-year intervention period (Rost et al., 2004; Rost, Fortney, & Coyne, 2005a). The uninsured in the treatment group also demonstrated greater improvements in the use of psychotropic medication than the usual care group, but that group's reported mental health quality of life improved less (Smith, Rost, Nutting, & Elliott, 2001; Smith, Rost, Nutting, Libby, Elliott, et al., 2002). Unfortunately, rural primary care practices were very difficult to recruit and maintain in the intervention, and although there appeared to be modest effects of increased use of psychotherapeutic modalities among rural residents, the positive outcomes were not observed in rural residents (Adams et al., 2006; Rost et al., 2000a; Smith, Rost, Nutting, Elliott, & Duan, 2000). Rost's quEST program is highly innovative and scientifically sound and has significant potential to be transferable to primary care settings and the populations that they serve. Among the large primary care depression trials, Rost's study is the first to include small rural practices and to evaluate the effect of rurality on outcome. While it is disappointing that significant improvement in outcomes in rural residents did not accrue, Rost's study provides many lessons about what is possible and needed in the delivery of high-quality depression treatment in rural primary care settings.

Hauenstein also conducted a study of depression treatment for rural women who used a rural community health center for routine health care (Hauenstein,

1996a, 1996b, 1997, 2003). This setting served a largely uninsured and impoverished population and at the time of the study offered no formal mental health services. Hauenstein developed a theoretical paradigm explaining depression and developed a treatment program paired to the theoretical targets for intervention. Using a manual derived from the theory, Hauenstein's research team provided 12 weekly sessions of cognitive-behavioral therapy with 12 sessions of follow-up to the intervention group; the nonintervention group received psychoeducation in 5 sessions over 10 weeks. There were no treatment differences between the two groups at 12 months following treatment; significant attrition in both treatment and comparison groups reduced the team's power to detect differences between the groups. In-depth interviews of respondents in both groups, however, revealed that the women in the intervention group had made substantial and positive changes in their personal lives (Hauenstein, 2003). While home visitation provides challenges to service delivery, women credited it with reducing the interpersonal and distance barriers that may have interfered with their ability to both engage and sustain treatment in more formal service settings.

Caregiver Interventions

Buckwalter and her research team also developed theory to guide several intervention studies with caregivers of individuals with dementia. The PLST, described earlier, guided the development of an in-home individual care plan that helped caregivers avoid and manage stressors that led to undesirable behaviors in their loved ones with dementia (Buckwalter, Gerdner, Kohout, Hall, Kelly, et al., 1999). Caregivers receiving the intervention were found to be less depressed at 6 and 12 months following intervention than caregivers in a comparison group. Depression level reported by caregivers in both groups was affected by measure used, educational level and age of the caregiver, and other contextual and illness-related variables. In a second study, Buckwalter and her team examined the effect of telephone intervention versus in-home intervention in the delivery of a similar PLST-based intervention on caregiver burden, distress, depression, social support, life satisfaction, and functional status over a 36-week period (Davis, Burgio, Buckwalter, & Weaver, 2004). They found that in-home treatment both effected positive outcomes sooner and engaged caregivers in treatment for longer periods of time. In a related study, family caregivers of residents of special care units for dementia were partnered with staff of those facilities to provide a negotiated plan of care (Maas et al., 2004). Here the PLST-based intervention also effected significant reductions in caregiver burden and distress. Buckwalter and her associates demonstrated the feasibility of the provision of PLST-based interventions for rural settings but provided little analysis of the effects of the rural context on either caregivers or needed modifications in the intervention as a result of the rural context. Still, the conceptual and methodological contributions to remediation of caregiver burden and distress provided by Buckwalter and her research team are considerable.

Other Intervention Studies

Two other intervention studies conducted in rural settings by rural mental health nurse researchers are notable for their innovation and their implementation with populations that are difficult to access and treat. Using the Program of Assertive Community Treatment (PACT) as the core intervention, SRMHRC investigator Kane made several modifications for rural and urban residents living in and around two small cities in Virginia (Kane & Blank, 2004). These modifications included the provision of nursing care that reduced physical and mental health comorbidity and promoted healthy lifestyles among the seriously mentally ill receiving care in community mental health. In order to implement this program, called NPACT, Kane created a joint position between the University of Virginia School of Nursing and the community mental health center that would be filled by what was then a new breed of health care provider, the psychiatric nurse-practitioner. Compared to PACT, recipients of NPACT at 6 months posttreatment had fewer psychiatric symptoms, better community functioning, and higher reported levels of consumer satisfaction. In addition to innovation in individual-level intervention programming, Kane's research demonstrates system modifications that are often necessary in rural research. Some 11 years after this research was first initiated, both the NPACT program and the psychiatric nurse-practitioner remain active components of the community mental health center's services.

Boyd conducted an intervention study with rural women with substance abuse disorders who also were infected with HIV and who had sought care from an HIV peer counseling service (Boyd et al., 2005). The peer counseling service has its own treatment protocol, and Boyd's substance abuse intervention was added to the existing protocol. The 4-session intervention was based on a readiness-to-change and motivational interviewing paradigm used in a major substance abuse study, Program MATCH. The substance abuse intervention began once the usual peer counseling protocol was completed. While 158 women were eligible to participate, the intervention could be completed with only 13 (8%) because of the lack of peer counselors available in rural areas. This is unfortunate because it is obvious from inspection of means reported in this study that the intervention had a substantial and positive effect on inducing change in substance abuse behavior.

OUTCOMES OF CARE

With the exception of Rost's efforts in examining workforce productivity, nurse scientists have not considered a wide range of potential outcomes for evaluation or evaluated the relevancy of these outcomes for rural populations. The Society for Research and Education in Psychiatric Nursing examined patient outcomes in psychiatric nursing in a survey of its members (Barrell, Merwin, & Poster, 1997). They found that symptom relief, behavioral changes, attaining goals, satisfaction, functional status, quality of life, and hospitalization-related factors were the most common outcomes measured. In a comprehensive review of the literature, Merwin and Mauck (1995) classified outcomes along five domains: humanitarian (level of well-being), public welfare (violence and its outcomes), rehabilitation (relapse prevention, social support), provider (burnout, attitudes) and clinical (symptom reduction). Merwin and Mauck pointed out the importance of properly specifying the outcomes of care as the anchor for evaluating the processes and quality of care offered by mental health care providers and notes the paucity of research directed to this objective. Outcome specification is further limited among rural populations, for whom environmental factors may influence achievement of outcomes as well as health care quality and processes. Rural residents are often unemployed, underemployed, self-employed, or employed in small businesses; as a consequence the outcome of work performance may have an entirely different meaning for rural dwellers than for urban residents. Social functioning in rural populations may be another outcome that is difficult to achieve in rural areas. The isolation of many rural areas and lack of privacy that often is evident in rural places may make it difficult for rural residents to achieve the level of social interaction that is considered desirable among urban populations. An important task of rural mental health nurse researchers is to determine individual-, community-, and population-level outcomes that are appropriate for rural settings.

CONCLUSIONS

The RMHS model is useful for organizing priorities for research that will promote the development of science in rural mental health and mental health service delivery in rural communities. Beginning in the area of access, rural mental health science will be advanced by studies that explore strategies that influence the uptake of mental health care and that describe the treatment sectors in which consumers seek care as well as the individual-, community-, and system-level factors that facilitate or inhibit engagement in treatment. For example, interventions that reduce stigma in rural communities and public education campaigns that seek to demystify mental health interventions may advance knowledge on how to deliver mental health care effectively in rural communities. A greater understanding of how professional and nonprofessional gateway providers communicate to promote mental health treatment would also advance the design and implementation of effective mental health services in rural settings that engage rural residents in treatment.

In the area of integration, little research has been conducted with rural communities and the myriad of organizations that provide formal and informal mental health services within them. While the original de facto model posited that the multiple sectors of care that provide mental health services in rural communities have evolved in response to an unanswered need, more data about the strengths as well as the limitations of the de facto system are needed (Fox et al., 1995). Studies of mental health service systems in rural areas suggest that the evolution of these systems reflects the resources available within the system; attempts to integrate services or otherwise alter the mechanisms of service delivery within these systems may further deplete the scarce resources that exist in rural communities (Calloway et al., 1999; Morrissey, Stroup, Ellis, & Merwin, 2002; Moscovice & Wholey, 2001; Provan & Milward, 1995; Topping & Calloway, 2000). Descriptive and intervention research of organizational and inter-organizational mental health services delivery using quality improvement strategies and qualitative data collection and analysis would significantly advance our knowledge on the extent to which services reach those who need them, as well as the quality of the services provided.

Very little work describing appropriate outcomes for rural consumers, quality indicators in the agencies in which they obtain their mental health care, or rural populations in general has been conducted. Research is needed on the quality indicators as outlined in the Institute of Medicine Quality Chasm reports (Institute of Medicine, 2001, 2005, 2006) and how these are evidenced in the rural health care agencies that deliver mental health care. While the values embodied in the quality indicators should be evident in all systems of care, how they are operationalized may need to vary across rural settings. Similarly, while population outcomes must be elucidated for all rural residents, priorities for achieving these outcomes will necessarily arise from local priorities.

Rural communities form the context for the RMHS, and these communities vary in characteristics across localities and regions. A key research priority is establishing how variation in the rural context affects individual, community, organizational, and mental health system outcomes. Our ability to answer this basic question is seriously impeded by conceptual limitations in how rurality is conceptualized and measured (Hart, Larson, & Lishner, 2005). For example, using several large nationally representative databases, SRMHRC investigators have been investigating the effects of various definitions of rurality commonly in use on services use and mental health outcomes. Findings show that the multi-dimensionality of currently employed definitions makes it difficult to discern the effects of rurality, especially in the most remote rural areas where sample sizes are small (Stern, Merwin, Hauenstein, Hinton, Rovnyak, et al., 2008). The available definitions of rurality make it unlikely that the effects of local and regional variation in geography, topography, culture, migration, and other features of the rural landscape on mental health outcomes will be captured (Bachrach, 1983; Philo et al., 2003). Rural mental health science may be advanced when researchers provide rich descriptions of the rural community context when discussing research findings. In addition, in-depth ethnographic studies of various rural communities and their mental health care systems are badly needed to improve our understanding of patterns of mental health utilization, quality mental health care, and individual outcomes within local systems of care.

A final comment about research methods seems warranted. Most rural mental health research has followed the form of traditional experimental and effectiveness research designs. These methods are expensive, are burdensome to rural mental health organizations that sponsor the investigators, and in the end have produced little in the way of positive outcomes for the rural residents they were commissioned to treat. The most compelling questions will require theoretical paradigms outside the more positivist framework that drives current research, including such diverse perspectives as critical social theory and constructivist theoretical paradigms. Research methods that integrate both quantitative and qualitative methodologies will be most useful in answering the multidimensional questions that are suggested here. Research methods that use participant observation such as multiple case study designs and ethnographic research are necessary in order to break down the cultural barriers between researchers and rural residents. Academic-community partnerships, action research, and community-based participatory research designs will be necessary to provide the expertise needed to tackle these difficult problems and ensure that interventions derived in this way are acceptable to community residents and sustainable in resource-poor rural health care agencies. While at least one NIH institute is considering this type of research approach, both research review groups and agencies that fund rural mental health research will need to take some risks to move to more novel research paradigms and methods in order to move rural mental health science forward (National Institute of Mental Health, 2006).

It is not surprising that nurses have provided leadership in rural mental health and made such rich contributions to the development of the science in this field. Nurses are the largest health care force evident in rural America and have seen firsthand the difficulties rural residents face in obtaining health care of any kind, but especially mental health care. Nurses will need to continue to provide leadership to move the field forward. But much is left to do. The RMHS model is necessarily a model of services use that requires a broad base of investigators to realize its objectives. To design interventions that improve access and treatment engagement, specialists in public health, organizational and management theorists, behaviorists, community developers, activists, and consumers must be engaged. Rural mental health systems are ripe for research investigation, and very few field reports describing them exist in the literature. While nurses are able to specify setting area variables that have an impact on their conduct of intervention and other research in these settings, an understanding of how rural organizations act and interact to provide mental health services is sorely needed. To enact change in these settings, nurse researchers will need to engage organizational theorists and behaviorists and will need to obtain the assistance of quality improvement specialists to be able to assess the impact of change within and across organizations. Development of outcomes that are specific to rural populations will also require cross-fertilization from other disciplines. Finally, the more recent action research paradigms require that nurses partner with a variety of interdisciplinary and community groups to specify research questions and designs and to engage in analysis. Rural mental health nurse researchers have provided leadership in developing the science thus far and, with partners in other disciplines and backgrounds, will build on the strength and resilience of rural communities to improve outcomes for the mentally ill.

REFERENCES

Adams, S. J., Xu, S., Dong, F., Fortney, J., & Rost, K. (2006). Differential effectiveness of depression disease management for rural and urban primary care patients. *Journal of Rural Health, 22,* 343–350.

Angold, A., Erkanli, A., Farmer, E. M., Fairbank, J. A., Burns, B. J., & Keeler, G. (2002). Psychiatric disorder, impairment, and service use in rural African American and White youth. *Archives of General Psychiatry, 59,* 893–901.

Anonymous. (2007, November 10). *What is rural?* Rural Information Center. Retrieved April 1, 2008, from http://ric.nal.usda.gov/nal_display/index.php?tax_level=1&info_center=5

Arcury, T. A., Preisser, J. S., Gesler, W. M., & Powers, J. M. (2005). Access to transportation and health care utilization in a rural region. *Journal of Rural Health, 21*(1), 31–38.

Asarnow, J. R., Jaycox, L. H., Duan, N., LaBorde, A. P., Rea, M. M., & Murray, P. (2005). Effectiveness of a quality improvement intervention for adolescent depression in primary care clinics: A randomized controlled trial. *Journal of the American Medical Association, 293*(3), 311–319.

Bachrach, L. L. (1983). Psychiatric services in rural areas: A sociological overview. *Hospital & Community Psychiatry, 34*(3), 215–226.

Barrell, L. M., Merwin, E. I., & Poster, E. C. (1997). Patient outcomes used by advanced practice psychiatric nurses to evaluate effectiveness of practice. *Archives of Psychiatric Nursing, 11,* 184–197.

Blank, M. B., Chang, M. Y., Fox, J. C., Lawson, C. A., & Modlinski, J. (1996). Case manager follow-up to failed appointments and subsequent service utilization. *Community Mental Health Journal, 32,* 23–31.

Blank, M. B., Mahmood, M., Fox, J. C., & Guterbock, T. (2002). Alternative mental health services: The role of the Black church in the South. *American Journal of Public Health, 92,* 1668–1672.

Bonari, L., Bennett, H., Einarson, A., & Koren, G. (2004). Risks of untreated depression during pregnancy. *Canadian Family Physician, 50,* 37–39.

Boyd, M. R. (2000). Predicting substance abuse and comorbidity in rural women. *Archives of Psychiatric Nursing, 14*(2), 64–72.

Boyd, M. R., Bland, A., Herman, J., Mestler, L., Murr, L., & Potts, L. (2002). Stress and coping in rural women with alcohol and other drug disorders. *Archives of Psychiatric Nursing, 16*(6), 254–262.

Boyd, M. R., & Hauenstein, E. J. (1997). Psychiatric assessment and confirmation of dual disorders in rural substance abusing women. *Archives of Psychiatric Nursing, 11*(2), 74–81.

Boyd, M. R., & Mackey, M. C. (2000a). Alienation from self and others: The psychosocial problem of rural alcoholic women. *Archives of Psychiatric Nursing, 14*(3), 134–141.

Boyd, M. R., & Mackey, M. C. (2000b). Running away to nowhere: Rural women's experiences of becoming alcohol dependent. *Archives of Psychiatric Nursing, 14*(3), 142–149.

Boyd, M. R., Mackey, M. C., Phillips, K. D., & Tavakoli, A. (2006). Alcohol and other drug disorders, comorbidity and violence in rural African American women. *Issues in Mental Health Nursing, 27,* 1017–1036.

Boyd, M. R., Moneyham, L., Murdaugh, C., Phillips, K. D., Tavakoli, A., Jackwon, K., et al. (2005). A peer-based substance abuse intervention for HIV + rural women: A pilot study. *Archives of Psychiatric Nursing, 19*(1), 10–17.

Brown, C., Schulberg, H. C., Madonia, M. J., Shear, M. K., & Houck, P. R. (1996). Treatment outcomes for primary care patients with major depression and lifetime anxiety disorders. *American Journal of Psychiatry, 153*(10), 1293–1300.

Buckwalter, K. C., Gerdner, L., Kohout, F., Hall, G. R., Kelly, A., & Richards, B. (1999). A nursing intervention to decrease depression in family caregivers of persons with dementia. *Archives of Psychiatric Nursing, 13*(2), 80–88.

Bush, T., Rutter, C., Simon, G., Von Korff, M., Katon, W. J., & Walker, E. A. (2004). Who benefits from more structured depression treatment? *International Journal of Psychiatry in Medicine, 34*(3), 247–258.

Bushy, A. (1998). Health issues of women in rural environments: An overview. *Journal of the American Medical Women's Association, 53*(2), 53–56.

Butcher, H. K., Holkup, P. A., & Buckwalter, K. C. (2001). The experience of caring for a family member with Alzheimer's disease. *Western Journal of Nursing Research, 23*(1), 33–55.

Butler, M. A., & Beale, C. L. (1993). *Rural-urban continuum codes for metro and nonmetro counties.* Washington, DC: U.S. Department of Agriculture, Economic Research Service.

Calloway, M., Fried, B., Johnsen, M., & Morrisey, J. (1999). Characterization of rural mental health service systems. *Journal of Rural Health, 15*(3), 296–307.

Costello, E. J., Keeler, G. P., & Angold, A. (2001). Poverty, race/ethnicity, and psychiatric disorder: A study of rural children. *American Journal of Public Health, 91,* 1494–1498.

Davis, L. L., Burgio, L. D., Buckwalter, K. C., & Weaver, M. (2004). A comparison of in-home and telephone-based skill training interventions with caregivers of persons with dementia. *Journal of Mental Health and Aging, 10,* 31–44.

Dembling, B., Li, X., Chang, W. Y., Mackey, S., & Merwin, E. (2001). Psychiatric health service areas in the southeast. *Administration & Policy in Mental Health, 28,* 407–416.

den Ouden, D. J., van der Velden, P. G., Grievink, L., Morren, M., Dirkzwager, A. J., & Yzermans, C. J. (2007). Use of mental health services among disaster survivors: Predisposing factors. *BMC Public Health, 7,* 173.

Downs, M. W., & Fox, J. C. (1993). Social environments of adult homes. *Community Mental Health Journal, 29,* 15–23.

Ekeland, T. J., & Bergem, R. (2006). The negotiation of identity among people with mental illness in rural communities. *Community Mental Health Journal, 42*(3), 225–232.

Esters, I. G., Cooker, P. G., & Ittenbach, R. F. (1998). Effects of a unit of instruction in mental health on rural adolescents' conceptions of mental illness and attitudes about seeking help. *Adolescence, 33*(130), 469–476.

Farmer, J. E., Clark, M. J., Sherman, A., Marien, W. E., & Selva, T. J. (2005). Comprehensive primary care for children with special health care needs in rural areas. *Pediatrics, 116*(3), 649–656.

Fichter, M. M., Narrow, W. E., Roper, M. T., Rehm, J., Elton, M., & Rae, D. S. (1996). Prevalence of mental illness in Germany and the United States: Comparison of the Upper Bavarian Study and the Epidemiologic Catchment Area Program. *Journal of Nervous & Mental Disease, 184*(10), 598–606.

Fortney, J., Rost, K., Zhang, M., & Warren, J. (1999). The impact of geographic accessibility on the intensity and quality of depression treatment. *Medical Care, 37,* 884–893.

Fox, J., Merwin, E., & Blank, M. (1995). De facto mental health services in the rural South. *Journal of Health Care for the Poor and Underserved, 6,* 434–467.

Fox, J. C., Blank, M., Berman, J., & Rovnyak, V. G. (1999). Mental disorders and help seeking in a rural impoverished population. *International Journal of Psychiatry in Medicine, 29,* 181–195.

Fox, J. C., Blank, M., Rovnyak, V. G., & Barnett, R. Y. (2001). Barriers to help seeking for mental disorders in a rural impoverished population. *Community Mental Health Journal, 37,* 421–436.

Francis, P., Merwin, E., Fox, J., & Shelton, D. (1995). Relationship of clinical case management to hospitalization and service delivery for seriously mentally ill clients. *Issues in Mental Health Nursing, 16,* 257–274.

Freiman, M. P., & Zuvekas, S. H. (2000). Determinants of ambulatory treatment mode for mental illness. *Health Economics, 9,* 423–434.

Gamm, L. D. (2004). Mental health and substance abuse services among rural minorities. *Journal of Rural Health, 20*(3), 206–209.

Ganguli, M., Mulsant, B., Richards, S., Stoehr, G., & Mendelsohn, A. (1997). Antidepressant use over time in a rural older adult population: The MoVIES Project. *Journal of the American Geriatrics Society, 45,* 1501–1503.

Gask, L. (2005). Overt and covert barriers to the integration of primary and specialist mental health care. *Social Science & Medicine, 61*(8), 1785–1794.

Gilbody, S., Whitty, P., Grimshaw, J., & Thomas, R. (2003). Educational and organizational interventions to improve the management of depression in primary care: A systematic review. *Journal of the American Medical Association, 289*(23), 3145–3151.

Givens, J. L., Katz, I. R., Bellamy, S., & Holmes, W. C. (2007). Stigma and the acceptability of depression treatments among African Americans and Whites. *Journal of General Internal Medicine, 22*(9), 1292–1297.

Hall, G. R., & Buckwalter, K. C. (1987). Progressively lowered stress threshold: A conceptual model for care of adults with Alzheimer's disease. *Archives of Psychiatric Nursing, 1*(6), 399–406.

Hart, L. G., Larson, E. H., & Lishner, D. M. (2005). Rural definitions for health policy and research. *American Journal of Public Health, 95,* 1149–1155.

Hauenstein, E. J. (1996a). A nursing practice paradigm for depressed rural women: Theoretical basis. *Archives of Psychiatric Nursing, 10*(5), 283–292.

Hauenstein, E. J. (1996b). Testing innovative nursing care: Home intervention with depressed rural women. *Issues in Mental Health Nursing, 17*(1), 33–50.

Hauenstein, E. J. (1997). A nursing practice paradigm for depressed rural women: The Women's Affective Illness Treatment Program. *Archives of Psychiatric Nursing, 11*(1), 37–45.

Hauenstein, E. J. (2003). No comfort in the rural South: Women living depressed. *Archives of Psychiatric Nursing, 17*(1), 3–11.

Hauenstein, E. J., & Boyd, M. R. (1994). Depressive symptoms in young women of the Piedmont: Prevalence in rural women. *Women & Health, 21*(2–3), 105–123.

Hauenstein, E. J., Merwin, E., & Topping, S. (2007, June). *The rural mental health systems model.* Unpublished grant application to the National Institutes of Health.

Hauenstein, E. J., & Peddada, S. D. (2007). Prevalence of major depressive episodes in rural women using primary care. *Journal of Health Care for the Poor & Underserved, 18,* 185–202.

Hauenstein, E. J., Petterson, S., Merwin, E., Rovnyak, V., Heise, B., & Wagner, D. (2006a). Rurality, gender, and mental health treatment. *Family & Community Health, 29,* 169–185.

Hauenstein, E. J., Petterson, S., Merwin, E., Rovnyak, V., Heise, B., & Wagner, D. (2007). Rurality and mental health treatment. *Administration and Policy in Mental Health and Mental Health Services Research, 24*(3), 255–267.

Hauenstein, E. J., Petterson, S., Merwin, E., Rovnyak, V., & Wagner, D. (2006b, August). *Patterns of mental health treatment in rural residents: Different pathways to care.* Unpublished presentation to the National Association of Rural Mental Health, San Antonio, TX.

Hemard, J. B., Monroe, P. A., Atkinson, E. S., & Blalock, L. B. (1998). Rural women's satisfaction and stress as family health care gatekeepers. *Women & Health, 28*(2), 55–77.

Hill, C. E., & Fraser, G. J. (1995). Local knowledge and rural mental health reform. *Community Mental Health Journal, 31*(6), 553–568.

Holmberg, S. K., & Kane, C. (1999). Health and self-care practices of persons with schizophrenia. *Psychiatric Services, 50,* 827–829.

Holt, F., Merwin, E., & Stern, S. (1996). Alternative statistical methods to use with survival data. *Nursing Research, 45,* 345–349.

Institute of Medicine. (2001). *Crossing the quality chasm: A new health system for the 21st century.* Washington, DC: National Academy Press.

Institute of Medicine. (2005). *Quality through collaboration: The future of rural health.* Washington, DC: National Academy Press.

Institute of Medicine. (2006). *Improving the quality of health care for mental and substance-use conditions.* Washington, DC: National Academy Press.

Kane, C., Blank, M., & Hundley, P. (1999). Care provision and community adjustment of rural consumers with serious mental illness. *Archives of Psychiatric Nursing, 13,* 19–29.

Kane, C. F., & Blank, M. B. (2004). NPACT: Enhancing programs of assertive community treatment for the seriously mentally ill. *Community Mental Health Journal, 40*, 549–559.

Kang, S. H., Wallace, N. T., Hyun, J. K., Morris, A., Coffman, J., & Bloom, J. R. (2007). Social networks and their relationship to mental health service use and expenditures among Medicaid beneficiaries. *Psychiatric Services, 58*(5), 689–695.

Kemper, P., Blumenthal, D., Corrigan, J. M., Cunningham, P. J., Felt, S. M., Grossman, J. M., et al. (1996). The design of the community tracking study: A longitudinal study of health system change and its effects on people. *Inquiry, 33*(2), 195–206.

Kerber, C. S., Dyck, M. J., Culp, K. R., & Buckwalter, K. (2005). Comparing the geriatric depression scale, minimum data set, and primary care provider diagnosis for depression in rural nursing home residents. *Journal of the American Psychiatric Nurses Association, 11*, 269–275.

Kessler, R. C., Chiu, W. T., Demler, O., Merikangas, K. R., & Walters, E. E. (2005). Prevalence, severity, and comorbidity of 12-month DSM-IV disorders in the National Comorbidity Survey Replication. *Archives of General Psychiatry, 62*, 617–627.

Kessler, R. C., McGonagle, K. A., Zhao, S., Nelson, C. B., Hughes, M., Eshleman, S., et al. (1994). Lifetime and 12-month prevalence of DSM-III-R psychiatric disorders in the United States: Results from the National Comorbidity Survey. *Archives of General Psychiatry, 51*, 8–19.

Kirkwood, A. D., & Stamm, B. H. (2006). A social marketing approach to challenging stigma. *Professional Psychology: Research and Practice, 37*, 472–476.

Larson, S. L., & Fleishman, J. A. (2003). Rural-urban differences in usual source of care and ambulatory service use: Analyses of national data using Urban Influence Codes. *Medical Care, 41*(7 Suppl.), III65–III74.

Leslie, L. K., Hurlburt, M. S., James, S., Landsverk, J., Slymen, D. J., & Zhang, J. (2005). Relationship between entry into child welfare and mental health service use. *Psychiatric Services, 56*(8), 981–987.

Logan, T. K., Stevenson, E., Evans, L., & Leukefeld, C. (2004). Rural and urban women's perceptions of barriers to health, mental health, and criminal justice services: Implications for victim services. *Violence & Victims, 19*(1), 37–62.

Maas, M. L., Reed, D., Park, M., Specht, J. P., Schutte, D., Kelley, L. S., et al. (2004). Outcomes of family involvement in care intervention for caregivers of individuals with dementia. *Nursing Research, 53*, 76–86.

McCrone, S., Cotton, S., Jones, L., Hawkins, T. A., Costante, J., & Nuss, M. (2007). Depression in a rural, free clinic providing primary care: Prevalence and predictive factors. *Archives of Psychiatric Nursing, 21*, 291–293.

Merwin, E., Hinton, I., Dembling, B., & Stern, S. (2003). Shortages of rural mental health professionals. *Archives of Psychiatric Nursing, 17*, 42–51.

Merwin, E., Hinton, I., Harvey, J., Kimble, K. E., & Mackey, S. (2001). *Mental health care in Virginia community mental health centers.* Report prepared for Virginia Primary Care Association. Retrieved April 1, 2008, from http://www.vpca.com/pdf/MentalHealth CHCscover.pdf

Merwin, E., & Mauck, A. (1995). Psychiatric nursing outcome research: The state of the science. *Archives of Psychiatric Nursing, 9*(6), 311–331.

Merwin, E., Snyder, A., & Katz, E. (2006). Differential access to quality rural healthcare: Professional and policy challenges. *Family & Community Health, 29*, 186–194.

Miranda, J., Chung, J. Y., Green, B. L., Krupnick, J., Siddique, J., Revicki, D. A., et al. (2003). Treating depression in predominantly low-income young minority women: A randomized controlled trial. *Journal of the American Medical Association, 290*(1), 57–65.

Morrissey, J. P., Stroup, T. S., Ellis, A. R., & Merwin, E. (2002). Service use and health status of persons with severe mental illness in full-risk and no-risk Medicaid programs. *Psychiatric Services, 53*, 293–298.

Moscovice, I., & Wholey, D. (2001). *The ecology of network organizations: Determinants of rural health network failure.* Abstracts of the Academy for Health Services Research and Health Policy Meeting. Retrieved April 1, 2008, from http://gateway.nlm.nih.gov/MeetingAbstracts/102273406.html

National Institute of Mental Health. (2006). *The road ahead: Research partnerships to transform services. A Report by the National Advisory Mental Health Council's Services Research and Clinical Epidemiology Workgroup.* Rockville, MD: Department of Health and Human Services.

Neese, J. B., Abraham, I. L., & Buckwalter, K. C. (1999). Utilization of mental health services among rural elderly. *Archives of Psychiatric Nursing, 18*(1), 30–40.

New Freedom Commission on Mental Health, Subcommittee on Rural Issues. (2004). *Background paper.* Report # DHHS Pub. No. SMA-04-3890. Rockville, MD: Department of Health and Human Services.

Ng, B., Bardwell, W. A., & Camacho, A. (2002). Depression treatment in rural California: Preliminary survey of nonpsychiatric physicians. *Journal of Rural Health, 18*, 556–562.

Nicholson, J., & Biebel, K. (2002). Commentary on "Community Mental Health Care for Women with Severe Mental Illness Who Are Parents"—The tragedy of missed opportunities: What providers can do. *Community Mental Health Journal, 38*(2), 167–172.

Norquist, G. S., & Regier, D. A. (1996). The epidemiology of psychiatric disorders and the de facto mental health system. *Annual Review of Medicine, 47*, 473–479.

Petterson, S. M. (2003). Metropolitan-nonmetropolitan differences in amount and type of mental health treatment. *Archives of Psychiatric Nursing, 17*, 12–19.

Philo, C., Parr, H., & Burns, N. (2003). Rural madness: A geographical reading and critique of the rural mental health literature. *Journal of Rural Studies, 19*, 259–281.

Posternak, M. A., & Miller, I. (2001). Untreated short-term course of major depression: A meta-analysis of outcomes from studies using wait-list control groups. *Journal of Affective Disorders, 66*(2–3), 139–146.

Provan, K. G., & Milward, H. B. (1995). A preliminary theory of interorganizational network effectiveness: A comparative study of four community mental health systems. *Administrative Science Quarterly, 40*, 1–33.

Provan, K. G., Veazie, M. A., Staten, L. K., & Teufel-Shone, N. I. (2005). The use of network analysis to strengthen community partnerships. *Public Administration Review, 65*, 603–613.

Pulice, R. T., McCormick, L. L., & Dewees, M. (1995). A qualitative approach to assessing the effects of system change on consumers, families, and providers. *Psychiatric Services, 46*(6), 575–579.

Reschovsky, J. D., & Staiti, A. B. (2005). Access and quality: Does rural America lag behind? *Health Affairs, 24*, 1128–1139.

Richardson, L. P., Lewis, C. W., Casey-Goldstein, M., McCauley, E., & Katon, W. (2007). Pediatric primary care providers and adolescent depression: A qualitative study of barriers to treatment and the effect of the black box warning. *Journal of Adolescent Health*, 40(5), 433–439.

Rigler, S. K., Perera, S., Redford, L., Studenski, S., Brown, E. F., Wallace, D., et al. (2003). Urban-rural patterns of increasing antidepressant use among nursing facility residents. *Journal of the American Medical Directors Association*, 4, 67–73.

Robinson, K. M., Buckwalter, K. C., & Reed, D. (2005). Predictors of use of services among dementia caregivers. *Western Journal of Nursing Research*, 27(2), 126–140.

Rosenblatt, R. A., Andrilla, C. H., Curtin, T., & Hart, L. G. (2006). Shortages of medical personnel at community health centers: Implications for planned expansion. *Journal of the American Medical Association*, 295(9), 1042–1049.

Rost, K., Adams, S., Xu, S., & Dong, F. (2007). Rural-urban differences in hospitalization rates of primary care patients with depression. *Psychiatric Services*, 58, 503–508.

Rost, K. M., Akins, R. N., Brown, F. W., & Smith, G. R. (1992a). The comorbidity of DSM-III-R personality disorders in somatization disorder. *General Hospital Psychiatry*, 14(5), 322–326.

Rost, K., Burnam, M. A., & Smith, G. R. (1993a). Development of screeners for depressive disorders and substance disorder history. *Medical Care*, 31(3), 189–200.

Rost, K. M., Dickinson, W. P., Dickinson, L. M., & Smith, R. C. (2006). Multisomatoform disorder: Agreement between patient and physician report of criterion symptom explanation. *CNS Spectrums*, 11, 383–388.

Rost, K., Fortney, J., & Coyne, J. (2005a). The relationship of depression treatment quality indicators to employee absenteeism. *Mental Health Services Research*, 7, 161–169.

Rost, K., Fortney, J., Fischer, E., & Smith, J. (2002a). Use, quality, and outcomes of care for mental health: The rural perspective. *Medical Care Research & Review*, 59, 231–265.

Rost, K., Fortney, J., Zhang, M., Smith, J., & Smith, G. R., Jr. (1999). Treatment of depression in rural Arkansas: Policy implications for improving care. *Journal of Rural Health*, 15, 308–315.

Rost, K., Humphrey, J., & Kelleher, K. (1994a). Physician management preferences and barriers to care for rural patients with depression. *Archives of Family Medicine*, 3(5), 409–414.

Rost, K., Kashner, T. M., & Smith, R. G., Jr. (1994b). Effectiveness of psychiatric intervention with somatization disorder patients: Improved outcomes at reduced costs. *General Hospital Psychiatry*, 16(6), 381–387.

Rost, K., Nutting, P., Smith, J., Coyne, J. C., Cooper-Patrick, L., & Rubenstein, L. (2000a). The role of competing demands in the treatment provided primary care patients with major depression. *Archives of Family Medicine*, 9, 150–154.

Rost, K., Nutting, P., Smith, J. L., Elliott, C. E., & Dickinson, M. (2002b). Managing depression as a chronic disease: A randomized trial of ongoing treatment in primary care. *BMJ*, 325, 934–940.

Rost, K., Nutting, P. A., Smith, J., & Werner, J. J. (2000b). Designing and implementing a primary care intervention trial to improve the quality and outcome of care for major depression. *General Hospital Psychiatry*, 22, 66–77.

Rost, K., Nutting, P., Smith, J., Werner, J., & Duan, N. (2001). Improving depression outcomes in community primary care practice: A randomized trial of the quEST intervention. Quality Enhancement by Strategic Teaming. *Journal of General Internal Medicine, 16,* 143–149.

Rost, K., Pyne, J. M., Dickinson, L. M., & LoSasso, A. T. (2005b). Cost-effectiveness of enhancing primary care depression management on an ongoing basis. *Annals of Family Medicine, 3,* 7–14.

Rost, K. M., Ross, R. L., Humphrey, J., Frank, S., Smith, J., & Smith, G. R. (1996). Does this treatment work? Validation of an outcomes module for alcohol dependence. *Medical Care, 34,* 283–294.

Rost, K. M., & Smith, G. R., Jr. (1997). Improving the effectiveness of routine care for somatization. *Journal of Psychosomatic Research, 43,* 463–465.

Rost, K., Smith, G. R., Burnam, M. A., & Burns, B. J. (1992b). Measuring the outcomes of care for mental health problems: The case of depressive disorders. *Medical Care, 30*(5 Suppl.), MS266–MS273.

Rost, K., Smith, G. R., & Taylor, J. L. (1993b). Rural-urban differences in stigma and the use of care for depressive disorders. *Journal of Rural Health, 9*(1), 57–62.

Rost, K., Smith, J. L., & Dickinson, M. (2004). The effect of improving primary care depression management on employee absenteeism and productivity: A randomized trial. *Medical Care, 42,* 1202–1210.

Rost, K., Smith, R., Matthews, D. B., & Guise, B. (1994c). The deliberate misdiagnosis of major depression in primary care. *Archives of Family Medicine, 3*(4), 333–337.

Rost, K., Williams, C., Wherry, J., & Smith, G. R., Jr. (1995). The process and outcomes of care for major depression in rural family practice settings. *Journal of Rural Health, 11*(2), 114–121.

Rost, K., Zhang, M., Fortney, J., Smith, J., Coyne, J., & Smith, G. R., Jr. (1998a). Persistently poor outcomes of undetected major depression in primary care. *General Hospital Psychiatry, 20,* 12–20.

Rost, K., Zhang, M., Fortney, J., Smith, J., & Smith, G. R., Jr. (1998b). Rural-urban differences in depression treatment and suicidality. *Medical Care, 36,* 1098–1107.

Rueter, M. A., Holm, K. E., Burzette, R., Kim, K. J., & Conger, R. D. (2007). Mental health of rural young adults: Prevalence of psychiatric disorders, comorbidity, and service utilization. *Community Mental Health Journal, 43,* 229–249.

Schultz, S. K., Hoth, A., & Buckwalter, K. (2004). Anxiety and impaired social function in the elderly. *Annals of Clinical Psychiatry, 16*(1), 47–51.

Sears, S. F., Danda, C. E., & Evans, G. D. (1999). PRIME-MD and rural primary care: Detecting depression in a low-income rural population. *Professional Psychology: Research and Practice, 30,* 357–360.

Sederer, L. I., Silver, L., McVeigh, K. H., & Levy, J. (2006). Integrating care for medical and mental illnesses. *Preventing Chronic Disease, 3*(2). Retrieved December 2007 from www.cdc.gov/pcd/issues/2006/apr/05_0214.htm

Sewitch, M. J., Blais, R., Rahme, E., Bexton, B., & Galarneau, S. (2005). Pharmacologic response to depressive disorders among adolescents. *Psychiatric Services, 56,* 1089–1097.

Sexton, R. L., Carlson, R. G., Siegal, H., Leukefeld, C. G., & Booth, B. (2006). The role of African-American clergy in providing informal services to drug users in the rural South: Preliminary ethnographic findings. *Journal of Ethnicity in Substance Abuse, 5*(1), 1–21.

Simmons, L. A., & Havens, J. R. (2007). Comorbid substance and mental disorders among rural Americans: Results from the national comorbidity survey. *Journal of Affective Disorders, 99*, 265–271.

Simon, G. E., Chisholm, D., Treglia, M., Bushnell, D., & LIDO Group. (2002). Course of depression, health services costs, and work productivity in an international primary care study. *General Hospital Psychiatry, 24*(5), 328–335.

Singh, G. K., & Siahpush, M. (2002). Increasing rural-urban gradients in U.S. suicide mortality, 1970–1997. *American Journal of Public Health, 92*(7), 1161–1167.

Smith, J. L., Rost, K. M., Nutting, P. A., & Elliott, C. E. (2001). Resolving disparities in antidepressant treatment and quality-of-life outcomes between uninsured and insured primary care patients with depression. *Medical Care, 39*, 910–922.

Smith, J. L., Rost, K. M., Nutting, P. A., Elliott, C. E., & Duan, N. (2000). A primary care intervention for depression. *Journal of Rural Health, 16*, 313–323.

Smith, J. L., Rost, K. M., Nutting, P. A., Libby, A. M., Elliott, C. E., & Pyne, J. M. (2002). Impact of primary care depression intervention on employment and workplace conflict outcomes: Is value added? *Journal of Mental Health Policy & Economics, 5*, 43–49.

Smith, M., Gerdner, L. A., Hall, G. R., & Buckwalter, K. C. (2004). History, development, and future of the progressively lowered stress threshold: A conceptual model for dementia care. *Journal of the American Geriatrics Society, 52*(10), 1755–1760.

Smith, M., Hall, G. R., Gerdner, L., & Buckwalter, K. C. (2006). Application of the progressively lowered stress threshold model across the continuum of care. *Nursing Clinics of North America, 1*(1), 57–81.

Stern, S., Merwin, E., Hauenstein, E., Hinton, I., Rovnyak, V., Wilson, M., et al. (2008). *The effect of rurality on mental and physical health.* (Under review.)

Stern, S., Merwin, E., & Holt, F. (2001). Survival models of community tenure and length of hospital stay for the seriously mentally ill: A 10-year perspective. *Health Services and Outcomes Research Methodology, 2*, 117–135.

Stiffman, A. R., Pescosolido, B., & Cabassa, L. J. (2004). Building a model to understand youth service access: The gateway provider model. *Mental Health Services Research, 6*(4), 189–198.

Stiffman, A. R., Striley, C., Horvath, V. E., Hadley-Ives, E., Polgar, M., Elze, D., et al. (2001). Organizational context and provider perception as determinants of mental health service use. *Journal of Behavioral Health Services & Research, 28*(2), 188–204.

Topping, S., & Calloway, M. (2000). Does resource scarcity create interorganizational coordination and formal service linkages? A case study of a rural mental health system. *Advances in Health Care Management, 1*, 393–419.

Wallace, A. E., Weeks, W. B., Wang, S., Lee, A. F., & Kazis, L. E. (2006). Rural and urban disparities in health-related quality of life among veterans with psychiatric disorders. *Psychiatric Services, 57*, 851–856.

Wang, J. (2004). A longitudinal population-based study of treated and untreated major depression. *Medical Care, 42*(6), 543–550.

Wang, P. S., Demler, O., Olfson, M., Pincus, H. A., Wells, K. B., & Kessler, R. C. (2006). Changing profiles of service sectors used for mental health care in the United States. *American Journal of Psychiatry, 163*, 1187–1198.

Wang, P. S., Lane, M., Olfon, M., Pincus, H. A., Wells, K. B., & Kessler, R. C. (2005). Twelve-month use of mental health services in the United States results from the National Comorbidity Survey Replication. *Archives of General Psychiatry, 62*, 629–640.

Yuen, E. J., Gerdes, J. L., & Gonzales, J. J. (1996). Patterns of rural mental health care: An exploratory study. *General Hospital Psychiatry, 18*, 14–21.

Zuvekas, S. H. (2005). Prescription drugs and the changing patterns of treatment for mental disorders, 1996–2001. *Health Affairs, 24*, 195–205.

Chapter 6

Improving the Quality of Rural Nursing Care

Kathleen Cox, Irma Mahone, and Elizabeth Merwin

ABSTRACT

The purpose of this chapter is to review the literature on quality of care in rural areas. Keywords related to rural quality of care were used to search CINAHL and MEDLINE databases for articles published between 2005 and 2007 (limited to studies occurring in the United States). The review consisted of a total of 46 articles. Limitations include inconsistent definitions of rural, the use of only articles available to the reviewers, an unclear understanding of the context of many of the studies, and lack of a clear operational definition of quality. The studies were grouped and discussed according to quality of workforce, practice, treatment, interventions, and technology in rural areas. Each study's contribution to the understanding of quality health care in rural areas and to determining what was effective in improving staff, patient, or organizational outcomes in rural areas was considered. This chapter also offers a discussion of ethical issues and data quality in rural research. Issues for future research include a focus on patient safety, mental health issues, and the use of technology to improve quality of care in rural areas. Future research should also focus on demonstration studies of model applications. The nursing profession has a unique opportunity to conduct research that will contribute to the development of knowledge that will ultimately improve the quality of health and health care for individuals in rural communities.

Keywords: rural; nursing; research; quality; outcomes; quality improvement

INTRODUCTION

Quality of care has been defined by the Institute of Medicine (1990) as "the degree to which health services for individuals and populations increase the likelihood of desired health outcomes and are consistent with current professional knowledge" (p. 4). The quality of health care in rural America falls far short of what it should be (Institute of Medicine, 2005). Core health care services in rural areas have been constrained by access issues, shortages of qualified health professionals, financial barriers, and an underresourced infrastructure. The Institute of Medicine has taken the lead in addressing quality-of-care issues in health care services nationally (Institute of Medicine, 2005). Their well-known aims identified in 2001 for all quality health care is to make care safe, effective, patient centered, timely, efficient, and equitable. Furthermore, the Institute of Medicine is taking the lead in addressing the unique health problems and special challenges of quality health care in rural America (Institute of Medicine, 2005). The final report from this initiative, titled *Quality through Collaboration: The Future of Rural Health*, addresses the need to improve the quality of both personal health care and the health care of the rural population as a whole, and to take into account the special characteristics and unique strengths of rural communities. This report recommends establishing a stronger quality-improvement support structure that involves adapting quality-improvement knowledge and tools to the unique characteristics and strengths of specific rural communities. It also clearly recommends greater flexibility and assistance in the coordination and improvement of quality of health care in rural areas.

In addition to the Institute of Medicine model with the six aims described above, other models have been used to study quality of care in rural settings. Thies and Ayers (2004) used the Donabedian framework of structure-process-outcomes to study service learning in nursing education at a small rural college. The inputs-outputs-outcomes logic model framework was used to evaluate a school-based teenage pregnancy prevention program in a rural community (Hulton, 2007). In a study of breast health in rural communities, Lane and Martin (2005) found that a logic model served as an excellent framework for developing a program that integrates service, practice, and research. Another framework that has been applied to rural health is the vulnerable populations conceptual model (Leight, 2003).

METHODOLOGY

Keywords related to rural quality of care were used to search CINAHL and MEDLINE databases for articles published between 2005 and 2007. Combining keyword searches for *quality, nursing, research,* and *rural* yielded 34 English-language articles; combining *nursing, research, rural,* and *outcomes* yielded 28 English-language; combining *nursing, research, rural,* and *quality of care* yielded 16 English-language articles; and combining *nursing, research, rural,* and *quality improvement* yielded 5 English-language articles published between 2005 and 2007. The key-word searches yielded a total of 83 English-language articles published between 2005 and 2007. Forty-eight articles remained after the elimination of duplicates and non-U.S. articles. Forty-six articles were accessible at UVA libraries and were analyzed for this report on nursing research on rural quality of care.

Limitations of this review include inconsistent definitions of *rural,* the use of only articles available to the reviewers, an unclear understanding of the context of many of the studies, and the lack of a clear operational definition of *quality.*

RESEARCH AREAS RELATED TO RURAL QUALITY OF CARE

Several studies focused on the education of providers or other workforce issues, as well as the education of clients. Rhyne, Daniels, Skipper, Sanders, and VanLeit (2006) evaluated the impact of attending a rural health program as part of professional education on individuals' future practice in rural settings. There were no differences in rural practice settings as the location of practice between nurses who completed such a program and a control group who did not. However, sample size was identified as a concern. Technology as a tool for education was described by Stanton and colleagues (2005) in their descriptive study of an Internet-based graduate nursing program focusing on case management. The challenges of technology were one of the problem areas faced by the students in the program, while increased access to graduate education was a strength. Wilson (2005) evaluated a management development educational program and demonstrated significant change in expected turnover among managers of health facilities.

Another study (Lea, Johnson, Ellingwood, Allan, Patel, et al., 2005) reported on a multiyear pilot project that used telemedicine to conduct clinical evaluations and consultations related to genetics. Although there was a low response rate on provider and patient satisfaction surveys, the program was well received. Anderko, Bartz, and Lundeen (2005) evaluated the effectiveness of a health and wellness intervention on advanced practice nurses' practice and on clients' outcomes in a nursing practice-based research network composed of nursing centers. Client knowledge improved and advanced practice nurses also improved their "assessment of physical activity and nutritional promotion" behaviors (p. 754).

There has been several studies related to the shortage of health professionals in many rural communities. Two studies included surveys of nurse practitioners in one state. Lindeke, Jukkala, and Tanner (2005) surveyed nurse practitioners and determined that there were obstacles to practice that lasted over time. They call for improving the work environment to better meet rural populations' health care needs. Green and Davis (2005) surveyed the population of nurse practitioners in Louisiana regarding the impact of nurse practitioners' caring behaviors on patient satisfaction. There were no differences in caring behaviors between nurse practitioners practicing in rural and urban areas.

A particularly well-designed study of nursing shortages in rural areas by Cramer, Nienaber, Helget, and Agrawal (2006) compared the need for RNs to the employment of RNs in 66 counties with hospitals in the state of Nebraska. Using secondary data and California-mandated staff-to-patient ratios as a measure of need, this study found greater shortages of RNs in rural areas when need for RNs was compared with RNs actually employed. The authors call for staffing targets specific to the needs for rural areas. Another study by Jiang, Stocks, and Wong (2006) compared two different data sources with information on staff-to-patient ratios and found differences for "small, rural, or nonteaching hospitals" (p. 187). However, the relationship between these variables and selected patient outcomes revealed similar relationships, although the strength of the relationships differed. The findings of this study suggest the importance of choice of data sets for secondary data studies and the need to examine the consistency of information between data sets when more than one provides information for the variable of interest.

PRACTICE, TREATMENT, AND INTERVENTIONS

The studies on practice, treatments, and interventions in rural areas involved a variety of patient populations, disease entities, interventions, staff and patient education programs, and initiatives and were grouped according to setting (acute care, nursing home, or community). The six goals of the Institute of Medicine mentioned earlier (care that is safe, effective, patient centered, timely, efficient, equitable) were considered in the review of the studies. Consideration was also given to each study's contribution to our understanding of quality health care in rural areas, and to effectiveness in improving staff, patient, or organizational outcomes in rural areas.

HOSPITALS

Disaster Preparedness/Patient Safety in Rural Health Care Facilities

Two studies demonstrate efforts to improve safety for individuals in rural areas. The goal of the Manley and colleagues (2006) study was "to assess the attitudes and experiences of rural hospital emergency departments (EDs) regarding threat preparedness and response to actual events" (p. 81). A team of subject matter experts developed a large pool of questions. The domains "dealt with all-hazard disaster experiences, frequency, type, and impact on the hospital; priorities and beliefs regarding where time and money should be spent on disaster training; self-assessment of preparedness for various types of disasters; and a very brief set of descriptive hospital characteristics" (p. 81).

A 20-question survey was sent to the ED nurse managers in the 1,975 hospitals that comprised the sample. After the original mailing of the survey, two additional mailings were sent to those who had not yet responded. The overall response rate was 48%. The results indicated "that rural hospitals have limited surge capacity" (Manley et al., 2006, p. 84). Many rural hospitals would be overwhelmed with as few as 10 critically ill or injured victims. Emergencies that would be considered routine in urban settings would be considered full-scale disasters in rural areas. The authors suggested that hospitals must move away from individual hospital preparedness and proceed to "active participation in a community-wide response" (p. 86).

Singh, Singh, Servoss, and Singh (2007) focused on system processes and patient safety in a primary care facility. The researchers adapted a Failure Modes and Effects Analysis (FMEA) to involve all team members in the identification and prioritization of safety and quality problems. The authors noted that the FMEA process is made up of 8 steps and is "time consuming, costly, and requires considerable expertise and experience" (p. 174). An anonymous survey was sent to staff in two rural primary care practices in New York State. Results indicated that 94% of staff at each practice completed the survey on their own time. A list of priorities was identified for each site. Comparisons were made among provider, nursing, and administrative groups. There was a 53% concordance at one site and 30% at the second site; however, there was only a 20% concordance among sites. The authors concluded that "the modified FMEA approach shows promise as a technique for identifying the most serious threats to patient safety in rural primary care practices" (p. 177).

Palliative Care in Rural Hospitals

In 1997, the Robert Wood Foundation created the program, Promoting Excellence in End-of-Life Care, to address deficiencies in care that is provided for patients in the final stages of life. From 1998 to 2004 the program provided funding and technical assistance for 22 demonstration projects located in both rural and urban areas. Byock, Twohig, Merriman, and Collins (2006) described the program impact of these 22 projects with respect to the practicality of palliative care service integration into existing clinical care settings, the availability and use of palliative care services, quality of care, and costs of care. The practicality of these models is suggested by the fact that hosting and adopting institutions sustained or expanded 20 of the 22 models. The availability and use of services is suggested by the fact that projects reached diverse populations "defined by a variety of diagnoses, ages, socioeconomic status, and location" (p. 140). Additionally, populations that would have had limited access to palliative care included "prison inmates; renal dialysis patients; Native Americans and Native Alaskans; African American patients in various settings; inner city medically underserved patients; and persons with serious mental illness" (p. 140). Quality of care is suggested by the implementation of new standards and clinical protocols. Finally, costs of care were "financially neutral or associated with measurable savings" (p. 142). The authors concluded that "creative, careful realignment of existing health system resources can improve the ability to meet patient and family needs without increasing costs" (p. 145).

Staff Education to Decrease Urinary Tract Infections in a Rural Hospital

The results of Ribby's (2006) study indicated that staff education was effective in decreasing UTIs in patients with indwelling catheters. An attractive poster was developed and left on nursing units for a period of 7 days. The poster was approved for continuing education units and "focusing on alternatives to urinary catheterization, early discontinuance of catheters, and proper insertion and care techniques" (p. 272). The study was conducted in a 650-bed level II trauma center in the South that was part of the third largest rural health system in the United States. As a result of the educational intervention there were 548 fewer UTIs in 2003 than had been reported in 2002. The use of innovative posters and videos may be an effective way to educate staff in rural hospitals to improve patient outcomes and to achieve the Institute of Medicine's goal of providing effective and efficient care.

COMMUNITY HEALTH

Nursing Intervention Processes in Nurse-Managed Clinics

Macnee and colleagues (2006) "evaluated the accomplishment of the Nursing Outcomes Classification outcome 'health-seeking behavior' in five nurse-managed clinics" (p. 243). The study was conducted in nurse-managed clinics located in northeastern Tennessee. Nurse practitioners in the clinics evaluated 556 patients for health-seeking behavior. Of the 556 patients who were evaluated, the majority (69%) were female and the average age was 28. Information about the providers' perceptions of their level of knowledge of the patients was also collected. Interestingly, the nurse practitioners indicated "they had very limited knowledge of 30% of patients" (p. 245). Nurse practitioners in student health service "rated their knowledge of patients the lowest while providers in the public high school clinic rated their knowledge of patients the highest" (p. 245). In addition, "knowledge of patients was significantly related to total health seeking score" (p. 245). The ratings of health-seeking behavior increased with the practitioner's knowledge of patients and also older patients. Results of this study indicate that health-seeking behavior may be valuable in evaluating nurse practitioner practice. This study also illustrates how nurse practitioners in nurse-managed clinics contribute to meeting the health care needs of individuals in rural areas.

Mental Health and Dementia in Rural Communities

There is evidence that depression may be more prevalent in rural and frontier patients than in nonrural patients (National Rural Health Association, 2007). The purpose of Fisher and Copenhaver's (2006) pilot study was to assess the prevalence of mental health disorders and cognitive impairment among rural older adults living in a public housing facility in Mount Union, Pennsylvania located in Huntingdon County where 69% of the population is rural. Individual interviews consisted of a "health history, review of current and past medical problems, past psychiatric illness or hospitalizations and review of current medications" (p. 29). The sample consisted of 38 older adults of which the mean age was 72. The majority were women (70%) and were White (95%). Results of the analysis indicated that there were "high correlations among the PRIME-MD, MADRS, GAS, and SF36" (p. 30). Findings indicated that depressive disorders were identified in 50% (n = 10) of participants. Of the patients who had depressive disorders, 25% were identified with major depression, 20% were identified with minor depression, and 5% were identified with dysthymia. In addition to the depressive disorders, cognitive impairment was identified in 15% of participants. The author acknowledged that limitations include the lack of randomization, self-selection of participants, reliance on self-reported data, small sample size, and no validations of instruments in the rural setting. However, findings support the PRIME-MD as possibly the most useful assessment tool "because it delivers a clear diagnosis and is extensively used in primary care" (p. 32).

The goals of Kosberg, Kaufman, Burgio, Leeper, and Sun's (2007) "exploratory study were to develop a research methodology for reaching a rural group of caregivers and to learn whether or not there are differences in the caregiving experiences" (p. 6) of African American and White family caregivers of dementia patients in rural Alabama. The caregiving stress model provided the theoretical basis for the study. A cross-sectional survey that consisted of a structured interview was used for data collection. Participants in the study came from 39 of the 45 rural counties in the state. A probability sampling strategy based on a power analysis was used to recruit a total of 141 study participants of which 67 were African American and 74 were White. The sample ranged in age from 22 to 82 with a mean age of 52.

"Using random digit dialing, the researchers located and interviewed rural dementia caregivers which is an understudied population" (p. 17). The methodology provided the researchers with a probability sample. Findings indicated that "white caregivers were more likely to be married and older, used acceptance and humor as coping styles, and had fewer financial problems" (p. 3), and "African American caregivers gave more hours of care, used religion and denial as coping styles, and were less burdened" (p. 3). Random digit dialing is an innovative methodology that may be used in other studies to reach rural caregivers.

End-of-Life and Palliative Care Programs in Rural Communities

Since "25% of the elderly in the United States live in rural communities" (Rural Assistance Center, 2008, para. 1), it is essential that quality end-of-life and palliative care services are available to elderly individuals in rural areas. In the review of the literature, two studies were found that focused on end of life and palliative care. VanVorst and colleagues (2006) conducted a study "to describe health care personnel's perceptions of care provided to dying patients and identify potential approaches to improving end of life care in rural health care facilities" (p. 248). The anonymous survey included an ordinal scale and open-ended questions on "beliefs about the effectiveness of and satisfaction with end-of-life care and the difficulties in identifying dying patients" (p. 249). The study was conducted in two rural practice-based research networks in Colorado and Kansas. A total of 363 surveys were returned. Of those surveys, 195 (54%) were from Colorado and the remaining 168 (46%) were from Kansas. Half of the personnel who responded to the survey "reported that palliative care could be improved at their facility (50.3%)" (p. 249). The majority (84%) were satisfied that palliative care is provided and 85% were satisfied that "patients are informed about care options" (p. 249). In response to the question about transition from curative to palliative care, 30% believed that the transition "was frequently or always too late" (p. 249). Seventy-six percent reported that "health care personnel do a good job of identifying a dying patient" (p. 250). Respondents indicated that there are barriers to initiating palliative care including "family members' avoidance of issues around dying," difference in opinion among health care personnel, and "patients' avoidance of issues around dying" (p. 251).

Schrader, Nelson, and Eidsness (2007) presented a profile of South Dakota palliative care teams. The researchers conducted a survey to determine the composition of palliative care teams, self-reported level of expertise, resources utilized for consultation, and perceived challenges and opportunities that face them in providing end-of-life care. Invitations were sent to 786 health care organizations of which 15% responded. Forty-nine teams of two or more individuals registered for the conference. Of the 49 teams, 40 completed surveys at the beginning and close of the conference. Of those 40 teams, 35 (88%) indicated that nursing was represented on the teams. Only 6% reported that a physician was part of the team. Social work, chaplaincy, volunteers, and pharmacy were other disciplines represented on teams. Respondents indicated that they would like to have other disciplines such as chaplaincy, pharmacy, and medicine added to the team. Results of the survey revealed that "42% of the team member's time was devoted to palliative care" (p. 38). The authors suggested that the insight gained from the survey of teams will increase the ability to enhance end-of-life care for rural residents in South Dakota. The insight may also increase the ability to enhance end-of-life care for rural residents in other states.

Impact of Medical Assistive Devices on Quality of Life of Rural Residents

Two studies explored the impact of medical assistive devices on the quality of life of rural residents. The purpose of Sossong's (2007) study was to determine if knowledge of implantable cardioverter defibrillators and uncertainty predict quality of life in individuals living with these devices. Selder's life transition theory provided the theoretical foundation for the study that was conducted in a cardiac clinic in a large rural northeastern state. The study used a "descriptive correlational design to investigate the relationships among implantable cardioverter defibrillator knowledge, uncertainty, and quality of life" (p. 100). The sample consisted of 90 implantable cardioverter defibrillator recipients of which 98% were White. The average age of the sample was 65 with a range of ages 36–88. Findings indicated that there were "statistically significant relationships between uncertainty and quality of life, but knowledge of implantable cardioverter defibrillators was not significantly related to uncertainty or quality of life" (p. 99). Also, "younger recipients reported a lower quality of life" (p. 99). "Education, ejection fraction, number of implantable cardioverter defibrillator shocks since implantation, and number of months since implantation were unrelated to knowledge of implantable cardioverter defibrillators, uncertainty, or quality of life" (p. 99).

Dickerson and Kennedy (2006) examined the "support-group experiences of individuals with sleep apnea who use continuous positive airway pressure devices (CPAP)" (p. 114). The goal was to determine shared meanings of seeking help by attending a CPAP support group and to describe difficulties group members encounter while accommodating CPAP treatment. The methodology for this study was Heideggerian hermeneutics, which is "a phenomenological approach whereby researchers uncover the common meaning of individuals' experiences through analysis of semi-structured interviews" (p. 116). The study was conducted in 12 urban medical centers and 5 rural hospitals. The sample consisted of 12 males and 5 females for a total of 17 participants of which the average age was 58.4 with a range from 40 to 73. The four themes that emerged were "becoming motivated to persist with help from the group" (p. 117), "accommodating to the device" (p. 118), "listening to and telling stories to gain practical knowledge" (p. 119), and "implementing a support group as a caring community" (p. 119). The authors indicated that "future research could examine the motivation to persist and how to encourage accommodation in people who do not attend support groups" (p. 121). "Interventions could be designed by implementing knowledge from support groups and features from this study to facilitate accommodation of CPAP into a person's lifestyle" (p. 121).

Breast Cancer Programs for Women in Rural Communities

Two studies explored programs to increase knowledge and awareness of breast cancer. The Health Belief Model provided the theoretical underpinning for Hall and colleagues' (2005) experimental posttest only control group study that was conducted to determine the effectiveness of breast cancer education program in the Arkansas Mississippi River Delta. The goal of the education program was to enhance breast cancer knowledge, beliefs, and behaviors. The sample consisted of 53 African American women of which 30 were in the experimental group and 23 were in the control group. After participants in the experimental group completed the educational intervention, participants in both groups completed the Breast Cancer Knowledge Test (BCK) and the Breast Cancer Screening Belief Scales (BCSBS). Results of the analysis indicated that the experimental group's mean score on the BCK test was significantly higher than the control group's as was the experimental group's mean score on the BCSBS. The mean score on the confidence scale of the BCSBS was also higher for the experimental group. The authors cautioned that the findings cannot be generalized to African American women in different geographic areas. Hall and colleagues suggested that replication is needed to evaluate the external validity of the study. However, the authors indicated that a "multifaceted culturally sensitive breast cancer education program may assist in enhancing African American women's knowledge and beliefs associated with early detection of the disease" (p. 857). These education programs also may be effective in increasing knowledge and beliefs about early detection of other forms of cancer.

Lane and Martin (2005) described the use of a logic model to guide the planning of a regionally based cancer health network. Since nurses play a key role in leading program development, the logic model methodology may be useful in the development of other programs and health networks that may improve outcomes for individuals in rural areas.

Use of Complementary Alternative Medicine in Rural Populations

Two studies focused on the use of CAM in rural populations. The purpose of Shreffler-Grant, Weinert, Nichols, and Ide's (2005) descriptive survey was to "explore use, cost, and satisfaction with the quality and effectiveness of complementary therapy" (p. 323). The study was conducted with older adults living in 19 rural communities in Montana and North Dakota. Power analysis indicated a sample size of 320 participants was required. Therefore, the goal was to interview 60 individuals from each state. The 325 participants were randomly selected from a list purchased from a commercial listing service. Interviews were conducted over a 5-month period.

The majority of the sample were White (95%) and included a slightly higher percentage of men (51%). The majority (83%) were between age 60 and 79. Interestingly, only 17.5% of the sample reported using complementary providers in the past year. Of those who used complementary providers, 54.4% sought care for chronic illness. In addition, of those who used complementary providers, 82.1% visited chiropractors. Further, 84.2% rated the care as good or excellent; and 76.8% reported that the care was quite helpful or extremely helpful with their health or health problem. The range of out-of-pocket costs was no cost to $240 with an average of $57. More than one-third (35.7%) of the sample reported using self-directed complementary practices. Vitamins, minerals, herbs, and magnets were the most frequently used self-directed practices. Self-directed practices were used more often for health promotion (73.9%) than for treatment of health problems.

The authors cautioned that results cannot be generalized to older adults living in other areas since participants in this study were rural residents of two rural states in the same region. The study sample was purchased from a commercial listing service and, therefore, eligible people may have been excluded. Also, data were collected by telephone interview; thus, those without telephones were excluded. The authors noted that the study has implications for "increased efforts to inform and educate rural consumers about safe methods for meeting health needs" (p. 329).

The purpose of another study was "to determine predictors of use of complementary and alternative medicine (CAM) therapies" among patients "with lung, breast, colon, or prostate cancer" in urban and rural communities in Michigan's lower peninsula (Fouladbakhsh, Stommel, Given, & Given, 2005, p. 1115). Andersen's Behavioral Model of Health Services Use provided the conceptual foundation for the study. Data for the secondary analysis came from two federally funded panel studies of cancer patients and caregivers. The sample included an equal number of men and women and consisted of 968 patients who ranged in age from 28 to 98 with a mean age of 70.6. Binary logistic regression was used in the analysis. Results indicated that females used CAM more than males, those who were separated or divorced had a greater tendency to use CAM than widows, and those who were in the early stages of cancer used CAM more than those in the late stages. Further, those patients who had surgery or chemotherapy were more likely to use CAM; however, radiation was not related to the use of CAM. Finally, those patients who experienced "three or more severe symptoms were more likely to use CAM therapies" (p. 1119). Both of these studies provide evidence that patients in rural areas are using CAM therapies. Therefore, it is essential for nurses to assess for CAM use and increase their own knowledge of CAM in order to educate patients about the risks and benefits of CAM.

Health and Safety Programs for Students in Rural Communities

Three studies that demonstrate efforts to improve the health and safety of students in rural areas were identified. The purpose of Horner's (2006) article was "to describe challenges with, and pose solutions for, implementing home visits to improve rural families' home asthma management" (p. 214). Although there are advantages to home visits, scheduling, locating the home, ensuring safety for home visitors, staying in contact with the families, and coping with the home environment were some of the challenges encountered in the pilot study. Solutions for these challenges were identified and incorporated into the implementation procedures for a subsequent larger intervention study. Although the article addressed home visits to improve rural families' asthma management, the strategies offered to confront the challenges of home visiting can be used for home visits in both rural and urban areas.

Winkelstein and colleagues (2006) conducted a study to determine the effectiveness of an asthma education program. The program consisted of a 6-hour training session and was designed to teach rural school nurses how to improve asthma management of children in the school setting using the Precede Health Behavior Model as a theoretical framework. Seven rural counties were randomized to the intervention or control condition. Forty-one schools and 46 school nurses participated. After the educational intervention, the mean asthma knowledge scores of the intervention group "increased from 15.57 points to 17.15

points whereas the mean score of the control group remained at 17.47" (p. 174). The study points to the need to educate rural elementary school nurses, which may ultimately result in the provision of more efficient and effective care for students with asthma in rural communities.

Lee et al. (2007) conducted a cross-sectional nonexperimental study in the small rural community of Monroe County, Kentucky, to describe fine-particle air pollution in a rural high school and other public places. Spectrometers were used to measure the fine-particle concentrations in the high school and 5 public venues. Findings indicated that "PM2.5 concentrations were 19 times higher in the boys' student restroom than the National Ambient Air Quality Standard for outdoor air (670 versus 35 microgram/meter^3)" (p. 224); "the staff restrooms adjacent to the student restroom where staff did not smoke also showed high PM2.5 levels" (p. 224); "average indoor air pollution in the public venues was 158 microgram/meter^3" (p. 226). The study has implications for the development of smoking cessation interventions and research to determine which interventions are most effective in decreasing smoking incidence.

IMPROVING ACCESS AND OUTCOMES

Use of Technology for Delivery of Interventions

Evidence suggests that technology is an effective way to deliver interventions and improve patient outcomes in rural areas. Lea et al. (2005) described the 3-year pilot outreach experience to provide clinical and educational genetics services via telemedicine. The data collected from October 1, 2000, through September 30, 2003, were presented. By the end of the third year, Southern Maine Genetics Services/Foundation for Blood Research, in collaboration with Maine Telemedicine Services (MTS), linked to 24 sites. Over the 3-year period, 93 genetics and related educational programs were presented to over 650 participants; 105 patients and approximately 250 family members received genetic consultations from March 1 through September 30, 2003. Most (64%) patients were pediatric patients. The most common reason for referral was to rule out an underlying genetic syndrome as a cause of developmental delay.

Unfortunately, only 18% of providers and 25% of patients responded to an evaluation of telemedicine sessions. Provider satisfaction received a mean rating of 3.83 on a 4-point scale. Patient satisfaction was rated with an overall mean of 3.56 on a 4-point scale. The authors noted that "telehealth approaches in Maine are enabling equity of access to services for rural, isolated, and underserved populations and introducing efficiency for the delivery of genetics educational and clinical services" (p. 27). The experience in Maine has implications for the development of telegenics models in rural areas in other states.

The purposes of the Carpenter and colleagues (2007) study were "to determine acceptability of a DVD intervention delivery platform and pilot test the efficacy of a new cognitive-behavioral intervention" (p. E2) to relieve hot flashes in women with cancer. A conceptual model developed by Carpenter was used to guide the study. The intervention was pilot tested using a quasiexperimental nonrandomized pretest–posttest design. The study was conducted at two sites, both of which were affiliated with the National Cancer Institute, one located in the Midwest and the other located in the southeast.

Of the 49 women who were recruited, 26 were at the first site while 23 were at the second site. Forty women completed the study. Of the 40 participants, 25% were African American and the remaining 75% were White. The mean age of the sample was 54.42. Only one participant was at high risk for breast cancer; the remaining participants were breast cancer survivors.

Results of the analysis indicated that the DVD was an acceptable way to deliver the intervention. In addition, results indicated that the intervention "significantly decreased (improved) worst severity, worse bother, Hot Flash Related Daily Interference Scale (HFRDIS) total, and HFRDIS average" (p. E5). Since the study had an unblinded single-group design, the investigators indicated that a placebo effect may have affected the findings and also note small sample size and the lack of a measure of the frequency of the intervention in the analysis as limitations. The investigators acknowledged that the intervention "will need refinement before it is ready for additional testing and use in clinical practice" (p. E7). However, the investigators suggested "other interventions could be developed and disseminated via a DVD platform" (p. E7).

Outreach Efforts and Programs in Rural Communities

The review of the literature indicated that there have been outreach efforts and programs that were initiated to meet the health care needs of individuals in rural communities. Crow, Lakes, and Carter (2006) described a cost-benefit analysis for expanding services at a rural health mobile medical unit. The expanded services would include a nursing case management program for low-income high-risk diabetic patients. The cost-benefit analysis suggested that the case management program could "potentially net a savings of $149,544 annually" (p. 97). "The benefit cost ratio was determined to be 2:9" (p. 97). "A benefit cost ratio greater than 1 generates more benefits than costs" (as cited in Penner, 2004). The data support the effectiveness of a nursing case management program in decreasing costs.

Hayward (2005) noted that "nursing schools are challenged to develop innovative methods for reaching older adults" in the community (p. 29). The author described the development of the Senior HealthMobile project that was started in July 2000 and funded through a grant award from the Quentin N. Burdick Interdisciplinary Program of the U.S. Department of Health and Human Services. Services for older adults can be accessed through their primary provider, senior centers, or self-referral. Interventions are delivered in teams of students from a variety of disciplines such as nursing, physical and occupational therapy, and dietetics. Group teaching sessions on a variety of topics are also presented.

In describing the outcomes, Hayward (2005) indicated that as of May 2004, "156 students from 9 disciplines had participated on the ISU Senior Health-Mobile, representing 9 disciplines, providing mobile services throughout rural Southeastern Idaho in an expanded 5 county area" (p. 32). In addition, services were provided to more than 750 individuals. Finally, a large percentage of the students expressed a desire to work with older adults in a rural community after graduation. The project is an example of an innovative outreach effort that not only benefits the elderly in a rural community, but also students who need the experience with older individuals.

Nursing Homes in Rural Communities

In the review of the literature, few studies were found that focused on nursing homes in rural communities. However, Hutt, Pepper, Vojir, Fink, and Jones (2006) focused on pain medication prescribed for patients in nursing homes in rural communities. Specifically, the researchers described the development and testing of the Pain Medication Appropriateness Scale (PMAS). Of significance is the finding that "the mean total PMAS was 64% of optimal," which suggests a generally poor score (p. 231). Findings of the study have implications for the inclusion of pain as a quality measure in nursing homes and point to the need for the use of evidence-based practices to improve pain management in nursing homes. Finally, few studies were found in the review of the literature that related to nursing homes in rural areas. Thus, nursing homes in rural areas may provide fertile ground for future nursing research.

SPECIAL ISSUES IN RURAL RESEARCH

Technology

Technology can be a transformational tool to improve health and health care, and rural areas stand to benefit enormously from the technology infrastructure being built (Institute of Medicine, 2005). Telehealth has been advanced as a means of augmenting health care services in areas experiencing generalist and specialist shortages, such as rural and geographically disperse areas (Demiris, Shigaki, & Schopp, 2005; Farrell & McKinnon, 2003). Technology may serve to improve health education, support and patient-provider connectedness in rural areas. The services gaps and health care access problems often encountered in rural areas may also be addressed in the future through the Internet versus the traditional face-to-face method (Farrell & McKinnon, 2003). Because people who live in rural areas far from large tertiary care centers have their own views of health care and health care practices, mechanisms that are culturally appropriate, reliable, and valid are needed to identify successful telehealth strategies in the delivery of mental health care services in rural areas. Holmes-Rovner and colleagues (2001), who have pioneered much of the work in patient decision aids, suggest that computer information technology could be used to provide important information for decision making via online patient choice modules. Initial testing in the School of Nursing–Rural Health Care Research Center has demonstrated the feasibility of using Web-based professional training, computer-based patient education, and interactive mental health screening with rural populations (Akan, Farrell, Zerull, Mahone, & Guerlain, 2006; Mahone, Farrell, Zerull, Guerlain, Akan, Hauenstein, et al., 2007). Technology has also been used in nursing education. One study examined Web-based graduate education in rural nursing case management, identifying both the difficulties and advantages encountered by students and faculty (Stanton et al., 2005).

Ethics

Although rural communities are enormously diverse, Nelson and colleagues (2007) discuss health care ethical issues based on common features of rural communities. They describe the work and accomplishments of the Coalition for Rural Health Care Ethics, an interdisciplinary group of ethicists who have defined rural health care ethics and proposed an ethics agenda with the goal of improving quality of care in rural America. They call for "evidence-informed, rural-attuned research" (Nelson, Pomerantz, Howard, & Bushy, 2007). Ethical issues in rural research are also discussed by Pierce and Scherra (2004), who cite social desirability factors, study participants' sense of obligation to participate and their desire not to alienate the providers who referred them, and lack of anonymity as ethical issues.

Data Quality

Concerns about data quality in rural research are also discussed by Pierce and Scherra (2004). The unique problems of rural research may compromise the process and the outcomes. They raise issues such as the use of appropriate tools, location of appropriate participants, rural health issues, and environmental barriers.

The "outsider" status of the researcher must be accounted for, yet use of insider connections may also challenge the integrity of the data.

CONCLUSIONS

Although great strides have been made in conducting research to improve the quality of health care in rural communities, much work remains to be done. Specifically, there is a need for additional research in rural health care facilities to determine best practices for patient safety and improvement in patient outcomes. Because of the prevalence of mental health issues in rural communities, study is needed to determine best practices to meet the mental health needs of individuals in rural communities. Research is also needed to identify mental health programs and services that provide cost-effective quality care for individuals in rural communities. Because of the high incidence of smoking and use of smokeless tobacco among rural youths (National Rural Health Association, 2007), research is needed to determine which smoking cessation programs are most effective. The use of technology to deliver interventions holds much promise, and additional research is needed to determine effective technological interventions for a variety of conditions. There continues to be a need for a better understanding of the role that service supply and accessibility and other factors play in the patterns and outcomes of rural long-term care. Research efforts should be directed at conducting studies that increase understanding of these issues.

Finally, Bigbee and Lind (2007) note that rural and frontier communities are often more different than they are alike. The authors stressed that rural researchers must be extremely cautious in making generalizations. They suggested that in addition to exploring rural-urban comparisons, the rich diversity within and among rural areas and groups must be explored.

It is important to keep in mind that the issues faced by health care providers and individuals in rural areas differ from those in urban areas. "Economic factors, cultural and social differences, educational shortcomings, lack of recognition by legislators and the sheer isolation of living in remote rural areas all conspire to impede rural Americans in their struggle for health and health care services" (National Rural Health Association, 2007, para. 1). The nursing profession has a unique opportunity to conduct research that will contribute to the development of knowledge that will ultimately improve the quality of health and health care of individuals in rural communities.

With improved research, demonstration studies of model applications, and evidence of outcomes, technologies could serve as tools to achieve the major goals of preventing, assessing, and treating health conditions in the rural communities. Ethical issues that have already been identified must be considered in future studies, with an eye to understanding them to a greater extent within the rural context. The special concerns regarding data quality discussed previously must also be considered with an emphasis on keeping the research as valid and reliable as possible while coming to a greater understanding of the factors associated with health care in the rural population.

ACKNOWLEDGMENT

The authors thank Ashley Jacob for providing expert research assistance for this review.

REFERENCES

Akan, K. D., Farrell, S. P., Zerull, L. M., Mahone, I. H., & Guerlain, S. (2006, April 28). *eScreening: Developing an electronic screening tool for rural primary care.* Presented at the 2006 Institute of Electrical and Electronics Engineers Systems and Information Engineering Design Symposium, International Forum for Student Design Projects. Charlottesville, University of Virginia.

Anderko, L., Bartz, C., & Lundeen, S. (2005). Practice-based research networks: Nursing centers and communities working collaboratively to reduce health disparities. *Nursing Clinics of North America, 40*(4), 747–758.

Bigbee, J. L., & Lind, B. (2007). Methodological challenges in rural and frontier nursing research. *Applied Nursing Research, 20*(2), 104–106.

Byock, I., Twohig, J. S., Merriman, M., & Collins, K. (2006). Promoting excellence in end-of-life care: A report on innovative models of palliative care. *Journal of Palliative Medicine, 9*(1), 137–151.

Carpenter, J. S., Neal, J. G., Payne, J., Kimmick, G., & Storniolo, A. M. (2007). Cognitive-behavioral intervention for hot flashes. *Oncology Nursing Forum Online, 34*(1), 37.

Cramer, M., Nienaber, J., Helget, P., & Agrawal, S. (2006). Comparative analysis of urban and rural nursing workforce shortages in Nebraska hospitals. *Policy, Politics, & Nursing Practice, 7*(4), 248–260.

Crow, C. S., Lakes, S. A., & Carter, M. R. (2006). A nursing case management program for low-income high-risk diabetic clients: A projected cost-benefit analysis. *Lippincott's Case Management, 11*(2), 90–98.

Demiris, G., Shigaki, C. L., & Schopp, L. H. (2005). An evaluation framework for a rural home-based telerehabilitation network. *Journal of Medical Systems, 29*(6), 595–603.

Dickerson, S. S., & Kennedy, M. C. (2006). CPAP devices: Encouraging patients with sleep apnea. *Rehabilitation Nursing, 31*(3), 114–122.

Farrell, S. P., & McKinnon, C. (2003). Technology and rural mental health. *Archives of Psychiatric Nursing, 17*(1), 20–26.

Fisher, K. M., & Copenhaver, V. (2006). Assessing the mental health of rural older adults in public housing facilities: A comparison of screening tools. *Journal of Gerontological Nursing, 32*(9), 26–33.

Fouladbakhsh, J. M., Stommel, M., Given, B. A., & Given, C. W. (2005). Predictors of use of complementary and alternative therapies among patients with cancer. *Oncology Nursing Forum Online, 32*(6), 1115–1122.

Green, A., & Davis, S. (2005). Toward a predictive model of patient satisfaction with nurse practitioner care. *Journal of the American Academy of Nurse Practitioners, 17*(4), 139–148.

Hall, C. P., Wimberley, P. D., Hall, J. D., Pfriemer, J. T., Hubbard, E., Stacy, A. S., et al. (2005). Teaching breast cancer screening to African American women in the Arkansas Mississippi River Delta. *Oncology Nursing Forum Online, 32*(4), 857–863.

Hayward, K. S. (2005). Facilitating interdisciplinary practice through mobile service provision to the rural older adult. *Geriatric Nursing, 26*(1), 29–33.

Holmes-Rovner, M., Llewellyn-Thomas, H., Entwistle, V., Coulter, A., O'Connor, A., & Rovner, D. R. (2001). Education and debate: Patient choice modules for summaries of clinical effectiveness: A proposal. *BMJ, 322*(7287), 664–667.

Horner, S. D. (2006). Home visiting for intervention delivery to improve rural family asthma management. *Journal of Community Health Nursing, 23*(4), 213–223.

Hulton, L. J. (2007). An evaluation of a school-based teenage pregnancy prevention program using a logic model framework. *Journal of School Nursing, 23*(2), 104–110.

Hutt, E., Pepper, G. A., Vojir, C., Fink, R., & Jones, K. R. (2006). Assessing the appropriateness of pain medication prescribing practices in nursing homes. *Journal of the American Geriatrics Society, 54*(2), 231–239.

Institute of Medicine. (1990). *Medicare: A strategy for quality assurance.* Washington, DC: National Academy Press.

Institute of Medicine. (2005). *Quality through collaboration: The future of rural health.* Washington, DC: National Academic Press.

Jiang, H. J., Stocks, C., & Wong, C. J. (2006). Disparities between two common data sources on hospital nurse staffing. *Health Policy and Systems, 38*(2), 187–193.

Kosberg, J. I., Kaufman, A. V., Burgio, L. D., Leeper, J. D., & Sun, F. (2007). Family caregiving to those with dementia in rural Alabama: Racial similarities and differences. *Journal of Aging and Health, 19*(1), 3–21.

Lane, A. J., & Martin, M. T. (2005). Logic model use for breast health in rural communities. *Oncology Nursing Forum Online, 32*(1), 105–110.

Lea, D. H., Johnson, J. L., Ellingwood, S., Allan, W., Patel, A., & Smith, R. (2005). Telegenetics in Maine: Successful clinical and educational service delivery model developed from a 3-year pilot project. *Genetics in Medicine, 7*(1), 21–27.

Lee, K., Hahn, E. J., Riker, C. A., Hoehne, A., White, A., Greenwell, D., et al. (2007). Secondhand smoke exposure in a rural high school. *The Journal of School Nursing, 23*(4), 222–228.

Leight, S. B. (2003). The application of a vulnerable populations conceptual model to rural health. *Public Health Nursing, 20*(6), 440–448.

Lindeke, L., Jukkala, A., & Tanner, M. (2005). Perceived barriers to nurse practitioner practice in rural settings. *Journal of Rural Health, 21*(2), 178–181.

Macnee, C. L., Edwards, J., Kaplan, A., Reed, S., Bradford, S., Walls, J., et al. (2006). Evaluation of NOC standardized outcome of "health seeking behavior" in nurse-managed clinics. *Journal of Nursing Care Quality, 21*(3), 242–247.

Mahone, I., Farrell, S. P., Zerull, M. L., Guerlain, S., Akan, D., Hauenstein, E. J., et al. (2007). *Electronic screening for mental health in rural primary care: Feasibility and user testing.* Unpublished manuscript.

Manley, W. G., Furbee, P. M., Coben, J. H., Smyth, S. K., Summers, D. E., Althouse, R. C., et al. (2006). Realities of disaster preparedness in rural hospitals. *Disaster Management & Response, 4*(3), 80–87.

National Rural Health Association. (2007). *What's different about rural health?* Retrieved December 18, 2007, from http://www.nrharural.org/about/sub/different.html

Nelson, W., Pomerantz, A., Howard, K., & Bushy, A. (2007). A proposed rural healthcare ethics agenda. *Journal of Medical Ethics, 33*(3), 136–139.

Penner, S. J. (2004). *Introduction to health care economics & financial management.* Philadelphia: Lippincott Williams & Wilkins.

Pierce, C., & Scherra, E. (2004). The challenges of data collection in rural dwelling samples. *Online Journal of Rural Nursing and Health Care, 4*(2), 10.

Rhyne, R. L., Daniels, Z. M., Skipper, B. J., Sanders, M., & VanLeit, B. J. (2006). Interdisciplinary health education and career choice in rural and underserved areas. *Medical Education, 40*(6), 504–513.

Ribby, K. J. (2006). Decreasing urinary tract infections through staff development, outcomes, and nursing process. *Journal of Nursing Care Quality, 21*(3), 272–276.

Rural Assistance Center. (2007). *Aging.* Retrieved December 18, 2007, from http://www.raconline.org/info_guides/aging/

Schrader, S. L., Nelson, M. L., & Eidsness, L. M. (2007). Palliative care teams on the prairie: Composition, perceived challenges & opportunities. *South Dakota Medicine, 604,* 47–149, 151–153.

Shreffler-Grant, J., Weinert, C., Nichols, E., & Ide, B. (2005). Complementary therapy use among older rural adults. *Public Health Nursing, 22*(4), 323–331.

Singh, R., Singh, A., Servoss, T. J., & Singh, G. (2007). Prioritizing threats to patient safety in rural primary care. *Journal of Rural Health, 23*(2), 173–178.

Sossong, A. (2007). Living with an implantable cardioverter defibrillator: Patient outcomes and the nurse's role. *Journal of Cardiovascular Nursing, 22*(2), 99–104.

Stanton, M., Crow, C., Morrison, R., Skiba, D. J., Monroe, T., Nix, G., et al. (2005). Web-based graduate education in rural nursing case management. *Online Journal of Rural Nursing and Health Care, 5*(2), 15.

Thies, K. M., & Ayers, L. R. (2004). Community-based student practice: A transformational model of nursing education. *Nursing Leadership Forum, 9*(1), 3–12.

Van Vorst, R. F., Crane, L. A., Barton, P. L., Kutner, J. S., Kallail, K. J., & Westfall, J. M. (2006). Barriers to quality care for dying patients in rural communities. *Journal of Rural Health, 22*(3), 248–253.

Wilson, A. A. (2005). Impact of management development on nurse retention: Leadership for the future. *Nursing Administration Quarterly, 29*(2), 137–145.

Winkelstein, M. L., Quartey, R., Pham, L., Lewis-Boyer, L., Lewis, C., Hill, K., et al. (2006). Asthma education for rural school nurses: Resources, barriers, and outcomes. *Journal of School Nursing, 22*(3), 170–177.

Chapter 7

Nursing Patient Safety Research in Rural Health Care Settings

Deirdre K. Thornlow

ABSTRACT

Adverse events occur in virtually all health care arenas, and while rural health care settings are no exception, these facilities often face unique financial burdens and personnel shortages. That may hamper patient safety efforts. Many of the interventions recommended to improve patient safety have largely been based on research conducted in urban hospitals. This chapter demonstrates the extent and type of nursing research being conducted to advance rural-specific patient safety research. The studies were conducted in various settings, with topics ranging from error reporting in hospitals to safety screening in the community. Limitations of these works are discussed, and the chapter offers guidance for a future nursing research agenda to include the need for interdisciplinary research; cross-national and international collaboration; and, at a minimum, the necessity for nurse researchers to sample rural hospitals in larger studies of patient safety.

Keywords: patient safety; rural; nursing; research

INTRODUCTION

Since the publication of the Institute of Medicine reports on quality and patient safety, investigators and providers alike have been searching for ways to improve the delivery and safety of patient care. The search may now reach a frenzied pace as the Centers for Medicare and Medicaid Services begin in October 2008 to eliminate payments for hospital-acquired infections and other "never events," defined as preventable adverse events that should never occur in health care (Centers for Medicare and Medicaid Services, 2007). This change in reimbursement is designed to motivate hospitals and nursing leaders to commit attention and resources to patient safety.

Patient safety may be defined as the prevention or amelioration of adverse outcomes or injuries stemming from the processes of health care (Cooper, Gaba, Liang, Woods, & Blum, 2000). The goal of patient safety efforts, therefore, is to reduce the risk of injury or harm to patients from the structures or processes of care (Battles & Lilford, 2003). While identifying factors that are associated with the provision of safe patient care is critical in all settings, this chapter focuses on patient safety research conducted by nurses in rural health care settings.

Challenges in Rural Health Care

Health care errors and compromised patient safety occur in virtually all health care arenas, and rural health care settings are no exception, yet rural communities, with nearly 20% of the population, confront a different mix of health and health care needs than urban and other less rural areas. Rural populations tend to be older than urban populations, and they experience more limitations in daily activities as a result of chronic conditions. Rural populations also show poorer health behaviors (i.e., higher rates of smoking and obesity and lower rates of exercise) than most urban populations (Institute of Medicine, 2005). In general, smaller, poorer, and more isolated rural communities experience greater difficulties ensuring the availability of high-quality health care services (Institute of Medicine, 2005).

A major reason for this difficulty is that rural facilities have little available capital and negative Medicare margins. Many small rural hospitals struggle to remain open in the face of accelerating capital and technical requirements, a dwindling population base, lagging economic growth, disproportionate rates of the uninsured and underinsured, health professional shortages, and federal reimbursement policies that disadvantage smaller, low-volume hospitals (Pink et al., 2004). These financial burdens pose serious implications for rural health care. First, the vast majority of federally designated health professions and nurse shortage areas exist in rural areas (Wakefield, 2002). Second, rural hospitals may commit fewer resources to information technology, an oft-cited component of patient safety programs, because of the financial burden of implementation (Ohsfeldt et al., 2005). In a recent study, Brooks, Menachemi, Burke, and Clawson (2005) reported that rural hospitals averaged 30% utilization for 10 IT applications installed to reduce medical errors, compared to 48% utilization in urban hospitals. In a related study, the same research team found that system-affiliated rural hospitals were significantly more likely than stand-alone hospitals to have installed information technology applications designed to reduce medical error. Financial barriers to successful IT implementation were noted by 69% of the stand-alone hospitals but only 20% of the system-affiliated rural hospitals (Menachemi, Burke, Clawson, & Brooks, 2005). Similarly, Longo and colleagues (2007) reported lower rates of computerized physician order entry implementation in rural hospitals than in urban hospitals, though differences in implementation of other patient safety initiatives were reduced over time.

Private organizations and federal agencies have begun to recognize the unique challenges of rural health care facilities. The Leapfrog Group explicitly excludes rural hospitals from their expectations, and the federal government has developed the Medicare Rural Hospital Flexibility Program, which designates small rural hospitals critical access hospitals (CAH) if they have fewer than 25 acute care beds, are located more than 35 miles from a hospital or another critical access hospital, and agree to limit stays to 96 hours or less. A hospital also may be certified a critical access hospital if it is deemed a necessary provider of health care services to area residents. The CAH program has revised the reimbursement model for rural hospitals from a prospective payment system to a fee-for-service model. Examining the impact of this reimbursement change, Casey and Moscovice (2004), in a national telephone survey of 72 critical access hospitals, found that cost-based Medicare reimbursement was a key factor in the ability of CAHs to fund additional staff, training, and equipment to improve patient care. Even so, Casey and Moscovice noted that critical access hospitals face many challenges in implementing quality improvement and safety initiatives; these challenges include "limited resources, low volume of patients, small staffs, and inadequate information technology" (p. 327), clearly all challenges that affect the delivery of nursing care.

Overview of Rural Patient Safety Research

Interventions recommended to improve patient safety have largely been based on research conducted in urban hospitals, though characteristics such as nurse staffing, organization of care, and even patient characteristics are often significantly different in rural facilities, limiting the ability to generalize findings (Burstin & Wakefield, 2003; Coburn et al., 2004). Recognizing the differences, researchers in various disciplines have sought to identify relevant patient safety interventions for small rural hospitals and other rural health care settings. For example, Coburn and colleagues (2004) assessed the current evidence regarding rural hospital patient safety and identified a set of patient safety interventions that the majority of small rural hospitals could readily implement. They concluded that many of the identified patient safety interventions were relevant to all types of hospitals, not just rural hospitals, but some, such as transfers to other facilities, were especially relevant to rural areas. In a follow-up study, Casey and investigators (2006) examined the relevance of and ability to implement these interventions in small rural facilities. The investigators found that adverse drug events and patient falls posed the greatest problems for rural facilities. In terms of interventions, the hospitals ranked using two patient identifiers and reading back verbal orders as easy to implement, but maintaining 24-hour coverage by a pharmacist as difficult to implement.

This chapter reviews relevant work of nurse researchers who have contributed to advances in patient safety research in rural health care. Reviewed patient safety studies range from reviews of care delivery models to analysis of processes developed to address clinical patient safety issues. Limitations of these works are also discussed, and guidance for a future nursing research agenda to follow up on the studies reviewed is offered.

METHODOLOGY

Several electronic searches of PubMed and CINAHL were conducted using different combinations of the keywords *patient safety, rural, nursing,* and *research.* These searches were limited to articles published since 2002, because those published prior to that year were focused less on patient safety than on quality, as was determined in a prior review (Merwin & Thornlow, 2006). An electronic search of CINAHL for articles published in English in 2002–2007 using the MeSH heading *patient safety* and the keyword *rural* (allowing the word *rural* to appear anywhere in the text) yielded 249 articles. Limiting articles to research resulted in 97 articles, and further limiting articles to those in which the truncated keyword *nurs* appeared reduced the number to 44.

A search of PubMed using the keywords *patient safety* and *rural,* and limiting articles to those published in English in 2002–2007, yielded 133 articles. Inclusion of the keyword *research* resulted in 83 articles, and inclusion of the keyword *nursing* further limited the number to 27. Of the 44 CINAHL and 27 PubMed articles, 5 articles were duplicates, which yielded 66 articles for review. Supplemental PubMed searches using combinations of the above keywords plus the terms *critical access hospitals, medical errors,* and *adverse events* were then conducted to locate additional research studies. This search yielded an additional 18 articles for review, of which 4 were duplicates.

Articles were selected for full review if they reported a research study and were available through a health science library or over the Internet. Articles that appeared to be conceptual or policy oriented, highlighted case examples, or focused on improving practice or quality of care with only an indirect relationship to patient safety were not selected for further review. In general, if the study focused primarily on nursing practice or nursing personnel, the article was selected for review. Articles were then reviewed so that patient safety research studies specific to nursing practice in rural health care settings could be identified. Research articles without a focus on rural health care settings and articles that did not at least sample rural health care settings were excluded. Several nurse researchers conducted studies in countries other than the United States, including Australia, Canada, and the United Kingdom, and these studies were included in the review.

These methods resulted in a total of 20 studies that were reviewed to determine the breadth of rural-specific patient safety nursing research. Research settings ranged from home health care to critical access hospitals. The articles were categorized by the research topic, regardless of the rural health care setting in which the research occurred, as review by topic served to highlight varied approaches to studying similar concepts.

LITERATURE REVIEW

Patient Safety Research in Rural Health Care Settings

As point-of-care providers, nurses in rural health care settings are in a position to design systems and processes that protect patients and accomplish the goals of patient safety management: to minimize the likelihood of errors and maximize the likelihood that errors will be intercepted before or when they occur (Battles & Lilford, 2003). In all, half of the studies ($n = 10$) were conducted in rural hospitals, 10% ($n = 2$) in nursing homes, and 40% ($n = 8$) in rural communities (Figure 7.1). Fifty percent of the research addressed medication safety and error reporting, with other topics ranging from safety screening to describing care environments (Figure 7.2).

Error Recognition and Reporting

Five patient safety studies addressed provider recognition and/or reporting of medical errors. The studies were descriptive: two research teams conducted survey research and/or participant interviews, and three reviewed incident report forms.

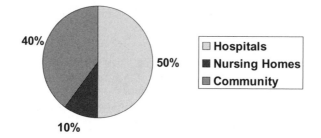

FIGURE 7.1   Rural nursing patient safety research (by setting).

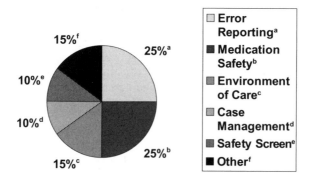

FIGURE 7.2   Rural nursing patient safety research (by topic).

Cook, Hoas, Guttmannova, and Joyner (2004) conducted a three-year cross-sectional multimethod study in 29 small rural hospitals in nine Western states to examine the organizational processes used to recognize medical errors and assign responsibility to resolve patient safety issues. The investigators used surveys, questionnaires, interviews, and case studies to gather data from nurses, physicians, administrators, pharmacists, and other health care workers (63% of the respondents were nurses). Participants were initially asked to complete a culture assessment and an error reporting tool; each subsequent month participants received two or three case studies involving errors and adverse events and were asked to identify the errors and describe protocols and "best practices" that might increase patient safety. The research team conducted quarterly follow-up interviews and at the 16-month point distributed an additional patient safety survey, which included questions about organizational culture, attitudes, and assignment of responsibility for patient safety. Respondents identified medication errors as the most common type of error, followed by patient falls. Interestingly, participants did not agree on what constituted error or what kinds of errors should be reported or disclosed to patients, and only 22% of respondents believed that physicians, nurses, pharmacists, and administrators shared equal responsibility for patient safety—most perceived patient safety to be primarily a nursing responsibility.

The Centers for Medicare and Medicaid Services funded a survey to assess health care providers' perceptions of medication errors in Nevada and Utah (Huber, 2002). Survey topics included error frequency, error detection and prevention, error reporting, patient harm, contributing factors, and nature of the error. Participating facilities ranged from rural/frontier facilities to large urban teaching hospitals. Response rates varied by facility, ranging from 10% to 80%, with a total of 825 responses received from 25 hospitals. Over 71% of the respondents were nurses, 11% were pharmacists, and 7% were physicians. Just over 30% of respondents had observed a medication administration error during the past month, yet only 33% of those respondents indicated that they had completed a written report for the errors described. The likelihood of reporting depended on the level of injury. For example, 79% of the errors described as having resulted in injury to the patient resulted in a written report, while near misses, or those errors that were prevented from reaching the patient, were 60% less likely to be reported.

Three research teams used incident reports to collect data on medication errors and other preventable adverse events. In the first study, a multidisciplinary team that included both pharmacists and nurses reported findings from a voluntary medication error reporting program developed by the Nebraska Center for Rural Health Research in six CAHs (Jones, Cochran, Hicks, & Mueller, 2004). Participating hospitals mailed copies of medication error reports to the Nebraska Center for Rural Health Research monthly, and the center then compiled quarterly summaries to allow each CAH to compare its reports by severity type, phase of the medication use process, contributing factors, and causes to those of its peers and to those in MEDMARX, a national medication error reporting program. Workshops were held to emphasize the importance of learning from errors by identifying system sources of variation in medication use and initiating change to achieve best practices. Results from the critical access hospitals indicated similar findings to those of MEDMARX: 99% of the medication errors reported by the Nebraska CAHs were not harmful, were most often cases of omission, and most frequently originated in the administration phase. However, the CAHs reported significantly smaller proportions of near-miss errors and errors originating in the prescribing phase than did MEDMARX. The investigators concluded that the limited presence of pharmacists in CAHs may have been a barrier to catching errors in the prescribing phase, implementing double checks, and learning about and improving medication use systems.

Madegowda, Hill, and Anderson (2007) examined medication error reporting in relation to differences in staffing patterns in a 100-bed rural midwestern hospital. The retrospective nonexperimental descriptive study compared three nursing shifts with regard to the number of reported medication errors, the types and severity of errors, and the units on which errors occurred. Staffing at the hospital was based on census, not acuity, and the pharmacy was not staffed around the clock. Investigators reviewed 120 of the 133 medication errors reported at the hospital over a 12-month period. No pediatric, incomplete, or illegible reports were included. Investigators found that the most frequent errors occurred with intravenous medications (53.5%). The majority of reported medication errors occurred on a general medical-surgical nursing unit (66.7%), and the fewest occurred in the operating room (1.7%). The majority of reported medication errors occurred on the second shift (52.5%), and one-third (32.5%) were classified as omissions. On a scale of 1 to 9, most reported medication errors were rated 3 (80%), defined as a medication error that reached the patient but caused no harm.

Using medical record review and incident reports, Schade, Hannah, Ruddick, Starling, and Brehm (2006) conducted a prospective cohort study of all adult discharges from a 200-bed rural acute care hospital in West Virginia during a 6-month period; outpatient and emergency department discharge records were included in the study. The investigators sought to determine the proportion of adverse drug events detected in chart surveillance that were reported through incident reporting. The team focused on the use of rescue drugs (e.g., narcotic reversal agents, vitamin K, Kayexalate, Benadryl, Digibind, intravenous/oral glucose solutions) as a means to flag potential adverse drug events. Of the 3,572 chart audits completed, 1,011 involved rescue drug administration. An adverse drug event was believed to have occurred in 109 of these cases, yet fewer than 4% of all adverse drug events involving the use of rescue drugs were reported. The investigators concluded that the rate of underreporting of preventable adverse drug events was comparable to published rates and that chart surveillance of adverse drug events to detect underreporting in small rural hospitals was feasible, albeit labor intensive.

In these studies, low response rates are a cause for concern. In the Huber (2002) study, response rates varied greatly, with no information on response bias. While response rates for the initial culture assessment and error reporting surveys in the study conducted by Cook and colleagues (2004) averaged 75% and 71% respectively, the response rate for the final culture survey averaged only 41%. The investigators did not address differences in response rates between the initial and final surveys, so response bias is unknown. Cook and team did use multiple methods, also known as triangulation, to address questions related to hospital patient safety, but because they did not articulate a priori hypotheses, systematic elimination of probable alternative explanations was not undertaken, which limited the strength of the study. Neither Huber nor Cook and colleagues validated survey instruments or compared the results to objective measures of adverse drug event rates. Although Madegowda, Hill, and Anderson (2007) reported interrater reliability and content validity for their self-developed Medication Error Audit Form, criterion-related validity was not addressed. This is important, as these investigators and an additional research team (Jones et al., 2004) used incident report forms to calculate the number of medication errors. Calculating incidents and errors in this manner is not always accurate because it is not known whether additional medication errors occurred but were not reported, as evidenced by Huber (2002) and Schade and colleagues (2006). Further research regarding medication error reporting, especially using validated instruments, is needed.

Findings from the five studies suggest that written incident reports for medication errors and adverse events are not always generated (Huber, 2002; Schade et al., 2006), and near misses are unlikely to be reported (Huber, 2002; Jones et al., 2004). Studies have found that lack of anonymity and fear of punishment may be reasons for not reporting (Mayo & Duncan, 2004; Weissman et al., 2005; Westfall, Fernald, Staton, VanVorst, West, et al., 2004). These factors may be even more pronounced in small rural health care facilities, where staff often perceive a lack of confidentiality; this is an area for further research. The impact of lack of pharmacist coverage on nursing and patient care is an additional area for further research. Jones and colleagues (2004) cited the lack of an on-site pharmacist as a potential barrier to medication error reporting, and Madegowda and colleagues (2007) reported that it may have even been a contributor to medication errors, as the most frequent errors occurred with intravenous medications; on a general medical-surgical nursing unit; and on the second shift, when the pharmacy was closed. Another area that would benefit from investigation is the use of information technology to support patient safety. For example, cost-effectiveness analyses and criterion-related validity studies of computerized error surveillance would be worthwhile. Computerized surveillance can be used to electronically capture or record adverse events, offering a much less labor-intensive method than chart review and enabling less burdensome reporting to external comparative agencies such as MEDMARX. Although many rural facilities currently lack the IT infrastructure to support such initiatives, the time saved and performance improvement information garnered from computerized surveillance may generate a significant return on investment.

Medication Safety

Five nursing studies addressed medication safety. In one study, pharmacists and nurses collaborated to describe medication safety infrastructure in critical access hospitals. Another team explored staff perceptions and concerns about medication safety in nursing homes, and a third team of researchers conducted a series of community studies to evaluate the medication administration practices of nurses working in rural and remote areas of Queensland, Australia.

Using self-assessment questionnaires and on-site visits, Winterstein and colleagues (2006) assessed the medication safety infrastructure in critical access hospitals in Florida. The self-assessment questionnaire included the Institute for Safe Medication Practices (ISMP) Medication Safety Self-Assessment and questions that addressed compliance with the four 2003 Joint Commission patient safety goals pertinent to medication use, use of health information technology, and processes related to medication use. Site visits were also conducted to inspect pharmacy facilities and interview personnel with safety responsibilities. Composite findings reflecting structural and procedural components were used to represent the CAH medication safety infrastructure. Based on investigator-weighted importance and feasibility, the researchers concluded that CAH improvement efforts should focus on enhancing medication order review systems, standardizing procedures for handling high-risk medications, promoting a culture of patient safety, creating seamless care, and investing in information technology.

In a qualitative study, Vogelsmeier, Scott-Cawiezell, and Zellmer (2007) interviewed 76 staff members from five nursing homes in three midwestern states regarding their perceptions of and concerns about medication safety processes; staff participated in informant interviews and focus groups. While the study was not rural specific, a rural nursing home was included in the sample. Investigators found common impediments to safe medication practices, including issues related to communication, competing demands for attention, and the challenges of a paper-based medication administration record. Staff provided insight as to how technology might improve the nursing home medication process; however, no description of differences among hospital types and their medication safety use processes was provided.

As in other rural health care settings, medication safety is a common topic in community and home care settings. Three studies evaluated the medication administration practices of nurses working in rural and remote areas of Queensland, Australia. In the first study, survey data were collected from 176 nurses to test a model linking organizational climate to unsafe medication administration behaviors (Fogarty & McKeon, 2006). Structural equation modeling was used to measure and model organizational climate, which was comprised of individual distress, quality of life, and individual morale. The study examined the possible mediating role of stress and morale in unsafe practices, as an earlier investigation by the same team had found that stress and morale were related to errors. The current study, however, only weakly supported these hypotheses. The only variable that directly contributed to medication errors was self-reported procedural violations, which explained 24% of the variance. While individual distress was found to be significantly associated with self-reported violations, neither individual distress, morale, nor quality of life directly contributed to medication errors.

In a follow-up study, members of the same team examined organizational factors that contributed to procedural violations by nurses during medication administration (McKeon et al., 2006). To understand why nurses deviated from established procedures, quantitative and qualitative data were collected from 627 nurses working in rural and remote areas. The data were used to build a model to demonstrate how organizational variables can produce work conditions unfavorable to following best practice standards. The model accounted for 19% of the variance in self-reported procedural violations. A higher level of knowledge was found to be associated with lower levels of violations. Heavier workloads and higher expectations by doctors were associated with a higher number of violations. Qualitative comments supported the conclusions drawn from the model and helped to explain the observed associations.

In the final study, investigators examined the medication practices of registered and enrolled nurses in rural and remote areas of Queensland after the introduction of the Australian Health (Drugs and Poison) Regulation Act (Hegney, Plank, Watson, Raith, & McKeon, 2005). The act increased the scope of nursing practice by allowing certified nurses to administer and supply (but not prescribe) drugs listed in a formulary to certain patients, using protocols. The impetus for the legislation was the recognition that many nurses in rural and remote areas were already practicing in this expanded role, albeit without the cover of legality and, more importantly, without the requisite training. Hegney and investigators (2005) compared practice patterns of nurses who had been through postgraduation training and certification for an expanded medication practice role to practice patterns of nurses who had not been certified. Certified registered nurses were more likely to believe they could explain the side effects of medications to clients in a way the clients were able to understand and thus were more likely to provide this information, and to more frequently use interpreters when needed.

Two of the studies used participant surveys or questionnaires (Fogarty & McKeon, 2006; Hegney et al., 2005), one used participant interviews and focus groups (Vogelsmeier et al., 2007), and three used a combination of quantitative survey data and either qualitative interview data or on-site observations (McKeon et al., 2006; Winterstein et al., 2006). The Australian research teams used survey data to design predictive models (Fogarty & McKeon, 2006; McKeon et al., 2006). The Queensland Public Agency Staff Survey was used to measure organizational climate, individual stress and morale, and quality of working life and had been validated in prior studies that assessed those characteristics in personnel working in the health care industry in Queensland. The primary characteristics of the tested models were derived from the structure of the survey, but with two outcome variables added—violations and errors. In the final study, the investigators developed their own questionnaire. A threat to the validity of the Australian studies is that response rates ranged from 31% to 33%, thus raising questions about nonresponse bias.

The hospital and nursing home studies (Vogelsmeier et al., 2007; Winterstein et al., 2006) highlight the need to explore the relationship of information technology to rural health care facility medication safety, while the Australian studies provide examples of patient safety research that can be conducted in rural communities. One way to improve upon the Australian studies is to assess the relationship between medication processes and patient outcomes. For example, research is needed to determine whether the provision of patient education is related to patient outcomes (e.g., adherence to medication, rehospitalization) and whether organizational climate and medication safety practices influence patient outcomes (and if so, to what extent). Further investigations should focus on enhancing medication order review systems and investigating barriers to safe medication practices.

Environment of Care

Three studies addressed the environment of care in rural health care facilities. One descriptive study provided rich detail on intensive care characteristics in critical access hospitals, another compared rural nursing homes that had created dementia special care units (DSCUs) to those that had not created such units, and the final study tested a theoretical model linking quality of the nursing practice environment to a culture of patient safety. Two of the three studies were conducted in Canada.

In hope of shedding light on the characteristics of intensive care units in critical access hospitals, Freeman, Walsh, Rudolf, Slifkin, and Skinner (2007) conducted semistructured interviews with nursing directors at 63 critical access hospitals to ascertain nurse-to-patient ratios, equipment availability, unit census, patient characteristics, and certification status of intensive care unit nursing staff. Although all 845 CAHs in the United States were included in the sampling frame, only 159 hospitals were considered to be providing intensive care at the time; a third were telephoned in random order to participate in interviews. Half of the respondents' hospitals were located in the Midwest, with a mean size of 23.6 beds. Two different pilot-tested semistructured interview forms were used: one for the 67% of hospitals that provided intensive care services in a unit designed or staffed specifically for that purpose, and another for the remaining hospitals that provided intensive care services using monitored medical-surgical beds or beds located for easy patient observation. The study provided detailed descriptive data on the characteristics of CAH intensive care units. Of interest is the fact that the majority (60%) maintained a nurse-to-patient ratio of 1:2, although ventilator patients received 1:1 care. The majority of the hospitals (71%) also reported that a physician was always on site and that they staffed respiratory therapists around the clock. All respondents listed more than one hospital to which they could transfer patients who needed care they could not provide, with an average transfer distance of 64 miles (range 12–309). Sixteen percent reported transferring patients to a hospital 100 or more miles away.

Morgan, Stewart, D'Arcy, and Werezak (2004) used analysis of variance to compare eight rural nursing homes that had created DSCUs to eight same-sized rural nursing homes that had not created DSCUs. The study was conducted in rural nursing homes with 100 beds or fewer in the Canadian province of Saskatchewan. Outcome measures included the Physical Environmental Assessment Protocol, which includes measures of resident safety and security, and the Nursing Unit Rating Scale, which assesses the social environment of dementia care settings. Investigators found that nursing homes with DSCUs were more supportive in maximizing awareness and orientation, safety and security, regulation of stimulation, quality of stimulation, opportunities for personal control, and continuity of self than nursing homes without DSCUs. Nursing homes with DSCUs also were found to have greater separation of residents with dementia from other residents for activities of daily living and programming, and better control of nonmeaningful stimulation. The authors concluded that rural nursing homes with DSCUs had measurable environmental benefits compared to facilities without DSCUs. These findings would have been strengthened had the investigators compared overall facility demographics and characteristics and then broken out residents with dementia to obtain more accurate comparisons. Further, although the team used previously tested instruments, they adjusted the Physical Environmental Assessment Protocol rating from a 5-point scale to a 13-point scale, on the premise that an earlier study of dementia care settings in the United States lacked sensitivity due to limited score ranges. This may have affected the findings.

Armstrong and Laschinger (2006) conducted an exploratory study in a small rural community hospital in central Canada to test a theoretical model linking the quality of the nursing practice environment to a culture of patient safety. The investigators used a predictive nonexperimental design and surveyed 79 nursing staff members regarding their work conditions. Three different tools were used: the Conditions of Work Effectiveness Questionnaire, which measures six components of structural empowerment (Laschinger, Finegan, Shamian, & Wilk, 2001); the Practice Environment Scale of the Nursing Work Index (Lake, 2002), which measures Magnet characteristics such as nursing participation in hospital affairs; and the Safety Climate Survey (Sexton, Thomas, & Helmreich, 2000). The investigators attained a response rate of 51% ($n = 40$) and concluded that strong relationships existed not only between structural empowerment and Magnet hospital characteristics, but also between the structural empowerment and Magnet hospital characteristics and perceptions of patient safety culture within the unit. This study provides a particularly strong example of well-designed rural patient safety research. The strengths are threefold: first, the investigators developed and tested a hypothesis; second, they used previously tested instruments to survey staff nurses; and third, the researchers attained a response rate of 51%, considered above average for survey research.

These three studies provide examples of varied methods that can be used to study the influence of nursing practice environments on patient safety in rural health care settings. Descriptive data on the characteristics of critical access hospitals and other rural health care facilities, like that provided by Freeman and colleagues (2007), can be used by administrators and policy makers to inform key funding decisions for essential resources. Similar studies or recurrent surveys can be conducted to routinely assess the characteristics of the more than 800 critical access hospitals in the United States, which would allow a comparative database of rural facilities to be compiled. This can be useful for benchmarking national quality and safety data. And finally, Morgan and colleagues' (2004) comparative study examined the relationship of a nursing care delivery model to patient safety outcomes, while Armstrong and Laschinger (2006) applied widely used instruments designed to measure safety climate and workplace environment to a rural health care setting. A logical next step would be to examine the relationship of these rural health care nursing practice environments to patient outcomes.

Case Management

Two nursing studies addressed case management models in rural health care settings. Further review of these studies found that they were not related to patient safety as defined by Cooper and colleagues (2000) and Battles and Lilford (2003), therefore only a brief overview is provided here. In one study, nurse researchers conducted a multisite randomized controlled trial to determine whether individualized nursing care management could decrease stress among pregnant women at risk for or in abusive relationships (Curry, Durham, Bullock, Bloom, & Davis, 2006). Two prenatal clinics in the Pacific Northwest and rural Midwest were included in the sample. In the other study, Horner (2006) described using home visits as part of an asthma self-management program for rural families who had a school-aged child with asthma. The intervention study involved randomizing the sample by elementary schools, then by baseline and postintervention data collection. The author concluded that home visits provided an opportunity to individualize asthma education to meet family needs and helped to retain participants for the year-long study.

Nurses have historically focused on the broader concept of patient safety in nursing intervention research, as evidenced in these two studies, yet specific patient safety outcome measures are often not included in the study designs. Incorporating these outcome measures into future studies is warranted; doing so will enable researchers to examine the association between nursing case management programs and the reduction of risk of injury or harm to patients.

Safety Screening

Two studies addressed the screening of patients for safety; one examined preterm infants, and the other the homebound elderly. Earlier studies had shown that preterm infants are at risk for apnea, bradycardia, and oxygen desaturations when they are transported from hospital to home in traditional car seats. To address such safety concerns, the American Academy of Pediatrics issued policy statements recommending that all infants less than 37 weeks of gestational age be monitored in a car seat safety test prior to hospital discharge. Williams and Martin (2003) surveyed newborn nursery and neonatal intensive care units across the United States to evaluate the status of the implementation of car seat safety testing programs. The sample included rural, suburban, and urban hospitals. Wide variation existed in testing program status: 19% of level III nurseries, 9% of level II nurseries, and 78% of level I nurseries had not established an infant car seat safety testing program. Lack of standardization was evident even among those hospitals that had implemented a program. Urban (46%) and rural (37%) hospitals performed car seat testing more often than suburban hospitals (17%), although suburban hospitals ($n = 9$) were underrepresented in the sampling frame in comparison to urban ($n = 25$) and rural ($n = 20$) hospitals. Further, level I nurseries, the least skilled level for newborn care, are generally found in the smallest facilities, but because nurseries were not differentiated by size, car seat testing status could not be determined in small rural health care facilities or critical access hospitals.

In the second safety screening study, Tanner (2003) assessed the safety risk for 288 homebound older adults living in rural Alabama. A variety of questions from existing home safety instruments, including those available from the Department of Health and Human Services, which were adapted to determine risk in participants, were used to assess home safety. Descriptive statistics provided a snapshot of the rural patients receiving home care: participants ranged from 60 to 100 years in age, with a mean of 78; their average educational level was 7.7 years, and 66.4% had a ninth-grade education or less. The investigators found that 44% of respondents were at moderate to high risk for falls: 41.3% of respondents had no grab bars around the bath/shower and toilet in the bathroom, 61% reported nocturia, and 59.7% reported use of medications that caused dizziness. The investigator offered no information regarding the validity or reliability of the instrument used.

These two studies point to ways in which nursing expertise can inform and benefit rural communities' safety efforts. Williams and Martin's (2003) survey regarding car seat safety testing programs expands the definition of patient safety but highlights the importance of transitions in care, a national patient safety goal (Joint Commission, 2007). Tanner's (2003) assessment of the rural homebound elderly most notably highlights their risk for falls and certainly suggests a number of areas where interventions such as installing grab bars in showers, assessing medication use, and addressing nocturia may prevent occurrence. Tailoring interventions to rural elderly residents' educational level would be necessary.

As evidenced by these two studies, nursing expertise is beneficial in developing rural community and public health programs, such as safety and other health care screenings. Additional research on patient safety screening programs and their effect on process redesign and patient outcomes is warranted. And finally, the descriptive data from these and other studies reviewed in this chapter provide a compelling case for the need for additional patient safety research targeted to rural residents. In particular, comparing rural communities with urban and suburban communities and differentiating remote critical access hospitals from other hospitals would help to inform policy makers and funding agencies about the unique needs of rural constituents.

Other Nursing Research in Rural Health Care Settings

The final three studies represent an eclectic mix, from a correlational study of prenatal care to surgical outcomes research to a nursing intervention study to reduce falls. In the cross-sectional correlational study, Chandler (2002) tested predictors of late entry into prenatal care among 176 women in a rural county in California. Social support, behavioral risk, and structural or demographic variables as well as acceptance of pregnancy were tested as predictors. Previously tested instruments were used to measure pregnancy-specific social support from family and friends and from partners and acceptance of pregnancy; during an interview, subjects were queried about behavioral risks such as poor nutrition and alcohol intake. Stress, lack of family support, Medicaid enrollment, age under 20 or over 34, low acceptance of pregnancy, and lack of a high school diploma were all predictors of late entry into prenatal care.

Williams and Jester (2005) retrospectively analyzed data from 381 patients admitted to a medium-sized general hospital in the United Kingdom with hip fracture to ascertain whether increased delays from admission to surgical repair were correlated with mortality in the first postoperative year. The hospital served a population of 320,000 in both urban and rural settings. Review of the literature and discussion with expert colleagues informed the decisions of which variables to include in the mortality model (e.g., anesthesia, deep vein thrombosis prophylaxis). Deaths were collected from hospital or community records, as applicable. Using multiple regression analysis, the investigators found no relationship between delayed surgery and postoperative mortality when all other independent variables were controlled; however, cognitive dysfunction and reduced prefracture mobility were both good predictors of increased mortality within the first year. The researchers conceded, however, that no data were available to assess the time between the fracture occurrence and admission to hospital, which may have been a factor in transfer time in rural areas and may have affected outcomes.

In the final study, using a quasiexperimental nonequivalent groups design, Meade, Bursell, and Ketelsen (2006) conducted a six-week nationwide evaluation of the effect of nursing rounds on patients' call light use, satisfaction, and safety. The participating hospitals were from 14 states, representing both rural and urban populations; the number of inpatient beds ranged from 25 to more than 600. Hospitals were given the option of rounding every hour or every two hours, and each hospital could determine which staff member would be ultimately responsible for rounding (e.g., CNA). The investigators found that a protocol that incorporated specific actions into nursing rounds conducted either hourly or once every two hours could reduce the frequency of patients' call light use, increase their satisfaction with nursing care, and reduce falls. The investigators concluded that a patient's perception of the quality of nursing care depends largely on the nurse's ability to meet the patient's needs. Several limitations, however, weakened this study. First, of the 22 hospitals that participated, 8 were excluded from the analysis because of poor reliability in data collection—the investigators could not ensure that every nurse carried out the protocol and recorded data. Furthermore, the researchers could not exclude the possibility that some contamination could have occurred between the experimental and control groups, as float staff may have performed additional rounding on the control groups, and some units experienced management changes over the course of the study. Finally, the use of a quasiexperimental design did not ensure equivalence between groups, and initial group differences may have accounted for the findings. Unit average daily census and nursing hours per patient day were recorded, but the investigators did not ascertain whether significant differences initially existed between the control and experimental groups.

The Chandler study provides an example of public health nursing research, while the Williams and Jester (2005) study provides an example of health services research. As with many studies in health care, Williams and Jester (2005) could not conduct a randomized prospective study because that would have involved deliberately delaying surgery for the control group; the investigators instead conducted a retrospective study using data collected from patient notes and care pathways. Proportional hazard regression analysis, frequently employed in survival analysis, allowed for calculation of the hazard or risk of death based on each independent variable. Additional effectiveness research that addresses surgical care, examines other health care populations, and applies to rural health care settings is needed. Time motion studies to determine how reduced call light use enables nursing staff members to redirect their time and energy to other patient care responsibilities would be interesting and informative, especially in light of the nursing shortage. In conclusion, more well-designed nursing research using sound theoretical frameworks is necessary to evaluate the influence of nursing care processes on patient safety outcomes.

Limitations

The use of multiple search methods represents a comprehensive approach to selecting articles reflective of the type of patient safety research being conducted by nurses in rural health care settings. It should be noted, however, that none of the selection modes for identifying research articles was completely objective—all required subjective decisions regarding the inclusion or exclusion of papers. Selection was challenging because of the broad scope of patient safety research, which is relevant to all clinical subspecialties and to all settings in the health system, and because nursing is a component of almost all patient safety studies; even those studies that did not focus primarily on nursing still had some relationship to nursing care. Only those articles considered relevant to the concept of patient safety, as defined earlier, were reviewed. Likewise, selecting only those studies that addressed patient safety in rural health care settings posed an additional challenge. To ensure that articles were not missed, one search strategy allowed inclusion of the word *rural* anywhere in the text. Although this strategy uncovered mostly national research studies, rural populations were sampled in some studies, and these were included for review. Despite these limitations, the selected studies typify nursing patient safety research conducted in rural health care settings.

Implications for Future Nursing Patient Safety Research in Rural Health Care Settings

Well-designed research using sound theoretical frameworks to evaluate the influence of nursing care processes on patient outcomes is essential. Multimethod studies and clearly linked studies that build on previous findings are especially important. Further research might follow the example of several of the studies reviewed here, such as Morgan and colleagues' (2004) work, which tested models of care to determine their impact on patient safety; Meade and investigators' (2006) study, which tested the effects of a nursing intervention on patient safety; Chandler's (2002) and Tanner's (2003) studies, which provide examples of nursing public health research in rural communities; and Williams and Jester's (2005) study, which provides an example of health services research. Additional research regarding patient safety culture similar to that conducted by Armstrong and Laschinger (2006) is also needed. Although not conducted by nurse researchers, two additional studies addressed patient safety culture in rural health care facilities.

The researchers conducted telephone interviews with administrators and rural health care providers in one U.S. state to assess organizational culture and the readiness of hospitals to adopt patient safety strategies (Demiris, Patrick, & Boren, 2004) and to examine differences between urban and rural facilities' patient safety system implementation over time (Longo, Hewett, Ge, & Schubert, 2007). Exploring the influence of patient safety culture on patient outcomes in rural settings would be an especially important endeavor for nurse researchers.

The majority of the nursing studies reviewed for this chapter addressed medication safety and error reporting. Further investigative efforts should focus not only on factors related to underreporting of medication errors in rural health care facilities, but also on enhancing medication systems and investigating barriers to safe medication practices. This work should be interdisciplinary, however, with Jones and colleagues' (2004) descriptive study serving as a model. Additional studies exploring the impact of lack of pharmacy coverage on nursing and patient care would further inform practice decisions in rural health care settings. In fact, pharmacists have evaluated a novel approach to address their limited after-hours staffing by designing a video verification process to reduce medication errors (Woodall, 2004). This research is exciting and suggests potential opportunities for collaboration between pharmacists and nurses.

Interdisciplinary Collaboration in Rural Patient Safety Research

Information technology in rural health care settings is another area that would benefit from interdisciplinary research. Initial studies conducted by information technologists have found that many rural facilities lack the necessary IT infrastructure to support patient safety (Brooks et al., 2005; Menachemi et al., 2005; Ohsfeldt et al., 2005). As IT becomes available in these rural areas, exploring its impact on patient safety will be critical. In one such study in primary care, information technologists analyzed the impact of introducing electronic medical records on patient safety (Singh, Servoss, Kalsman, Fox, & Singh, 2004). This study exemplifies the type of research in which nurses should be involved. Future collaborative research may also investigate the use of information technology to collect, analyze, and aggregate clinical data that can then be used for point-of-care nursing decisions and made available for reporting to external comparative agencies. Using information technology to help nurses incorporate cutting-edge knowledge and evidence-based care into practice is essential in rural health care facilities that may otherwise lack access to such information.

In addition to pharmacists and information technologists, several investigators from other disciplines have conducted rural patient safety research that is applicable to nursing care. For example, physician investigators piloted a home-based comprehensive geriatric assessment and found that an urban model could be successfully adapted to rural areas (Cravens et al., 2005). In two studies, rural community and primary care patients were queried about their perceptions of harm from medical mistakes and interviewed to ascertain reports of preventable problems and harm (Kuzel, Woolf, Gilchrist, Enge, LaVeist, et al., 2004; Van Vorst et al., 2007). In a series of interviews with emergency department patients, researchers found that patient concerns about medical errors varied by patient and hospital characteristics; four rural hospitals were included in the sample (Burroughs et al., 2005).

Other disciplines' research can serve as a model for nursing research, and the field of rural patient safety research could be more quickly advanced through improved planning and coordination among the many disciplines conducting such research. As this review demonstrates, the topics nurses are interested in studying are similar to those of researchers in other disciplines. Nurses bring considerable expertise to the field of patient safety research, and the contributions of nurse researchers to improving patient safety in rural health care facilities and communities are evident in the literature. Providing further training and encouraging nurses to conduct interdisciplinary research to improve patient safety will amplify these contributions.

It is possible for researchers in universities in rural locations in different states and even in different nations to develop collaborative relationships to advance the field of rural patient safety research. As noted in this review, several nurse researchers have conducted studies in countries other than the United States, including Australia, Canada, and the United Kingdom. Similar interdisciplinary studies are being undertaken throughout the world. For example, investigators in Australia have examined the impact of the Threats to Australian Patient Safety initiative on the incidence of reported errors and the effectiveness of targeted follow-up (Makeham et al., 2006). Researchers in Northern Ireland evaluated the feasibility and long-term outcomes of home versus hospital-initiated thrombolysis in acute myocardial infarction patients (McAleer & Varma, 2006), while Swedish researchers found that patients in urban areas had a higher ejection fraction and fewer symptoms of heart failure 30 days after discharge and a lower one-year mortality rate than patients in nonurban areas—a difference the investigators associated with delay time in prehospital thrombolysis between urban and rural areas in Sweden. Canadian researchers evaluated the effectiveness and safety of procedural sedation and analgesia in a community emergency department that was staffed primarily by family physicians using capnometry (Mensour, Pineau, Sahai, & Michaud, 2006), and occupational therapy researchers in Sweden examined whether active intervention using a checklist for wheelchair checkups increased user satisfaction and decreased accidents, near accidents, and pressure sores (Hansen, Tresse, & Gunnarsson, 2004). Prospects for additional national multisite and international rural patient safety studies should be identified, and federal agencies should support such research, given that global opportunities may exist for improved health care in rural communities.

Finally, at a minimum, researchers must incorporate rural health care communities and facilities into the sampling frame of their national patient safety studies. Comparative yet rural-relevant patient safety research will establish standards and interventions and highlight challenges that are unique to rural communities. Doing so may enhance purchaser and public perceptions of rural hospitals, eventually bolstering their financial stability (Pink et al., 2004). Given the high proportion of the elderly residing in rural areas, The Centers for Medicare and Medicaid Services and other health insurance programs have a compelling interest in ensuring their beneficiaries have access to safe care. The forthcoming change in Medicare reimbursement loudly signals this interest, which should in turn lead to additional funding for patient safety research, particularly for rural-specific patient safety research. Nurse researchers must be involved in conducting this important work. Studies that address patient safety in rural health care have the potential to be lifesaving—not only for patients, but for the rural facilities struggling to remain open amidst substantial challenges.

CONCLUSION

This chapter demonstrates the extent and type of nursing research being conducted to advance rural-specific patient safety research. The studies were conducted in various settings, with topics ranging from error reporting in hospitals to safety screening in the community. More well-designed research using sound theoretical frameworks to evaluate the influence of nursing care processes on patient outcomes in rural health care settings is necessary. At a minimum, more nurse researchers need to at least sample rural hospitals in their larger studies of patient safety. Further investigative efforts should focus on exploring factors related to underreporting of medication errors in rural health care facilities; evaluating barriers to safe nursing care, including how a lack of pharmacy coverage and information technology affects nursing care and patient outcomes; examining the relationship between rural health care nursing practice environments and patient outcomes; and addressing transitions in care, especially given the great distances between providers, facilities, and patients in rural areas. Nurses bring considerable expertise to the field of patient safety research. Encouraging nurses to conduct interdisciplinary, cross-national, and even international rural patient safety research will amplify these contributions.

REFERENCES

Armstrong, K. J., & Laschinger, H. (2006). Structural empowerment, Magnet hospital characteristics, and patient safety culture: Making the link. *Journal of Nursing Care Quality, 21*(2), 124–134.

Battles, J., & Lilford, R. (2003). Organizing patient safety research to identify risks and hazards. *Quality and Safety in Health Care, 12*(Suppl. 2), ii2–ii7.

Brooks, R., Menachemi, N., Burke, D., & Clawson, A. (2005). Patient-safety related information technology utilization in urban and rural hospitals. *Journal of Medical Systems, 29*(2), 103–109.

Burroughs, T. E., Waterman, A. D., Gallagher, T. H., Waterman, B., Adams, D., Jeffe, D. B., et al. (2005). Patient concerns about medical errors in emergency departments. *Academic Emergency Medicine, 12*(1), 57–64.

Burstin, H., & Wakefield, M. (2003). The importance of safety and quality in rural America. *Journal of Rural Health, 20*(4), 301–303.

Casey, M. M., & Moscovice, I. (2004). Quality improvement strategies and best practices in critical access hospitals. *Journal of Rural Health, 20*(4), 327–334.

Casey, M. M., Wakefield, M., Coburn, A. F., Moscovice, I. S., & Loux, S. (2006). Prioritizing patient safety interventions in small and rural hospitals. *Joint Commission Journal on Quality & Patient Safety, 32*(12), 693–702.

Centers for Medicare and Medicaid Services. (2007). *HHS reports to Congress on value-based purchasing of hospital services by Medicare.* Retrieved November 16, 2007, from http://www.hhs.gov.news/press/2007/11/pr20071126a

Chandler, D. (2002). Late entry into prenatal care in a rural setting. *Journal of Midwifery & Women's Health, 47*(1), 28–34.

Coburn, A. F., Wakefield, M., Casey, M., Moscovice, I., Payne, S., & Loux, S. (2004). Assuring rural hospital patient safety: What should be the priorities? *Journal of Rural Health, 20*(4), 314–326.

Cook, A. F., Hoas, H., Guttmannova, K., & Joyner, J. C. (2004). An error by any other name. *American Journal of Nursing, 104*(6), 32–44.

Cooper, J. B., Gaba, D. M., Liang B., Woods, D., & Blum, L. N. (2000). National Patient Safety Foundation agenda for research and development in patient safety. *Medscape General Medicine, 2*(4), 14. Retrieved October 1, 2007, from http://www.medscape.com/viewarticle/408064

Cravens, D. D., Mehr, D. R., Campbell, J. D., Armer, J., Kruse, R. L., Rubenstein, L. Z., et al. (2005). Home-based comprehensive assessment of rural elderly persons: The CARE project. *Journal of Rural Health, 21*(4), 322–328.

Curry, M. A., Durham, L., Bullock, L., Bloom, T., & Davis, J. (2006). Nurse case management for pregnant women experiencing or at risk for abuse. *Journal of Obstetric, Gynecologic, & Neonatal Nursing, 35*(2), 181–192.

Demiris, G., Patrick, T. B., & Boren, S. A. (2004). Assessing patient safety awareness and needs in rural hospitals in one U.S. state. *Informatics in Primary Care, 12*(3), 157–162.

Fogarty, G. J., & McKeon, C. M. (2006). Patient safety during medication administration: The influence of organizational and individual variables on unsafe work practices and medication errors. *Ergonomics, 49*(5–6), 444–456.

Freeman, V. A., Walsh, J., Rudolf, M., Slifkin, R. T., & Skinner, A. C. (2007). Intensive care in critical access hospitals. *Journal of Rural Health, 23*(2), 116–123.

Hansen, R., Tresse, S., & Gunnarsson, R. K. (2004). Fewer accidents and better maintenance with active wheelchair check-ups: A randomized controlled clinical trial. *Clinical Rehabilitation, 18*(6), 631–639.

Hegney, D., Plank, A., Watson, J., Raith, L., & McKeon, C. (2005). Patient education and consumer medicine information: A study of provision by Queensland rural and remote area registered nurses. *Journal of Clinical Nursing, 14*, 855–862.

Horner, S. D. (2006). Home visiting for intervention delivery to improve rural family asthma management. *Journal of Community Health Nursing, 23*(4), 213–223.

Huber, D. (2002). Nevada nurses participate in medication errors survey. *Nevada RNformation, 11*(3), 18–19.

Institute of Medicine. (2005). *Quality through collaboration: The future of rural health care.* Washington, DC: National Academy Press.

Joint Commission. (2007). *2008 national patient safety goals.* Retrieved from http://www. jointcommission.org/PatientSafety/NationalPatientSafetyGoals

Jones, K. J., Cochran, G., Hicks, R. W., & Mueller, K. J. (2004). Translating research into practice: Voluntary reporting of medication errors in critical access hospitals. *Journal of Rural Health, 20*(4), 335–343.

Kuzel, A. J., Woolf, S. H., Gilchrist, V., Enge, J. D., LaVeist, T., & Franke., R. (2004). Patient reports of preventable problems and harms in primary health care. *Annals of Family Medicine, 2*(4), 292–293.

Lake, E. (2002). Development of the practice environment scale of the nursing work index. *Research in Nursing and Health, 25*, 176–188.

Laschinger, H., Finegan, J., Shamian, J., & Wilk, P. (2001). Impact of structural and psychological empowerment on job strain in nursing work settings: Expanding Kanter's model. *Journal of Nursing Administration, 31*(5), 260–272.

Longo, D. R., Hewett, J. E., Ge, B., & Schubert, S. (2007). Rural hospital patient safety systems implementation in two states. *Journal of Rural Health, 23*(3), 189–197.

Madegowda, B., Hill, P. D., & Anderson, M. A. (2007). Medication errors in a rural hospital. *MEDSURG Nursing, 16*(3), 175–180.

Makeham, M., Kidd, M. R., Saltman, D. C., Mira, M., Bridges-Webb, C., Cooper, C., et al. (2006). The Threats to Australian Patient Safety (TAPS) study: Incidence of reported errors in general practice. *Medical Journal of Australia, 185*(2), 95–98.

Mayo, A. M., & Duncan, D. (2004). Nurse perceptions of medication errors: What we need to know for patient safety. *Journal of Nursing Care Quality, 19*(3), 209–217.

McAleer, B., & Varma, M. P. (2006). Feasibility and long term outcome of home vs hospital initiated thrombolysis. *International Journal of Medical Science, 175*(4), 14–19.

McKeon, C. M., Fogarty, G. J., & Hegney, D. G. (2006). Organizational factors: Impact on administration violations in rural nursing. *Journal of Advanced Nursing, 55*(1), 115–123.

Meade, C. M., Bursell, A. L., & Ketelsen, L. (2006). Effects of nursing rounds on patients' call light use, satisfaction, and safety: Scheduling regular nursing rounds to deal with patients' more mundane and common problems can return the call light to its rightful status as a lifeline. *American Journal of Nursing, 106*(9), 58–71.

Menachemi, N., Burke, D., Clawson, A., & Brooks, R. (2005). Information technologies in Florida's rural hospitals: Does system affiliation matter? *Journal of Rural Health, 21*(3), 263–268.

Mensour, M., Pineau, R., Sahia, V., & Michaud, J. (2006). Emergency department procedural sedation and analgesia: A Canadian community effectiveness and Safety Study (ACCESS). *Canadian Journal of Emergency Medicine, 8*(3), 147.

Merwin, E., & Thornlow, D. (2006). Methodologies used in nursing research designed to improve patient safety. *Annual Review of Nursing Research, 24,* 273–292.

Morgan, D. G., Stewart, N. J., D'Arcy, K. C., & Werezak, L. J. (2004). Evaluating rural nursing home environments: Demential special care units versus integrated facilities. *Aging & Mental Health, 8*(3), 256–265.

Ohsfeldt, R., Ward, M., Schneider, J., Jaana, M., Miller, T., Lei, Y., et al. (2005). Implementation of hospital computerized physician order entry systems in a rural state: Feasibility and financial impact. *Journal of the American Medical Informatics Association, 12,* 20–27.

Pink, G. H., Slifkin, R. T., Coburn, A. F., Gale, J. A., Pink, G. H., Slifkin, R. T., et al. (2004). Comparative performance data for critical access hospitals. *Journal of Rural Health, 20*(4), 374–382.

Schade, C. P., Hannah, K., Ruddick, P., Starling, C., & Brehm, J. (2006). Improving self-reporting of adverse drug events in a West Virginia hospital. *American Journal of Medical Quality, 21*(5), 335–341.

Sexton, J. B., Thomas, E., & Helmreich, R. (2000). Error, stress, and teamwork in medicine and aviation: Cross-sectional surveys. *British Medical Journal, 320,* 745–749.

Singh, R., Servoss, T., Kalsman, M., Fox, C., & Singh, G. (2004). Estimating impacts on safety caused by the introduction of electronic medical records in primary care. *Informatics in Primary Care, 12*(4), 235–241.

Tanner, E. K. (2003). Home health care: Assessing home safety in homebound older adults. *Geriatric Nursing, 24*(4), 250.

VanVorst, R., Araya-Guerra, R., Felzien, M., Fernald, D., Elder, N., Duclos, C., et al. (2007). Rural community members' perceptions of harm from medical mistakes: A High Plains Research Network (HPRN) study. *Journal of the American Board of Family Medicine, 20,* 135–143.

Vogelsmeier, A., Scott-Cawiezell, J., & Zellmer, D. (2007). Technology innovations: Barriers to safe medication administration in the nursing home: Exploring staff perceptions and concerns about the medication use process. *Journal of Gerontological Nursing, 33*(4), 5–12.

Wakefield, M. (2002). Patient safety and medical errors: Implications for rural health care. *Journal of Legal Medicine, 23*(1), 43–56.

Weissman, J. S., Annas, C. L., Epstein, A. M., Schneider, E. C., Clarridge, B., Kirle, L., et. al. (2005). Error reporting and disclosure systems: Views from hospital leaders. *Journal of the American Medical Association, 293,* 1359–1366.

Westfall, J. M., Fernald, D. H., Staton, E. W., VanVorst, R., West, D., & Pace, W. D. (2004). Applied strategies for improving patient safety: A comprehensive process to improve care in rural and frontier communities. *Journal of Rural Health, 20*(4), 355–362.

Williams, A., & Jester, R. (2005). Delayed surgical fixation of fractured hips in older people: Impact on mortality. *Journal of Advanced Nursing, 52*(1), 63–69.

Williams, L. E., & Martin, J. E. (2003). Car seat challenges: Where are we in implementation of these programs? *Journal of Perinatal & Neonatal Nursing, 17*(2), 158–163.

Winterstein, A. G., Hartzema, A. G., Johns, T. E., De Leon, J. M., McDonald, K., Henshaw, Z., et al. (2006). Medication safety infrastructure in critical-access hospitals in Florida. *American Journal of Health-System Pharmacy, 63*(5), 442–450.

Woodall, S. C. (2004). Remote order entry and video verification: Reducing after-hours medication errors in a rural hospital. *Joint Commission Journal of Quality and Safety, 30*(8), 442–447.

PART III

Improving Cultural Relevance of Rural Nursing Research: Methodological Issues, Constraints, and Opportunities

Chapter 8

Conducting Culturally Competent Rural Nursing Research

Angeline Bushy

ABSTRACT

The face of America is changing. In efforts to provide services to and meet the needs of consumers of different ethnicities and cultures, cultural competence has become a driving force not only in health care but also in business, education, and research. Lack of cultural competence among caregivers has been linked to health disparities, decreased client satisfaction, and decreased client adherence to recommended medical regimens. The depth of rural research in general, and by nurse researchers focusing on rural cultural groups in particular, is limited. This chapter focuses on conducting rural nursing research with rural cultural groups, highlights methodological issues that are commonly encountered with rural populations, and proposes strategies to address them. Addressing methodological challenges will contribute to the limited knowledge base related to culture and ethnicity in rural nursing research.

Keywords: rural nursing research; rural cultural groups; rural research methodologies

INTRODUCTION

The focus of this chapter is nursing research with various rural cultural groups. To understand this topic, it is necessary to understand the context of rural nursing research and the methodological challenges in conducting this research. These challenges are identified and are discussed within the context of nursing research conducted with various rural cultural groups. This chapter has two goals: to identify methodological challenges unique to rural nursing research and to consider these challenges for studies of various rural cultural groups in rural nursing research. First, culture will be discussed. Then issues concerning methodological challenges of rural research will be identified. Then the literature on nursing research with different rural cultural groups will be presented and discussed within the context of challenges of conducting rural research. Finally, strategies for overcoming the challenges of rural research will be presented, with implications for furthering the research knowledge base of nursing and cultural groups in rural areas. This approach will provide the reader with an understanding of the influence of rurality on nursing research related to various cultural groups.

Before we discuss rural nursing research, it is important to examine the meaning of culture and cultural competence. In March 2002, the Institute of Medicine released the report *Unequal Treatment: Confronting Racial Disparities in Health Care*. The report concluded that there is evidence suggesting that bias, prejudice, and stereotyping on the part of health care providers may contribute to disparities in health care (Institute of Medicine, 2002). While the Institute of Medicine's report focused on racial and ethnic minority groups, the American Psychological Association (2002) identifies 10 subgroups of their ethics code: different age groups, (e.g., the very young, the elderly), gender groups, racial groups, ethnic groups, groups of different national origins, religious groups, sexual orientation groups, ability groups (i.e., the disabled), language groups, and socioeconomic groups. Not included but perhaps inferred in the APA list could be place of residence as a factor that can have an impact on access to health care and health status for an individual or community.

Sparsely populated rural settings have features that are different from those of urban and suburban settings with denser populations within a defined geographical area. Ultimately, contextual variations can affect activities in the day-to-day lives of people in a particular setting, as well as studies that are designed to investigate a health concern among a given population or within a particular setting. In reality, every individual could potentially be part of one or more of the aforementioned APA subgroups. Some individuals, however, experience two or more risk factors that interact and make them vulnerable to certain health conditions.

Ideally, each of the aforementioned groups should be listed along with *rural nursing research* as keywords for a focused and comprehensive state-of-the-science report. The purpose of this chapter, however, is not to provide a comprehensive report on nursing research focusing on all the groupings that are listed in the APA report. Rather, this chapter focuses only on a general review of cultural groups and rural nursing research.

Madeline Leininger was one of the first nursing scholars to use the term *cultural competence* (Burcham, 2002; Leininger & McFarland, 2002). She offers the following definition of culturally competent nursing care: "The explicit use of culturally-based care and health knowledge in sensitive, creative and meaningful ways to fit the general life ways and needs of individuals or groups for beneficial health and well-being, or, to face illness, disabilities or death" (Leininger, 2002, p. 84). Leininger used the term *cultural congruence* to describe nursing care that is appropriate and safe for clients of minority cultures. Recently, Spector (2004) described cultural competence as the ability of health care providers and organizations to understand and respond effectively to the cultural and linguistic preferences brought to the health care experience—a complex combination of knowledge, attributes, and skill. Andrews and Boyle (2002) emphasize that cultural competence is a process rather than an end point, while Campina-Bacote (2003) explains that cultural competence involves a process of working effectively within the cultural context of an individual, family, or community. To that end, Satcher and Rubins (2006) and DeChesney and Anderson (2008) caution caregivers on the potential to misinterpret an individual's verbal and physical cues and thus ignore variations within a cultural group.

The Bureau of Primary Health Care (2005) describes cultural competence as a journey and has partnered with the National Center for Cultural Competence to enhance and measure culturally competent services. Cultural competence refers to the ability to demonstrate cultural awareness, knowledge, and skill and apply these components in interactions with others. An individual must continuously undertake self-assessment and adjust to dynamic and challenging opportunities in remaining culturally aware and effective (Seright, 2007). Culture per se does not only affect individuals who are ethnically, racially, or socioeconomically different from the nurse. Rather, a culturally competent researcher is aware that culture is a component of all aspects of human life, including health and illness. These dimensions need to be considered when one is designing and implementing a nursing study focusing on a particular rural population.

Cultural competence has become a driving force not only in health care but also in business (Trompanaars & Wooliams, 2004), education (Silverman, Bharathy, Johns, Eidelson, Smith, et al., 2007), and research. Lack of cultural competence among caregivers has been linked to health disparities, decreased client satisfaction, and decreased client adherence to recommended medical regimens. To that end, the Commission on Collegiate Nursing Education, the National League for Nursing, and state boards of nursing as well as other accrediting and certification bodies recommend inclusion of dimensions of cultural care in nursing curricula and in measuring health care provider competencies.

METHODOLOGY

The depth of rural research in general, and by nurse researchers focusing on rural cultural groups in particular, is limited. This chapter focuses on nursing research with rural cultural and ethnic minority groups. Four processes were undertaken in the preparation of the content literature reviews. Initially, the key terms *rural nursing* and *research* (delimiters: English language, humans) were used to conduct a broad search of MEDLINE for articles published in the last five years; this search yielded more than 500 citations. In the second search the keywords *culture* and *rural nursing research* (delimiters: English language, humans) were used to target the last 5 years; this yielded 60 articles. The third search focused only on the last 2 years, again using the keywords *rural nursing research* and *culture* (delimiters: English language, humans), which yielded 35 citations. Of these, 15 citations had an international focus. Twenty of the articles cited focused on a U.S. population or setting. Of these, only 8 were research-based reports; these are reviewed in the subsequent discussion. Even though all the journals were U.S. publications, it was surprising to note the high proportion of citations with an international perspective—all of which used a qualitative or mixed-methods approach. Particular methodological challenges related to rural research are part of the reason that the knowledge base in this area is so sparse. These challenges, and strategies to address them, were identified through an extensive literature search for articles specifically addressing methodological considerations that must be taken in rural nursing research in the United States.

LITERATURE REVIEW

Definition of Rural

Methodological challenges posed by rural health research are associated with inconsistent and imprecise definitions of rurality and the social and cultural preferences inherent in rural communities, coupled with the contextual diversity of rural communities. Definitions of *rural* have been established by the U.S. Department of Commerce–Bureau of the Census, the Office of Management and Budget, and the U.S. Department of Agriculture Economic Research Service. Recently, the Institute of Medicine's (2005) *Report on the Future of Rural Health Care* reinforced the inconsistencies among the multiple definitions. Consequently, an oft-cited methodological concern in rural health research is the imprecise and conflicting definitions of *rural*. More specifically, there is no universally accepted definition of rurality, and quite often rural-focused research reports fail to specify how *rural* is defined for that particular study. Imprecise definitions limit the comparative value and potential to replicate a study. Different definitions are used by various governmental and policy bodies. Some focus only on population density, while others focus on communities' access to urban-based services or level of urban influence. Rural nursing scholars argue that these approaches fail to capture the inherent diversity of rural communities, including structural, ecological, social, and cultural dimensions (Bigbee & Lund, 2007).

In recent years the term *frontier* has come into use to describe the most remote and sparsely populated geographical settings, that is, six or fewer individuals per square mile. This definition can provide a more definitive baseline with which to evaluate research methodologies and empirical findings of a small segment of rural-focused studies. Without a consistent definition, the comparability and generalizability of the rural research body of nursing knowledge are limited. For the sake of comparison and to highlight the ambiguity, the next few paragraphs provide examples of the manner in which rurality is described by investigators in several recent nursing research studies.

Culture of Rural Areas

Brown and Hill (2005) and Brown and Van Hook (2006) used a qualitative descriptive design to focus on rural and small-city African Americans who use cocaine and their perceptions of HIV risks and prevention strategies. Data were collected with focus groups consisting of "respondents recruited from a rural county and a small city within a semi-urban county located in north central Florida. The population of the counties was 13,500 and 242,000 respectively; and the population of the city was 92,000" (p. 44).

In another study by Williams-Brown and colleagues (2005), a qualitative phenomenological design was used to investigate the descriptions of mammogram quality provided by African American women "living in rural West, South and Northeast Georgia" (p. 232). No additional details are provided about the definition or characteristics of the rural setting for this study.

In the third example, Caldwell's (2007) qualitative study was designed to use storytelling and ballad elements of the culture, as well as Moustakas's heuristic phenomenological approach, to reveal the life stories of nurse practitioners in rural Appalachia. This report provides an elaborate and picturesque description of the setting.

> The rural community is located in southwestern Virginia bordering Kentucky, West Virginia and Tennessee. The terrain is rugged, steep and rocky. The misty blue hills are nestled within the Allegheny Plateau of the Appalachian Mountains. The results of the 2000 census revealed the population as 1,175 people living in the town and 31,333 people living in the county. The community and the county have one hospital with 144 beds, three clinics, 16 physicians, 5 dentists and 12

nurse practitioners. The community remains isolated and many of the residents have never traveled outside the county. (p. 73)

The description of *rural* in the Caldwell study is elaborate. However, the array of health care resources described herein might seem similarly elaborate to someone living in a frontier community that does not have even one doctor to enable the small local hospital to keep its doors open and provide health care services.

Considering the enormous diversity within and among rural communities, it is not likely that there is one rural culture. Even within a given region or the smallest rural town, there are likely to be numerous subgroups and multiple subcultures. One of the sociocultural features that exists in many smaller communities is a homogeneous population consisting of individuals who are acquainted or even related. Other characteristics often attributed to rural residents include a distrust of outsiders, a strong sense of independence and self-reliance, and a preference for interacting with other local residents as opposed to someone from outside the community. Considering the diversity among rural communities, these sociocultural features may or may not characterize a particular population of interest. Nonetheless, those preferences should be taken into consideration by investigators from outside the community, as their activities could be perceived to be an invasion of privacy or interference into a local issue.

Culture and Accessing and Recruiting Rural Populations

Gaining entrance into a community and inviting members of another culture or a subgroup of a rural community to participate in a study are time-consuming and critical processes. A major challenge for studies is recruitment of participants who represent the community's population or who are underserved as a result of their minority status. Participant recruitment has always been a challenge with non-English-speaking minorities, who often are more marginalized than English-speaking minorities (Anderson & Hatton, 2000; Bigbee & Lund, 2007). The challenges to accessing these groups can be even more profound than those who are more proficient with the English language. Nurses commonly provide care to individuals who fall in one or more of the APA groups (hereafter referred to as vulnerable populations). However, nurse investigators usually must negotiate entrée into sites not typically used for clinical nursing practice to access participants for a study.

Not only can a researcher have difficulty locating and recruiting participants, but subject attrition always is a consideration. Individuals who are vulnerable, for instance, often experience pressing socioeconomic needs that can limit their time and energy, which can interfere with their participation in a study. Further, these individuals and the nurse researcher may differ with regard to socioeconomic status, education, language, and/or ethnicity—all of which can pose barriers to the implementation of an unbiased study. Such differences can have consequences in terms of how the researcher and the participants view the importance and the purpose of the research. In other words, interpersonal and cultural differences affect communication between the two parties, which in turn can influence the quality of the data and the findings of the study. The next paragraphs highlight recruitment and retention challenges that presented in two recent nursing research studies focusing on a rural racial and ethnic minority group.

Hendrickson (2007) describes the process for developing a short videotape designed to support the recruitment of monolingual, low-literacy Hispanic mothers as participants in their study. The contextual expertise of women from the target community was enlisted, and the videotape was culturally congruent while providing clarity about the recruitment process. The video, narrated in Spanish, portrayed the home visit interviews used in the study. From the pilot study, the investigators found that 40% of the mothers were not accustomed to reading, and the use of a video offered a consistent presentation of the study, thereby reducing recruitment variance. While video recruitment was deemed to be successful in this study, potential pitfalls of this approach are associated with sites that lack electricity or are not otherwise conducive to the use of a video because the room is crowded and noisy. Production barriers relate to time, money, and technical support.

In another rural study, Jacobson and Wood (2006) highlight lessons learned about recruitment of participants to their pilot study focusing on the feasibility of an in-home educational intervention for African Americans with diabetes living in rural Alabama. Despite a careful explanation to diabetes educators, all of whom were known by the investigators, the recruitment process did not go smoothly or rapidly. The inclusion requirements of the study required participants to be African American, with type 2 diabetes, children in the home, and a willing and available adult support person. These requirements ruled out a large share of many diabetes educators' caseloads, who were, for the most part, older individuals. Of the 11 families who were referred and contacted, only 5 qualified. Of these 5, only 3 families completed the study. As for the 2 families who did not complete the study, one young mother smilingly consented and completed the baseline data but could never identify a good time for a follow-up visit despite numerous telephone calls from the investigators. Another woman with diabetes expressed an interest in participating in the study; however, her adult support person (a daughter) was present for only a few minutes following the first and second intervention sessions. Shortly thereafter, she moved away from the community and could no longer continue to participate in the study. After several months of trying to recruit families with a nondiabetic adult support person, the investigators realized that the inclusion requirements were inappropriate given the high prevalence of diabetes in the African American community. Subsequently, that particular criterion was relaxed in order to include one more family in the study. The total time required to acquire 3 eligible families who completed the study was 9 months.

Conducting Culturally Sensitive Research

Investigators' Relationship With Community

Regardless of the design, establishing rapport is critical for the nurse researcher who is working with rural residents or the community as a whole. Building initial community trust usually requires considerable time and travel on the part of the investigator. There also are issues one must anticipate with carrying out a study in a community where most residents know or are acquainted with each other.

Privacy Concerns

Threats to anonymity and confidentiality persistently emerge among residents in small rural communities. Even when large state- or county-level data sets are used, reporting of such events could threaten the anonymity of those who are affected by the condition being studied. In an effort to address this concern, the federal government codes large data sets with 9999 for counties with populations of fewer than 100,000 individuals—which greatly limits the reliability of data for rural and frontier counties (Aide & Fahs, 2001). Similarly, the national Behavioral Risk Factor Surveillance System includes health indicator data only from counties with at least 250 respondents, which limits its usefulness in studies of rural and frontier populations.

Research Designs

Both qualitative and quantitative studies are necessary to enhance the theoretical and empirical foundation for rural practice. Findings from the two kinds of studies must be integrated to yield a full picture of the phenomenon of interest. Recognizing the uniqueness of an individual's experiences (qualitative approaches) while simultaneously identifying commonalities from which to make predictions (quantitative approaches) is important. Both approaches must be equally valued, and each one's unique contributions must be carefully weighed. Thus the problem statement, along with what is known about the variables of interest, preempts the choice of the methodology to be used in a study with a particular population.

With rural-focused research, methods must be responsive to and congruent with the values, beliefs, customs, and nuances of the culture of the participants in the study. The expanding interest in and concern for the health of rural populations has resulted in nurse scholars posing questions that require primary data from rural residents. To that end, an emic approach attempts to describe a phenomenon from inside a culture or from the viewpoint of members of a culture (Munhall, 2007) or a culturally specific perspective, while an etic approach is from the vantage point outside a culture, or from the observer's viewpoint, and thus is considered by some a "culture-free" perspective (Munhall, 2007).

To elicit either type of information, it would be prudent for a nurse researcher to first learn about the various elements of a community to effectively plan culturally sensitive and appropriate research methods. For instance, the investigator could conduct an assessment prior to planning and implementing a study to learn about the values, beliefs, and behaviors of the population and phenomenon of interest and then work with members of the group to address methodological concerns that could emerge with a particular research design.

The majority of nursing research studies focusing on rural areas and populations have used qualitative or mixed methods to provide beginning insights about what is little known about rural nursing. Close scrutiny of the abstracts elicited in the broad literature search showed phenomenology, ethnography and grounded theory, and participatory approaches to be the most often cited designs. Data sources included focus groups, interviews, and surveys of various types, and combinations of two or more of these approaches were used in several recent nursing studies focusing on high-risk minority populations.

In a study by Heuer, Lausch, and Bergland (2006), a phenomenological approach was used to explore the experiences of diabetes lay educators who worked with migrant farmworkers traveling from state to state. While this study makes an important contribution to our understanding of the lifestyle of migrant farmworkers, the self-management of diabetes while traveling, and the roles of diabetes lay educators and access to health care of migrant farmworkers, additional research is needed on the impact of the diabetes lay educators on access, use of services, and farmworkers' knowledge and behavior changes in relation to the self-management of their diabetes.

More recently, Harrison and Scarinci (2007) used focus groups to identify perceptions of Latino parents living in rural Alabama related to their children's health needs. The groups were led by native Spanish speakers, and classic qualitative data collection and analysis methods were used. Focus groups can provide important insights into the perspectives and experiences of "hidden" groups that can be useful to the development of services to reduce health disparities. In this instance, the study served as an impetus to develop a Latino health community partnership in the county in which the study was conducted; the partnership represented a collaboration between the university and more than 75 individuals and community groups. This was a preliminary step in the development of culturally appropriate community-based programs to address the priority health needs of the Latino community within one rural Alabama community.

In yet another study, Guo and Phillips (2006) undertook a systematic assessment using a participatory action research design to gain an understanding of aging in a rural community along the U.S.-Mexico border. Interviews were conducted with key informants, including health care and social service providers and community leaders. Content analyses focused on identifying common themes and concerns of rural elders. Three major themes were identified: social infrastructure issues, community awareness of health, and socioeconomic problems. The study found that elders living on the border are a particularly vulnerable population with strong cultural affiliations and health disparities. Although the population of elders at the U.S. border has been growing, the focus has traditionally been on youths and children. This study provided insights from key community informants about the health care needs and priorities of aging community members along the Mexican-U.S. border.

Contextual, social, and cultural features of rural settings can also pose challenges to researchers conducting quantitative studies. For example, survey research is often relied on as a relatively cost-effective method for collecting data in rural settings, in particular for frontier regions with populations that are dispersed over a large geographical area. Classic references on conducting survey research by mail offer standards for commonly accepted procedures regarding approach letters and follow-up reminders but offer few guidelines for tailoring these approaches to different cultural groups.

Shreffler (1999) describes adaptations and adjuncts to conventional survey research methods based on knowledge of and respect for the characteristics and qualities of rural culture. In addition to adjustments in timing of methodologic procedures, additional activities may need to be implemented to reach residents in more remote settings. Likewise, access to telecommunication and postal services may be restricted, which could create barriers to researchers' ability to reach potential subjects and to the return rate. These are a few of the contextual features that should be taken into consideration when researchers are identifying and contacting potential subjects. To enhance sample sizes in rural areas with low populations, mailed or telephone surveys may be used. These survey methods can reduce the depth of the data and may impair the building of trust with an individual or community. Telephone survey methods may also be problematic because of the higher rate of rural ethnic minority and low-income residents who do not have a telephone in their homes (Fahs, Feinholdt, & Daniel, 2001).

Online surveys may not be effective in rural communities due to limited penetration of information technology, in particular telephonic and cable-modem access. Adoption of conventional approaches that are preferred or most often used by those to be surveyed can increase response rates, thereby enhancing the validity of the results, as well as demonstrate respect and sensitivity for the culture of participants in the study, regardless of the setting.

Challenges: Influence of Rural Culture and Geography

Conducting Human Subjects Research in Rural Areas

Protection of human subjects must be ensured in all types of research. However, rarely do institutional research review boards that can present issues that need to be addressed within human subjects research proposals exist in rural health care facilities. Along with university institutional review boards' approval, other approaches may also be needed to obtain approval to implement the study and ensure protection of human subjects in rural minority groups. For example, someone planning to implement a study in a very small hospital may need to obtain a letter of approval from the institution's chief executive officer, administrator, or perhaps the board of directors. When a study is being implemented in the community, a letter of support may be needed from the city council, mayor, or some other official leader, such as the tribal chairperson or a leader of a faith community.

Establishing Trust

Whether the rural-focused study is quantitative or qualitative in nature, a distrust of "outsiders" along with strong values of independence, self-reliance, and privacy may hinder efforts to recruit participants for a study. Coupled with a low population density, these cultural preferences make it difficult, if not impossible, to achieve a sample size that meets the requirements identified in the statistical power analysis. Recruiting an adequate sample becomes particularly problematic when studies are focusing on health events that are relatively rare, such as maternal deaths, or conditions with associated stigma, for example a mental illness, HIV/AIDS, or substance abuse.

Small Sample Sizes

Methodological and statistical issues must be addressed when rural research is being planned and conducted. For instance, often the sample size is inadequate as a result of a low population, especially in regions designated frontier areas. Developing sampling frames in rural communities from telephone or voter registration listings may be problematic due to incomplete addresses. Use of census tract or zip code data may be helpful for determining denominators; however, residents' names generally are not included in these rosters. Some rural health researchers use existing state or national data sets for epidemiological or health services research. This approach poses inherent challenges as well because of sampling size and small numbers. For example, in nursing workforce research, the National Sample of Registered Nurses data collected by the Division of Nursing in the Health Resources and Services Administration often are used. The usefulness of this data set, however, is limited because the sample may include few nurses residing in very low population density areas.

The effect of small sample numbers, along with confidentiality, has been addressed by some rural scholars through the use of "spatial smoothing" to correct projection biases that may occur among small populations with small or sporadic occurrence rates of a particular event, health problem, or condition. This approach calculates the population number and mortality rate by county, along with the population number and mortality rates for all surrounding counties. The total is then divided by the number of counties to obtain an average occurrence rate by county (Aide & Fahs, 2001).

Measures

Instrumentation also presents unique challenges for the rural researcher. For example, rarely are standardized instruments developed, tested, or normed with rural populations in general, much less with a particular ethnic or cultural group. Thus the reliability and validity of the instrument may also be questionable when used with rural subjects. Urban bias in questions or overall insensitivity may be offensive to rural residents, further threatening the validity of the data and lowering the response rates. The wide diversity within and among rural and frontier areas mandates that researchers be cautious in making generalizations of findings. Conversely, investigators must go beyond general rural-urban comparisons and examine the diversity within and among rural communities and subpopulations.

Other Strategies for Overcoming Methodological Challenges

Inclusiveness in Clinical Trials

Rural representation in clinical trials is imperative; however, the challenges are similar to those posed by the recruitment and retention of participants in national studies. Historically, rural populations in general, and minorities in particular, have been underrepresented in all phases of the biomedical research process. Racial minorities traditionally have been excluded both in planning and implementing biomedical and health-related research, including epidemiological, behavioral, and community-based research and clinical trials. Rural people have not been included in adequate numbers to provide statistically valid estimates of health outcomes and differences. Greater inclusiveness requires the development and implementation of processes to increase funding for programs designed for and by rural communities and researchers. Emphasis must be placed on working with the communities to find out what they believe their problems are, then providing the necessary financial and technical support to solve those concerns.

Innovative Statistical and Data Analysis Approaches

Statistical challenges with rural-focused research studies are related to low event rates, which make it difficult to ascertain the severity of the problems (for example, the incidence and prevalence of HIV/AIDS in a frontier county). Typically rates are followed over time, or compared to similar counties. With very low numbers, a change of only one or two individuals could represent a 50% or even 100% change in the rate of a particular condition. Along with the spatial smoothing previously discussed, longitudinal smoothing may be used with events considered in three-year rolling averages. With both of these approaches, the researcher may not be able to study the geographic area or time period that is of the highest interest. Bayesian statistical methods, in which an a priori estimate is compared to a post-period observation, are sometimes helpful.

Mapping technology holds potential for health intervention studies, especially in more remote rural settings. Gesler and colleagues (2004) focused on a geographical analysis of diabetics. The purpose of the article was to show how maps of where people live and carry out their daily activities can be used by health care providers to plan prevention programs. Global Positioning Systems and Geographic Information Systems technologies were used to map residences and activity spaces and sites where diabetes information has the potential to be welcomed by low-income African American, Latino, and White males and females in a small rural southern town. Maps can provide an in-depth orientation to a study community in visually striking ways. In this study they provided data on the best locations for diabetes prevention programs and the provision of educational materials to target individuals at high risk for the development of type 2 diabetes.

Disseminate and Utilize Evidence-Based Findings

In spite of unprecedented growth in research, and even with the phenomenal expansion of communication capabilities, the greatest challenge that remains is dissemination of findings to clinicians. It is, after all, those who care for client systems who can make the most use of that information. Once a study is completed, the findings may be applied to practice immediately or, as often is the case, may contribute to a body of evidence over a period of time. Regardless of the time needed to implement the findings, the goal of evidence-based data is improving client care in a cost-effective manner. Utilizing research findings and implementing evidence-based practice in rural settings can be a challenge, and while opportunities for professional dialogue among clinicians may be limited, communication technology may not be as reliable.

A major limitation to the dissemination of empirical findings is that researchers are primarily based in institutions of higher learning. On one hand, researchers are mostly found in urban settings associated with the expertise and funding necessary to create and fund research. Rural practitioners, on the other hand, tend to be more clinically and service oriented, as opposed to having a research focus. The interfacing link of these two entities is the dissemination of research findings. Then, too, a research report must fit the particular needs and interests of specific audiences—clinicians, scholars, consumers. A serious barrier for rural clinicians is the cost and time required and the distance one must travel to attend a research conference. For this reason, effective strategies must be used to deliver information to peers who live and work in rural catchment areas.

CONCLUSIONS

The depth of rural research in general, and by nurse researchers focusing on a cultural group in particular, is limited. The U.S. studies that have been published definitely make a contribution to the profession's knowledge base. However, as a result of imprecise definitions and methodological challenges, comparing the findings and expanding empirical evidence for particular foci is problematic. As research begins to link health disparities to the lack of cultural competence, the mandate for cultural competence is reinforced by the design and implementation of all studies with human subjects. Researchers who are not culturally competent may produce studies that do not have valid and reliable findings relative to the population or phenomenon of interest.

To enhance the empirical knowledge base, it would be prudent to develop an agenda that focuses on select health-related phenomena. Subsequently, incentives should be put in place to motivate nurse researchers to study these situations within and across different rural cultural groups. Addressing methodological challenges identified in this review, and incorporating some of the methodological strategies identified, will contribute to the limited knowledge base related to culture and ethnicity in rural nursing research. Then, the research findings must be disseminated to various consumer bodies, including other researchers as well as rural clinicians. In light of the limited number of studies that focus on rural cultural groups in the rural context, the sky is the limit as to the topics for the nurse researcher.

REFERENCES

Aide, M., & Fahs, P. (2001). A secondary analysis of cardiovascular mortality among rural Native American women. *Journal of Multicultural Nursing and Health, 7*(2), 42–47.

American Psychological Association. (2002). *Code of ethics*. Retrieved January 2008, from http://www.apa.org/ethics/code.html

Anderson, D., & Hatton, D. (2000). Issues in clinical nursing research: Accessing vulnerable populations for research. *Western Journal of Nursing Research, 22*(2), 244–251.

Andrews, M., & Boyle, J. (2002). Transcultural concepts in nursing care. *Journal of Transcultural Nursing, 13*, 178–180.

Bigbee, J., & Lund, B. (2007). Methodological challenges in rural and frontier nursing research. *Applied Nursing Research, 20*, 104–106.

Brown, E. J., & Hill, M. (2005). Perceptions of HIV risks and prevention strategies by rural and small city African Americans who use cocaine: Views from the inside. *Issues in Mental Health Nursing, 26*, 359–377.

Brown, E. J., & Van Hook, M. (2006). Risk behavior, perceptions of HIV risk and risk-reduction behavior among a small group of rural African American women who use drugs. *Journal of the Association of Nurses in AIDS Care, 17*, 42–50.

Burcham, J. (2002). Cultural competence: An evolutionary perspective. *Nursing Forum, 137*(4), 5–15.

Bureau of Primary Health Care. (2005). *Transforming the face of health professions through cultural and linguistic competence education: The role of the HRSA centers of excellence.* Retrieved January 2008 from http://www.yvcc.edu/coe/pdf/competence.pdf

Caldwell, D. (2007). Bloodroot: Life stores of nurse practitioners in rural Appalachia. *Journal of Holistic Nursing, 25*(2), 73–79.

Campina-Bacote, J. (2003). Many faces: Addressing diversity in health care. *Online Journal of Issues in Nursing, 8*(1), 3.

DeChesney, M., & Anderson, B. (2008). *Caring for the vulnerable: Perspectives in nursing theory, practice and research.* Boston, MA: Jones & Bartlett.

Fahs, P., Feinholdt, N., & Daniel, S. (2001). Themes and issues in rural nursing research. In M. S. Collins (Ed.), *Teaching/learning activities for rural community-based nursing practice.* Binghamton, NY: Binghamton University.

Gesler, W., Hayes, M., Arucry, T., Skelly, A., Nash, S., & Soward, A. (2004). Use of mapping technology in health intervention research. *Nursing Outlook, 52*(3), 142–146.

Guo, G., & Phillips, L. (2006). Key informants' perceptions of health care for elders at the U.S.-Mexico border. *Public Health Nursing, 23*(3), 224–233.

Harrison, L., & Scarinci, I. (2007). Child health needs of rural Alabama Latino families. *Journal of Community Health Nursing, 24*(1), 31–47.

Hendrickson, S. (2007). Video recruitment of non-English speaking participants. *Western Journal of Nursing Research, 29*(2), 232–242.

Heuer, L., Lausch, C., & Bergland, J. (2006). The perceptions of diabetes lay educators working with migrant farm workers. *Online Journal of Rural Nursing & Health Care, 6*(1), 63–73.

Institute of Medicine. (2002). *Unequal treatment: What health care providers need to know about racial and ethnic disparities in health care.* Retrieved October 10, 2007, from http://www.iom.edu/?id=4475&redirect=0%20

Institute of Medicine. (2005). *Quality through collaboration: The future of rural health care.* Washington, DC. Retrieved October 15, 2007, from http://www.iom.edu/?id=29734

Jacobson, S., & Wood, F. (2006). Lessons learned from a very small pilot study. *Online Journal of Rural Nursing & Health Care, 6*(2), 18–28.

Leininger, M., & McFarland, M. (2002). *Transcultural nursing: Concepts, theories, research and practice.* New York: McGraw-Hill.

Munhall, P. (2007). *Nursing research: A qualitative perspective.* Boston, MA: Jones & Bartlett.

Satcher, D., & Rubins, P. (2006). *Multicultural medicine and health disparities.* New York: McGraw-Hill Medical Publishing Division.

Seright, T. (2007). Perspectives of registered nurse cultural competence in a rural state: Part I & Part II. *Online Journal of Rural Nursing & Health Care, 7*(1), 47–69.

Shreffler, J. (1999). Culturally sensitive research methods of surveying rural/frontier residents. *Western Journal of Nursing Research, 21*(3), 426–435.

Silverman, B. G., Bharathy, G., Johns, M., Eidelson, R. J., Smith, T. E., & Nye, B. (2007). Sociocultural games for training and analysis. *Man and Cybernetics, Part A, 37*(6), 1113–1130.

Spector, R. (2004). *Cultural diversity in health and illness.* Upper Saddle River, NJ: Pearson Prentice Hall.

Trompenaars, F., & Wooliams, P. (2004). *Business across cultures.* Chichester, UK: Capstone.

Williams-Brown, S., Meinersmann, K., Baldwin, D., & Phillips, J. (2005). Rural African American women's description of mammogram quality. *Journal of Nursing Care Quality, 20*(3), 231–237.

Chapter 9

Establishing the Public's Trust Through Community-Based Participatory Research: A Case Example to Improve Health Care for a Rural Hispanic Community

Deborah Shelton

ABSTRACT

This chapter describes the contextual nature of contemporary rural America to provide the background for the case example of a 4-year community-based participatory research project to enhance community capacity building in a rural New England community with a large Latino/Hispanic population. The changing nature of rural populations and implications for rural health care and nursing research are discussed.

Keywords: community-based participatory research; health disparities; community capacity building

INTRODUCTION

Efforts to enhance the health and well-being of rural communities have been met with obstacles, among which is an over-30-year history of mistrust among rural residents of outsiders and programming that come from the "outside" (Sawyer, Gale, & Lambert, 2006). For example, the efforts that are made to recruit health professionals to rural areas to address the chronic problem of health professional shortages have been countered by the difficulties of retention, which then result in rapid turnover that exacerbates the mistrust of the health care system that already exists. With an underlying fiscal foundation for rural health services dependent upon state and federal government funding (Wellever, Wholey, & Radcliff, 2000), the need to collaborate for improved community outcomes is clear. The sad thing is that not every community knows how to collaborate. Collaboration may prove difficult in rural areas because of the very values rural communities hold dear— fierce independence and mistrust of others to help meet their needs.

Heyman (1982) has a different view and suggests that rural culture may be especially conducive to citizen participation in addressing health care problems because rural residents are community oriented and more likely to utilize natural helpers and support systems than their urban counterparts. Moscovice (1989) also asserts that the self-sufficiency of rural residents supports a tradition of self-help that can be capitalized upon to enact social and health system change. It is for these very reasons that use of community-based participatory processes is an important strategy for nursing and nursing research, which has a long history and tradition of being with and in the community.

The aim of this chapter is threefold: first to describe the contextual nature of contemporary rural America so that the reader is familiar with the environment in which community-based participatory research (CBPR) is conducted; second, to present a review of rural CBPR literature documenting the work by nurses and others who have been using CBPR for the purpose of supporting community health; and lastly, to present a case example of the community capacity building that has been done over the last 4 years in a rural New England community with a large Latino/Hispanic population. The discussion focuses upon the changing nature of rural populations and implications for rural health care and nursing research. The challenges and paradoxes presented by the experiences of this author's researcher-community relationship provide an example of how CBPR holds significance for nursing researchers who engage in translational research to demonstrate that nursing interventions can and do reduce health disparities. Community-based nurses have a long history of demonstrating clinical knowledge and skill in developing collaborative partnerships within communities and among vulnerable populations. Through CBPR, the best of two worlds can meet. The new cadre of advanced practice nursing researchers can bring their research and community clinical nursing experience to the process.

Community-Based Participatory Research

The description of CBPR provided by Wallerstein and Duran (2006) is based on two assumptions. The first assumption is that interventions can be strengthened when they benefit from community insight and when community theories of etiology and change are incorporated into the empirical science base. The second assumption is that there is an added value in participation for enhancing health. The CBPR effects have shown to ensure cultural and local sensitivity, to facilitate sustainability, and to enhance productivity of programs (Isham, Narayan, & Pritchett, 1994).

The Changing Nature of Rural Populations

The ebb and flow of rural populations is more volatile than the shifting census numbers in urban areas (Kandel & Cromartie, 2004). Most increases in the metropolitan census are the result of immigration, whereas most of the rural census growth results from domestic migration, as more people move from cities to rural areas than vice versa. Rural migration patterns reflect an exodus of youths and a growth in retirement communities (Johnson, 2006). An important trend in the recent population growth of rural America is immigration from foreign countries to rural areas of the United States. Data on the rates of population growth among the various immigrant groups suggest that the South American Hispanic population in rural areas grew at the fastest rate of any racial or ethnic group during the 1990s, a pattern that has continued (Lichter & Johnson, 2006). Such changing demographics have implications for rural health care needs and for nursing research.

The dispersion of the foreign-born population outside the traditional gateway metro and border areas into rural areas exceeded 5% for the first time in 2000 (Kandel & Cromartie, 2004). At first, many of these rural counties were on the peripheries of regions that already had large concentrations of foreign-born individuals (e.g., regions spreading out from the Southwest). Lichter and Johnson (2006) found that more recently, new immigrants are bypassing the gateway cities and regions for more geographically dispersed locations. Currently, half of all nonmetro Hispanic immigrants in the United States live outside traditional settlement areas (Guzmán, 2001). The significance of this lies in the demand for culturally designed social and health programming for the disproportionate share of the rural growth by immigrants, more specifically Hispanic immigrants. Many Hispanics in counties that have experienced rapid Hispanic growth are recent U.S. arrivals with relatively low education levels, weak English proficiency, and undocumented status. This recent settlement has increased the visibility of Hispanics in many regions of rural America with populations that have long been dominated by non-Hispanic Whites. Kandel and Cromartie (2004) note that in smaller cities and towns, the level of residential separation between Hispanics and non-Hispanic Whites has increased. At the neighborhood level, this residential separation is even greater. Hispanic settlement patterns warrant attention by policy makers because they put an added strain upon the already limited resources in rural areas. It is possible that the well-being of both Hispanics and the rural communities themselves are in jeopardy. There is potential for a conflict between rural culture, which has historically been a non-Hispanic White culture, and the new immigrant Hispanic culture as the fight over sparse resources heats up.

The most prominent demographic differences between Hispanics and non-Hispanic Whites are in age and sex distributions. The disproportionate number of young and male (ages 15–39) Hispanics can be attributed to the international labor migration (Kandel & Cromartie, 2004). These younger age groups, combined with higher Hispanic fertility rates, result in a large growth in the numbers of families (Downs, 2004). Child statistics confirm this, as children under age 10 make up 24% of the Hispanic population, compared to the 12% in the non-Hispanic White population (Grieco & Cassidy, 2001). Age and sex composition have important economic and public policy ramifications. These youthful Hispanic populations attend schools, enter the labor force in relatively greater numbers, vote infrequently, and require different social services than older populations (Holder, 2006). With a high proportion of young males, there is also potential for higher rates of high-risk behaviors (Hernandez & Charney, 1998).

Legal status has perhaps the most significant influence on the economic and social well-being of these rural immigrant populations. Legal status has an impact on everything from social and health service eligibility and employment to working conditions and wages, housing, and mobility. Naturalization rates offer limited information regarding the acculturation of Hispanic immigrants into U.S. society. Census data provide only three general legal status categories for immigrants: undocumented immigrants, who comprise a large portion of the low-skill labor force; documented immigrants, who possess legal status to work and live in the United States; and naturalized individuals, who are citizens (Guzmán, 2001). For some, being an undocumented worker causes anxiety and acts as a barrier to needed social and health services. The likelihood that these individuals will report incidents of violence and crime is low due to their fear of being deported.

Apart from legal status, the amount of time one has spent in the United States influences the acquisition of language skills, which is critical for employment mobility. Roughly half of all working-age native Spanish speakers claim good English-language proficiency (Guzmán, 2001). Low English-language proficiency is more pronounced among new immigrants and poor working-age residents and the elderly. Formal education, which also heavily influences economic outcomes, is more difficult to attain for those with limited English-language proficiency. Generally, education increases one's chances of being employed. Migratory patterns indicate that Hispanic immigrants move to follow employment opportunities through social networks (Hernández-León & Zúñiga, 2000). Despite their relatively high employment rates, household incomes remain lower than those of non-Hispanic Whites, particularly for undocumented new immigrants. Numerous studies attribute income gaps to differences in education, English-language skills, legal status, and U.S. work experience (Schoeni, McCarthy, & Vernez, 1996). Poverty, defined by the U.S. Census Bureau (2007) as a threshold of $19,157 for a family of two adults and two children, is more prominent in nonmetro counties.

Hispanic newcomers have forged communities in areas in which residents are unaccustomed to seeing large numbers of foreign-born individuals. Hispanics in these communities include disproportionate numbers of young men who come from economically depressed regions of Mexico and other countries and begin migrating as single teenagers or young adults without documentation. These recent immigrants typically have fewer years of formal education and often speak little English. Despite these disadvantages, employment rates are high. Immigration to rural areas results in residential separation, as Hispanics tend to live in more culturally concentrated neighborhoods. This segregation has implications for the location and distribution of public resources and less tangible public goods. Long-term effects will be significant for individuals as well as communities if this separation acts to restrict access to resources. The urban "White flight" in previous decades illustrates how the depopulation of neighborhoods by typically better-educated and higher-income individuals leaves behind increasingly concentrated minority populations whose lower earnings reduce the tax base necessary for adequate social services. While large cities are sufficiently diverse to absorb such shifts in population, rural places are less likely to be insulated from changes posed by rapid demographic shifts. For example, a notable impact from a health services perspective would be the trickle-down effect of state budget cuts upon local budgets, which hurt fragile community-based programs. Without a solid tax base, there is little fiscal recourse for local community health care providers or consumers. This is particularly difficult for communities with few jobs or jobs that pay poorly, and communities with high rates of unemployment. These issues will be magnified in scope and importance as Hispanics increasingly populate nonmetro counties.

One view is that the Hispanic population growth has helped to stem decades of population decline and revitalized many rural communities (Kandel & Cromartie, 2004). This viewpoint is countered by a perspective that rural communities are economically and culturally unprepared for the rapid growth of large numbers of culturally distinct and low-paid newcomers who struggle to speak English. Rural residents, who are fiercely independent and have up to now lived in closed communities (particularly those in the Northeast), have little experience with people of different backgrounds. Numerous reports suggest pervasive social conflict among communities that have experienced rapid influxes of Hispanic residents (Fennelly & Frederico, 2007). Such population infusions may affect the allocation of state and federal program funding to rural areas for education, health, other social services, and infrastructure projects. On a positive note, in addition to increasing the local tax base and spending money on local goods, services, and housing, recent migrant workers may fill labor market demands that otherwise might force employers to relocate domestically or internationally or even abandon certain industries. Finally, new migrants clearly provide social and cultural diversity and introduce native residents to new cultures, languages, and cuisine.

Prospects for social and economic mobility among Hispanics in rural America hinge on their ability to overcome the same barriers faced by earlier generations of U.S. immigrants. These immigrants must work to attain legal status, U.S. work experience, English skills, training, and education and to overcome discrimination and prejudice. Long-term success in the United States will depend on the degree to which the education of Hispanic children corresponds to that of their peers (Hernandez & Charney, 1998). Some local communities have addressed these issues in targeting basic public services and assisting new residents to acclimate to their civic environment. In rural America, acculturation experiences occur against the backdrop of an aging, mostly White population that will increasingly rely upon the productivity, health, and civic participation of Hispanic migrants. Consequently, the social and economic adaptation, integration, and mobility of new Hispanic rural residents and their children are critical public policy issues that merit attention.

The Changing Nature of Rural Health Care

The health care industry is inextricably tied to economics. The health care system has changed dramatically over the last 15 years as health care financing has been transformed, new technologies have been introduced, and health services have been clustered together within various networks. Yet the principle concern in rural health care remains the maintenance of the availability of necessary services within communities. Key rural health care issues include access to care, supply of health care providers, health promotion and disease prevention, health care technology, organization of services for vulnerable rural populations, and consumer choice (Agency for Health Care Policy and Research, 1996).

Changes in the health care sector that threaten providers—both hospitals and individual practices—have serious implications for rural communities. Alternative sources of care in the community or within reasonable proximity are scarce; this makes each provider critical to health care in the community. Additionally, for many rural communities, the health care infrastructure is inextricably intertwined with the community's economy. Closure of a rural hospital, for example, can seriously threaten the health of the residents as well as the economic stability of the community. For this reason, in most rural communities, all providers are considered part of the health care safety net, whether they provide care for vulnerable populations or contribute to the community's health care infrastructure and economy (Ormond, Wallin, & Goldenson, 2000).

Local access to health care is most critical for vulnerable populations who are unable to travel to obtain services, such as the elderly, the poor, and recent immigrants. Local control of services is highly valued in rural communities and ensures that local expenditures are for services retained by the community. Estimated nationally at more than $4,000 per capita per year (Anderson & Hussey, 2001), these expenditures are not insignificant and represent substantial local, state, and federal resources that come in the form of reimbursement for services and direct support for local health care institutions.

The dynamics of rural communities and the current organizational structures of the health care system result in challenging dilemmas for local providers. Local health care services are tied to the economics of the rural community and are part of what attracts new residents and new businesses and creates new jobs. To maintain local health services, communities must recruit and retain health care professionals and ensure the financial viability of local hospitals and other services. The increased demand for primary care providers by urban-managed care systems has left rural communities in stiff competition for these professionals. The smaller patient base of rural hospitals makes it difficult to match the financial incentives offered by urban hospitals. The low population density of rural communities suggests low volume, which can translate into high average costs, a factor that rural health officials historically have felt is not taken into account in reimbursement (Wakefield, 2000). Low patient volume may affect quality, or the perception of quality, which may encourage residents who are able to look outside the community for care to seek care elsewhere, reducing the number of available patients even lower. Transportation to health care providers is critical, given the greater distances involved. Public transportation systems are usually lacking in rural areas, and private transportation may be quite costly.

The demographic and socioeconomic profile of rural community residents influences the demands placed on the health care system. The occupations in rural environments tend to be in agriculture, mining, and fishing, which are attractive to immigrant populations. As a result, the high number of work-related injuries creates a challenge for emergency medical systems (Ricketts, 2000). The poverty, limited English-language proficiency, and lower educational levels of these immigrant populations may hamper health education and preventive health efforts. Health literacy, which has gained recent attention, is yet another barrier to efficacy of health services.

Patterns of insurance coverage cannot be ignored. High rates of self-employment influence the availability of employer-sponsored health insurance and result in a large number of people who are underinsured (Wakefield, 2000). As a result of high prescription drug costs, the elderly, those living in poverty, and the working poor may not have access to the medications they need. Public insurance programs are especially important to rural communities, given the older age structure and higher poverty levels, but the social structure of rural communities may attach stigma to participation in these programs. The importance of public insurance makes rural health care providers more dependent on revenues from these programs than are their urban counterparts.

Changes in public insurance have clear consequences for rural communities. A change in the funding of local community-based mental health services has resulted in dramatic changes in the way services are organized, leaving rural residents scrambling for services. Further, rural health care providers have long felt that reimbursement rates under public programs are based on a faulty assumption of lower costs in rural areas and that these programs are thus biased against rural areas. One reason for this is the competition with urban areas for health care professionals, which drives competitive salaries. The inability of rural communities to compete with these salaries reduces their ability to recruit health care professionals and results in high provider turnover, which drives recruitment costs higher. In summary, the persistence of skewed resource distribution is a salient characteristic of rural health care (Ricketts, 2000).

Citizen Participation in Rural Health

The cultural characteristics of the people and the geographic dimensions of the communities themselves in combination with the limitations of the health care system create a need for citizen participation in rural areas. Community-based participatory research (CBPR) (Metzler et al., 2003), participatory action research (PAR) (Morris, 2002), and empowerment research (EPR) (Page & Czuba, 1999) are all approaches that involve participants as full partners in the research process and have been successfully used to engage citizens in community development. CBPR has had as its focus health issues, and has brought the community members into the research process as complete research partners, including the design and immediate benefits; PAR has its roots in phenomenology, and is a recognized form of research where the focus is on the effects of the researcher's actions within a participating community; and within EPR framework, the researcher targets a community group that would be excluded because of some characteristic, then through assessment identifies and utilizes strengths of the group to work for mutual benefit. Although each of these approaches has a slightly different emphasis, they all involve shared decision making, shared power, shared responsibility, and shared benefits. In these research approaches, conducting the research is in itself considered transformative for participants, with the goal of immediate benefit from their participation. Wallerstein and Duran (2006) offer perspectives on the value of participatory research in empowering rural communities by describing CBPR as a process of training and education to improve employment opportunities, income, and the potential for advocacy or policy changes. Israel, Schulz, Parker, and Becker (1998) define it as

> a collaborative approach to research that equitably involves community members, organizational representatives, and researchers in all aspects of the research process. The partners contribute unique strengths and shared responsibilities to enhance understanding of a given phenomenon and the social and cultural dynamics of the community, and integrate the knowledge gained with action to improve the health and well being of community members. (p. 4)

A central component of the empowerment of rural people is the goal to improve their capacity to take control of their health care, draw upon their strengths, and cope with their own problems. These empowerment and community capacity strategies result in positive health outcomes (Morford, Robinson, Mazzoni, Corbett, & Schaiberger, 2004). As Wallerstein and Duran (2006) point out, empowering strategies create empowerment and capacity outcomes, and these have a direct impact on health outcomes and effectiveness—all of which occur within the unique sociocultural, racial, and environmental contexts of the local community. The importance of CBPR is that it addresses power dynamics and relationships. CBPR must involve representatives of the affected population in the research process in order for the assessment, evaluation, or research to represent at least some of the voices in the community from an insider's perspective. To be authentic, relevant, and sustainable, it must involve community members and provide some benefit to the community.

Brehm (2002) summarizes the things one must consider before doing community development. He suggests checking the fit between the researcher and the community. Values and vision need to be shared. The project taken on must be practical and within the community's capacity and resources. An agreed-upon strategy for getting the work done and assessment of risk is important, as the consequences of failure are detrimental to future work. The community must be involved in all stages of planning. Much time, energy, and emotion can be expended by the community as it moves through the phases of its development.

CBPR has its origin in the social and political movements of the 1940s, when Kurt Lewin introduced the idea of action research as a means to overcoming social inequalities (O'Brien, 1998). Lewin dismissed the idea that researchers needed to remove themselves from the community in order to be objective. Later, Paulo Freire, in his book *Pedagogy of the Oppressed* (1970), introduced the idea of having communities identify their own problems and solutions. Building upon this history, communities and researchers today are increasingly turning to CBPR approaches to research because research designs often fail to incorporate the multiple domains in their explanations of health, which limits our understanding of the social and economic complexities motivating individual and family behavior. Further, community members feel used when little or no direct benefit is returned to them for their efforts. Community input is invaluable in the determination of the research adaptations that are necessary to address the unique characteristics of a given community, particularly where large cultural groups exist. In adherence with the basic principles of CBPR, the outcomes must provide information that is of use to the community so community members can develop their own solutions. Moreover, to do this, public trust and respect—things that can be challenging in closed rural communities—are required. The idea is that if the research design and methods actively engage community members in an equitable manner, public trust is likely to develop.

Hartwig, Calleson, and Williams (2006) summarize the eight key characteristics of successful community-based partnerships. These partnerships:

- Recognize community as a unit of identity
- Build on strengths and resources within the community
- Facilitate collaborative partnerships in all phases of the research
- Integrate knowledge and action for mutual benefit of all partners
- Promote a co-learning and empowering process that attends to social inequalities
- Involve a cyclical and iterative process
- Address health from both positive and ecological perspectives
- Disseminate findings and knowledge gained to all partners

These principles are useful as a guide to a community process that is essential for building the infrastructure of the partnership.

METHODOLOGY

The primary goals of CBPR are to strengthen an intervention and to add value to the community. A review of the literature was conducted to explore use of CBPR in rural areas by nurses and other health care professionals with Latino and Hispanic individuals and to determine whether or not the studies reviewed met these two goals (Shelton, 2007). A search of 11 search engines was conducted (Academic Search Premier, CINAHL, EconLit, ERIC, LGBT Life with Full Text, MasterFILE Premier, Nation Archive, Professional Development Collection, PsycARTICLES, Psychology and Behavioral Sciences Collection, PsycINFO, Religion and Philosophy Collection, Social Work Abstracts, Women's Studies International, MEDLINE) using the keywords *participatory research, CBPR, Latino, Hispanic, rural* and *nursing*. In order to be included in the review, studies had to be accessible online and present the experience and findings of a community intervention, with an aim to discover how health disparities were reduced in the community, particularly for Latino and/or Hispanic populations, if available. The search yielded 21 articles; of these, 7 were written by nurses. One additional article described a study conducted by an interdisciplinary team that included a nurse. None of the nursing articles focused on rural Latino/Hispanic populations. Sixteen of the articles described an intervention providing some benefit to a rural Latino or Hispanic community. The articles that discussed rural Latino or Hispanic populations focused on environmental justice (2 articles); HIV/AIDS projects (6 articles); diabetes, cancer, and violence (1 article each); school dropouts (3 articles); and lay health advisors (2 articles). All but 3 articles focused on adults, primarily males.

LITERATURE REVIEW

Forty-five percent of the 16 intervention studies focused on Latino/Hispanic rural populations attributed the reduction of health disparities to researchers' access to a population in need, such as undocumented or gay Hispanics, and another 45% attributed it to the creation of culturally relevant adaptations to clinical services, such as the provision of educational materials. One article discussed the creation of social change. The authors of these articles described the benefits to the community as empowering people in terms of "giving voice," "developing commitment," and "fostering pride and self-sufficiency." Others stated that the intervention was a way to mobilize the community and move them toward social change.

The high number of articles that cite the researchers' access to the population as the benefit of the CBPR intervention reflects the issue of gaining public trust. The articles that discuss the development of culturally relevant clinical services imply that the initial steps necessary to gain public trust had already occurred. Most of the articles discuss the lengthy process of gaining trust, which frequently takes up to 3 years. The articles share commonalities in their discussion of immigrant and cultural experiences of stigma, whether related to race and ethnicity, legal status, or health status (as in the case of mental illness or HIV/AIDS). Stressors related to acculturation experiences and oppression are also mentioned.

At the root of these interventions lies the issue of power and the negative outcomes experienced by people targeted by the biases of society or a social group. Negative stereotypes result in resistance and render communities unable to enact some change for the common good. Empowerment strategies are the prescription for these immobilized communities, and as such, expertise with empowerment strategies is a vital component of the CBPR researcher's toolkit.

As a nursing strategy, empowerment refers to increasing the spiritual, political, social, and/or economic strength of individuals and communities. It often involves helping community members develop confidence in their own capacities. Strategies include identification and recognition of community strengths. Empowerment is then the process of obtaining basic opportunities for marginalized people, either directly by those people or through the help of nonmarginalized others who share their own access to these opportunities. It also includes actively thwarting attempts to deny those opportunities. Empowerment also involves encouraging and developing the skills for self-sufficiency, with a focus on eliminating future need for charity or welfare. This process can be difficult to start, and challenging to implement effectively, but there are many examples throughout the nursing literature of empowerment projects that have succeeded. As will be discussed, research needs to be conducted to validate the methods and approaches in a more rigorous way.

A CASE EXAMPLE

The case that will be examined involves an eastern Connecticut rural community approximately 12 miles from the University of Connecticut. With a population of approximately 16,000 people, this community is the largest town in the immediate area. It is categorized as rural because of its isolation from other population centers, and the surrounding towns are agricultural in character. Described by the U.S. Census Bureau (2003) as a "micropolitan" area, this community met the Human Resources and Services Administration's criteria of rurality. In addition, this community was recognized as a Governor Service area due to its 2004 designation as one of 25 "distressed municipalities" by the state's economic and community development commissioner, a designation based on demographic and economic indicators. Further, the community met federal criteria to be designated a "medically underserved population" (U.S. Census Bureau, 2002).

The town is quite diverse by rural standards, with a significant Latino/Hispanic population comprising 33% of the total population. Nearly 70% of immigrants were of Puerto Rican origin, followed by 20% recent arrivals from Mexico. The remaining 10% of Latino/Hispanic immigrants came from several countries, a number of them from Guatemala. Whereas people of Puerto Rican heritage were often more acculturated, other recently arrived Latino/Hispanic immigrants tended to work on farms in surrounding towns. An appraisal of the community found the Latino/Hispanic minority vulnerable to health disparities.

The town was an economically stressed community facing challenges in several areas. The passing of the textile industry in New England had impoverished the town, and this was evident in its dilapidated appearance and antiquated and poorly maintained housing. Despite the presence of a hospital, medical care was largely inaccessible to much of the community because of language and cultural barriers or lack of insurance. The community also suffered from a reputation for once having been a haven of drug use. Although resources were brought to the community, sustainability remained an issue primarily because of their dependency upon state funding. A core group of health care providers remained in the community. They reported that the poor and uninsured continued to be underserved. Access to services due to limited bilingual health care providers and lack of transportation was one of the primary problems reported. A gap in the service structure existed for mental health services and prevention services (Shelton, Fitzgerald, & Amendola, 2007).

Other community concerns were the undocumented migrant workforce and the growing number of homeless people, many of whom faced multiple physical health and mental health problems as well as problems with violence and abuse. For some services, particularly mental health services, residents had to travel 125 miles round trip to the nearest urban area. Insufficient communication between community agencies was identified as a stressor. This was in part fueled by confidentiality of records and the undocumented status of the migrant population. Personal relationships and informal networks among churches and families filled gaps in services (Shelton & Piotr, 2007).

Before a CBPR process was implemented, an assessment of the community's existing coalitions, their target populations, and their level of functioning or productivity was conducted. It was not our intent to supplant existing resources. A match between the researcher's interests and that of the community is a necessary first step. How to structure participation depends upon the history of collaboration within the community (Wallerstein, Duran, Minkler, & Foley, 2005). Typically, CBPR projects have community advisory boards; in communities that already have community-based coalitions, networking with these existing identities may be a strategy for engaging the community. In the rural Hispanic community studied, following several months of networking through telephone and personal meetings, and following the rural community appraisal (Shelton, Fitzgerald, & Amendola, 2007), the researcher, who was new to the community, distributed a flier inviting community health care providers and community social and religious leaders to meet to explore how they might work together. In response, 24 individuals, primarily health and mental health agency representatives attended, some out of interest in collaborating, and some out of curiosity, none of them wanting to be left out should resources become evident. The majority of these individuals had collaborated with university faculty prior to this time, but less frequently with the School of Nursing. Following an introduction and a presentation on the education and community service mission of the university, the group was asked, "How can we partner with the community?" The question was met by silence. One community member stated that they had never been asked before. At this meeting, it was discovered that the history of collaboration with the university had to be undone. Unhappiness with past participation in projects and a lack of access to information and other interventions left some uninterested in further involvement. This became obvious after two meetings, when attendance dropped dramatically. Seven individuals remained loyal to the process: four agency employees (one mental health agency, one child agency, one community health agency, and one homeless shelter agency), two advocacy people, and one private citizen. For those who remained in the group, the next challenge, one of control and competition, surfaced.

Wallerstein and Duran (2006) point out that participation and control are never static. Levels of participation vary by levels of ownership, with greatest participation by partners who have a stake and authority in the decision making. It is not unusual for a CBPR project to start with a university-driven agenda and move toward a community-driven agenda over time. For this rural community, this is exactly what occurred. Over several years, the competing priorities of the various players arose. It became evident that the "who" representing the community was an issue. No community is homogeneous, and community organizations and leaders may not fully represent the range of community interests. The researchers realized that to have an impact on the challenges of the Hispanic community, they would have to engage Hispanic residents in the project. However, this was not a view held by all the health care provider participants.

Yet another challenge was the level of participation over time. True CBPR methods go beyond minimal or superficial involvement. In the case of this rural community, it took three years to engage the Hispanic residents in the process, and the same number of years for the health care providers to understand the importance of their role for this process. Participants needed to come to understand that they had to be more inclusive, and that they were to have equality in the process. Hall (2001) refers to this as a challenge to "unpack the role of power and privilege" in the research relationship. Researchers may perceive that they have the "expert" power. The recent focus on evidence-based interventions, which are (for the most part) tested in the dominant (White) culture, may have the effect of minimizing the importance of the knowledge that comes from within the local community. In this rural community example, the challenge involved helping the community participants understand that they had experiential knowledge about the community that was as important to the process as the expert power of the researchers. Miller and Shinn (2005) refer to this as the "experience of culturally supported interventions." These experiences are the indigenous theories of etiology, practices, and programs that emerge from communities that have not been formally evaluated but are widely accepted.

Responsibilities and levels of collaboration can be expected to shift, as the ebb and flow of day-to-day work activities in the community and CBPR processes proceed, particularly around entry to the community, data analysis, and dissemination. In the researchers' experience, during phases of the research for which permission to enter the community was needed from community-based organizations, or when data analysis was in need of interpretation, the community partners had more power and responsibilities. However, when data entry and statistical analyses were needed, the responsibility fell to the researchers. In this rural community, the interpretation was made difficult by the different perspectives held by the health care providers and the residents themselves. These perspectives often had to be obtained in separate meetings. The health care providers were open to having community residents come to their meetings, but few if any Hispanic residents attended, despite extensive outreach efforts. Resistance on the part of the Hispanic residents manifested as "community shyness." While researchers were readily accepted into their homes and churches, Hispanic residents seemed intimidated by the health care provider group, and therefore unwilling to join in meetings with them.

Dissemination, on the other hand, was easier. The Hispanic community had well-defined cultural networks, and community leaders, identified by residents, were those in the community who owned small businesses and had access to the local media (radio and newspapers). The Hispanic participants who owned the Spanish-language newspaper and Spanish-language radio station were very supportive and the researchers had easy access to the population through those mechanisms. These participants felt comfortable in this role and took on the dissemination with little assistance. It was expected that the church would have some influence, and it too provided a forum for dissemination.

Although shown in the literature, it was surprising how the challenges associated with race, racism, and ethnic discrimination were strongly evidenced in this small rural community in the form of resistance to change. It was expected that work by White researchers in a community dominated by Hispanic people might raise issues of racism or at least unintentionally obscure cultural concerns. Taking an approach of "cultural humility," described by Tervalon and Murray-Garcia (1998) as "a lifelong commitment to self-evaluation and self-critique," the researchers sought to reduce power imbalances and "develop and maintain mutually respectful and dynamic partnerships" (p. 118) with the community. Effort was made to identify differences in perspectives based upon differences in culture and to support a creation of mutual knowledge. These actions were embraced by the Hispanic residents, but never focused on by the health care providers, who seemed uncomfortable with the leveling of the playing field.

After several years of effort and a natural evolution during which partners were changed, an opportunity to collaborate with a group of three male Hispanic community leaders who had formed an advocacy group emerged. The fact that they were respected within their own cultural community as leaders greatly facilitated efforts to enact social change. Simple persistence and having a physical presence in the community over time, combined with self-reflection and dialogue, rewarded the researchers with the privilege of having the Hispanic community as allies in research. Labonte (2005) points out that it is necessary to engage in a process of self-reflection about historic and changing positions of power, and to do so with various partners, to build relationships and make each stakeholder feel valued. Efforts to create safe opportunities for reflection and to define the agendas and abilities of community partners were both stimulating and draining. People needed to feel safe and to be given permission to voice their opinions, and to move beyond words to social action. Spivak (1990) refers to this as moving beyond "ventriloquism," or speaking for community members, to a place where all partners can be heard and valued. This experience heightened awareness of the power and privileges tied to different roles, and the importance of recognizing this before any relationships are built. Much is said about resistance on the part of researchers in the literature (Rhodes et al., 2006), but in this situation, it was the health care providers who showed greater resistance to the shift in roles and boundaries. Given the limited number of health care providers in the community, the demands upon their time contributed to this resistance. And although health care providers could recognize the need to make changes in order to improve access and services, there was concern among them that they would create a need that could not be served. There was little acknowledgment that the need existed despite their recognition of it, and that there were few ideas on how to make the changes that the system needed. An underlying concern that was never voiced was economics. Key health providers such as the lead community public mental health provider did not want competition for fear of loss of funding, even if this left people underserved.

CONCLUSIONS

Participatory strategies are thought to affect health by empowering participants, which produces psychological, community, and cultural outcomes (Wallerstein & Duran, 2006). Only a few published studies, each with different research designs, have tested and validated the hypothesis that community participation provides additional health benefits at the community level. Studies of youth interventions provide good examples for participatory outcome measures on self-efficacy, bonding, and civic behavior (Streng, Rhodes, Ayala, Eng, Arceo, et al., 2004). At a systems level, participatory strategies have led to improved mental health and school performance (Holden, Messeri, Evans, Crankshaw, & Ben-Davies, 2004; Lerner & Thompson, 2002).

As the growth of CBPR provides evidence that participation makes a difference, and science seeks to understand these differences, the value of local community groups themselves identifying outcomes has not been lost on the World Health Organization's Healthy Cities (WHO, 2006) and Communities movement (O'Neill & Simard, 2006). Five characteristics of healthy cities (participation, interagency collaboration, healthy public policy, sustainability, and healthy structures and good governance) and potential changes in material, social, and cultural conditions that are linked to health outcomes have been identified (O'Neill & Simard, 2006). The added value of participation in the intervention and outcomes remains a critically important question and the primary point of using CBPR methods. Through consciousness raising and empowerment, participants not only come to value such things as intuitive knowledge and knowledge from shared experiences but use this knowledge and experience in an active and focused way to reach an agreed-upon community goal.

As evidenced by the brief review of online journal articles, nursing researchers who are interested in these methods need to collaborate to develop a more focused and organized body of literature to document the important aspects of CBPR as it applies to topics of interest to nursing. Within the profession, we must demonstrate the evidence that supports the two beliefs that CBPR strengthens interventions and adds value. Although known intuitively by many, it needs to be demonstrated scientifically. Many of the nursing articles found that were not discussed in this review focused on the process of CBPR. It is indeed a difficult and time-consuming process. But, as with other types of research, different designs need to be tested and replicated across communities. CBPR is commonly utilized and appears to be a successful strategy for cultural populations. What conclusions can be drawn? And what models developed and strategies tested?

The partnership approach described here has fostered interaction and involvement among many collaborators (the university, the researchers, community agencies, Hispanic residents, and the media). CBPR provides a process for meeting research goals as well as for developing long-term partnerships to promote the health of communities. In the community discussed, researchers and three Hispanic men initiated a partnership to promote Hispanic health within the community. After many years of effort, the power base has shifted.

The need for reflection on processes is real. Reflection is needed to center the process and meet the first goal of CBPR—to strengthen the intervention. But it must be done ever so gently. Wisdom gained from the use of CBPR methods to conduct successful community research to reduce health disparities for Hispanic populations may be applicable to work done with other community groups. Researchers should remember to involve members of the targeted group as equal partners in the process. Be sure to level the playing field by including existing community networks, such as advocacy groups as well as social and health agencies. The inclusive nature of this work means that the network will grow and expand as the collaboration with other community programs, religious organizations, and lay organizations become partners. Empowerment strategies and community ownership do foster community pride and self-sufficiency (McQuiston, Choi-Hevel, & Clawson, 2001). In order to support community pride and self-sufficiency, participants must demonstrate flexibility and constant attention to the processes as they unfold. Acquisition of resources, whether those resources are financial or volunteer time, is necessary. Remuneration for efforts is one way of demonstrating respect for the commitment made and helps sustain interest and work efforts. Demonstrating cultural responsiveness—for example, speaking the language of the community, making an effort to be nonthreatening, validating understandings and meanings, and approaching the situation as a listener and one who is learning—was found to impart a message that the researchers were interested in and committed to the community.

Challenges

Challenges for use of CBPR methods present themselves at the outset of the process. The time spent at the beginning is well worth the effort. Plan ahead, and allow sufficient time to gain entry into the community and to formulate and confirm research interests. Constant and fluid interactions with community collaborators are required to complete a study and to effect a positive health outcome, the second goal of CBPR. These approaches allow researchers to address problems as they arise, and to keep the project on course. The value of food should not be underestimated. Food, a common language for many cultures, was found to be one way that people felt comfortable sharing, and an effective strategy for gaining access to people's cultural expertise. Further, researchers conducting studies with low-income communities need to recognize that food is often scarce and should be part of what they plan. People cannot think and work when they are hungry.

In this day and age, in light of required economic efficiencies in health care and in the conduct of research studies, finding out what works and for whom is important. Grassroots collaboration is increasingly relied upon to improve health and the quality of life, in part as a response to increasing sociopolitical complexities. Solutions to critical community problems require a collaborative approach. While this is not a new concept, the focus of the National Institutes of Health on translational research has pushed this issue forward and has created expectations that the benefits to the public should be tangible. This movement matches well with CBPR approaches that engage citizens in their own health care. In addition, the participatory nature of CBPR is a good fit for cultural populations that value social and family networks.

Future Directions

The nurse researchers of tomorrow need to utilize their skills to analyze and synthesize on behalf of the community as they use their expert power and knowledge of community development to advance community goals, bridge differences between partners, and facilitate communication. Marois (2006) aptly reported climates characterized by mistrust, inequity, constant change, competition, and scarcity; culture clashes; identity and role confusion; and a lack of shared vision and decision making to be barriers to health partnerships. Successful strategies to handle these conflicts include equalizing power, strengthening relationships through dialogue and responsive action, and learning to navigate the different cultures of communities and institutions. The first step in this process, however, is to gain public trust.

The significance of CBPR methodology for nursing lies in the opportunities offered through its iterative processes, which allow for reflection and positive exchange, which encourage modifications that strengthen projects, benefit community partners, and create environments of mutual respect and trust. Herein also lies the methodological challenge—balancing responsiveness with the responsibilities of rigor. Many questions face the profession as it expands its use of CBPR methodologies. What criteria are used to evaluate CBPR methodologies? Which research strategies are preferred, or recommended? How is the quality of this research to be assessed? Few nursing studies report CBPR processes in totality; frequently they are presented as disjointed ethnographic studies. The contextual and historical richness of the process is lost. This may be a result of what is accepted for publication, or of what we as authors think is important to include in publications. A suggestion would be to publish a sequence of articles that describe a network's CBPR process from inception through several cycles of projects so that readers come away with a full understanding of the dynamics (an excellent example can be found in Powers, Cumbie, & Weinert, 2006). Given the popularity of interdisciplinary research, nursing doctoral education will continue to call for rigorous methodological training, and an appreciation for mixed methods. No one method serves all purposes, particularly when one is immersed in the community. When in a participatory process, the researcher is a participant, as the subject is a researcher. Always remember the CBPR motto—responsiveness and rigor.

CBPR seems a natural fit methodologically, for what nurses have been doing and will continue to do. Nurse researchers are in the unique position to collaborate with each other to promote rapid methodological development leading to national nursing research centers focusing on CBPR methodology. Nursing has the National Institute for Nursing within the National Institutes for Health at the federal level, and the ability to capitalize upon the well-developed community clinical nursing networks already developed at the local level. This discipline-specific partnership could develop national models of excellence in CBPR research methodology.

This writer finds CBPR an easy framework for working with cultural communities. With some reflection, it seems CBPR is a methodology that exemplifies the blending of the art and science of nursing—that which makes this profession so wonderfully fulfilling and unique.

REFERENCES

Agency for Health Care Policy and Research. (1996). *Improving health care for rural populations*. Research in action fact sheet (Pub. No. 96-P040). Rockville, MD: Agency for Health Care Policy and Research. Retrieved November 25, 2007, from http://www.ahrq.gov/research/rural.htm

Anderson, G., & Hussey, P. S. (2001). Comparing health system performance in OECD countries. *Health Affairs, 20*(3), 219–232.

Brehm, J. M. (2002, June). *The multidimensional nature of community attachment in a changing rural landscape*. Presented at the Ninth International Symposium on Society and Resource Management, Bloomington, IN. Retrieved December 2, 2007, from http://www.indiana.edu/~issrm/9thISSRM.pdf

Downs, B. (2004). Fertility of American women: June 2002. *Current Population Reports* (P20-548). U.S. Department of Commerce, Economics and Statistics Administration, U.S. Census Bureau. Retrieved December 1, 2007, from http://www.census.gov/population/www/socdemo/fertility.html

Fennelly, K., & Federico, C. M. (2007). *Rural residence as a determinant of attitudes toward U.S. immigration policy*. Minneapolis: University of Minnesota. Retrieved December 4, 2007, from http://www.hhh.umn.edu/img/assets/3755/ruralresidence_determinant.pdf

Freire, P. (1970). *Pedagogy of the oppressed*. New York: Herder and Herder.

Grieco, E. M., & Cassidy, R. C. (2001). *Overview of race and Hispanic origin, 2000*. (C2KBR/01-1). U.S. Department of Commerce, Economics and Statistics Administration, U.S. Census Bureau. Retrieved December 1, 2007, from http://www.census.gov/prod/2001pubs/c2kbr01-1.pdf

Guzmán, B. (2001). *The Hispanic population: Census 2000 brief*. Washington, DC: U.S. Census Bureau. Housing and Household Economic Statistics Division. Retrieved December 2, 2007, from http://www.ncsl.org/programs/immig/demographics2000census.htm

Hall, G. C. (2001). Psychotherapy research with ethnic minorities: Empirical, ethical, and conceptual issues. *Journal of Consulting and Clinical Psychology, 69*(3), 502–510.

Hartwig, K., Calleson, D., & Williams, M. (2006). Community-based participatory research: Getting grounded. In J. Kauper-Brown & S. Seifer (Eds.), *The examining community-institutional partnerships for prevention research group. Developing and sustaining community-based participatory research partnerships: A skill-building curriculum*. Retrieved November 18, 2007, from http://www.cbprcurriculum.info

Hernandez, D. J., & Charney, E. (1998). *From generation to generation: The health and well-being of children in immigrant families*. Washington, DC: National Academy Press. Retrieved November 15, 2007, from http://books.google.com

Hernández-León, R., & Zúñiga, V. (2000). *Mexican immigrant communities in the South and social capital: The case of Dalton, Georgia*. Working Paper 64. University of California, San Diego: The Center for Comparative Immigration Studies. Retrieved November 28, 2007, from http://ccis.ucsd.edu/PUBLICATIONS/wrkg64.pdf

Heyman, S. R. (1982). Capitalizing on unique assets of rural areas for community interventions. *Rural Community Psychology, 3*(3), 5–48.

Holden, D. J., Messeri, P., Evans, W. D., Crankshaw, E., & Ben-Davies, M. (2004). Conceptualizing youth empowerment within tobacco control. *Health Education & Behavior, 31*(5), 548–563.

Holder, K. (2006). Voting and registration in the election of November 2000: Population characteristics. *Current Population Reports* (P20-556). U.S. Department of Commerce, Economics and Statistics Administration, U.S. Census Bureau. Retrieved December 1, 2007, from http://www.census.gov/prod/2006pubs/p20-556.pdf

Isham, J., Narayan, D., & Pritchett, L. (1994). *Does participation improve project performance: Establishing causality with subjective data*. Policy Research Working Paper #1357, World Bank. Retrieved December 2, 2007, from http://www-wds.worldbank.org/servlet/WDSContentServer/WDSP/IB/1994/09/01/000009265_3970716141732/Rendered/PDF/multi0page.pdf

Israel, B. A., Schulz, A., Parker, E., & Becker, A. B. (1998). Review of community-based research: Assessing partnership approaches to improve public health. *Annual Review of Public Health, 19*, 173–202.

Johnson, K. (2006). *Demographic trends in rural and small town America*. Durham: Carsey Institute, University of New Hampshire.

Kandel, W., & Cromartie, J. (2004). *New patterns of Hispanic settlement in rural America* (RDRR-99). Washington, DC: Department of Agriculture. Economic Research Service. Retrieved November 28, 2007, from http://www.ers.usda.gov

Labonte, R. (2005). Community, community development, and the forming of authentic partnerships: Some critical reflections. In M. Minkler (Ed.), *Community organizing and community building for health* (pp. 88–102). New Brunswick, NJ: Rutgers University Press.

Lerner, R. M., & Thompson, L. S. (2002). Promoting healthy adolescent behavior and development: Issues in the design and evaluation of effective youth programs. *Journal of Pediatric Nursing, 17*(5), 338–344.

Lichter, D. T, & Johnson, K. M. (2006). Emerging rural settlement patterns and the geographic redistribution of America's new immigrants. *Rural Sociology, 71*,109–131.

Marois, D. (2006). *Beyond polarities: Collaboration and conflict in community health partnerships*. Unpublished thesis. State University of New York, Plattsburgh.

McQuiston, C., Choi-Hevel, S., & Clawson, M. (2001). Protegiendo nuestra comunidad: Empowerment participatory education for HIV prevention. *Journal of Transcultural Nursing, 112*(2), 275–283.

Metzler, M. M., Higgins, D. L., Beeker, C. G., Freudenberg, N., Lantz, P. M., Senturia, K. D., et al. (2003). Addressing urban health in Detroit, New York City, and Seattle through community-based participatory research partnerships. *American Journal of Public Health, 93*(5), 803–811.

Miller, R. L., & Shinn, M. (2005). Learning from communities: Overcoming difficulties in dissemination of prevention and promotion efforts. *American Journal of Community Psychology, 35*(3/4), 169–183.

Morford, S., Robinson, D., Mazzoni, F., Corbett, C., & Schaiberger, H. (2004). Participatory research in rural communities in transition: A case study of the Malaspina-Ucluelet Research Alliance. *BC Journal of Ecosystems and Management, 5*(2), 39–43. Retrieved November 25, 2007, from http://www.forrex.org/jem/2004/vol5/no2/art5.pdf

Morris, M. (2002). *Participatory research and action: A guide to becoming a researcher for social change*. Ontario, Canada: Canadian Research Institute for the Advancement of Women.

Moscovice, I. (1989). Strategies for promoting a viable rural health care system. *Rural Health, 5*, 216–230.

O'Brien, R. (1998). An overview of the methodological approach of action research. In R. Richardson (Ed.), *Theory and practice of action research*. João Pessoa, Brazil: Universidade Federal da Paraíba. Retrieved December 2, 2007, from http://www.web.ca/~robrien/papers/arfinal.html

O'Neill, M., & Simard, P. (2006). Choosing indicators to evaluate Healthy Cities projects: A political task? *Health Promotion International 2006, 21*(2), 145–152. Retrieved December 2, 2007, from http://heapro.oxfordjournals.org/cgi/content/full/21/2/145

Ormond, B. A., Wallin, S., & Goldenson, S. M. (2000). *Supporting the rural health care safety net, 36*. Assessing the New Federalism. Washington, DC: The Urban Institute.

Page, N., & Czuba, C. E. (1999). Empowerment: What is it? *Journal of Extension, 37*(5), 1–5. Retrieved December 4, 2007, from http://www.joe.org/joe/1999october/comm1.html

Powers, J., Cumbie, S. A., & Weinert, C. (2006). Lessons learned through the creative and iterative process of community-based participatory research. *International Journal of Qualitative Methods, 5*(2), Article 4. Retrieved January 31, 2008, from http://www.ualberta.ca/~ijqm/backissues/5_2/pdf/powers.pdf

Rhodes, S. D., Hergenrather, K. C., Montaño, J., Remnitz, I. M., Arceo, R., Bloom, F. R., et al. (2006). Using community-based participatory research to develop an intervention to reduce HIV and STD infections among Latino men. *AIDS Education & Prevention, 18*(5), 375–389.

Ricketts, T. (2000). The changing nature of rural health care. *Annual Review of Public Health, 21*, 639–657.

Sawyer, D., Gale, J., & Lambert, D. (2006). *Rural and frontier mental and behavioral health care: Barriers, effective policy strategies, best practices* (contract # 02-0279P). Waite, MN: National Association for Rural Mental Health.

Schoeni, R., McCarthy, K., & Vemez, G. (1996). *The mixed economic progress of immigrants*. Santa Monica, CA: Rand.

Shelton, D. (2007). *An integrative review of the benefits attributed to CBPR with Hispanic communities*. Unpublished manuscript. Storrs, CT: University of Connecticut.

Shelton, D., Fitzgerald, L., & Amendola, M. G. (2007). *Compañeros Por Salud: Initial phases of a rural community-based participatory process*. Manuscript submitted for publication.

Shelton, D., & Piotr, P. (2007). *Rural Latino and Hispanic mental health networks*. Manuscript submitted for publication.

Spivak, G. (1990). Criticism, feminism and the institution. In S. Harasym (Ed.), *The postcolonial critic* (pp. 1–16). New York: Routledge.

Streng, J. M., Rhodes, S. D., Ayala, G. X., Eng, E., Arceo, R., & Phipps, S. (2004). Realidad Latina: Latino adolescents, their school, and a university use photovoice to examine and address the influence of immigration. *Journal of Interprofessional Care, 18*(4), 403–415.

Tervalon, M., & Murray-Garcia, J. (1998). Cultural humility vs. cultural competence: A critical distinction in defining physician training outcomes in medical education. *Journal of Health Care for the Poor and Underserved, 9*(2), 117–125.

U.S. Census Bureau. (2002). *U.S. census 2000*. Washington, DC: U.S. Department of Commerce, Economics and Statistics Administration, Systems Support Division.

U.S. Census Bureau. (2003). *Metropolitan and micropolitan statistical areas*. Washington, DC: U.S. Census Bureau, Housing and Household Economic Statistics Division. Retrieved December 4, 2007, from http://www.census.gov/population/www/estimates/metroarea.html

U.S. Census Bureau. (2007). *Poverty thresholds, 2004*. Washington, DC: U.S. Census Bureau, Housing and Household Economic Statistics Division. Retrieved December 4, 2007, from http://www.census.gov/hhes/www/poverty/poverty.html

Wakefield, M. (2000). *Rural hospitals and rural economic development*. Testimony before the Agriculture, Rural Development and Related Agencies Subcommittee of the Senate Committee on Appropriations. Center for Health Policy, Research & Ethics. Fairfax, VA: George Mason University. Retrieved December 2, 2007, from http://chpre.gmu.edu/briefspublications/Wakefield_testimony.pdf

Wallerstein, N., Duran, B., Minkler, M., & Foley, K. (2005). Developing and maintaining partnerships with communities. In B. Israel, E. Eng, A. Schulz, & E. Parker (Eds.), *Methods in community based participatory research methods* (pp. 31–51). San Francisco: Jossey-Bass.

Wallerstein, N. B., & Duran, B. (2006). Using community-based participatory research to address health disparities. *Health Promotion Practice, 7*(3), 312–323.

Wellever, A., Wholey, D., & Radcliff, T. (2000). *Strategic choices of rural health networks: Implications for goals and performance measurement* (Working paper #31). Minneapolis, MN: University of Minnesota Rural Health Research Center. Retrieved November 30, 2006, from http://www.hpm.umn.edu/rhrc/pdfs/wpaper/working%20paper%20031.pdf

World Health Organization. (2006). *WHO European healthy cities*. Retrieved December 1, 2007, from http://www.euro.who.int/healthy-cities/introducing/20050202_1

Chapter 10

Rural Health Nursing Research Review: Global Perspectives

Doris S. Greiner, Doris F. Glick, Pamela A. Kulbok, and Emma McKim Mitchell

ABSTRACT

The CINAHL and MEDLINE databases were used to conduct a review of international rural nursing research published between 2003 and 2007. In total, 41 articles were reviewed and organized based on the United Nations Human Development Index, which categorizes countries based on development status. Critical review of international rural nursing research yielded three major organizational themes: clinical issues, aspects of nursing practice, and nursing and health policy research. Despite the variety in international locale of the research, these themes and other common findings emerged. The need for increased access to specialized nursing knowledge, resources, and support is an ongoing issue facing nurses in rural and remote settings.

Keywords: review of nursing research; rural health; review of literature; international rural health; international nursing; global health nursing; research in rural global health

INTRODUCTION

This review of international rural nursing research was undertaken in response to the observation of other contributors to this volume that a noticeable quantity of the research publications on their topics of interest was completed outside the United States. The aims of this review are to critique current literature focusing on international rural nursing research; identify approaches to clinical issues, nursing practice, and policy issues challenging nursing colleagues abroad; further our understanding of rurality as a variable that informs analysis of nursing research; and identify needed next steps for rural nursing research.

Papers selected for this review included research from countries across a wide range of levels of development, although the greatest number came from highly developed countries such as Australia and Canada. One method of comparing development and the well-being of populations is through the use of the Human Development Index (HDI). This index, developed in 1990, provides a standardized means to compare quality of life among countries and to measure the impact of social and economic policies on quality of life. The HDI is used by the United Nations Development Programme to list and rank countries as a means to assess overall well-being and child welfare. The index is a single statistic expressed as a value between 0 and 1, derived from the following measures (United Nations Development Programme, 2007):

- Life expectancy—measured by life expectancy at birth
- Education—measured by the adult literacy rate (two-thirds weight) and the combined primary, secondary, and tertiary gross enrollment ratio (one-third weight)
- Standard of living—measured by gross domestic product per person

To provide context and perspective for this review, the HDI for the countries addressed are listed in Table 10.1. The United States is included as a benchmark for comparison.

Eleven Australian articles and 13 Canadian articles met inclusion criteria and are discussed in separate sections. Ten research articles from highly developed countries are discussed as a group; these include reports from Sweden, Japan, Taiwan, Crete as a distinct part of Greece, and Korea. Eight studies represent work in medium-developed countries and are also discussed as a discrete group.

METHODOLOGY

A wide variety of articles describing rural health research conducted in an international context are available in nursing literature. Thus, a review of international nursing research of rural health issues was conducted. CINAHL and

TABLE 10.1   Human Development Index and Ranking for Countries Represented

Country	Level of Human Development	Rank Among 177 Countries	Human Development Index
Australia	High	3	0.962
Canada	High	4	0.961
Sweden	High	6	0.956
Japan	High	8	0.953
United States	High	12	0.951
Greece (Crete)	High	24	0.926
Korea	High	26	0.921
Philippines	Medium	90	0.771
Indonesia	Medium	107	0.728
Nicaragua	Medium	110	0.710
South Africa	Medium	121	0.674
Lesotho	Medium	138	0.549
Bangladesh	Medium	140	0.547
Swaziland	Medium	141	0.547
Zimbabwe	Medium	151	0.513
Gambia	Medium	155	0.502
Tanzania	Low	159	0.467
Malawi	Low	164	0.437

Note: HDI data for Taiwan is not available.
Source: United Nations Development Programme (2007).

MEDLINE databases were used to search for the keywords *rural areas*, *rural health*, *rural health nursing*, and *rural health services*. These searches yielded 10,152 articles. Computerized searches were then limited to research articles, publications in English, and research conducted in geographic regions outside the United States. The review was limited further to literature published between 2003 and 2007. The resulting 259 articles and all available abstracts were reviewed for relevance. Articles that focused on international rural nursing education were excluded, as this was viewed as an important topic warranting separate review. Once dissertations, evaluative reviews, conference proceedings, articles with an historical focus, and those articles inaccessible to reviewers were excluded, the remaining 42 articles were reviewed. Three categories emerged from the review of international rural research articles: clinical issues (e.g., medication errors, clinical practice for specific diseases or populations), nursing practice in rural areas (e.g., collaborative practice models), and policy issues. These categories provide the organizing framework for the subsequent review and discussion of articles. (Refer to Table 10.2 for study characteristics by focal category and country.)

NURSING RESEARCH IN RURAL AND REMOTE AUSTRALIA

Search of the literature identified 11 unduplicated manuscripts from Australia. This literature uses the terms *rural* and *remote* to refer to areas that are not densely populated. In contrast to *rural, remote* describes areas that are extremely isolated and distanced from resources. In Australia 30% of nurses work in rural and remote areas and are removed from the resources of the large urban teaching hospitals. These nurses work in facilities ranging from base rural and provincial hospitals that have medical and other health care professionals available to remote health facilities with only one nurse, who must depend on communication with the Royal Flying Doctor Service or other off-site medical support (McKeon, Fogarty, & Hegney, 2006). Australia has more remote areas than most other developed countries. Negative terms such as *isolation, poor facilities and communities, violence,* and *fear* are commonly used to describe the experience of nursing in remote areas of Australia (O'Brien & Jackson, 2007). Prior research shows that nurses working in remote areas tend to be professionally isolated and detached from professional practice and organizations. This geographic disadvantage calls attention to the need for special education and support for remote area nurses.

Among the 11 manuscripts that were reviewed, 7 described qualitative research methods, 2 reported quantitative research studies, 1 used a mixed-methods approach, and 1 used program evaluation to test the translation of nursing research into practice. The focus of interest of this literature was clinical management, nursing practice, and policy, and the populations of interest were patients and nurses in rural areas. In 2 of the studies, patients were the unit of analysis, while 9 focused on nurses. Sample size ranged from 6 to 627. Exploration of the concept of rurality primarily related to its impact on access to health resources for patients in remote areas. In addition, these articles examined the impact of isolation from colleagues and support resources on nurses and nursing practice.

Clinical Focus

Medication Errors

Using a survey of 627 nurses employed in rural or remote settings, McKeon, Fogarty, and Hegney (2006) investigated the impact of organizational issues on

TABLE 10.2 Focus and Selected Study Characteristics

			CLINICAL FOCUS	
Author and Date	Country	Design	Sample and Size	Focus and Findings
Ahn & Kim, 2004	Korea	Quantitative	$N = 97$, all elderly living alone in one rural county	Identified needs of elderly living alone. Called for health and social services to be combined
Bauer, 2006	Australia	Qualitative (in-depth interviews, naturalistic paradigm)	$N = 30$ (11 RNs, 9 ENs, 10 personal care attendants) in metropolitan and rural nursing homes	Examined how nursing home staff construct family involvement and how they work with residents' families (Used rural nursing homes in sample selection but rurality was not discussed)
Bennett et al., 2006	Australia	Quantitative (tool reliability assessment)	$N = 112$ HD patients in 9 nonhospital HD units (7 metropolitan and 2 rural)	Assessed reliability of a nurse-administered nutrition screening tool for HD patients to identify nutritionally at-risk patients
Bucknall, 2003	Australia	Qualitative (naturalistic observations/semi-structured interviews)	$N = 18$ critical care nurses in private and public hospitals (6 rural)	Investigated environmental influences on nurses' decisions in the critical care setting. Addressed issues unique to rural hospitals

(Continued)

TABLE 10.2 Focus and Selected Study Characteristics (*Continued*)

			CLINICAL FOCUS	
Author and Date	Country	Design	Sample and Size	Focus and Findings
Chen et al., 2005	Taiwan	Cross-sectional descriptive	$N = 37$ mothers with birth age below 18	Investigated health-related behaviors and life stresses of adolescent mothers. Found high dependence of parents, low rate of health-related behaviors
Culp et al., 2007	The Gambia	Exploratory descriptive	$N = 21$ rural nursing service employees, $N = 20$ farmers and field workers	Examined health and safety of farmers. Found congruence between health workers and farmers. Determined use of pesticides to be in need of intervention
Duffy, 2005	Zimbabwe	Ethnography	Ethnographic methods, including 41 interviews	Explored factors that influence rural Ndau women's participation in HIV prevention. Found women's oppression through gender inequality to be the dominant theme
Ellis et al., 2005	Australia	Program evaluation using pretest–posttest/interviews	Nurses in rural hospitals	Used a model to test process of translation of evidence into practice
Jelinek et al., 2006	Australia	Comparison of medical history and EKGs	$N = 71$ people from rural Australia at risk for cardiovascular disease	Examined use of 3-lead ECG assessment by community nurses in remote settings. Found implications of rural nursing practice

Study	Country	Method	Sample	Findings/Purpose
Karaolis et al., 2007	South Africa	Quantitative observational	N = 93 (all admissions for malnutrition in time period)	Assessed feasibility and actual use of WHO guidelines for inpatient management of severe malnutrition
Kohi et al., 2006	Lesotho, Malawi, South Africa, Swaziland, Tanzania	Descriptive qualitative	N = 251 total (111 individuals living with AIDS, 114 nurses, 26 volunteers)	Investigated the experience of stigma. Identified multiple forms of violation of human rights
Li & Chang, 2004	Taiwan	Quantitative (descriptive/correlational)	N = 195 (124 urban, 71 rural; mean age of 74.8)	Investigated home health care needs of patients with cardiovascular disease in both rural and urban settings
McCann & Baker, 2003	Australia	Qualitative (interviews/observation)	N = 24 community mental health nurses in three community mental health centers	Identified models of general practitioner collaboration used by nurses and analyzed the implications of these models for promoting continuity of care (Used rural mental health centers in sample selection but rurality was not explored)
McKeon et al., 2006	Australia	Quantitative/Qualitative (questionnaire)	N = 627 nurses working in rural or remote areas (481 BSNs, 140 ENs, 6 unknown)	Investigated effect of organizational issues in rural and remote environment on nurses' ability to follow procedures for safe or approved medication administration

(*Continued*)

TABLE 10.2 Focus and Selected Study Characteristics (*Continued*)

CLINICAL FOCUS

Author and Date	Country	Design	Sample and Size	Focus and Findings
Nordberg et al., 2005	Sweden	Quantitative (nurse and physician evaluation of patients)	N = 740 (living in rural areas)	Determined formal and informal care for older adults living in rural areas both with and without dementia
O'Brien & Jackson, 2007	Australia	Qualitative (interpretative approach)	N = 6 remote area mental health nurses in remote Aboriginal communities	Explored how mental health nurses experience working in remote communities and how they developed relevant knowledge and skills
Ritchie, 2003	Canada	Qualitative (descriptive/ exploratory interviews)	N = 21 elders; n = 7 caregivers; n = 4 RNs; Elders: male = 3; female = 18 Caregivers: female = 7; RNs: female = 4	Investigated perceptions of utility of adult day care programs in north. Found need for respite and aging in place. Offered recommendations concerning staff characteristics, roles, and challenges
Shawn et al., 2005	South Africa	Cross-sectional survey	N = 64 HIV-positive patients in palliative care	Identified symptoms
Steven et al., 2004	Canada	Qualitative/ quantitative (interviews, survey)	N = 105 women between the ages of 40 and 65	Used multiple media sources/ education to inform women. Used reminders when screenings due. Patients reported Pap tests were uncomfortable and frightening. Found that gynecologists,

Author and Date	Country	Design	Sample and Size	Focus and Findings
				family practitioners, and nurses must work collaboratively to design effective and efficient breast/cervical cancer screening services for rural regions (Used rural and urban settings, but rurality was not examined as a variable)
Svensson et al., 2003	Sweden	Quantitative (prospective program evaluation)	N = 16 hospitals in both urban and rural settings, where program is already in place (64 urban, 90 rural)	Evaluated a program implemented to treat cardiac patients with sinus tachycardia segment elevation prior to hospital admission (en route)

PRACTICE FOCUS

Author and Date	Country	Design	Sample and Size	Focus and Findings
Arthur et al., 2006	Philippines	Husserlian phenomenology	N = 5 professional nurses who are faculty and provide service	Described the remarkable work of rural community health nurses in country where little comparable information is available. Identified and compared four themes to similar themes in a 2002 Canadian remote community health study

(Continued)

TABLE 10.2 Focus and Selected Study Characteristics (*Continued*)

			PRACTICE FOCUS	
Author and Date	Country	Design	Sample and Size	Focus and Findings
Bailey et al., 2006	Canada	Qualitative (narrative analysis)	$N = 13$ family physicians; 5 nurse practitioners	Described differences in scope of practice; role clarity/trust; ideology r/t disease prevention/health promotion; perceptions of operation of practice. Found that collaboration requires ed. r/t expectation of partnerships
Chu et al., 2006	Taiwan	Cross-sectional survey	$N = 231$ (87.2%) of all 265 public health nurses in rural Taiwan	Found relationship between job stress, social support, and organizational citizenship behaviors. Found supervisor support to be a significant factor
Fogarty & Mckeon, 2006	Australia	Structural equation modeling	$N = 176$ nurses working in 11 rural hospitals	Measured organizational climate and tested a model with hypothesized links between climate and unsafe medication administration behaviors. Examined possible mediating role of stress/morale
Gould et al., 2007	Canada	Qualitative (interviews)	$N = 7$ (out of 9) female nurse practitioners with mean age of 46.8 (range 36–60)	Assessed perceptions of acceptance by rural patients and satisfaction with work. Found that a shortage of physicians, aging of population, and increased health care demands have led to accessibility problems, decreased satisfaction with care, and fears that the system is flawed

Hu et al., 2003	Taiwan	Quantitative (questionnaire)	N = 940 (86.4%) of all 1,121 community nurses of the 174 government health stations in rural Taiwan	Identified willingness to provide in-home palliative care. Found need for additional education, both in basic program and continuing education, in order to do so
Jewell, 2007	Nicaragua	Qualitative (interviews to develop a grounded theory)	N = 10 women (age 18–65)	Developed a grounded theory of contextual empowerment. Learned that the meaning of empowerment to the rural women is defined by the collectivist culture in which they live
MacLeod & Zimmer, 2005	Canada	Qualitative action research in three towns in northern British Columbia	N = 24 of 60 registered and licensed practical nurses	Found "We're it" described experience of being nurses in small rural hospitals. Found influential factors to be teamwork, decision support, education, administrative and clinical support. Nurses reluctant to take action.
Markaki et al., 2006	Crete	Psychometrically tested questionnaire	All 112 nursing personnel in 14 rural health centers (84.4% response rate)	Determined that assessment study of nursing personnel is needed. Found to be in need of continuing education, support from supervisors and environment

(*Continued*)

TABLE 10.2 Focus and Selected Study Characteristics (*Continued*)

PRACTICE FOCUS

Author and Date	Country	Design	Sample and Size	Focus and Findings
Mills et al., 2007	Australia	Qualitative (grounded theory; semistructured interviews)	N = 9 rural nurses (3–33 years experience)	Explored rural nurses' experiences of mentoring
Parkhurst & Rahman, 2006	Bangladesh	Qualitative	N = 31 rural women who recently delivered in a health facility (ages 16–35)	Aimed to understand process of decision making and engagement with health care of pregnant women. Found distrust of doctors and disagreement and between doctors and midwives
Yamashita et al., 2005	Japan	Ethnography, primarily interview	N = 16 adults (5 public health nurses, 7 clients, 4 allied health)	Described activities of public health nurses in one rural community. Linked commitment to identification of real needs, prompt and appropriate response, and establishing trust key findings

POLICY FOCUS

Author and Date	Country	Design	Sample and Size	Focus and Findings
Andrews et al., 2005	Canada	Quantitative (subset of national survey—see Stewart et al., 2005)	N = 412 RNs working alone in rural and remote regions (11.5% of all survey respondents)	Found work satisfaction to be influenced by diploma versus higher education, availability of face-to-face contact with colleagues and necessary equipment, fewer barriers to continuing education, fewer psychological demands, greater decision latitude

Barber et al., 2007	Indonesia	Quantitative (subset of Indonesian Life Survey)	7,000 households (representative of 83% of population of Indonesia)	Evaluated the quality of care given by physicians, nurses, and midwives. Determined that professional nurses could play a key role in promoting quality
Kosteniuk et al., 2006	Canada	Quantitative (mailed survey)	N = 3,933 RNs living in rural Canadian provinces (69% response rate)	Learned that most RNs in rural areas used at least one evidence-based information source to inform their nursing practice. Determined that central sources of information (i.e., nursing colleagues, non-nursing colleagues, in-service, newsletters) were used more frequently, and peripheral sources (i.e., Internet, library, journal subscription, continuing education) were used less frequently. Found factors associated with information use to be age and geographic location
LeSergenta & Haney, 2005	Canada	Qualitative (analysis of one work-related stressor)	N = 87 RNs (3 males, 84 females) with mean age of 44 (25–65 years); in rural acute care hospitals	Found stressors similar for rural and urban nursing: death and dying (6%), interpersonal conflicts with health care professionals (23%), fear of failure/professional confidence (6%), interpersonal problems with patients/families (4%), work-load/overload (46%), concerns about adequate care (12%)

(Continued)

TABLE 10.2 Focus and Selected Study Characteristics (*Continued*)

POLICY FOCUS

Author and Date	Country	Design	Sample and Size	Focus and Findings
Minore et al., 2004	Canada	Qualitative/ quantitative (open- and close-ended questionnaire)	N = 237 nurses (random sample)	Explored feasibility of establishing a relief pool of nurses from nearby small industrial towns. Posed strategies for nursing recruitment in northern Aboriginal communities
Minore et al., 2005	Canada	Qualitative (chart reviews/structured interviews)	N = 135 chart reviews; 30 interviews with professionals and paraprofessionals	Used Donabedian's structure, process, and outcome. Found that turnover detrimentally affected communication, medication management, range of services offered, follow-up, engagement of clients, illness, and burden of care for family and community members
Penz et al., 2007	Canada	Qualitative (open-ended survey)	N = 2,547 nurses who perceived barriers to participation in continuing education and described the nature of those barriers	Determined nursing continuing education to be integral to highly competent nursing workforce and safe health care environment. Learned that barriers in practice have made ongoing participation in continuing education challenging and are a greater concern in rural practice settings due to geographic isolation, limited accessibility, financial/time constraints

Stewart et al., 2005	Canada	Quantitative (national survey of RNs in rural and remote settings across California; mailed survey)	Target sample = 7,065 RNs in 10 provinces and three territories (68% response rate)	Found sample to be representative of population of RNs in Canada: 94.8% female; 66.5% between 35 and 54 years of age; 17–41% held Bacc. Ed.; 39% worked in hospitals; 28% worked in outposts, home care, or community/public health agency. Found average satisfaction levels for work and community to be positive. Found pay to be a significant contributor to work satisfaction
Tilleczek et al., 2005	Canada	Program evaluation (open- and close-ended questions)	Target sample = 472 nurse practitioners; N = 227 returned surveys; 146 completed	Learned respondents preferred face-to-face modalities and recognized the challenges of delivery of continuing education to rural and remote areas
Turner et al., 2007	Australia	Qualitative (critical discourse analysis/focus group)	N = 15 nurse practitioners in rural practice. Literature and policy documents.	Examined social discourses of nursing within health care as these produce understandings about autonomy for nurse practitioners, where autonomy refers to the ability of nurse practitioners to practice as professionals in their own right. Found gaps between policy and practice

TOTAL = 42

nurses' ability to follow procedures for safe or approved methods of medication administration in rural and remote environments. The nature of the environment determines the scope of nursing practice in rural and remote areas. Because of professional isolation in remote areas, nurses are likely to assume an expanded or advanced practice role in order to fill the gaps caused by the shortage of medical and other health care professionals. The following comments directly address the professional environment in which these nurses must practice:

> The number of doctors available in our district is totally inadequate—they have too many demands made on them. . . . Nurse is obligated to fill the gap left by doctors.
>   Pressure of workload, small numbers of GPs, and emergency situations lead to staff doing what is best for the patient at the time even if it is outside the guidelines. Nobody deliberately flouts the rules, but staff knows that the GPs would burn out if they were called every time someone presents to the hospital after hours (p. 120).

These researchers found that higher levels of knowledge correlated with lower levels of violations, and that knowledge protected against unsafe practices. This finding is consistent with previous research suggesting that one of the most common system failures is lack of knowledge.

Similarly, Fogarty and McKeon (2006) examined patient safety during medication administration using structural equation modeling with a sample of 176 nurses in 11 rural hospitals. Focus was on the impact of organizational and individual factors on unsafe practices and medication errors. Findings showed that violations are more likely to occur when nurses are distressed and morale is low. Moreover, the climate of the organization influences these personal states. These results support previous findings that heavy workloads and physicians' high expectations—conditions that tend to prevail in rural and remote areas—contribute to increased frequency of medication violations.

Mental Health Nursing

O'Brien and Jackson (2007) noted a paucity of research that explores how remote area practice affects nurses professionally and personally and recognized a need for better understanding of the experiences of nurses who develop and deliver mental health nursing care to remote indigenous communities in Australia. Recognizing that nurses working in very remote areas of Australia could not use the same models of care that are used in metropolitan areas, these researchers held conversational-style interviews with six remote area mental health nurses who had experience working with remote Aboriginal communities. The aim was to explore the experiences of mental health nurses working in remote communities and how they develop relevant knowledge and skills. While this study is small, it identifies some of the major issues and themes for nurses working in remote rural areas.

Findings showed that developing relationships was central to nurses' practice, and this included developing effective communication skills (O'Brien & Jackson, 2007). The focus was more on developing a relationship with the community rather than with an individual. The difficulty of adapting to the culture was a major theme, clearly characterized by the title of the article: "It's a Long Way from the Office to the Creek Bed." This included learning how to integrate Western medicine with traditional healing practices. These nurses had to learn how to deal with trauma and grief from losses that resulted from a history of colonization and, currently, suicide. They discussed the difficulties of moving between two cultures: the remote culture of their patients and their own personal lives, professional context, and bureaucracy. On a more positive note, all the nurses interviewed talked about developing a strong connection to the land and a sense of place. Finally, the nurses interviewed felt transformed by their experience; they felt that their experience gave them a greater awareness of the role of culture in shaping their own worldviews and values and a sense of their own roots.

In some articles, rurality provides a context for the research, but the implications of this context are not explored in the narrative. For example, McCann and Baker (2003) interviewed 24 community mental health nurses in three regional and rural community mental health centers to identify models of collaboration used by nurses and to analyze the implications of the models for promoting continuity of care. Two models were described by the study: in the Shared Care model, the nurse and physician maintain close communication while the psychiatric patients are having symptoms, and in the Specialist Liaison model, the community mental health team maintains responsibility for care and treatment with only intermittent contact with the physician. While rural areas provide a setting for sample selection, the researchers do not address the relevance of this setting.

Clinical Practice for Specific Diseases

Bucknall (2003) examined the impact of environment on critical care nurses' practice. This researcher used observations in natural settings and semi-structured interviews with 18 critical care nurses in private and public hospitals (six of them rural) in Australia to investigate environmental influences on nurses' decisions in the dynamic critical care setting. Results demonstrated that the context in which decisions are made greatly influences clinical decision making. Three fundamental environmental influences were identified: the individual patient situation, availability of resources, and interpersonal relationships. For example, critical care nurses in all settings focus on obtaining staff for the next shift; however, the stress caused by this responsibility intensifies for nurses in the rural hospital. In the rural areas studied, there were no nursing agencies from which to obtain staff, and nurses could be required to work double shifts. In addition, rural nurses have to predict a patient's situation and likely trajectory, because medical staff are not available at night. Before the medical staff leave the hospital, nurses must anticipate medical orders needed for problems that may arise. Bucknall concludes that decision making results from the environmental context, and that to improve health care outcomes, we need to measure the impact of contextual variables on nurses' decision making.

Cardiovascular disease is a major cause of death in both Australia and the United States. It is estimated that by the year 2010 there will be at least 25 patients with heart failure for every general practitioner, and that this ratio will be greater in rural and remote regions (Jelinek, Warner, King, & De Jong, 2006). Jelinek and colleagues investigated the value of community nurses' use of 3-lead ECG assessment in rural and remote health settings. This study examined the medical history and EKGs of 71 people living in rural Australia who were over age 45 and not diabetic. Twelve percent of the asymptomatic individuals screened had potentially serious cardiovascular disease. These researchers concluded that more informed evaluation of asymptomatic individuals is possible with in-depth assessment of cardiovascular risk factors combined with 3-lead ECG tracing to provide early recognition of cardiac anomalies that may be amenable to treatment. Having nurses with suitable expertise is especially important in isolated rural areas.

Bennett, Breugelmans, and Parkhurst (2006) tested the reliability of a simple nutrition screening tool used by hemodialysis nurses to identify nutritionally at-risk patients. Based on the testing of 112 hemodialysis patients in seven metropolitan and two rural nonhospital hemodialysis units, the tool accurately identified the nutritional status of 88% of participants, while 12% were incorrectly classified (sensitivity = 0.84; specificity = 0.9). Although the concept of rurality was not directly discussed in this paper, the relevance for rural nursing is implied. The researchers conclude that the tool is particularly effective in screening patients not requiring intervention by a dietitian and recommend that the tool be used in satellite hemodialysis units that have limited access to dietetic services.

Bauer (2006) used conversational in-depth interviews with 30 nursing home personnel (including 11 RNs) working in both metropolitan and rural nursing homes in Australia to examine the experiences of nursing home staff working with residents' families. Findings showed that while some nursing home staff develop a notable family orientation and adopt practices that are inclusive of the family, others have attitudes that cast the family in an adversarial and competitive role. Some of the interviewees described practices that suggested a need to control the family. The researchers concluded that while some nursing homes use a rhetoric of family partnerships, the staff focuses primarily on provision of physical care. Family needs become secondary to getting the work done. While some of the data were collected in rural areas, there was no discussion of the implications.

Nursing Practice

The development of evidence-based practice for nurses in rural areas of Western Australia was examined in a study reported by Ellis, Howard, Larson, and Robertson (2005). Using a conceptual framework titled Promoting Action on Research Implementation in Health Services, these researchers explored the importance of context and facilitation in the implementation of an evidence-based clinical protocol and examined the establishment of lasting change. A pretest and post-test of workshop content and follow-up interviews were used to assess the context and facilitation of transfer of evidence to workplace practice for nurses from six rural hospitals. Nurses working in these rural hospitals tended to be generalists, with limited resources and support for staff development and quality improvement. Five of the six rural hospitals adopted the new protocols for practice. Findings demonstrated the need for support for nurses who are responsible for developing the practice protocols for their staff.

Recruitment and retention of rural nurses is an issue of concern in Australia. Mentoring has been favored as a strategy to improve retention of nurses in the rural workforce because it is cost effective and draws on local resources. Its effectiveness, however, has not been measured. Mills, Francis, and Bonner (2007) used a grounded theory design with nine rural nurses in Australia to examine rural nurses' experiences mentoring. The nurses had an average of 19 years of experience in rural nursing (range 3–33), and eight of the participants had taken part in a mentor development program and defined themselves as rural nurses. As experienced rural nurses, they cultivate supportive mentoring relationships with novices. The outcomes of this approach for novice nurses include orientation to the local cultural mores and an increase in confidence to practice. Rural nurses living and working in the same community must use multiple perspectives of self to manage a complex web of relationships and interactions. The researchers use the phrase "live my work" to describe their multiple roles as community members, nurses, and health care consumers. The authors conclude that the process of mentoring assists novice nurses to more successfully face the complex challenges posed by living and working in the same community and thereby promotes staff retention.

Implementation of the role of nurse practitioners in Australia has been slow due to numerous obstacles, including strong opposition from the Australian Medical Association. This nursing role was only recently introduced in rural and remote Australia in 2001. Turner, Keyzer, and Rudget (2007) used critical discourse analysis to examine the differences between policy and the reality of implementation of the role of nurse practitioners. Their research focused on understanding the degree of autonomy of nurse practitioners, meaning the ability of nurse practitioners to practice in their own right as professionals. Findings reveal that in rural and remote Australia, there is a considerable gap between rhetoric of the policy and implementation of nurse practitioner roles. Policy supports the concept of autonomy; however, nurses experience only a small shift in the traditional boundaries of nurses' roles. In the words of one nurse practitioner, "Basically the health service did not know what to do with me," and management as well as other nurses in the health service "had difficulty in understanding the relative autonomy of the role." The researchers conclude that there is a need for further exploration of the real meaning of autonomy in practice in addition to a need to legitimize the already existing role of rural and remote nurses in areas where practice has traditionally crossed nebulous professional boundaries.

NURSING RESEARCH IN RURAL AND REMOTE CANADA

A systematic search of nursing research on rural health outside the United States identified 13 unduplicated articles from Canada that met the review inclusion criteria and focused on rural and remote nursing practice. Of the 13 studies of nursing practice in rural and remote regions in Canada, 5 were qualitative investigations that used different approaches, including narrative analysis (Bailey, Jones, & Way, 2006), hermeneutic interpretation (MacLeod & Zimmer, 2005), descriptive exploratory interviews (Gould, Johnstone, & Wasylkiw, 2007; Ritchie, 2003), and a combination of chart reviews and in-depth interviews (Minore, Boone, Katt, Kinch, Birch, et al., 2005). One study used a qualitative approach to identify a major work-related stressor and a questionnaire on demographics, coping styles, and nursing stress scales (LeSergenta & Haney, 2005). Another study used both a qualitative interview and a questionnaire (Steven et al., 2004). Three quantitative studies analyzed data from a national survey of registered nurses working in rural and remote settings across Canada (Andrews, Stewart, Pitblado, Morgan, Forbes, et al., 2005; Kosteniuk, D'Arcy, Stewart, & Smith, 2006; Stewart et al., 2005). Two studies used questionnaires with both open- and close-ended questions (Minore, Boone, & Hill, 2004; Penz, D'Arcy, Stewart, Kosteniuk, Morgan, et al., 2007). Another study that used an open- and close-ended questionnaire involved a needs assessment, program implementation, and evaluation (Tilleczek, Pong, & Caty, 2005).

The primary focus of interest of these articles was work life and issues related to satisfaction with nursing practice in rural and remote regions of Canada. This is similar to the focus reported in the Australian literature. Eleven of the Canadian studies examined working conditions, satisfaction with nursing practice and resources, and/or opportunities for collaboration; only 2 articles focused on clinical patient care. The sample sizes ranged from 7 to 3,933. Three studies using data from the national survey of nurses in rural and remote Canada had the largest sample sizes, which ranged from 412 to 3, 933 respondents.

Clinical Focus

Only 2 of the 13 articles focused on clinical practice issues. Ritchie (2003) examined adult day care in northern regions of Canada by interviewing 21 elders, 7 caregivers, and 4 RNs about their perceptions of the utility of existing adult day care programs and recommendations and challenges for the future. Steven and colleagues (2004) explored knowledge, attitudes, beliefs, and practices related to breast and cervical cancer screening in different ethnic groups in northern Ontario. The sample ($N = 105$) consisted of females ranging in age from 40 to 65 years. Themes emerged related to the importance of using multiple sources of information to educate women and remind them when screenings are due. Practitioners should address the discomfort and fear associated with particular screening tests. In rural and remote communities, gynecologists, family physicians, and nurses must collaborate to design effective and efficient ("one-stop shopping") breast and cervical cancer screening.

Nursing Practice

Three articles focused on the challenges of advanced nursing practice models and the importance of partnerships between nurse practitioners and other health care professionals and with patients in rural communities. Bailey and colleagues (2006) used narrative analysis of the experiences of nurse practitioners and family physicians working in shared practice settings in four rural primary care agencies ($N = 18$; 13 nurse practitioners and 5 family physicians). They told stories of collaboration involving issues such as scope of practice, the roles of clarity and trust, ideological differences related to health promotion and disease prevention, perceptions of how to operate in a collaborative practice, and understanding that collaborative relationships evolve over time. Collaborative practice requires an intentional orientation and educational strategies related to role expectations in health care delivery partnerships.

Another qualitative study of nurse practitioners' practice with rural patients focused on perceptions of acceptance by patients and satisfaction with work (Gould et al., 2007). Seven out of nine female nurse practitioners, with a mean age of 46.8, participated in the study. Themes emerging from the analysis were the importance of a holistic approach to care that differed from the approach of medical care, barriers encountered in the establishment of advanced practice nursing in rural provinces, and an overall pioneering outlook and pride in their work. These nurse practitioners emphasized the need for acceptance by the public and for other health care providers to effectively reduce costs and increase access to care.

An interpretive action research study built upon an understanding of stressful work environments of nurses in small rural hospitals (MacLeod & Zimmer,

2005). Twenty-four of 60 registered and licensed nurses practicing in three hospitals with 12–16 beds took part in the study. These hospitals had only 2 nurses on each shift. The authors explored the meaning of working with minority patient populations, factors that facilitate or hinder development of expertise in the care of minority patient populations, and strategies to increase flexibility and responsiveness of nursing practice in small rural hospitals. The phrase "We're it" captured the nurses' experiences. These nurses were reluctant to take action, recognizing an existing pattern of Band-Aid approaches. They felt a tremendous burden of responsibility in their practice and wanted nurse researchers to tell their stories to employers, health care planners, and the community.

Policy Issues

Nursing Practice and Policy Implications

Five studies addressed closely related nursing practice and policy issues. The first three of these studies used data from the national survey of registered nurses in rural and remote settings across Canada (Stewart et al., 2005). Stewart and colleagues described the characteristics of the work environment, nursing practice roles, the context of practice, and issues related to the rural nursing work life. The target sample was 7,065 RNs in 10 provinces and 3 territories. Of the 5,782 eligible nurses, 3,933 completed the mailed questionnaire (68% response rate). Stewart and colleagues patterned the questionnaire after surveys used in Australia. The study included psychometric refinement and validation of the instruments for Canadian nurses. Of the rural RNs, 94.8% were female, 66.5% ranged in age from 35 to 54 years, and only 17% had a baccalaureate degree. Overall, these characteristics are representative of the population of RNs in Canada. The majority (39%) of rural nurses worked in hospitals; 28% worked in outposts, home care, or community/public health agencies. The average satisfaction levels for work and the community were positive. The study emphasized that the context of the community—that is, "being in and of the community"—shapes nursing practice, and that nursing practice in a rural community differs from practice in urban settings.

Andrews and colleagues (2005) analyzed data from a subset of the respondents of the national survey of RNs in rural Canada who indicated there were one or fewer RN positions at their place of work ($n = 412$). These nurses were older than the total sample. Most solitary positions were in community health/public health agencies or outpost nursing stations, face-to-face interaction with peers was less frequent, and community residents frequently sought their advice outside work. However, barriers to continuing education and perceptions of their roles as advanced practice nurses did not differ from those reported by the total sample.

Kosteniuk and colleagues (2006) analyzed data from the national survey of RNs living in rural and remote regions to assess the type and quality of information sources. Rural RNs used central sources such as nursing and other health professional colleagues, in-services, and newsletters most frequently, while they used peripheral sources such as the Internet, libraries, and journals less frequently. This article identified the challenges in recruiting and retaining nurses in rural areas due to isolation, heavy workloads, small professional networks, limited availability of clinical services, and increased numbers of uninsured patients.

Two qualitative studies examined the experiences of nurses in small rural hospitals. LeSergenta and Haney (2005) focused on work-related stressors and coping strategies of nurses ($N = 87$ RNs) in rural acute care hospitals. The mean age of the respondents was 44 years; the sample was 96.5% female. The nurses identified six categories of work-related stressors that fit into a framework previously used with urban nursing students (Parkes, 1986): workload or overload (46%), interpersonal conflicts with health care professionals (23%), concerns about adequate nursing care (12%), fear of failure (6%), death and dying (6%), interpersonal problems with health care professionals (4%), and other stressors (3%). Nurses who felt stressed tended to rely on emotion-focused coping and increased social support. The authors suggested that stress-management intervention programs could benefit nurses in rural, often isolated practice settings.

Needed Support for Nurses in Rural Areas

Four studies focused on sources of support for nurses practicing in rural settings. Minore and colleagues (2004) used a questionnaire with open- and close-ended questions to examine the feasibility of nurses in nearby communities providing short-term relief in remote regions. A stratified random sample of 622 registrants of the College of Nurses of Ontario who lived in the northern part of the province but did not work in the region received the survey; 237 nurses completed the survey (38.1% response rate). The findings suggest that recruiting nurses to provide short-term relief in these isolated regions will entail the provision of personal support, flexible work schedules, and links to community leaders. Orientation of nurses to nursing practice in isolated northern regions must address the clinical demands and realities of the region that are potential causes of fear as well as joy. This involves learning about Aboriginal culture and communities and opportunities to make clinical decisions.

Minore and others (2005) examined the effects of turnover on continuity of care in three isolated communities in northern Ontario. Using Donabedian's framework for quality care assessment, they conducted reviews of a random sample of 135 oncology, diabetes, and mental health patients' charts and 30 in-depth structured interviews with professionals and paraprofessionals. Findings showed that nursing turnover negatively affected structural factors such as interprofessional and patient communication. Process factors detrimentally affected were preventive care, management of medications, establishment of client trust, holistic assessment, and cultural awareness. Negative outcomes included essential follow-up, disengagement of clients in their care, illness exacerbation, and an increased burden of care and stress for both family and community members.

Penz and colleagues (2007) focused on perceptions and the nature of barriers to participation in continuing education among rural nurses by analyzing data from the national survey of RNs in rural and remote settings across Canada (Stewart et al., 2005). Data were from 2,547 nurses who reported perceiving barriers to participation in continuing education. Themes that emerged from open-ended responses about the nature of these barriers included rural community and work life, time constraints, and financial constraints. In addition, there were barriers related to participants' energy, motivation, and health status; lack of awareness of educational opportunities; and perceived lack of importance of continuing education participation. Overall, barriers to continuing education were a greater concern in rural and remote nursing practice settings than in urban settings due to isolation, limited access to educational offerings, and the financial and time constraints of nurses practicing in rural regions.

A needs assessment and program evaluation used a mailed survey with open- and close-ended questions to explore issues associated with the delivery of continuing education to nurse practitioners in rural and northern communities of Canada (Tilleczek et al., 2005). The target sample was 472 nurse practitioners working in the rural and northern regions of Ontario. Of the 227 questionnaires returned, 146 had complete data and were included in the analysis (30.9% response rate). The findings showed that continuing education was critical for nurse practitioners in rural and remote communities to maintain competency, but barriers such as travel cost, work, and family obligations hindered access. Overall, the respondents preferred face-to-face learning and networking for continuing education. Health care managers in rural communities face challenges to use innovative approaches "to encourage learners to proactively integrate their practice networks into a support system for learning" (Tilleczek et al., 2005, p. 158).

NURSING RESEARCH IN RURAL SWEDEN, PHILIPPINES, JAPAN, KOREA, CRETE, AND TAIWAN

A systematic search of nursing research on rural health identified 10 articles from developed countries other than Australia and Canada. Two were qualitative and conducted for the purpose of describing the activities of rural public health nurses. A study conducted in Crete had a similar purpose but used a psychometrically tested questionnaire. The other 8 were quantitative studies; 5 focused on health issues of specific populations, and 3 focused on clinical practice issues.

A study of safety and delay time in prehospital thrombolysis of acute myocardial infarction conducted by physicians in Sweden was exceptional in its detailed definition of *rural* and *urban* and the degree to which the analysis of the data addressed differences between the two (Svensson, Karlsson, Nordlander, Wahlin, Zedigh, et al., 2003). "Urban areas included hospitals with a city catchment population of more than 90,000 inhabitants. The remaining hospitals, in which the city catchment population varied between 9,000 and 44,000 inhabitants were classified as being rural" (p. 263). Prehospital thrombolysis is administered by the nurses who staff the ambulances, both regular nurses and staff nurses. The latter have a one-year education. Law prohibits personnel other than nurses and physicians from administering drugs in the ambulance. Rarely are physicians in the ambulance; consequently, the nurses assess patients and administer interventions based on protocols. Assessment includes ECG readings transmitted electronically to a physician on call for interpretation. The practice was found to be safe in both urban and rural areas. Not surprisingly, all components of delay times in rural areas were longer, though not always significantly, and symptoms of heart failure were more severe for the rural patients.

Cerebrovascular disease was the focus of a descriptive correlational study undertaken by two nurses in Taiwan (Li & Chang, 2004). The purposes were to quantify the home care needs of cerebrovascular disease patients and to identify predictors of services required. Li and Chang point out that most home care services are delivered in urban areas and that there are few resources for rural areas. Three services in Taipei and one in a rural county agreed to participate in the study, providing a sample of 124 and 71 subjects respectively with the diagnosis of cerebrovascular disease. The study effectively documents the needs of the subjects, though differences between urban and rural populations were not identified. The cultural factors that influence the care given to ill relatives by family members and needed changes to the National Health Insurance reimbursement policies were emphasized in the discussion.

Two studies—one in rural Sweden and one in rural Korea—addressed the health care needs of the elderly. The Swedish study, which was conducted from an aging research center, specifically addressed the dramatic rise in elderly populations as a developed country phenomenon and described the amount of formal and informal care for all 740 nondemented and demented elderly individuals 75 years of age and older living in a rural community (Nordberg, von Strauss, Kareholt, Johansson, & Wimo, 2005). Nurses were the primary data collectors. The discussion focused on the degree to which informal care substitutes for rather than complements formal care and increases with dementia severity. No specific nursing implications were drawn.

Nurses in Korea examined the need for health and social support services of elderly individuals living alone in a rural Korean community (Ahn & Kim, 2004). Eight public health nurses interviewed and assessed all 97 individuals in the community, using standardized instruments. A follow-up study focusing on community capacity building to encourage integrated health care and social welfare care was strongly recommended for the next phases of this work.

Nurses in Taiwan interested in a younger population explored health-related behaviors of adolescent mothers in a rural area of the country using a cross-sectional and descriptive design (Chen, James, Hsu, Chang, Huang, et al., 2005). In Taiwan, public health nurse visits to these mothers are a priority of public health policy. The findings of the study are useful for focusing the con-tinuing work of the public health nurses. The authors call for similar rural inter-national studies, which could contribute significantly to the development of intervention strategies that positively influence the health of this population.

Two cross-sectional design studies with practice and policy foci were con-ducted in Taiwan. The first sampled all 265 public health nurses in two rural Taiwan counties to examine the relationship between job stress, social support, and organizational citizenship behaviors of public health nurses (Chu, Lee, & Hsu, 2006). Mailed questionnaires using standardized measures of the variables yielded a response of 231 (87.2%) for the multiple regression analysis. Supervi-sor support was revealed to be the important variable. The results were related to other recent research. Cultural differences were effectively specified. The second study used a similar design to determine the willingness of rural district nurses to provide palliative care to rural community-dwelling individuals with terminal disease (Hu, Chiu, Dai, Chang, Jaing, et al., 2003). All district nurses of every rural community were sent surveys, which were returned by 968 respondents (86.4%) from 162 (93.1%) government health districts. The knowledge required for nurses to effectively care for terminally ill patients in their homes was not part of the basic education of the nurses, and the nurses felt the lack. These results can be used in the design of education for these nurses, whose work covers 80% of the geographic area of the country.

Similarly, a needs assessment study of nursing personnel employed in public sector primary health care in Crete was undertaken in 2001 (Markaki, Antonakis, Philalithis, & Lionis, 2006). All 112 registered nurses, midwives/health visitors, and licensed practical nurses in 14 rural health centers received a newly developed psychometrically tested questionnaire by mail. There was an 84.4% response rate. This was a first effort to uncover the hidden profile of practice patterns of public health nursing in this setting. Clinical care is the primary responsibility of the nurses, and they reported high satisfaction with that aspect of their work. Work with colleagues and supervisors was less satisfying and is reported to contribute to a high expected turnover of nurses. The absence of clear reporting channels and unclear job descriptions—both potentially solvable problems—create major frustration. The authors specify implications for practice and policy.

One ethnographic study was conducted in Japan with the intention of describing an effective public health nursing role (Yamashita, Miyaji, & Akimoto, 2005). A health insurance system change effective in 2000 requires the nurses to interact with other health care workers who provide home services. The 16 interviewees were nurses ($n = 5$), clients ($n = 7$), and allied health workers ($n = 4$). From the results, a model was developed that places commitment at the center and emphasizes the three characteristics of trusting relationships, assessing real needs, and promptly and appropriately addressing individual needs first and then community needs.

A study grounded in phenomenology from the Philippines, a country defined as a developing country based on the UN Development Index, closely parallels the study conducted in Japan and thus is included here. Arthur and associates (2006) used data from in-depth interviews with five nursing faculty members to reveal the previously unreported highly effective work of rural public health nurses in the Philippines. The findings in this study were likened to those of Vukic and Keddy (2002), who investigated the nature of nursing work in northern indigenous communities in Canada. The uniqueness of nursing experiences in different cultures around the world is emphasized.

NURSING RESEARCH IN RURAL AND REMOTE DEVELOPING COUNTRIES

Eight studies undertaken in rural areas of developing countries are reported in this section. Five address health issues of specific populations, one addresses nursing practice, and two address policy issues. The studies were evenly divided between qualitative and quantitative methods.

Clinical Focus

A carefully designed study involving observation of the direct practice of physicians and nurses and psychometrically detailed analysis addressed the care of children with severe malnutrition in two rural South African hospitals (Karaolis et al., 2007). The report begins by reporting the sobering fact that malnutrition contributes to 50–60% of all childhood deaths in developing countries. Effective treatment has been known for 50 years, and comprehensive WHO guidelines for inpatient management of malnutrition have been developed. This study was undertaken to determine whether the guidelines were feasible and whether they were being implemented by physicians and nurses in two rural hospitals, where these professionals had been taught to use the guidelines in a workshop setting.

Findings indicate that they are feasible; however, they have not been effectively implemented as a result of major staffing shortages and high levels of turnover. The implications of this work for education and practice reform are well documented.

Researchers from the University of Iowa and the University of Texas Health Science Center at Houston worked with nursing colleagues in The Gambia, where they observed nurses to be the backbone of the rural health care delivery system (Culp, Kuye, Donham, Rautiainen, Umbarger-Mackey, et al., 2007). The study was designed to describe agricultural-related injury and illness in the country. Though farming is the most prevalent type of employment worldwide, the number of workers engaged in farming is greatest in developing countries. In this exploratory descriptive study, a convenience sample of nurses (n = 21 RNs, community health nurses, and certified nursing assistants) and farmers and field workers (n = 20) provided data. The former group completed questionnaires, and the farmers, most of whom were illiterate, were interviewed by four well-educated farm extension workers in their native language. The study represents a first attempt at documenting these injuries and illnesses and highlights the education needed for nurses and farmers. The prevention and treatment of malaria and injuries related to the use of government-issued spraying equipment were highlighted.

A second study in South Africa was undertaken by U.S. nurses with local colleagues (Shawn, Campbell, Mgnuni, Defilippi, & Williams, 2005). The purpose was to collect information about the prevalence and frequency of symptoms experienced by the 64 HIV-positive patients in four rural regions in the Ugu District of KwaZulu Natal. Care of these patients in the community is provided by professional nurses and community caregivers with minimal medical or nursing experience. The results effectively document needed care planning and management and can be used to develop models for providing care in similar settings.

Two additional African studies focused on HIV/AIDS. An ethnographic study conducted in Zimbabwe by a nurse from the University of New Brunswick sought to understand the factors that facilitated or hindered the participation of women in health promotion and prevention of HIV (Duffy, 2005). A core group of 11 women and additional focus groups with other community members (6 men and 11 women) provided the data from which rich conclusions that reveal multiple dimensions of social and cultural life were drawn. The findings are directly related to the poverty of the participants, which must be addressed if any change is to be made that will empower women. This is the central recommendation of the study.

The focus of a study that originated from the University of California–San Francisco's African stigma study was on violations of human rights (Kohi et al., 2006). Individuals living with HIV/AIDS and nurses in five African countries (Lesotho, Malawi, South Africa, Swaziland, and Tanzania), a total of 251 informants, were interviewed. Both Malawi and Tanzania fall below the medium level in the HDI and thus represent the only countries in that category included in this review. Six categories of violations of human rights were identified and the cultural implications of these violations were discussed. A distinct effort was made to include urban and rural participants; however, the analysis did not identify distinctions, if there were any, between the two cohorts.

Nursing Practice

In Bangladesh the incidence of caesarean births (2.4%) is unusually low and the maternal mortality rate is very high (Parkhurst & Rahman, 2006). The goal of a study conducted by members of the Health Systems Development Programme, funded by the UK Department for International Development, was to understand the perceptions of the women in need of maternity care that influenced their care choices. At the time of the study, Bangladesh was ranked 138th (of 177 countries) in terms of human development by the United Nations Development Programme. The practices of nurses and doctors with whom 30 pregnant women interacted are described in detail. Qualitative interviews were conducted within the year following the birth of their children. The cultural beliefs and practices of the women and the health care professionals are carefully related to the researchers' finding of a high level of distrust regarding recommendations for both normal and caesarean deliveries from both physicians and nurse-midwives.

Policy Issues

The following two studies are diverse and important for different reasons. The first documented the country-wide need for nurse staffing in Indonesia to meet the governmental plan to achieve desired quality objectives. The second described in detail the importance of the culture-specific learning for U.S. nurses involved in international practice and research in a developing country.

Using public facility survey data from the 1993–1997 Indonesia Family Life Surveys, the study took advantage of an exogenous shock to the system imposed by central government policy changes related to physician and nurse staffing to analyze the impact on prenatal, child, and adult care indicators (Barber, Gertler, & Harimurti, 2007). The methods are exquisitely detailed and involved interviews of subsets of the population at two points in time that yielded a response rate of 99% both times. Rural and urban differentiation is thoroughly described. A central finding was that increasing the number of nurses resulted in larger quality gains for curative care than did increasing the number of physicians and midwives. The authors call for careful skill-mix considerations in the future and for the roles and responsibilities of nurses in remote areas to be expanded, in lieu of attempts to post physicians in remote areas.

Contextual empowerment was the central finding of a qualitative descriptive study of how working with health brigades in a rural Nicaraguan community influenced the lives of the local women (Jewell, 2007). Following Hurricane Mitch, faculty and students from a Michigan school of nursing sought to provide primary health care and health promotion services to victims in one rural village by organizing health brigades. They initially spent six clinical days, and in collaboration with community leaders at the end of the first brigade, three additional brigades were planned and implemented. During the last brigade, the investigators secured permission to conduct interviews with the local women who worked with them in the hopes of developing a grounded theory to explain the contextual empowerment of the women they had observed. Ten women were interviewed. Two findings discussed eloquently in the report are noted here. First, the idea of autonomy was foreign to their collectivist culture. When their personal actions could be seen as leading to the improvement of the community, they felt empowered and could act with more self-assurance in multiple contexts. Second, all five researchers admitted to personal and professional biases as a result of the "wise teachings of the women of Miraflora" (Jewell, 2007, p. 55). This report provides an accessible and valuable resource for any nurse considering implementing research in another culture.

DISCUSSION

Health care resources clearly influence the amount and type of rural nursing research conducted internationally. The UN Human Development Index illuminated the comparative differences and proved useful in explaining the context of this review. For example, the clinical symptom focus on cardiovascular treatment in the more highly developed countries of Australia and Sweden contrasts vividly with malnutrition treatment and symptom identification in the studies done in less developed African countries. Thematic identification of nursing practice and policy-related research was also useful for understanding the work reviewed in its entirety and the ways in which resources influence the delivery of health care across a range of international countries.

The use of rurality and remoteness as concepts gave particular meaning to international research. Some studies used rurality as a demographic variable but provided little analysis of the meaning of rurality to the data. More often, rural was a defining characteristic of the research context. In the Indonesian study of the assignments of doctors and nurses to rural settings and the Swedish study of myocardial infarction transport, population characteristics that differentiated rural from urban were specified. Both studies could serve as models for future research. Most frequently, the discussion of rurality focused on the work of nurses in settings where they have few colleagues, insufficient knowledge to meet the patients' needs, and little access to continuing education. Staffing was a significant concern in both inpatient and community settings in rural and remote regions. The importance of the nurse as a member of the community served was a consistent theme in these studies.

CONCLUSIONS

The educational needs of nurses practicing in rural areas revealed by these studies demonstrate the need for a separate review of the educational rural nursing education research identified in the selection process for this review. It will be necessary to increase the availability, quality, and level of basic nursing education before a significant cohort of nurse researchers become available in each country worldwide. Although a number of specific research and policy agendas were specified based on the data already available, the research indicates many instances in which further description is warranted. The pairing of researchers from developed countries with colleagues in resource-poor countries makes a distinct contribution to our understanding of the realities of health care needs and rural nursing. Cultural learning is a never-ending process. All nursing researchers who choose to engage in research with international colleagues are well advised to continually examine personal biases and to draw heavily from the wisdom of those who live in the culture.

REFERENCES

Ahn, Y. H., & Kim, M. J. (2004). Health care needs of elderly in a rural community in Korea. *Public Health Nursing, 21*(2), 153–161.

Andrews, M. E., Stewart, N. J., Pitblado, J. R., Morgan, D. G., Forbes, D., & D'Arcy, C. (2005). Registered nurses working alone in rural and remote Canada. *Canadian Journal of Nursing Research, 37*(1), 14–33.

Arthur, D., Drury, J., Sy-Sinda, M. T., Nakao, R., Lopez, A., Gloria, G., et al. (2006). A primary health care curriculum in action: The lived experience of primary health care nurses in a school of nursing in the Philippines: A phenomenological study. *International Journal of Nursing Studies, 43*, 107–112.

Bailey, P., Jones, L., & Way, D. (2006). Family physician/nurse practitioner: Stories of collaboration. *Journal of Advanced Nursing, 53*(4), 381–391.

Barber, S. L., Gertler, P. J., & Harimurti, P. (2007). The contribution of human resources for health to the quality of care in Indonesia (Web exclusive). *Health Affairs*, w367–w379.

Bauer, M. (2006). Collaboration and control: Nurses' constructions of the role of family in nursing home care. *Journal of Advanced Nursing, 54*(1), 45–52.

Bennett, P., Breugelmans, L., & Parkhurst, D. (2006). A simple nutrition screening tool for hemodialysis nurses. *Journal of Renal Nutrition, 16*(1), 59–62.

Bucknall, T. (2003). The clinical landscape of critical care: Nurses' decision-making. *Journal of Advanced Nursing, 43*(3), 310–319.

Chen, M. Y., James, K., Hsu, L. L., Chang, S. W., Huang, L. H., & Wang, E. K. (2005). Health-related behavior and adolescent mothers. *Public Health Nursing, 22*(4), 280–288.

Chu, C., Lee, M., & Hsu, H. (2006). The impact of social support and job stress on public health nurses' organizational citizenship behaviors in rural Taiwan. *Public Health Nursing, 23*(6), 496–505.

Culp, K., Kuye, R., Donham, K. J., Rautiainen, R., Umbarger-Mackey, M., & Marquez, S. (2007). Agricultural-related injury and illness in The Gambia. *Clinical Nursing Research, 16*(3), 170–188.

Duffy, L. (2005). Culture and context of HIV prevention in rural Zimbabwe: The influence of gender inequality. *Journal of Transcultural Nursing, 16*(1), 23–31.

Ellis, I., Howard, P., Larson, A., & Robertson, J. (2005). From workshop to work practice: An exploration of context and facilitation in development of evidence-based practice. *World Views on Evidence-Based Practice, 2*(2), 84–93.

Fogarty, G. J., & McKeon, C. M. (2006). Patient safety during medication administration: The influence of organizational and individual variables on unsafe work practices and medication errors. *Ergonomics, 49*(5–6), 444–456.

Gould, O. N., Johnstone, D., & Wasylkiw, L. (2007). Nurse practitioners in Canada: Beginnings, benefits, and barriers. *Journal of the American Academy of Nurse Practitioners, 19*, 165–171.

Hu, W. Y., Chiu, T. Y., Dai, Y. T., Chang, M., Jaing, T. H., & Chen, C. Y..(2003). Nurses' willingness and the predictors of willingness to provide palliative care in rural communities of Taiwan. *Journal of Pain and Symptom Management, 26*(2), 760–768.

Jelinek, H., Warner, P., King, S., & De Jong, B. (2006). Opportunistic screening for cardiovascular problems in rural and remote health settings. *Journal of Cardiovascular Nursing, 21*(3), 217–222.

Jewell, G. (2007). Contextual empowerment: The impact of health brigade involvement on the women of Miraflor, Nicaragua. *Journal of Transcultural Nursing, 18*(1), 49–56.

Karaolis, N., Jackson, D., Ashworth, A., Sanders, D., Sagaula, N., McCoy, D., et al. (2007). WHO guidelines for severe malnutrition: Are they feasible in rural African hospitals? *Archives of Disease in Childhood, 92*, 198–204.

Kohi, T. W., Makoae, L., Chirwa, M., Holzemer, W. L., Phetlhu, R., Uys, L., et al. (2006). HIV and AIDS stigma violates human rights in five African countries. *Nursing Ethics, 13*(4), 404–415.

Kosteniuk, J. G., D'Arcy, C., Stewart, N., & Smith, B. (2006). Central and peripheral information source use among rural and remote RNs. *Journal of Advanced Nursing, 55*(1), 100–114.

LeSergenta, C. M., & Haney, C. J. (2005). Rural hospital nurse's stressors and coping strategies: A survey. *International Journal of Nursing Studies, 42*, 315–324.

Li, I. C., & Chang, T. S. (2004). Predictors of home health care services for cerebral vascular disease patients in Taiwan. *Public Health Nursing, 21*(1), 41–48.

MacLeod, M. L. P., & Zimmer, L. V. (2005). Rethinking emancipation and empowerment in action research: Lessons from small rural hospitals. *Canadian Journal of Nursing Research, 37*(1), 68–84.

Markaki, A., Antonakis, N., Philalithis, A., & Lionis, C. (2006). Primary health care nursing staff in Crete: An emerging profile. *International Nursing Review, 53,* 16–18.

McCann, T. V., & Baker, H. (2003). Models of mental health nurse-general practitioner liaison: Promoting continuity of care. *Journal of Advanced Nursing, 41*(5), 471–479.

McKeon, C. M., Fogarty, G. J., & Hegney, D. G. (2006). Organizational factors: Impact on administration violations in rural nursing. *Journal of Advanced Nursing, 55*(1), 115–123.

Mills, J., Francis, K., & Bonner, A. (2007). Live my work: Rural nurses and their multiple perspectives of self. *Journal of Advanced Nursing, 59*(6), 583–590.

Minore, B., Boone, M., & Hill, M. E. (2004). Finding temporary relief: Strategy for nursing recruitment in Northern Aboriginal communities. *Canadian Journal of Nursing Research, 36*(2), 148–163.

Minore, B., Boone, M., Katt, M., Kinch, P., Birch, S., & Mushquash, C. (2005). The effects of nursing turnover on continuity of care in isolated first nation communities. *Canadian Journal of Nursing Research, 37*(1), 86–100.

Nordberg, G., von Strauss, E., Kareholt, I., Johansson, L., & Wimo, A. (2005). The amount of informal and formal care among non-demented and demented elderly persons—Results from a Swedish population-based study. *International Journal of Geriatric Psychiatry, 20,* 862–871.

O'Brien, L., & Jackson, D. (2007). It's a long way from the office to the creek bed: Remote area mental health nursing in Australia. *Journal of Transcultural Nursing, 18*(2), 135–141.

Parkes, K. R. (1986). Coping in stressful episodes: The role of individual differences, environmental factors, and situational characteristics. *Journal of Personality and Social Psychology, 51*(6), 1277–1292.

Parkhurst, J. O., & Rahman, S. A. (2006). Life saving or money wasting? Perceptions of caesarean sections among users of services in rural Bangladesh. *Health Policy, 80,* 392–401.

Penz, K., D'Arcy, C., Stewart, N., Kosteniuk, J., Morgan, D., & Smith, B. (2007). Barriers to participation in continuing education activities among rural and remote nurses. *Journal of Continuing Education in Nursing, 38*(2), 58–66.

Ritchie, L. (2003). Adult day care: Northern perspectives. *Public Health Nursing, 20*(2), 120–131.

Shawn, E. R., Campbell, L., Mgnuni, M. B., Defilippi, K. M., & Williams, A. B. (2005). The spectrum of symptoms among rural South Africans with HIV infection. *Journal of the Association of Nurses in AIDS Care, 16*(6), 12–23.

Steven, D., Fitch, M., Dhaliwal, H., Kirk-Gardner, R., Sevean, P., Jamieson, J., et al. (2004). Knowledge, attitudes, beliefs, and practices regarding breast and cervical cancer screening in selected ethnocultural groups in northwestern Ontario. *Oncology Nursing Forum, 31*(2), 305–311.

Stewart, N. J., D'Arcy, C., Pitblado, J. R., Morgan, D. G., Forbes, D., Remus, G., et al. (2005). A profile of registered nurses in rural and remote Canada. *Canadian Journal of Nursing Research, 37*(1), 123–145.

Svensson, L., Karlsson, T., Nordlander, R., Wahlin, M., Zedigh, C., & Herlitz, J. (2003). Safety and delay time in prehospital thrombolysis of acute myocardial infarction in urban and rural areas in Sweden. *Journal of Emergency Medicine, 21,* 263–270.

Tilleczek, K., Pong, R., & Caty, S. (2005). Delivery of continuing education to nurse practitioners in rural and northern communities. *Canadian Journal of Nursing Research, 37*(1), 146–162.

Turner, C., Keyzer, D., & Rudget, T. (2007). Spheres of influence or autonomy? A discourse analysis of the introduction of nurse practitioners in rural and remote Australia. *Journal of Advanced Nursing, 59*(1), 38–46.

United Nations Development Programme. (2007). *UN Human Development Report 2007–2008: Table 1* (pp. 230–232). New York: Palgrave Macmillan. Retrieved January 18, 2008, from http://hdr.undp.org/en/media/hdr_20072008_en_complete.pdf

Vukic, A., & Keddy, B. (2002). Northern nursing practice in a primary health care setting. *Journal of Advanced Nursing, 40*, 542–548.

Yamashita, M., Miyaji, F., & Akimoto, R. (2005). The public health nursing role in rural Japan. *Public Health Nursing, 22*(2), 156–165.

Index

Contents of Previous
10 Volumes

VOLUME 19: Research on Women's Health

Joyce Fitzpatrick, Series Editor; Diana Taylor and Nancy Fugate-Woods, Volume Editors

SPRINGER / PUBLISHING COMPANY

Rural Nursing
Concepts, Theory, and Practice
Second Edition

Helen J. Lee, PhD, RN
Charlene A. Winters, DNSc, APRN, BC, Editors

This thoroughly revised second edition chronicles the path to creating a coherent, conceptual framework for rural nursing practice. By bringing together research, theory, and narratives from rural nursing practice, the authors and contributors provide readers with a foundation for understanding the special dimensions of rural nursing and health, including:

RURAL NURSING
Helen J. Lee & Charlene A. Winters

2nd Edition
CONCEPTS, THEORY AND PRACTICE

• The need for nurses to play multiple autonomous
  and team-centered roles
• Negotiating issues of confidentiality and over-familiarity
  with the lives of patients
• Self-reliant rural dwellers often seeking health care as a last resort
• Life-or-death roles that remote locations often play in
  whether health care is accessed in a timely manner
• Environmental health hazards due to hazardous waste in rural areas

Partial Contents:

Part I: The Rural Nursing Theory Base • Rural Nursing • Examining the Rural Nursing Theory Base • Exploring Rural Nursing Theory Across Borders

Part II: Perspectives of Rural Persons • Health Needs and Perceptions of Rural Persons • Health Perceptions, Needs, and Behaviors of Remote Rural Women of Childbearing and Childrearing Age • Strategizing Safety • Rural Family Health

Part III: The Rural Dweller and Response to Illness • Patterns of Responses to Symptoms in Rural Residents • Updating the Symptom-Action-Time-Line • The Chronic Illness Experience

Part IV: Rural Nursing Practice • The Distinctive Nature and Scope of Rural Nursing Practice • Rural Health Professionals' Perceptions of Lack of Anonymity • Rural Nurse Generalist in Community Health • Men Working as Rural Nurses • Continuing Education and Rural Nurses

Part V: Rural Public Health • Public Health Emergency Preparedness in Rural/Frontier Areas • Rural School Health • Improving the Health Literacy of Rural Elders

Part VI: Looking Ahead • Further Development of the Rural Nursing Theory Base • Implications for Education, Practice, and Policy

2005 · 376 pp · 978-0-8261-6955-6 · softcover

**11 West 42nd Street, New York, NY 10036-8002 • Fax: 212-941-7842
Order Toll-Free: 877-687-7476 • Order Online: www.springerpub.com**